11-26 [...] fears of Romanticism
to the seemingly more
controlable boundaries
of Realism

173-220

Ana's
Resistance to and
Partial Overcoming re-writing
of Romanticism in
LR

Realism as Resistance

Realism as Resistance

Romanticism and Authorship in Galdós, Clarín, and Baroja

Denise DuPont

Lewisburg
Bucknell University Press

Associated University Presses
2010 Eastpark Boulevard
Cranbury, NJ 08512

The paper used in this publication meets the requirements of the American National Standard for Permanence of Paper for Printed LIbrary Materials Z39.48-1984.

Library of Congress Cataloging-in-Publication Data

DuPont, Denise, 1966–
    Realism as resistance : romanticism and authorship in Galdós, Clarín, and Baroja / Denise DuPont.
        p. cm.
    Includes bibliographical references and index.
    ISBN 0-8387-5638-7 (alk. paper)
    1. Spanish fiction—19th century—History and criticism. 2. Romanticism—Spain. 3. Pârez Galdâs, Benito, 1843–1920. Episodios nacionales (Alianza Editorial). Primera serie. 4. Alas, Leopoldo, 1852–1901. Regenta. 5. Baroja, Pâô, 1872–1956. Lucha por la vida. I. Title.

PQ6144.D86 2006
863'.509145—dc22

                                                                    2005055321

Contents

Acknowledgments

I would like to thank Biblioteca Nueva for permission to quote from the works of Pío Baroja, and *Letras Peninsulares* for permission to use material from my article, "Modernity and the Public in Galdós's *La corte de Carlos IV* and *El 19 de marzo y el 2 de mayo*," Fall 1998, 625–35.

Faced now with the task of acknowledging the advice, readings, and patience of so many people who helped in the writing of this book, I would like to thank them collectively for demonstrating to me the importance of belonging to an intellectual community.

Most of all, I wish to thank my professors from Wesleyan and Yale, who continue to inspire me so many years later.

Realism as Resistance

Introduction:
Romanticism, Realism's Companion

It is as difficult . . . to trace the dividing-line between the real and the romantic as to plant a milestone between north and south.
—Henry James, Preface to *The American*, 283

Madame Bovary, c'est moi.
—Gustave Flaubert, Letter to Amélie Bosquet

IN THIS STUDY OF BENITO PÉREZ GALDÓS'S FIRST SERIES OF *EPISODIOS nacionales,* Leopoldo Alas (Clarín)'s *La Regenta,* and Pío Baroja's *La lucha por la vida,* I examine realistic novels that portray periods important to Spain's self-definition.[1] The novels engage the debates of their day, giving particular attention to the questions of realism vs. romantic idealism, and rationality vs. irrationality (or "quixotism"). Rather than returning to the contentions of Lovejoy and Wellek about the validity of the term "romanticism," in this study I take my definition of romanticism from the realists, who believed that it was, simply, all that realism was not. For example, M. H. Abrams articulated the realist's point of view in the following way: "Realistic fiction is often opposed to romantic fiction: the *romance* is said to present life as we would have it be, more picturesque, more adventurous, more heroic than the actual; realism, to present an accurate imitation of life as it is." According to Walter Kaufmann, romanticism may be dismissed as "flight from the present, yearning for deliverance from the cross of the here and now, an escape into the past, preferably medieval, or the future, into drugs or other worlds, either night or twilight," since romanticism "can face anything except the facts."[2] Finally, F. W. J. Hemmings detailed the stereotypes of both schools, listing generalizations relevant to the study of realism as a confrontation with romanticism:

11

The realist is supposed to deal with contemporary life and commonplace scenes; the romantic succumbs to the lure of the past and delights in dreaming of far-off places. The realist fixes his gaze on the world of men, the streets where they jostle and the rooms where they meet and converse; the romantic seeks solitude and finds it in nature, in the woods, the fields, the lonely seashore and the lonelier mountain crag. The realist is drawn into the social vortex, charts the cross-currents of ambition and self-interest, is familiar with all the processes of getting and spending; the romantic disdains such prosaic preoccupations; instead, he idealizes the purer passions and cultivates the darker ones, having leanings towards the satanic as well as the spiritual; whereas the typical realist, more especially in France, levels passion down to the play of the senses and has no patience with intimations of immortality. The romantic exalts the creative spirit and puts his faith in intuition; the realist's approach to his material is detached and analytic. On a strictly literary plane, the value the realist sets on stylistic sobriety contrasts with the romantic's cultivation of exuberance and emotive imagery; the former, in short, sticks to prose, while poetry remains the authentic, if not the exclusive, medium for the expression of the romantic mood and the romantic world view.[3]

Here, I want to explore these contrasting images in order to examine realism's reaction to romanticism—that is, realism's construction of the romanticism to which it opposes itself.

I take a similar approach to the terms "quixotism" and "quixotic," associating these ideas with the realistic, pragmatic reaction to romantic (some would argue, distorted) readings of the *Quijote*. Saying that he believes the romantic interpretation to be "misguided in each of its basic tendencies," Anthony Close listed the characteristics of this vision of *Don Quijote* as

a) the idealisation of the hero and the denial of the novel's satiric purpose.
b) the belief that the novel is symbolical and that through this symbolism it expresses ideas about the human spirit's relation to reality or about the nature of Spain's history
c) the interpretation of its symbolism, and more generally, of its whole spirit and style, in a way which reflects the ideology, aesthetics, and sensibility of the modern era.[4]

The realist vision of romantic quixotism is clearly negative, featuring a disdain driven by the realists' need to compete with romantic discourse.

Looking beyond the novels studied here, we note that the historical engagement of realism and idealism in Spain mirrors the intratextual realist preoccupation with the poetry of romanticism-quixotism.[5] In the wake of the Revolution of 1868, with idealism linked in the minds of many Spaniards to social unrest, philosophical idealism fell out of favor with many intellectuals. Nevertheless, even though many Spanish thinkers embraced positivism and practical sociopolitical solutions after 1875, many romantic or idealistic habits of thought remained in the philosophy of the Restoration in the form of "hilos conductores" (connecting threads) between the idealist and positivist mentalities.[6] In the 1875 debate over idealism and realism in the Spanish Ateneo, the dialogue "reveals the general tendency toward an idealism which is willing to compromise in order to meet the scientific age."[7] Still, at no time did idealism completely disappear: it persisted in the aesthetic realm through the 1870s and 1880s, as writers found this form of idealism safer than the political variety.[8] For this reason, idealism (or romanticism) colored even the historical period in which the realist novel dominated, in that the transition from romanticism to realism was incomplete: "el realismo nace preñado de romanticismo" [realism is born pregnant with romanticism].[9] In Spain, as elsewhere, instead of realism making a sharp break with romanticism, "Charlotte's homely bread-and-butter . . . stuck for ever to the Romantic sleeve of Werther."[10] It is the persistence of romanticism and the anxiety it causes that I explore in this study of Spanish fiction.

The novels I analyze here probe the romantic heritage of realism by focusing on a particular character—the protagonist who acts as an author. Realism's author-character, while unremarkable, is nevertheless a hero, because, in this sort of novel, "the artist is the form that the heroic takes."[11] Given that this character acquires his or her status as author by composing texts for others, we must also look at the figure of the reader. The author-protagonist courts various reading characters with a complicated synthesis of didacticism, entertainment, and competition. Although the author-character recognizes realism as the contemporary world's dominant discourse, and often demonstrates her superiority as a realist in opposition to other, less rational characters, she also notes the seductive powers of romance narratives, even as they affect the author-character herself. It is this autobiographical turn of realist romance that concerns us, in that the realist author-character who is still drawn to romantic narratives mirrors the external authors Galdós, Clarín, and Baroja. Thus, the novels are historical not just because they portray important events, but also because they give us a compelling picture of the preoccupations of the historical, biographical authors.

These three external authors lived the dichotomy of competing literary styles, navigating a course of textual production that straddles realism and romanticism, and working through their divided loyalties by way of the internal authors of their novels.[12] Galdós, Clarín, and Baroja explore the precariousness of their position, consequently revealing the dilemmas faced by the creators of romantic-realist fiction. They, and their protagonists as surrogates, fight for the integrity of their very selves, at one moment claiming authority and supremacy as objective, impartial converts to realism, and in the next, attempting to recover the identity of the traditional romantic hero.[13] The authors, both internal and external, become painfully aware that their legitimacy hangs in the balance, for they must reconcile the hegemony of realism with the irresistible pull of romanticism. Spanish realist authors are typical of the Victorian age in which many writers were drawn to the romantic spirit, but then imagined for themselves the project of taming the wild romantic free will.[14]

Let us look closely now at the workings of this relationship between author-character and reader-characters. In the novels I analyze, the protagonist acts as an author on the model of Don Quijote, imitating both the idealistic dreamer and the eventually chastened realist of Cervantes's masterwork. This recuperation of Cervantes's character echoes extra-textual developments in Spanish cultural history. In Spain, the late nineteenth and early twentieth centuries featured a "reinvention" of the *Quijote,* after its absence from the Spanish narrative itinerary between 1615 and the 1870s.[15] Whereas he reduced the duration of the dormancy period, and referred to *Quijote* criticism rather than fictional reworking and imitation, Anthony Close also remarked on the difference between the continuous international critical attention to *Quijote* and Spanish *Quijote* criticism, which "seems to have gone to sleep" in the early 1800s.[16] The novels I analyze here appeared when Spain was reclaiming the *Don Quijote* as national text, with Galdós's "Observaciones sobre la novela contemporánea en España" (Observations on the Contemporary Novel in Spain, 1870) as one representative gesture of this larger impulse. I suggest that Spanish realist authors read and wrote the *Quijote* into their novels as a metaphor for their own divided loyalties to romanticism and realism.

The quixotic author, as I define him, is first a reader, as is Don Quijote.[17] The readings he prefers initially are as extravagant as chivalric novels, and he attempts to "author" his own texts according to this romantic model. Whether this authoring gesture takes the form of actual textual composition or is merely an acting out of, or living by romanticism, the author-character suffers difficulties, just as does Don Quijote, because these sorts of texts do not have a place as models for modern life. Defiant readers mock the unfortunate author-character, and this negative reception of his creative work persists as an injury that drives the next stage of his behavior. Scarred by the rejection of his romantic narratives, which are associated with youth, the author-character "matures" into an identification with realism, like Don Quijote at the end of the second part of Cervantes's novel. Still, this reactive turn to realism does not resolve the author-character's dilemmas, as he has insufficiently worked through his own identification with romanticism. Just as Cervantes's text brings new life to the chivalric novels it parodies, the realist novel recuperates as its subtext the narratives of romanticism, and the author-character must recognize their haunting presence. At the base of the author-protagonist's alliance with realism, there lie the readers' disrespect and the author-character's resulting self-doubt. This trauma is the trace of romanticism the realist author-character cannot disavow, and must eventually confront and resolve. The romantic residue takes several forms.

First, the realist author-character seems chastened by the power of the people (his "readers"), and he makes amends by according them presence and voice in his text. However, in addition to deferring to his public, the author-character rebels against them. He is driven to compete with his readers, in order to erase their earlier ridicule and to show his eventual dominance over them. This is the persistence of the author-character's romantic self, which masquerades as an objective, almost self-effacing realist, but ultimately insists on its protagonism. As part of this domination of the unruly reader, the realist author-character effects a sort of revenge when he reveals the romanticism that his readers—the "others" who originally mocked him—harbor in themselves. And yet, finally, in much of the action of these novels, the author-character is anything but vengeful and self-righteous, and instead revisits the romanticism he admits he still harbors. I end the study of each of these works by focusing on the author-character's stepping away from his competition with other (reader) characters, and his turning to an analysis of his own covert romanticism. The author-protagonists in these novels by Galdós, Clarín, and Baroja have various reactions to their residual romanticism, as I explain in the body of this study.

Fittingly, although the works of these three novelists engage in a defense of personal identity, they also take up the question of national self-definition, in that for the nineteenth century, national and personal history blended.[18] These historical novels depict three important junctures in Spanish history—specifically, the founding of the modern nation during the War for Independence from France, the period of uneasy political accommodation with the reinstatement of the Bourbon monarchy after the disappointments of the First Republic, and the loss of hope for radical solutions to social problems at the close of the nineteenth century. I chose to examine these particular novels because they issue from different historical moments in Spanish realism, and portray the boundaries of Spain's nineteenth century. Galdós's First Series of *Episodios* tells the story of the early 1800s, and the War for Independence from Napoleonic France, which is often considered the origin of modern Spain. *La lucha por la vida* covers the last years of the nineteenth century and the first years of the twentieth, and demonstrates that even as the country moves into a new century, the confrontation with the quixotic mindset continues to be a relevant topic for Spanish fiction.[19] Looking at *La Regenta* after Baroja's trilogy is a chronological step backwards, since Clarín's novel is set in Restoration Spain. *La Regenta* chronicles the cultural lethargy after the disappointment of the September Revolution of 1868 ("La Gloriosa") and the subsequent failed experiment in republican government.[20] Recalling the model we use to examine the author-character's relationship to his readers, we can easily see the historical correlative in all of these periods portrayed in the various novels. Whether we look to the War for Independence, or to the years after the Revolution of 1868 when calls for reform clashed with a desire for order, each epoch features a struggle between the popular (equivalent to the internal readers) and some sort of authority figure or figures (mirror image of the novels' author-character).

The tension between the people and an authority figure is a model that permits us to discuss both the internal workings of the novels and the historical periods they portray; I would also like to consider the extratextual figure of the biographical authors, Galdós, Clarín, and Baroja. In fact, these "authorities" exhibit the same dialectic of manipulation and liberation of their readers as do their textual surrogates, both controlling and freeing the implied reader. Whether they articulate this goal or not, novelists such as Galdós, Clarín, and Baroja connect history with contemporary life, and encourage their readers to reexamine the issues of their present. As typical of the nineteenth century, novelistic representations of national history anticipated further growth of a reading public that would continue to look for information about itself in novels that provided images of the historical origins of the nation and its people.[21] Clearly, even if external authors of such texts expressed their own assessments of historical events, they also ceded considerable autonomy to readers. When authors blended historical information with fiction, they allowed novels to speak for themselves, in all their uncertainty and potential for diverse interpretation, and handed control to readers now empowered to imagine the nation's history. These same popular novels, while providing much-needed information about the nation, provoked readers. The open nature of fiction responded to readers' critical thinking skills, encouraging them to "play with" and debate history. Regardless of novelists' controlling gestures, once authors articulated their ideas in the form of a novel, readers had the last word in textual interpretation.

Galdós, for example, had high expectations for the readers of his *Episodios nacionales*. The *Episodios* expose historical writing as "an act of creation," or "a literary undertaking,"[22] while at the same time the author takes advantage of the poetic register as a vehicle to interrogate Spanish history. Galdós lamented the uncritical acceptance of commonplaces in national history, and called for a skeptical processing of Spanish history.[23] While Galdós expected a young public, he did not provide them with an uncomplicated vision of the past.[24] Galdosian literary examination of history never leads to simple answers, but it does speak to the author's faith in the ability of his readers to think critically. Clarín's open-ended interrogation of Restoration society has a similar flavor, and Baroja's work seems even less didactic. E. Inman Fox discussed Baroja's differences from the generation of novelists preceding him, emphasizing his break with the realist novel's conception of the human being as a social animal, with individual existence inseparable from the sociohistorical background: in Baroja, the individual is typical of no larger tendencies or entities at all.[25] Baroja and Clarín wrote historically based novels and expected them to be read, which allows us to pose questions about the relationship of author to reader configured by their texts.[26]

Once we have established that these external authors challenge their readers to conceptualize national and personal history, we must now ask who exactly this reader was. Prepared by the *novela por entregas,* or "novel by installment," the nineteenth-century Spanish readership demanded information about itself from the fiction it consumed.[27] The reader also wished to imagine him or herself as part of a collective national project, and novels of the recent past, such as those I examine here, provided a vehicle for the reader's direct engagement with the nation's history. In the intersection of national history and fiction, the imaginative reader plays an important and active role. It is here, in the realist novel's involvement of the reader with national history, that we encounter extra-textually the same overlapping of romanticism and realism that we found in the relationship of the novel's author-characters with its internal readers. In focusing on characters who read the history they have lived, the realist novels of Galdós, Clarín, and Baroja recuperate the very romanticism that realist genres at times appear to reject; the romantic history recovered by realist novels is the construction of a rational narrative in conjunction with the fabrication of the self.[28]

Ordinarily, the notion of "romantic history" conjures up images of stereotypical, picturesque national topics, however, it is important to remember that European romanticism changed the concept of national history from "un patrimonio recibido a una confrontación meditativa y consciente con la tradición" [a received heritage to a meditative and conscious confrontation with tradition].[29] For the romantic, unfailingly "a devotee of history,"[30] national history becomes an active process as citizens seek to understand their nations and themselves. This "desire for history" is the people's imaginative conceptualization of their relationship to history, and is a feature of the nineteenth-century rise of history, when for the first time historical information became accessible and useful to the growing reading public through texts, and to the illiterate through pictorial imagery.[31] Expressing a desire for historical discourse in the form of dramatic representation, the people actively participated in this construction by influencing the historian who generated the images of history. Thus, the consumer of national history was also, indirectly, its producer, taking part in the investigation and fabrication of a personalized national history. Through the dialogue between historical novelist and the public, the representation of national history allowed the readership a good deal of control over the "stagings" of history. Even though the dialectical production of historical discourse as a project shared by the historian and the consuming public began with romanticism, it persisted long after the eclipse of that movement.[32]

Continuing with this examination of the relation of extratextual authors to an increasingly powerful reading public, I turn now to the reservations expressed by many authors about the potential corruption of these readers. Spanish novels of the 1870s and beyond emerged in a climate of concern about reading which began years before their appearance.[33] Here, I suggest that the fear of dangerous influences on the reader relates directly to the greater power of that reader, who had gained voice in the form of public opinion. After 1808, the expansion of the printing industry and the increased production of political literature coincided with a preoccupation with public opinion in Spain.[34] Although Spanish readers remained primarily of the middle classes, the growth of this reading audience was undeniable.[35] Because the explosion of available reading material coincided with the increase in the number of potential readers, cultural authorities worried about the democratization of reading. As the rise of the popular novel went hand in hand with the extension of popular education, this increase in literacy motivated an anxiety about the critical skills of the new reader.[36] Apprehensive about the public's judgment, many writers spoke out about popular novels' pernicious effect on naive readers. Ramón de Mesonero Romanos, Modesto Lafuente, Ramón de Navarrete, and Francisco Javier Moya, from the 1840s; Vicente Barrantes in the 1850s; and the Duque de Rivas and José España Lledó in the 1860s expressed such reservations.[37] As in the following passage, these critics—many of whom were also authors of fiction—often decried the contamination of the Spanish reader by the importation and serialization of French novels:

> Luego que se quitó a la imprenta todo freno, tradujéronse a destajo las producciones de los novelistas franceses más señalados por su libertinaje e impiedad, y con pretexto de poner estos libros al alcance de todas las fortunas (como se dice en la germanía corriente) se publicaron por entregas, facilitando así su expendición y la introducción de la ponzoña en muchas familias que de otro modo no se hubieran contagiado.

> [As soon as controls over the printing press were removed, the works of the French novelists best known for their licentiousness and impiousness were hurriedly translated, and under the pretext of making these books available to

all fortunes (as is said in common slang). they were published in installments, facilitating in that way their dissemination and the introduction of the poison into many families who otherwise would not have been contaminated].[38]

Recalling the at times adversarial relationship between author and readers which we found in the realist novel, it is tempting to suggest that at least some of the Spanish authors who lamented the French novel's popularity were actually expressing regret that they themselves did not have such access to, and thus, control over, Spanish readers. Rather than revealing the concrete reasons for their resistance to the foreign novel, Spanish authors used vague, poetic images to convey their fears related to the success of the genre: "The novel's popularity was everywhere attested, but usually in terms that betrayed cultural anxiety, with metaphors of floods, invasions, and epidemics."[39] As another tactic to deflect attention from their concern with increased competition, Spanish authors often related independence in reading to the threat of social unrest. Spanish writers who made this argument departed from the cultural phenomenon of increased literacy, and suggested that readers' access to serialized novels (particularly translations from the French) would have social and political consequences far beyond Spanish authors' loss of control of their native readers. Competition from French authors was no small matter for Spanish writers of the mid-nineteenth century. According to Elisa Martí-López, "in the mid-nineteenth century the French novel was the center of Spanish publishing activity; all commercial publishing resources were invested in promoting and disseminating the French novel in Spain. As a result, the French novel determined the habits and expectations of the Spanish readers and deprived the incipient Spanish novel of the domestic resources that could have supported it."[40] In his 1869 essay, José España Lledó bemoaned the conversion of the novel, thanks to Eugenio Sue, into a "libelo infamatorio y cátedra de socialismo" (defamatory libel and pulpit for socialism).[41] Stephanie Sieburth discussed the social and political implications of serialized fiction, succinctly elaborating the connections made by España Lledó: "The new availability of serialized fiction was assumed to lead to corruption, and the development of this kind of mass cultural product was often seen as a metaphor for the development of an organized working class. Mass culture therefore meant, in the eyes of the dominant class, a threat to social control. In response, bourgeois discourses from the most conservative to the radical associated mass culture with corruption, triviality, and decay."[42]

Again, I wonder if the Spanish critics' fear of the political and cultural "corruption" of the masses was not at least in part unease about their own threatened position as intellectual authorities and privileged producers of the novel. Reinforcing this idea, other attacks on the unwelcome novel focus less on social peril and more on discourse and literary style. Despite pessimism about the genre, some critics offered suggestions for the reformation of the novel. For example, José España Lledó called for a new Cervantes to end the unbridled idealism of popular literature: "tiempo es ya de que nazca un nuevo Cervantes que concluya con esta literatura, y que aprovechando el carácter de nuestro siglo y los elementos dispersos que en él existen, dé a la novela un nuevo giro, una nueva tendencia." [It is time now for the birth of a new Cervantes, who would put a stop to this literature, and who, taking advantage of the character of our century and the varied elements that exist in it, would give the novel a new twist, a new direction.][43] España Lledó's conjuring of a nineteenth-century Cervantes echoes Galdós's seminal essay, "Observaciones sobre la novela contemporánea en España" (Observations on the Contemporary Novel in Spain, 1870), in which Galdós recognized that Spaniards were currently "idealistas desaforados" (unbounded, outrageous idealists), but cited Cervantes and Velázquez as great Spanish realists who attested to Spain's innate capacity for honest observation and realistic art: "Puede asegurarse que en este punto la citada disposición [idealista] es más bien accidental, hija sin duda de condiciones del tiempo, que innata y característica." [It can be assured that at this point the above-mentioned idealist tendency is in fact circumstantial, a product undoubtedly of the conditions of the age, rather than innate and characteristic.][44] For this reason, Galdós hopes for a reform of the Spanish novel, and suggests that the incorporation of a greater degree of realism would be a healthy starting point for such a restorative project. This agenda coincides with a pattern wherein authors and author-characters use realism to defend themselves from unruly readers; such "authorities" designate realism as salubrious in order to present their own creations as superior to those of their competitors.

Indeed, it is not difficult to identify the personal insecurity motivating these novelists' retreat to realism. Tellingly, the cultural critics' complaints about the lack of realism in the novel often form part of an attack on women novelists: "The objections to the novel's popularity, seditiousness, and exoticism, and also the perception of its possible usefulness for the middle class, surfaced at the same historical juncture that witnessed the emergence of the first generation of Spanish women writers, who began to publish in 1841."[45] These women (along with the French novelists mentioned earlier), then, are some of the writers producing the idealistic, romantic (non-realist) texts to which Galdós, for example, objects. Situating Galdós's promotion of the realist novel within his need to clear a space protected from competition with the novels of women writers (Jagoe) or *costumbristas* (Santana), we realize that what appears to be concern for the well-being and morality of the vulnerable reader may in fact be motivated by a sense of competition with other authors for the right to control that reader.[46]

To extend this hypothesis, when working through female or naive reader-authors such as the protagonists Gabriel Araceli (the First Series of *Episodios*), Ana de Ozores (*La Regenta*), and Manuel Alcázar (*La lucha por la vida*), I suggest that the apprehensions expressed by Galdós and other novelist-critics might have been motivated by fear of *lack* of difference between themselves as reformed Quijotes and the "weak" internal authors of their novels. We must keep in mind the intellectual baggage carried by the external authors: they are committed realist authors, but they are also vulnerable to the seductions of fantasy, and are perpetually marked by an early association with romanticism. One might urge also that the Spanish external authors' complaints about French novelists be seen in a similar light: perhaps Spanish authors feared their own proximity to, rather than difference from, these foreign authors. In their own entertainment of naive readers, Spanish authors could easily have incurred charges of lack of patriotism due to manipulation or corruption of readers, and thus be accused of not being "genuinely" Spanish.

For these Spanish realist authors, painfully aware of their own romantic "weaknesses" and of the possibility that they could be replaced by other authors, the notion of exclusivity came under attack. This leveling trend affected readers, as more and more people had access to books, and novels themselves countered claims to privilege.[47] But clearly authors were also touched, and in their novels reveal their anxiety about competition from new authors. It is logical, then, that novels of the period would portray characters obsessed with differentiating themselves from their presumed inferiors through their cultural awareness and ability to read critically and write realistically. Even as they compose realist texts, author-characters engage in a thoroughly romantic, self-oriented project, attempting to be heroes in a world that makes heroism impossible. Although protagonists fight to maintain their distinctions from others, the very "specialness" they assert is undermined by their own habits of reading. Stephanie Sieburth discusses this leveling in Galdós's *La desheredada:* "Opposite to this tendency of the *one* to fragment into the *many,* and equally alarming to the narrator, is the creation of uniformity out of diversity. As the many melt into one undifferentiated mass or into identical units, individuality is threatened."[48] Whereas Galdós, Clarín, and Baroja engage in a critique of Spanish society and history when they select their protagonists, they also participate in a project of self-examination, in which they confront their continuing attraction to idealism. These authors are afraid not only of social unrest or the unfriendly reception of their work. They also fear their own idealistic debilities, lingering romanticism, association with femininity, and expendability.

Although each of the three authors is known for his primary identification with realist narration, all three display an attraction to non-realist elements exemplified by idealism, romanticism, melodrama, or a style approximating that of the *folletín* or *novela por entregas*.[49] For example, Laureano Bonet and Walter Pattison discussed Galdós's interest in romanticism in his early life. With regard specifically to the *Episodios,* Sainz de Robles explained that Galdós's First Series is "la que más emoción y simpatía despierta en nosotros" [the one that awakens the most emotion and sympathy in us]. Montesinos, on the other hand, specified that the novels are able to elicit strong reactions from readers because of the melodramatic force of the narrative: "Arrastra, sí, arrastra al lector, pero como arrastra el folletín." [It drags, yes, drags the reader, but in the way that the folletín drags (the reader).] Bonet recognized the influence of the *folletín* in Galdós, while Gustavo Correa studied Galdós's platonic idealism, and Emily Letemendía connected Galdós to Bécquer. Victor Fuentes broadened the definition of realism ("realismo integral") to discover dreams, myth, and idealism in Galdós and Clarín, explaining that after rejecting Restoration society, Galdós's and Alas's novels connect the transhistorical, imaginative search for creative solutions to the mythological register. John Kronik's "La retórica del realismo: Galdós y Clarín" also reexamines realism in light of romanticism and idealism, while Daria J. Montero-Paulson, in her article "Nombres, símbolos, personajes, y textos literarios" (170), stated that "Pérez Galdós debe mucho al Romanticismo" (Pérez Galdós owes much to Romanticism), and studied romantic traces in four of Galdós's characters. According to Wadda C. Ríos-Font, "Galdós's work is always in dynamic relationship with melodrama, the serial novel, popular theater."[50]

Others have written on romanticism, idealism, and melodrama in Clarín. Because *La Regenta* transcends a simple realist paradigm, critics, such as Sánchez and Valis, have questioned the presumptive characterization of Alas's realism as unqualified mimeticism or naturalism. For some, such as John Kronik, Alas's most successful works are his stories of idealized and idealizing characters defeated by reality. According to Kronik ("Retórica del Realismo," 55), because poesis is as important as mimesis in the rhetoric of realism, the author acts as a sort of pastry chef in fashioning the novelistic world. According to Kevin Larsen, in the banquet at the Casino (*La Regenta*'s chapter 20), Clarín dramatized the conflict between idealism and materialism, rejecting both in their extreme form. Believing that lyric poetry could expose one's interior life, says Gifford Davis, Clarín departed from the naturalism espoused by Émile Zola, who strictly condemned lyric poetry. Germán Gullón tells us that Clarín exhibited varied antirealist techniques which, given Alas's personality and the rest of his work, problematize reading the end of *La Regenta* as the destruction of the idealist soul and romantic love.[51] Clarín lived "la compleja dialéctica de la cultura decimonónica europea entre tradicionalismo y liberalismo, idealismo y positivismo, romanticismo y realismo" [nineteenth-century European culture's complex dialectic between traditionalism and liberalism, idealism and positivism, romanticism and realism], refusing to choose between spirit and matter, and taking up a position "which is both anti-idealist and anti-materialist."[52] He incorporated romantic works such as *Don Juan* into *La Regenta,* paying literary homage, and demonstrating his persistent idealism—his "predilección por una tradición romántica e idealista" [predilection for a romantic, idealist tradition].[53] Just as did Galdós and Baroja, Clarín relied on *folletín*-style plotting (Sieburth, *Reading* La Regenta; and Rivkin, "Plotting in *La Regenta*").

Finding idealistic, melodramatic, or other nonrealistic elements in Baroja is even easier, justifying the characterization of his fiction as fundamentally different from that of Galdós and Clarín. Because Baroja's romantic idealism "ran deep,"[54] he has been described as sentimental and romantic.[55] His attraction to symbolism drew him close to Machado, while his narrative art displays many antirealist, grotesque "trazos goyescos" (Goyesque features).[56] Baroja struggled with divided allegiances to both an "idealismo de corte romántico" (idealism of a romantic sort) and an "escepticismo de pequeño burgués" (petty-bourgeois skepticism). If Baroja was an indefatigable reader of *folletines,* this form of the novel has particular importance in *La lucha por la vida,* where Roberto's resolution of Manuel's dilemmas can be seen as a *folletín*esque act by a deus ex machina. The proximity to the *folletín* of certain moments in *Aurora roja,* demonstrated by the author's interest in "los bajos fondos" (the dregs), is in part a historical feature of Baroja's epoch, because a "corriente folletinesca" (*folletín*esque current) extended through late nineteenth-century Europe.[57] Still, Baroja's interest in representing the world mimetically authorizes us to explore his connections to realism as well as his ties to romanticism.[58] Indeed, *La lucha por la vida* has been called "la descripción más realista de una ciudad en toda la literatura española" [the most realistic description of a city in all of Spanish literature].[59]

* * *

In their novels, then, these authors process their dual allegiances to realism and romanticism. In my examination of these texts, I devote three chapters to Galdós's First Series of *Episodios nacionales,* whereas my studies of Baroja and Clarín occupy one chapter apiece. Although this division is unequal, I believe the ten *Episodios* require such an exposition in the interest of responsible literary analysis. At the same time, in permitting my readings of the Galdós novels to occupy the majority of this study, I do not mean to suggest that Clarín and Baroja are not worthy of equal attention. Accordingly, I situate the Clarín and Baroja chapters after my examination of Galdós, allowing these other authors the "last word," and demonstrating that Baroja and Clarín make an invaluable contribution to the novelization of realism's dialogue with romanticism.

As the foundation of this book, the *Episodios* (1873–75) deserve significant critical attention for three reasons: they were written at the beginning of the realist boom of the 1870s and 1880s, they were some of Galdós's earliest novels, and they portray the events that shaped modern Spain's national consciousness. In these novels of the Spanish War for Independence, the narrator Gabriel Araceli battles for autonomy by defending his status as authority and author, but also by coming to terms with the interior demons of romanticism, a heritage he learns he cannot escape by projecting it onto others. In the first of the three chapters on Galdós, covering the novels *Trafalgar, La corte de Carlos IV,* and *El 19 de marzo y el 2 de mayo,* I follow Gabriel as he discovers what a reader is and how to captivate one. He contemplates notions of "lying" and the fabrication of fiction, and juxtaposes quixotism and realism. Finally, he realizes—as his nation begins the struggle that will be the War for Independence from France—that he will also have to fight: he must acquire cultural authority in order to argue his legitimacy as an author. In chapter 2, in which I read *Bailén, Napoleón en Chamartín, Zaragoza,* and *Gerona,* Gabriel's memoirs cover a significant portion of the war's battles, and much of Gabriel's own competition with other authors. Gabriel is now committed to realism, and usually lives according to this worldview. However, at the same time he realizes that the phenomenon of authorial self-focus is a sort of quixotism—a self-proclaimed heroics of the author. This behavior is new to him, and a cause of discomfort when he recognizes that it distracts him from patriotic action. Concurrently, and somewhat contradictorily, he becomes aware of the importance of romantic or quixotic models for heroic action—a fitting realization for the novels that treat the majority of the war. Gabriel ends *Gerona,* the last of these four novels, apparently secure in his rationality, but having devoted much attention to the specter of romantic quixotism, which haunts him as a necessary component of triumphant authorship, and as the spontaneous expression of self-sacrificing patriotism. In this way, Gabriel increases the complexity of his presentation of the quixotic imagination. Whether quixotism forms the basis for a heroics of authorship or a program of patriotic self-defense, it cannot be summarily dismissed in favor of strict realism. The novels discussed in chapter 3 delve deepest into the essence of self and nation, and the quixotic residue that lies at the heart of both entities. I first follow Gabriel's return to his birthplace in Cádiz. I trace his observance of the birth of the nation at *las Cortes* as correlative to his own renaissance, in full awareness of the quixotism that persists within him and his country. On behalf of Spain, Gabriel confronts the extravagant *Quijote* don Pedro and betters the strong but savage *guerrilleros,* only to have his unresolved romanticism highlighted by the English tourist of the picturesque, Miss Fly. As I explain, the series ends with Gabriel anything but confident in his authorial powers, despite his nominal identification with realism.

In chapter 4, I jump ahead to the end of the nineteenth and the beginning of the twentieth century to follow the development of reformed *pícaro* Manuel Alcázar in Pío Baroja's *La lucha por la vida* (1904). As soon as young Manuel arrives in Madrid from provincial Spain, he is immersed in an environment of fantasy and romantic readings. He then meets, however, the champion of his own brand of realism, Roberto Hasting. Throughout the trilogy, Roberto gives Manuel lessons in the domestication of inclinations toward romantic love, evidencing a Nietzschean will-to-power that manifests itself as a commitment to daily effort and unheroic action. Despite Roberto's forceful character, Manuel clings to make-believe, denying this formidable icon of self-control three times before becoming a submissive disciple. Manuel imposes romanticism on a ragpicker's pedestrian domain, participates in an elaborate masquerade as the son of an impoverished baroness, and follows a dissipated misfit into social and political anarchy. When these rebellions subside, Manuel settles down, deferring to Roberto, and to the woman who becomes his (Manuel's) wife, la Salvadora. Manuel is now quite passive, and his creative spirit seems to transfer to his brother Juan. While Manuel drifts from political activity, Juan becomes a committed anarchist in his stead, channeling his romantic readings and hopes into this amorphous political program. Although he survives his brother, and no longer needs to be jealous of Juan's emotional intimacy with Salvadora, Manuel nevertheless mourns at the end of the trilogy his own loss of ideals, however quixotic they might have been. I suggest that this regret is also motivated by nostalgia for the (romantic, authorial) self, in that the "true" self is again seen as tied to the conception of the romantic hero, and this component of his identity is what Manuel has suppressed.

In chapter 5, I return to Galdós's generation of realists to look at Leopoldo Alas's *La Regenta* (1884–1885), because I believe this novel provides information necessary for conclusions about the realist author-character's confrontation with romanticism. The primary action of Clarín's novel is the attempted seduction of Ana de Ozores—*la Regenta,* or the judge's wife—by both the small-town don Juan Álvaro Mesía and the corrupt *Magistral* and *Provisor,* Fermín de Pas.[60] These three primary characters negotiate a textual battle based on their readings and their skill at creating narrative, and enter into an unstated literary pact. Both men wish to seduce Ana and each seems to realize, however inconsistently, that to do so he must become an author and convince her to protagonize his narrative. At first Fermín appears to enjoy a greater facility for narrative invention and progresses more quickly toward conquering Ana than does

Álvaro. The problem is that Ana also desires to be a writer. Both suitors struggle with Ana's independence, as she strives to invent her own personal narratives. Álvaro and Fermín often succumb to the temptation of conceiving the battle to possess Ana as a purely physical contest rather than a textual one, and Ana outdoes them in authorial skill. Eventually, the male protagonists confront their own lack of words and their ineffective authorship. Although Álvaro succeeds in seducing Ana, both men fail as authors. Even in her solitude at the end of the novel, Ana is the master author, and her durability and persistence are the lessons of romanticism the external realist authors must confront.

Thus, whereas I began this introduction by focusing on the internal and external authors' relationship to their readers—also internal and external—the *Episodios* lead us to the realization that the greater preoccupation of the novels in question is the author. The readers are important, because their ridicule of the internal author's early romanticism sparks the conflicted development of the authorial project, but we see that the author-character engages ultimately in self-analysis, concerning him or herself with the internal reader only as a component of this introspection. The external authors reveal in their comments about readers' vulnerability their own insecurity about threats from competing female and foreign authors, due to their insufficient differentiation from these competitors. Mirroring this extratextual anxiety, the internal authors reveal the self-doubt caused by their lingering romanticism. In all cases, the authors would like to champion realism, but they worry about the romantic skeletons in their closets. I turn now to the novels, to explore how these vestiges of romanticism in the realist novel undergird the self-analysis of the figure of the romantic-realist author, who must come to terms with the incomplete separation of the two mentalities and styles.

1

Setting the Stage:
Exploring Authorship in *Trafalgar, La corte de Carlos IV,* and *El 19 de marzo y el 2 de mayo*

IN THE FIRST THREE NOVELS OF THE FIRST SERIES OF *EPISODIOS,* WE become acquainted with the young narrator, Gabriel Araceli. Gabriel composes as an old man his memoirs of encounters with Spanish history from 1805 to 1814, and chronicles his personal development during those years. In this first chapter, I examine the novels *Trafalgar, La corte de Carlos IV,* and *El 19 de marzo y el 2 de mayo,* in which young Gabriel discovers and develops his authorial consciousness, meets his first audiences of readers, debates the attractions of romanticism and the good sense of realism, and realizes that he is only beginning the literary apprenticeship that will provide him cultural authority and legitimacy.[1] As Gabriel is learning to act as an author, he is also living the historical events leading to the War for Independence which will be the focus of the rest of the series. In this way, a sense of impending struggle accompanies both the political developments and Gabriel's becoming an author. To begin with, these are Gabriel's first collisions with resistant and unaccommodating readers, and he fights to win over these unreceptive audiences. Also, in many instances, the older Gabriel, who authors the memoirs and benefits from readings done in years subsequent to the events portrayed, plays an important role. By subduing the competing artists and historical events which would overshadow Gabriel as cultural authority, he comes to his younger self's aid, eclipsing such figures as Goya, Moratín, and Godoy. At the same time, older Gabriel's interventions make evident that while the narrator's younger self is "sensibly" turning toward realist narrative structures and away from quixotic ideations, young Gabriel lacks the basic skills of literacy that

27

would complement his native good sense and allow him to act and speak with authority. *Trafalgar* is the first of the three novels that chronicle this preliminary stage of the two wars for independence: Spain's from France, and Gabriel's from his baggage of romantic extravagance and literary naivete.

TRAFALGAR

Set in 1805, when the combined naval forces of France and Spain fought the British in the Battle of Trafalgar, *Trafalgar* is much more than a historical preface to the rest of the series. The novel tells the story of the first stage of Gabriel's occupation as author of his memoirs and of national history, with military action serving as an allegory for writing. The series opens with Gabriel's account of his picaresque childhood, and a meditation on his creation of the *Episodios*.[2] The protagonist now speaks from old age, but "reading" the past (207–8) revives him like no other activity, until he is young again (208).[3] Here, the creation of a written text gives Gabriel back his life, and allows him to fight the history that weighs him down with age. This rejuvenation of Gabriel is paralleled by that of his master and protector, don Alonso, and Alonso's friend Marcial. When the seventy-six-year-old retired sailor Marcial (who is known as *Medio-hombre*—Half-Man—because he has lost a leg, part of an arm, and an eye in battle) arrives, he confirms the pattern of old age planning to be young again through ambitious action. Gabriel observes this recapture of youth as the men play at being soldiers, commenting that the enthusiasm of old age turns old men into children (217). In this way, the two quixotic warriors, "half-man" each of them because of their injuries and the handicaps of old age, compose together one whole that parallels the Gabriel of the 1870s, writing to recover a lost past just as the elderly companions of his youth fight to relive their own glories.[4]

Although they concern themselves primarily with the recovery of their military status, Gabriel's two alter egos also teach the young narrator much about authorship and dependence on readers. Gabriel learns a hard lesson about "difficult" readers by observing the two old men with their target audience, don Alonso's wife, doña Francisca, who is a defiant "reader" of her husband's fantasies. Francisca (or Paquita) remains firmly opposed to her husband's dream of again participating in naval action. She blames Marcial for corrupting Alonso, and associates her husband's decrepit friend with the self-proclaimed "pícaro" Gabriel by calling him a "pica-rón" (209). Francisca thus plays a role in the drama of authorial concern with readers' attitudes in her undermining of the authority of both these men. However, Gabriel observes Marcial's recapturing of his listener's (reader's) interest, when the old man shifts to an account of his earlier experiences in battle (213). After Marcial gives a gripping description of the conflict, embellished with his personalized version of the Spanish language, which serves as a vivid reminder of the color, fantasy, and fictionality of the narrated history, Francisca reacts positively. Marcial now has her attention, and relishes his control of the story as she demonstrates her continued interest by asking several questions (214).

When Francisca concludes that the Spaniards should have stayed home, regardless of the valor they displayed, don Alonso joins in as co-author of the story. Alonso recognizes that his wife is an audience for the two men's joint narrative of patriotic action, and takes responsibility for retaining her as a willing "reader" (214). At a point in which Marcial appears disposed to conclude the account of his adventures, Alonso incites him to continue. Marcial is careful to cater to his audience, conveying that her involvement in his story is important to him. When he recounts the loss of his leg, she demonstrates that she has been "seduced" by the story of a man she earlier professed to hate, and now sympathizes with him (215). Ultimately, however, her opinion about war has not changed. Although she admires Marcial's bravery, she also admonishes him, and warns of the dangers of war (216–17).

Thus, Gabriel has learned several things from watching the two men engage Francisca. He has seen that in order to capture her interest, they package historical information in a dramatic form. He has heard how they revive and sustain her curiosity, and he has seen the fading of their control over her as they shift from old battle stories to debating the current military situation. In other words, Gabriel acquaints himself with the experience of past masters, not just in the military arena, but in the construction of tales. He observes the power of dramatized history over an audience, but he also notes the waning of that influence and the reassertion of the "reader's" defiant attitude. Despite the lessons learned, Gabriel demonstrates that he is not as adept at handling this particular reader as are his two experienced companions. The threat of the unruly audience confronts Gabriel when he, don Alonso, and Marcial plan and act out a naval battle. Gabriel joins in happily, and all play enthusiastically until they hear doña Francisca's steps, at which point Marcial and Alonso put away their maps and contain their excitement (217). Gabriel, however, does not curtail his activity, and Francisca punishes him severely, causing him great shame (217–18).

Considering this brief episode carefully, we notice that Gabriel's crime is to continue elaborating the same fantasy that Francisca earlier tolerated in the form of a quasi-historical account. Gabriel's first error is his unwelcome introduction of make-believe into real life by acting out a narrative that should have remained a literary adventure. His second mistake is to overlook the presence and miscalculate the impact of his audience. For

Gabriel, the moral of this particular contretemps is that a hostile audience can present a formidable obstacle for an author of fiction. This lesson remains important for him throughout the series, and he returns often to the threat of the renegade reader.

At this stage in the text, Gabriel strikes out on his own in the textual battle for his readers' approval by cultivating his own favored audience, since Francisca already "belongs" to Alonso and Marcial. His "amita," Rosita, is the only daughter of Alonso and Francisca, and is Gabriel's adored playmate. At the time that Gabriel hears of the potential adventure in Cádiz, Rosita has turned from her childhood companion Gabriel to her fiancé, Rafael, and Gabriel is struggling with his rejection by the girl who used to be his faithful friend. This estrangement is significant to Gabriel's initiation into authorship, because Gabriel begins at this point to imagine Rosita as an audience for his tales, and to wish to recover her with his stories, because he can no longer have her as a companion. In the same way that Alonso and Marcial try to interest Francisca in their narratives, as Gabriel grows in independence from his teachers in life and literature, he cultivates his own ideal reader and listener as he imagines writing his adventures and recounting his thoughts.

When they arrive in Cádiz, where Gabriel was born, the young man becomes more independent of Marcial and Alonso. He has observed their storytelling, has been aroused by their accounts of battle, has found his own ideal reader, and now begins a new stage in his development as an author, which coincides with his return to his birthplace.[5] In Cádiz, and also on board various warships, Gabriel negotiates his literary style and principles, recognizing his debt to his two protectors, but also defining his own text of national adventure as produced expressly for the recruitment and retention of an audience. Involved in this elaboration of textual goals is the reconciliation of history, action, and fiction, which begins with Gabriel's encounter with a new set of purveyors of fiction, whom he sets up as negative role models. The poets of Cádiz, whom Gabriel describes as "encopetados" (haughty), "discretos y elegantes" (discreet and elegant), of "afeminados gestos" (effeminate gestures and expressions) and "trajes . . . extravagantísimos" (excessively elaborate outfits), were inclined to use monocles, "para que tales figuras fueran completamente mamarrachos" (232). [so that they achieved an utterly ridiculous appearance.] All of these characters write inferior poetry and spend their time in the Academia, where they meet to "tirotearse con sus estrofas, entretenimiento que no hacía daño a nadie" (233). [take shots at each other with their stanzas, an entertainment which harmed no one.] In contrast to their vacuous literary works, Gabriel would like to think of himself as offering fiction based on historical (and autobiographical) fact. Gabriel's choice of the word "tirotearse" to describe what the poets do with their verses mocks the notion of real gunfire, and the final clause, "que no hacía daño a nadie," instead of rationalizing approval of the poets' activity, becomes a critique of their indolence in a time of national peril. Gabriel also suggests that the texts these authors produce are worthless because of their lack of ties to history, and confirms his contrasting role as responsible historical narrator by recounting the story of the visit of the military leader Churruca, soon to be Spain's martyr at Trafalgar.

Nevertheless, if we are inclined to consider Gabriel's decision to go to war as self-sacrifice for the sake of the glories of national history, we should remember that he in fact participates in battle as a search for something personal. He wishes to distinguish himself from the foppish, empty-headed poets by creating literature about historical events, but particularly about those encounters with history that he himself will protagonize. Gabriel covets the starring role of the author, and dreams of enjoying absolute control of his narrative, which he will use to seduce his audience. He confirms this agenda once on board the ship:

Ver cómo era la batalla, cómo se disparaban los cañones, cómo se apresaban los buques enemigos . . . , ¡qué hermosa fiesta!; y luego volver a Cádiz cubiertos de gloria . . . Decir a cuantos quisieran oírme: "Yo estuve en la escuadra; lo vi todo . . ." Decírselo también a mi amita, contándole la grandiosa escena y excitando su atención, su curiosidad, su interés . . . Decirle también: "Yo me hallé en los sitios de mayor peligro, y no temblaba por eso." Ver cómo se altera, cómo palidece y se asusta, oyendo referir los horrores del combate, y luego mirar con desdén a todos los que digan: "¡Contad, Gabrielito, esa cosa tan tremenda! . . ." ¡Oh!, esto era más de lo que necesitaba mi imaginación para enloquecer . . . ; digo francamente que en aquél día no me hubiera cambiado por Nelson. (236)

[To see what battle was like, how the cannons fired, how enemy ships were captured. What a beautiful party! And then to return to Cádiz covered with glory. To say to anyone who would listen to me: "I was in the squadron; I saw it all." To say it all also to my little mistress, telling her about the great scene and exciting her attention, her curiosity, her interest. To say to her also: "I was in the most dangerous places, and I was not afraid." To see how she would get upset, turn pale, and become frightened, hearing me recount the horrors of combat, and then I would look with disdain at all those who might say: "Tell, Gabriel, that tremendous story!" Oh!, this was more than my imagination needed in order to go crazy, I say sincerely that on that day I would not have changed places with Nelson himself.]

Clearly, Gabriel is motivated by the potential scene of his adoring "amita" as audience. When he says that he would not change places with Admiral Nelson, the commander of the British fleet, he means that it is less important to him to be the actual hero of the battle than it is to survive the engagement and return to land as the glorious historian of the event. Perhaps he has learned from the mendacious José María Malespina (226) that the author of an adventure can present himself as its hero, no matter the historical reality. Later, when he recounts his awakening and the fading of his lofty illusions and even of the glories of reality (258), the reference to Calderón's *La vida es sueño* is obvious. Perhaps he realizes that if even reality is a dream, then the only thing left is dreams of literature, like Calderón's play. In this way, by writing the story of the event, Gabriel can be as much a battle hero—or at least as much a hero of his own account— as he wishes.

As the battle rages, there is a gradual shifting of physical (and textual) power away from the two old men and onto Gabriel. Gabriel transposes oral tradition into his written text, capturing "todo lo que nos cuentan" (all that is told to us) by characterizing his acquaintance with these classical stories as an exclusively oral (aural) experience, so that he can present himself as the only author of written stories. He takes over firing a cannon from Marcial, thereby replacing Alonso as Marcial's partner in action, and portraying himself as actor rather than spectator. Gabriel complements this increase in action in both his naval and textual endeavors by imagining Rosita watching his acts of heroism (245). In other words, the purpose of Gabriel's participation in this entire military operation is to be able to recount the adventure, and to have the adoring attention of Rosita. Thus, Gabriel is embarking on a new life in which the ebbing physical ability of both Alonso and Marcial transfers to himself (young Gabriel), in the form of potential literary power actualized later by the elderly Gabriel in the writing of the *Episodios*.

When Gabriel discovers that Rosita's fiancé, Rafael, has been slightly wounded but is alive, he focuses on his role as bearer of good news for his audience Rosita (254–55). Although his rival remains a threat, Gabriel is consoled by the thought of himself in a position of narrative power. He increases his narratorial control by making Rafael the narrator of news from other ships—specifically the death of Churruca—but then subordi- nates Rafael's information within his own frame, as main narrator of the novel.[6] Just as the compelling portrayal of Churruca functioned earlier in this episode as confirmation of Gabriel's new identity as historical novel- ist, now his death provides the story that allows Gabriel to replace Rafael as storyteller and console himself for his inability to be Rosita's lover. In this passage that focuses on Rafael's injury, the young Malespina becomes a vehicle for Gabriel the novice author to gain access to his beloved audience, Rosita. By extension, Rafael facilitates the establishment of a connection between Gabriel and future readers.

Gabriel appears particularly agitated by the idea of Churruca (258). His preoccupation with the martyr of Trafalgar recalls for his readers that this is the same Churruca whose story has been controlled for a time by Rafael, Gabriel's rival for Rosita, even though Gabriel introduced Churruca to readers of the *Episodios* in an earlier passage. At one point, Gabriel falls asleep, and obsessive thoughts of combat color his dreams: "Excuso decir que en aquel reñido combate, forjado dentro de mi propio cerebro, derroté a todos los ingleses habidos y por haber con más facilidad que si sus barcos fueran de cartón y de miga de pan sus balas" (258). [It goes without saying that in that bitter combat, forged inside my own brain, I destroyed all English who ever lived with more ease than if their ships had been made of cardboard and their cannonballs of bread crumbs.] Of course, this is a dream about controlling the story of various battles, and Gabriel will attain the power to do so when he chronicles the events of the day. When he ends his account of his imaginary battle by referring to the games he played as a child with his friends (258), Gabriel establishes a parallel with his diversions with Marcial and Alonso at the beginning of the novel. His various exercises in make-believe were not just about the battle, but prepared him for the challenge of storytelling.

When the Spaniards on board the occupied *Santa Ana* fight to recover their ship from the English, Gabriel muses that this example of Spanish bravery is largely ignored in traditional historical accounts of the battle (259). Here, in telling the tale himself, Gabriel is remedying the lack of historical attention to the retaking of the ship, while also acknowledging the power implicit in writing history. Just at this moment Gabriel witnesses his master Alonso make a similar assertive gesture, a military action that echoes Gabriel's celebration of himself as author of a lost episode of the battle of Trafalgar. Alonso clumsily fires a cannon, and shakes with joy as he asserts that Paca will no longer be able to laugh at him (259). In the same way that Alonso commits a last act of heroism for the benefit of his beloved yet resistant audience, Gabriel offers his own public a tale of Spanish bravery which he salvaged from an otherwise crushing defeat. When Gabriel observes that obsessive concern with his reluctant reader has become monomania in Alonso, he realizes that he alone must continue the fight to captivate his audience through rational means, because Alonso has lost his mind (262). This vision of Alonso, now as mad as Don Quijote, reminds Gabriel of the dangers of untrammeled fantasy.

Nevertheless, Gabriel also acknowledges the difficulty of separating fact from fiction. The novel closes with his recognition of the paradox that some of the outrageous lies told by the older Malespina (Rafael's father), such as his stories of huge steam-powered warships, have actually come true (265). At the same time, the "fact" he thought was true—that his rival Rafael was dead—turns out to be false. Increasing awareness of the dangers of oversimplifying categories of truth and fiction thus forms a part of Gabriel's complex examination of the power of narrative. Whereas the blurred boundaries of reality and fantasy have already unsettled Gabriel, he is further destabilized when he arrives at the house of the newlyweds Rafael and Rosita, and overhears his "amita" giving all of her attention to another storyteller: her new husband (275). Scorned by his former audience, Gabriel departs for Cádiz, intending then to go to Madrid, presumably in search of a new public of "readers." Perhaps because he knows he can never win the attention he desires, Gabriel gives up that particular fight. Thus, in this first novel of the series, the protagonist-narrator learns about the powers he possesses as an author when he convincingly articulates his project of writing national history for an audience. At the same time, Gabriel realizes that this intended reader can easily escape authorial control. The next two novels continue to explore the topic of the legitimacy of Gabriel's authority.

La corte de Carlos IV

In *La corte de Carlos IV,* which opens in 1807, Gabriel addresses some of the insecurities that plagued him as a novice author in *Trafalgar.* We return to the complex topic of Gabriel's "specialness," the quality that might allow him to distinguish himself on the basis of his skill in the project of interpreting and creating texts. Gabriel himself raises this issue when he explains that he has found his job by advertising in the newspaper, and that he feels recognized for his "natural qualities" because he has been hired by the actress Pepa González (277). From the first paragraph, then, this novel offers Gabriel as noteworthy, then quickly deflates notions of the protagonist as distinguished, consigning him to less than illustrious company. Still, Gabriel presents himself as having innate good taste, in the sense that he is able to look down on the inferior inclinations of Pepa. According to Gabriel, Pepa's taste in theater is quite bad, in that she prefers inferior sentimental literature to the modern works of Moratín (279–80). While Pepa, "rancia e intransigente española por los cuatro costados" (in every respect an old-fashioned and uncompromising Spanish woman) rejects Moratín's school as foreign, Gabriel suggests that the Spanish works by Comella which she praises lack literary merit. From his vantage point in the 1870s, he can safely conclude that none of the plays Pepa admired survived the nineteenth century with any degree of respect. When Pepa does turn to Spanish works that have achieved canonical status, it is only to rebuff her enemies, not because she recognizes the works' quality (280).

As he denigrates Pepa, Gabriel subtly distinguishes himself as a connoisseur of national literary treasures. His description of Pepa as opposing Moratín, given within the same paragraph in which he laments her bad taste, allies Gabriel with this controversial, yet celebrated playwright of the

Spanish Enlightenment.[7] In addition, Gabriel's account of his daily tasks—going on errands in search of elixirs, drugs, and clothing items, cleaning his *ama*'s costumes, spying on Isidoro Máiquez (the director of Pepa's acting troupe), and playing roles—recalls the occupations of Celestina, the protagonist of the *Tragicomedia de Calisto y Melibea*. Futhermore, embedded in the list of activities in imitation of Celestina is an echo of *Lazarillo de Tormes,* which we know from his narration of *Trafalgar* that Gabriel has read. Every day, Gabriel takes food to the starving playwright Comella, who writes the plays Pepa loves.[8] In the same way that Lazarillo must beg for food for his starving master the proud squire, Gabriel provides for the primary figure in his adoptive family—the man who should be "feeding" his adherents Pepa and Gabriel with his success in the theater. Finally, the chapter closes with a statement in which Gabriel identifies with Galdós himself, borrowing the celebrated novelist's own words: "De buena gana me extendiera aquí haciendo algunas observaciones sobre los partidos dramáticos de entonces y sobre los conocimientos del pueblo en general y de los que se disputaban su favor con tanto encarnizamiento" (280). (I would gladly have elaborated here, making observations about the factions in the Spanish drama of the day, about the knowledge possessed by the public in general, and about those whose favor was sought so fiercely.) In this one clause, Gabriel echoes the title as well as the content of Galdós's 1870 essay, "Observaciones sobre la novela contemporánea en España," (Observations on the Contemporary Novel in Spain) and manifests the same desire to be an arbiter of literary style that Galdós exhibits in "Observaciones."

Thus, with a preponderance of examples, the older Gabriel who composes the *Episodios* demonstrates his abundant knowledge of Spanish literature.[9] Nevertheless, the reliance of Gabriel's narrative on the readings subsequent to his early adventures begs the question of the cultural acuity of the younger Gabriel. The innocent Gabriel employed by the unenlightened Pepa must still pass through a series of tests before he can attain the cultural competence of his older self. With these literary contests and competitions, young Gabriel attempts to establish himself as both a sensible author and a capable reader. The primary feature of Gabriel's literary apprenticeship is his drive to distinguish himself from other characters, as we shall now see.

In the novel's second chapter, Gabriel turns to his role, which he now regrets, in the 1806 premiere of Leandro Fernández de Moratín's *El sí de las niñas* (280).[10] Here, Gabriel continues in his identification with canonical cultural texts. This is not an easy task because the young Gabriel, in service to the anti-Moratinist Pepa, conspires with unsavory accomplices in an attempt to disturb the performance. Gabriel manages to separate himself from the others in his group by emphasizing his good instincts—

he liked the play in spite of himself—as well as the temporal distance between the adolescent servant and the elderly, experienced reader
and cultural critic penning the memoirs that constitute the *Episodios*. In
a sense, Gabriel benefits in these passages from his dual nature, and
his historical perspective allows him to present himself as superior to
those around him. The poet-playwright who leads the conspiracy in which
Gabriel is involved is the primary target of Gabriel's ridicule (281).

If Gabriel speaks condescendingly of the leader of the literary rebels, he
also critiques the rest of the audience. Led by the bad poet to the *cazuela*
(the "gods," or gallery of the theater), in the physical sense, Gabriel looks
down on the entire spectacle, while the reduced cost of the seating in this
area draws him into contact with the lowest stratum of spectators. Gabriel
notes this paradox: "Ocupamos los mejores asientos de la región para-
disíaca, donde se concertaban todos los discordes ruidos de la pasión
literaria y todos los malos olores de un público que no brillaba por su
cultura" (281). [We occupied the best seats of the highest part of the
theater, which combined all the discordant noise of literary passion and all
the evil odors of an audience that was not known for its refinement.] Yet
despite their foul smell, Gabriel emphasizes the natural talent of these
people to judge works of art—they are grotesque in their outer manifestations, but they have a great artistic instinct. Here the novel makes an
important connection of this innate aesthetic taste to fairness in reception
of art works, in the sense that the people are not afraid to boo and reject bad
authors; at the same time, they are pliable in the hands of the talented
(281). Gabriel argues that because this audience is but a feeble child with
respect to the artist, spectators should not be blamed for a playwright's
failure: "Si alguien no pudo jamás tenerle propicio, culpa suya fue" (281).
(If anyone was unable to win them over, it was his own fault.) Here, the
apprehensions of the fledgling author Gabriel are subjugated, countered by
the ambitious challenge that it is an author's responsibility to captivate an
audience.[11] As in this passage, we will see that the narrator does not
consistently maintain this magnanimous attitude, and occasionally berates
the uncouth public. Two of his challenges as an author are defending
himself from misunderstanding and "selling" his work to an audience.
Gabriel's vulnerability on these two points at times leads him to make
hostile statements about the public he imagines as his adversary.

If we turn back to Gabriel and his co-conspirators, we note that by
separating himself from his companions Gabriel suggests to his readers
that he will, in the end, approve of the play. However, he does not merely
criticize the literary taste of the bad poet, but incorporates *El sí de las niñas*
into the very fabric of his description of the theater, thus anticipating,
approving, and appropriating Moratín's plot, in a continuation of the al-

liance with cultural canonical texts which he began in the first chapter of *El corte de Carlos IV*. Gabriel describes the theater in the following way:

Mirando el teatro desde arriba, parecía el más triste recinto que puede suponerse. Las macilentas luces de aceite, que encendía un mozo saltando de banco en banco, apenas le iluminaban a medias, y tan débilmente, que ni con anteojos se descubrían bien las descoloridas figuras del ahumado techo, donde hacía cabriolas un señor Apolo con lira y borceguíes encarnados. Era de ver la operación de encender la lámpara central, que, una vez consumida tan delicada maniobra, subía lentamente por máquina, entre las exclamaciones de la gente de arriba, que no dejaba pasar tan buena ocasión de manifestarse de un modo ruidoso (281–82)

[Looking down at the theater from above, it seemed the saddest place imaginable. The wan oil lights, lit by a boy jumping from bench to bench, barely illuminated the theater, and did it so weakly that even with opera glasses the discolored figures of the smoky ceiling—including an Apollo scampering about wearing half-boots and carrying a lyre—could not be seen well. It was something to see the lighting of the main lamp, which, as soon as the delicate maneuver was performed, was raised slowly by a machine, amidst the exclamations of the people seated above, who did not miss the opportunity to noisily make their presence known.]

This description is a metaphorical representation of the action of Moratín's play. The first scenes are plagued by a darkness that hides the love relationship (represented by the mythological scene on the ceiling) growing between Paquita and Carlos. The last night of the play's action—the third act—is marked by a gradual dawning, and don Diego's realization that he must grant Paquita the freedom to choose her lover even over himself, her fiancé. Just as the "gente de arriba" exclaim as light is forced upon them, perhaps even protesting the change, don Diego alters his position, at first uncomfortably, while doña Irene resists more tenaciously. In this way, by reproducing *El sí de las niñas,* and anticipating it in a re-authoring gesture, Gabriel presents himself as the hero of a new drama of enlightenment. Here, then, the older, well-read Gabriel steps in to support his younger self, whose alliance with quality literature might have been less definitive without the assistance of his older incarnation.

When the play begins, the bad poet at Gabriel's side attacks Moratín for the use of pedestrian scenification, boring characters, and lowly ideas, and inserts passages from one of his own plays as a contrast, with overblown language that calls into question his fitness as a critic (282–83). However, despite the conspirators' loud yawns, whistles, and complaints, to Gabriel's secret satisfaction, good artistic instincts predominate among the sensible audience that surrounds him and his ignoble companions. In a pattern that repeats itself in this novel, Gabriel juxtaposes himself with an inferior judge of literature, and the absurdities this figure utters showcase Gabriel's good sense. When Gabriel attempts to disagree with the poet, praising the play's lack of artificiality and tentatively suggesting that Moratín's recommendations for reform in the education of girls are laudable, his companion mocks him. Gabriel counters with the idea that the theater should provide entertainment as well as be didactic, and the bad poet again dismisses him (285).

Yet the head conspirator receives a just punishment in the end. Members of the audience pull his large hat over his eyes, leaving him in the darkness he has consistently chosen over Moratín's illumination. Others free him from the hat, and he swears he will avenge himself in the next showings of *El sí de las niñas.* He is prevented from doing so, though, by the presence of a powerful protector of Moratín—a historical personage who is central to this *episodio*—the prime minister Manuel Godoy, *Príncipe de la Paz* (285).[12] Godoy thus identifies with Moratín, whom *La corte de Carlos IV* classifies at this point as a "good" writer, and becomes the playwright's patron, as Gabriel wishes he could do.[13] If Gabriel is unable to silence the inferior judge of his culture at the time they attend the premiere, his surrogate Godoy effectively preserves a work of art that Gabriel favors.

In this way, while the older Gabriel, who has in the intervening years become literate and cultured, supplants Moratín, the younger Gabriel is left in a more subservient position, as he places his hopes for justice in the criticism of art in the hands of a sensible public, and watches the powerful Godoy protect the artist Moratín. In other words, young and relatively helpless, Gabriel is forced to rely on the rest of the audience to express his taste in art, on Godoy to protect the artist he favors, and on his older incarnation to reauthor and compete with Moratín.

With his attendance at the premiere of *El sí de las niñas,* Gabriel raises the issue of the public's good judgment. Gabriel's examination of the dilemmas of the author shapes his ambivalent portrayal of the audience as at times sensible and on other occasions misguided. On one hand, he trusts the audience's capacity to judge an artwork fairly, and, as seen above, holds the artist responsible for pleasing the public. However, Gabriel also includes less flattering images of the play's audience, as when he comments on their raucousness and foul odor. This contradictory presentation of the public is the result of authors' apprehensions about the people's power, as examined in the introduction: the audience interprets works of art and literary representations of the nation, yet the degree of liberty possessed by that same public threatens any artist or writer who produces artworks for the public's consumption. Gabriel the author exhibits obvious anxiety about the fickleness of readers, as they listen to another author of tales at a meal Pepa hosts near the beginning of the novel. Seated near the marqués, Gabriel observes how the older man's mocking audience—the actor Isidoro, the duchess Lesbia, the nobleman Mañara, and even the countess Amaranta—treats him. Gabriel juxtaposes this disdain with Pepa's reaction to the marqués. Pepa suffers from jealousy as Isidoro and Lesbia engage in intimate, exclusive conversation, and she refocuses her unexpressed passion for Isidoro on the marqués. Instead of discussing love, she encourages him in his fantasies of diplomatic power (298). Incited by Pepa, the self-important marqués regales the party with diatribes on Godoy's influence, the minister's conspiracies with Napoleon, the French invasion of Portugal and Spain, and the future of the royal family, protesting all the while that he should not be revealing such guarded secrets.[14] By ridiculing the marqués, the text (Gabriel) pokes fun at didactic literature, and at the addled author's drive to teach and thus control the capricious reader.

Eventually, when the marqués requests yet again that his audience not beg him for information, Isidoro tires of the charade, and promises they will ask him no more, in an effort to embarrass him. The marqués then turns his attention to his meal, attempting from time to time to captivate Pepa, who displays a complete lack of interest, and merely stares at the two lovers (299). In this way, Isidoro breaks the marqués's spell over Pepa, and she acts as the consummate fickle audience, rejecting the older man's narratives and deserting the person who was her preferred storyteller. Indeed, in this arena, Lesbia parallels Pepa. Both have an interest in Máiquez—Pepa's presumably more genuine than Lesbia's—and display a changeable nature, with Lesbia alternating between Máiquez and Mañara, and Pepa quickly turning from attentive audience to unreceptive listener. By establishing this specularity,[15] the novel calls attention to the inconstant reader, implicitly comparing her to a deceitful lover. In this context of fickle readers and rejected authors, Gabriel tries to prove both his discrimination in reading and his authorial control over the public. As we will see throughout this *episodio,* though, the fact that Gabriel wishes for cultural supremacy does not mean that he can easily attain a position superior to that of the general public, either as a skilled reader or as an authoritative producer of national literature. Gabriel's situation is precarious: he is at once an older cultural commentator benefited by the wisdom provided by hindsight and subsequent readings, and a younger participant in the collective demonstrations of ignorance featured in the *episodio.*

In *La corte de Carlos IV,* there are several instances in which the public reads badly, and Gabriel struggles to distinguish himself from them. The first of these showcases for public misjudgment is the marketplace. When Gabriel arrives at the market, he hears many opinions about Godoy's alleged negotiations with Napoleon. The one view that seems to be shared by all is that Godoy is evil—married to and living with two women at once, plotting to murder the king, and expecting with Napoleon's help to make himself ruler of Portugal (309). One of Godoy's harshest critics is the friar Father Salmón, who focuses on Godoy's assaults on religious institutions in Spain, all the while stealing fruit from Gabriel as they talk (310).

In the marketplace, Gabriel also encounters Comella, the unfortunate playwright whom he and Pepa supported. Comella informs Gabriel that he requires an account of certain details of the battle of Trafalgar, because he intends to compose a play about the battle, romanticizing and distorting it beyond recognition. As Comella describes his play, Gabriel interrupts him with laughter (311), thereby suggesting his superiority to the inept poet. Using Comella as a contrast, Gabriel shores up his own version of the battle, and claims authority as a narrator. Comella also attacks Godoy, exclaiming that no worse man exists in all the land, and citing a previously unmentioned crime as Godoy's most egregious—his protection of "bad" poets. Together with Comella's ridiculous comparison of himself to Cervantes, the playwright's critique of Godoy's tendency to favor so-called inferior poets serves to further ridicule Comella as an unqualified reader, or judge of art of any sort. Lest we wonder which side Gabriel takes in the nearly unanimous condemnation of Godoy, the older Gabriel defends Godoy, and characterizes him as a Quijote figure, imagining and implementing reforms that only meet with resentment and incomprehension (312).

Still at the market, Gabriel speaks finally with one last person whose opinion he values above all others. The illiterate knife grinder Pacorro Chinitas is a character who appears several times in the second and third *episodios,* and whose "good sense" and lack of formal schooling make him a mirror image of Gabriel. In this instance, Gabriel and Chinitas discuss Napoleon's arrangements with Godoy. Many of the speakers in the marketplace have argued that Napoleon is coming to Spain merely to remove Godoy and crown the Prince of Asturias, but Chinitas opines that anyone who believes in Napoleon's beneficence is crazy. Chinitas distinguishes Gabriel and himself from the gullible hordes by emphasizing his and Gabriel's illiteracy (313). Here, Chinitas suggests that the young Gabriel's lack of culture lends him a certain political wisdom, or at least, good sense.

In addition to their extravagant misjudgments of Godoy, the public also engages in misreading at the staging of *Othello,* near the end of the novel. In Gabriel's description of the setting for this production, *La corte de Carlos IV* fictionalizes the painter Francisco de Goya.[16] Specifically, the narrator incorporates Goya into this *episodio* as evidence of his preeminence. The characters prepare for the production of *Othello* at the marquesa's mansion, which has been decorated by Goya in a style of which Gabriel approves (354). However, the mansion's furniture is an artistic

French invasion, and contextualizes Goya's work in a jarring stylistic mix, mocked by Gabriel, but unnoticed by the majority of the guests (354–55). Thus, we see the upper class that sponsors ill-advised artistic productions paralleling the misguided, weak readers Gabriel meets in the marketplace. Although, according to Gabriel, Goya's specific work is in good taste, it is situated in a setting that summarily degrades it, and speaks to the lack of aesthetic sense among the aristocracy.

The final interpretive act of a community in *La corte de Carlos IV* is the spectators' immersion in the end of *Othello*. In earlier gatherings of actors and nobility, such as the dinner at Pepa's, members of *Othello*'s audience have attended social functions with Isidoro Máiquez, who plays the protagonist, so they know him personally. When he discovers that his "wife" Edelmira (the equivalent of Shakespeare's Desdemona) has deceived him, the audience identifies with his genuine grief (366).[17] When Isidoro (Otelo) confronts Lesbia (Edelmira) in her bed, intending to kill her, the audience remains unable to distinguish reality from fantasy, but now defends Edelmira. As Isidoro pursues Lesbia with the real knife that Pepa has substituted for the stage knife, the audience loses control. Led by the aristocratic Lesbia's example, the audience members become artists, acting directly in the play, and begging for mercy for Edelmira and punishment for Pésaro (367). In this way, this interpretive community, which politely ignored the real-life intrigues of Lesbia and her lovers, now attempts to take desperate action when the drama is recast as fiction. Clearly, this is an audience of misreaders, despite their provenance in the upper social classes.

Now, if we return to the marketplace, we find a discussion that allows us some insight into the obstacles Gabriel faces when trying to stand out from the various crowds portrayed in *La corte de Carlos IV*. Pacorro Chinitas makes an oblique reference to Gabriel's greatest challenge in this *episodio,* which is intimately tied to his ability to "read." Chinitas calls the Portugal that Godoy is purported to desire "un reino chiquito" [a tiny kingdom] (313), echoing Gabriel's exact words on the previous night, when he reveled in his own dreams of governing a small kingdom.[18] In this way, Chinitas associates Godoy with Sancho Panza, and implicitly with Gabriel. Thus, while he praises illiteracy, Chinitas also suggests paradoxically that questions of reading and critical sensibility may not be so simple, because ignorance of the written word does not protect one from the seductions of impossible dreams, as in the case of Sancho Panza. In the next chapters, as Gabriel navigates life in the palace, his most significant challenge is resisting the quixotic narrative of Godoy.

Indeed, Godoy figures as important throughout this *episodio* because Gabriel dreams of imitating his rise to power. Gabriel's girlfriend, the seamstress Inés, makes explicit the connection of this pipedream to the

Quijote. She surprises Gabriel with her wise skepticism about his plans for a quick ascent in court, then explains that other than religious texts, she has only read Cervantes's novel. She astutely compares Gabriel to Cervantes's protagonist, yet ranks her young friend below the knight-errant because Gabriel lacks the "wings" that Don Quijote possessed, but was unable to use in his particular environment (289). Gabriel recognizes that she is right, and implicitly that she is the better reader of the *Quijote.* In addition, Inés's comparing Gabriel to Don Quijote reminds Gabriel of his need to resist quixotism.

Still, temptations to live according to impossible chivalric models abound in the text. Beginning when Godoy supplants Gabriel in the protection of Moratín against inferior rivals, Gabriel and Godoy parallel each other in several instances in the *Episodios,* and Gabriel's quixotic imagination cultivates their similarities. Whether at Pepa's dinner with the marqués, in the Royal Palace, or on errands while merely thinking about her, Gabriel's association with Amaranta brings him into close contact with the legends of Godoy. Amaranta plays on her page's weakness and vanity, presenting herself as a powerful benefactress who might accord him such favors as the queen had purportedly bestowed on Godoy. Gabriel fantasizes about imitating Godoy's meteoric rise to power (308), and Amaranta tells Gabriel a coded version of the same story, featuring a Sultan, Sultana, and Grand Visir (324, 333–34). Godoy's biography does temporarily seduce Gabriel, but when he discovers the duplicity he will have to practice in order to acquire power in the court, he ultimately renounces such a course of action.[19]

Gabriel's success in resisting the attraction of the Godoy story relates to his recognition of the implausible nature of the narratives inspired by the mysterious minister. In this sense, Gabriel makes progress toward the rejection of quixotism, thanks to his awareness of the lack of concrete information about Godoy, and his desire to distinguish himself from the "misreaders" who fabricate the Godoy legends. As a vaguely discernible figure in *La corte de Carlos IV,* Godoy presents himself as open to interpretation.[20] The one time the prime minister actually appears in the second *episodio,* dressed in a wide black cape, he can only be seen from the back. Gabriel observes only a shape wrapped in a wide cape, and admits that he was unable to discern the person's features (331). In acknowledging that he cannot offer here a precise description of Godoy, Gabriel retreats from the task of incorporating a definitive version of Godoy into his memoirs, yet also eschews the temptation to elaborate fantasy based on very little evidence.[21]

In contrast to Gabriel's apparent "reserve," other characters, such as the actors and aristocrats at Pepa's dinner (301–2), and the *pueblo* Gabriel encounters in the streets of Madrid (309–12), relish the recounting of

Godoy's sensational biography. The various groups who figure in Galdós's novel turn their (un)critical attention to the raw material of the young minister's vague life story, and they form a contrast with Gabriel's interpretation and use of the Godoy stories. The people gossip incessantly about Godoy's terrible crimes, assigning him meaning in their production of stories. Gabriel records their list of accusations and observes their hatred of Godoy, whom they accuse of being "corrompido, dilapidador, inmoral, traficante en destinos, polígamo, enemigo de la Iglesia" [corrupt, wasteful, immoral, a trafficker in positions of employment, a polygamist, an enemy of the Church], and of wanting to usurp the throne (311). With his report of their varied and extravagant charges, Gabriel leads his readers to observe that while he ultimately renounces the melodrama of inventing Godoy, many other characters continue in their quixotic self-deception, blithely producing stories that feature Godoy as a larger-than-life villain.

Gabriel returns to Inés and to Madrid once he has become disillusioned with the palace, the misreadings, and Amaranta, who wanted to employ him as a spy. In conversation with his beloved seamstress, Gabriel admits his earlier errors in judgment, and resolves that he will now learn a trade instead of trying to find shortcuts to positions of power (349). He also rejoins Pepa, in time for the production of *Othello* at the house of the marquesa, aunt of Amaranta. Gabriel accepts the role of Pésaro (Iago), and rehearses with gusto, motivated by the payment he will receive, and by vanity (351). This decision to act in a play confirms—perhaps ironically— his rejection of fantasy. Gabriel's agreement to participate in a dramatic work cements his successful renunciation of quixotism's contamination of his everyday life, and his relegation of the drive to play roles to the theatrical stage itself.

Having resisted the temptations of quixotic thought, Gabriel returns to the marketplace, the setting of his earlier characterization as the ambitious Sancho Panza, and now confidently asserts his superiority over not only the general public, but also the wise Pacorro Chinitas, precisely because Gabriel has in fact mastered the skill of "reading." By doing the exact opposite, a crowd of misreaders of the *Gaceta de Madrid* showcases Gabriel's good sense in rejecting life's infection by extravagant narrative. They discover that Prince Fernando has retracted his challenge to the throne, and they blame Godoy for the frustration of the plan to crown the popular heir as replacement for his disrespected father. The theory that prevails among the people Gabriel interviews is that Godoy forced Fernando to sign the retraction letters in order to humiliate the prince. As Gabriel explains, this cherished hypothesis blinds the people to the prince's faults and to his responsibility for his own actions: "Nadie veía en las citadas cartas una manifestación espontánea del príncipe, sino, antes bien, una denigrante confesión arrancada por sus carceleros para ponerle en ridículo a los ojos del país" (353). [No one saw in said letters a spontaneous declaration by the prince, but rather, a denigrating confession forcibly elicited by his jailers in order to humiliate him in the eyes of the country.]

Gabriel observes that his fellow citizens attribute all manner of ills to Godoy—failed crops, hailstorms, shipwrecks, yellow fever, and whatever other calamities Heaven could visit on the Peninsula (353). In contrast, Pacorro Chinitas, whom Gabriel feels obligated to see before returning home, reacts differently. He is aware of the information in the *Gaceta* (353), but believes that the prince is responsible for what he signs. Gabriel acknowledges his good sense, and calls attention to his illiteracy (354). At first glance, it seems that even after passing the test of the appealing Godoy narrative Amaranta offered him at El Escorial, Gabriel continues to portray favorably the unlearned character Pacorro Chinitas, suggesting that it is preferable to remain illiterate than to fall into the trap of quixotic reading. Nevertheless, we must examine this passage a second time. Here, the older Gabriel places himself above Chinitas, because he (Gabriel) has eventually dominated the written word, retaining his critical skills even after acquiring the ability to read. Gabriel asserts this dominance by incorporating the interchange between himself and Chinitas into his text, the *Episodios,* which must be read. For all of his defense of Chinitas's illiteracy, then, Gabriel's words reach his audience only because he has acquired the ability to write—because he has not, in fact, lived like Chinitas.

To confirm his superior position, Gabriel returns, at the time of the staging of *Othello* and after he has resisted the attractions of the Godoy-Quijote narrative, to the assessment of the playwright Moratín. In the same chapter in which Gabriel discusses Goya's participation in the construction of a monument to bad taste, he addresses the entertainment offered after the first act of the play—verses by Moratín, Arriaza, and Vargas Ponce (356). The narrator digresses in a long description and assessment of Moratín, which balances with its cynicism any idealization of Moratín Gabriel might have offered in his account of the premiere of *El sí de las niñas*. Moratín is a pale, serious man of about forty-five, with a soft voice and a certain "expresión biliosa en su semblante, como hombre a quien amarga la hipocondría y entristece el recelo" (357). [bilious expression on his face, like a man embittered by hypochondria and saddened by distrust.] Gabriel explains that no one can dispute Moratín's responsibility for the restoration of Spanish drama, and that *El sí de las niñas* has always seemed to him a work of most perfect wit. Gabriel praises Moratín for remaining loyal to Godoy even after the minister's fall, when many of his former supporters deserted him, and he reminds his readers of Godoy's expansive support of Moratín. However, ultimately Gabriel finds Moratín's aesthetics limited by his epoch, judges his poetry inferior to his drama, and wishes that Moratín had spent more time producing literature and less time criticizing others. Finally, Gabriel observes that when the public examined his papers after Moratín's death, they found him unaware of international literary developments (357).

Thus, even if he did revive Spanish drama, Moratín is for Gabriel a somewhat pathetic character. He is petty, dependent on the protection of Godoy, inferior as a poet, uninformed about developments in world literature, and scarce in his literary contributions. After this unflattering description, Gabriel recounts Moratín's participation in the program staged along with *Othello*. Moratín reads his "romance" *Cosas pretenden de mí,* which pleases his audience, but ultimately consists only of self-promotion. Gabriel concludes dismissively, leaving Moratín to the empty comforts of flattery (357). In this way, we see the campaign waged by the older Gabriel—benefited by the experience of living long years after the playwright's death—to deflate Moratín. Gabriel's qualification of his earlier praise of Moratín reduces the playwright's threat as rival artist within the *Episodios.*

Moreover, after the production, the spectators discuss Isidoro Maiquez's violent display of jealousy during the play, and Gabriel finds another opportunity to mock Moratín. Most of the audience believes that Isidoro's emotional excess inspired him to identify with his role perfectly (367). Moratín, however, feels differently, arguing that loss of emotional control leads to the corruption of taste and extinguishes "decorum and grace" in fiction, so that the fiction in question becomes confused with "repugnant" reality (367–68). This portrayal of Moratín contrasts provocatively with Gabriel's earlier account of the premiere of his play. While Gabriel praised the "naturalness" of *El sí de las niñas,* here we see Moratín rejecting significant aspects of realism, in favor of more stylized literary representations. In this way, the same chapter that subjects Goya to the degrading whims of his patrons qualifies the earlier positive assessment of Moratín by ridiculing his artistic theory. These two acts of deflationary criticism leave (the older) Gabriel as the arbiter of style in the wake of the other artists' degradation.

When Gabriel leaves the mansion, he formally renounces his former life of *comedias.* Once he arrives at the stairs that lead to Inés's home, he begins to change his outward appearance as well, throwing off the components of his costume (372). In this way, he leaves make-believe in its place in the theater, and resolves to live fiction-free. He rushes to Inés, just as her adoptive mother, Juana, dies. Before losing consciousness, Juana has revealed to Celestino that she rescued Inés when the child's aristocratic mother abandoned her, and Gabriel suspects the connection to Amaranta. He approaches Juana's body, hoping that the dead woman might definitively resolve the issue of Inés's parentage, but then realizes the futility of this wish, and recognizes his madness (374). Gabriel's realization of the impossibility of his desire and his acknowledgment of his own (temporary) insanity mark a shift in the narration. The young man's renunciation of his plans to imitate the stories of Godoy as well as his shedding of his theatrical trappings have anticipated Gabriel's change of heart with respect to the application of literature to life. Gabriel appears to have defeated various obstacles presented by quixotic thinking, and has rejected "locura" (insanity) along with his costume.

Still, in the final chapter, the narrator reopens the question of life's contamination by literature, preparing us for the continued examination of these issues in the rest of the series. In this last chapter, Gabriel takes stock of his youth and of the specific adventures narrated in *La corte de Carlos IV*, likening his experiences to a play. He also compares his life to a novel, adding that this is not a quality special to his adventures, and thereby signaling quixotism's permeation of universal life (374). Gabriel blurs the line between literature and life, and emphasizes the possibility of reading another's life story as a means of entertainment, even as a means of escape. "Todo hombre es autor y actor de algo que, si se contara y escribiera, habría de parecer escrito y contado para entretenimiento de los que buscan recreo en las vidas ajenas, hastiados de la propia por demasiado conocida" (374). [Every man is author and actor of something that, if it were told or written, would necessarily seem written and told for the entertainment of those who, bored with their own excessively familiar lives, look for diversion in the lives of others.] In so doing, he recalls the *Quijote*. Finally, Gabriel confirms the universality of the novelesque aspects of life, arguing that all lives contain literary elements, while all novels feature grains of truth: "No hay existencia que no tenga mucho de lo que hemos convenido en llamar *novela* (no sé por qué), ni libro de este género, por insustancial que sea, que no ofrezca en sus páginas algún acento de vida real y palpitante" (374). [There is no existence that does not have much of what we have agreed to call the *novel* (I do not know why), nor is there a book of that genre, however trite it may be, that does not offer in its pages some degree of real, palpitating life.]

In this way, the *Episodios*' narrator ends this second novel with an implicit question. Although he has successfully navigated a number of temptations to imitate Don Quijote, Gabriel recognizes that there is much more to be said on this topic, and that his own battles are not over. Gabriel's persona as older chronicler and author of the *Episodios* has allowed him to appropriate artists and readings into his text for the purpose of demonstrating his critical superiority, but the young adventurer who constitutes the other half of Gabriel must still face a number of literary challenges, which mirror the vicissitudes of his life during the War for Independence. Gabriel's confrontations with the quixotic mindset, and with his own lack of culture and literacy, continue in *El 19 de marzo y el 2 de mayo*.

EL 19 DE MARZO Y EL 2 DE MAYO

The third novel of the series begins in March 1808, when Gabriel has been employed for months as a typesetter for the *Diario de Madrid,* having kept his promise to Inés to learn a trade. Although he is now in direct contact with literature, Gabriel remains skeptical of the value of the minute, mechanical tasks that he performs, even though his work is basic to the formation and sustenance of a literary culture.[22] This, then, becomes the central question of this third *episodio,* and is a fitting continuation for Gabriel's apprenticeship in realism: Is Gabriel really literate? Perhaps realizing his lack of genuine literacy, young Gabriel finds his job unfulfilling and unimportant, and escapes into the fantasies he earlier resisted. Fictions of Inés allow him emotional and mental release even on workdays, and his spirit frees itself as the letters slip from his fingers to the press. At the same time as he indulges his escapism, Gabriel is aware of the power he has as he controls the words that issue from the printing press (375):

"Las letras pasaban por mi mano, trocándose de brutal y muda materia en elocuente lenguaje escrito. ¡Cuánta animación en aquella masa caótica! En la caja, cada signo parecía representar los elementos de la creación, arrojados aquí y allí, antes de empezar la grande obra. Poníalos yo en movimiento, y de aquellos pedazos de plomo surgían sílabas, voces, ideas, juicios, frases, oraciones, períodos, párrafos, capítulos, discursos, la palabra humana en toda su majestad; y después cuando el molde había hecho su papel mecánico, mis dedos lo descomponían, distribuyendo las letras; cada cual se iba a su casilla, como los simples que el químico guarda después de separados; los caracteres perdían su sentido, es decir, su alma, y tornando a ser plomo puro, caían, mudos e insignificantes, en la caja" (375).

[The letters passed through my hands, turning from crude, mute material into eloquent written language. What animation in that chaotic mass! In the box, each sign seemed to represent the elements of creation, tossed here and there, before beginning the great work. I put them in motion, and from those pieces of lead came syllables, voices, ideas, judgments, sentences, prayers, periods, paragraphs, chapters, discourses, the human word in all its majesty; and afterwards, when the form had played its mechanical role, my fingers would dismantle it, distributing the letters; each one in its pigeonhole, like the simple chemicals the chemist puts away after isolating them from each other; the characters lost their meaning—that is to say, their soul, and becoming pure lead again, they fell, mute and insignificant, into the box.]

In this way, Gabriel experiences several internal conflicts: he senses the power of the written word, he recognizes his own shortcomings and limitations in the fabrication of texts, and he is still attracted by poetic fantasy.

Thus, the first scenes of this novel identify the obstacles young Gabriel will have to face on his journey to become author of the *Episodios*.

Celestino and Inés are now living in Aranjuez, and weekly visits to them further remind Gabriel of his cultural insufficiencies. On one afternoon, Celestino reads Gabriel and Inés a long poem he has composed in praise of Godoy. Celestino explains his motives for reading it to Gabriel by acknowledging the young man's good sense and his devilish knack for understanding things, while at the same time characterizing him as uneducated. For Celestino, then, Gabriel is still a *pícaro*, naturally quick and perceptive, but unstudied. When Gabriel protests Celestino's forcing him to judge the poem, because he does not know a word of Latin, Celestino continues to insist, saying that Gabriel's incomprehension is unimportant. Of course, the reading of four hundred lines of Latin verse makes little impression on Gabriel, even though Celestino takes pains to explain his use of rhetorical figures (378). Despite Celestino's explanation, Gabriel and Inés understand none of the composition, although they listen politely (379). Whereas Gabriel appears unashamed of his ignorance, and the *Episodios* do not show much respect for Celestino's poetry, this incident serves as an additional reminder of young Gabriel's lack of culture.

At the same time, we note that Gabriel's indulgence in fantasies while working at the press mirrors the continued influence of quixotic thinking about his future. When Gabriel insists that he plans to marry Inés, Celestino reminds him that he would be unable to support her. Gabriel informs Inés's "uncle" that he will look for a "destinillo" (a position), a goal Celestino compares to Gabriel's earlier ambitions: "Eso es como cuando se te puso en la cabeza que te iba a caer un principado" (387). [That is like when you got it into your head that a principality was going to fall into your lap.] Gabriel tries to make a distinction between these two dreams, saying that he just wants one of those modest positions they give to any old person—nothing fancy (387). Fortuitously, Celestino has on the following day an appointment with the Prince of Peace, at which time he plans to read his Latin poem. Tempted again by the idea of magical social advancement without the acquisition of education, Gabriel decides to accompany him so that Celestino will be able to request for him the coveted "destinillo." As he goes in pursuit of a quixotic dream, Gabriel again confronts his alter ego Godoy. We now see that whereas Godoy uses art to subdue young Gabriel, the older Gabriel who authors the *Episodios* uses his novel to reduce Godoy and defend the young protagonist.

As a reminder of the continuing importance of the learned and artistic culture Gabriel initially disregards, the *Episodios* present Godoy as enjoying dictatorial control over his subjects' requests. His ability to control his public is directly related to his patronage of art, and Godoy's commanding presence in his government has much to do with his contributions to the art world. When Gabriel and Celestino arrive at the palace, they pass through a hall of tapestries, paintings, statues, vases, and other fine art (391), a setting that reminds the reader of the historical Godoy, whose antechamber was filled with "all that is great and distinguished and beautiful" in Spain.[23] The sight of Godoy's art collection silences Gabriel, who is overcome with shyness at the prospect of meeting the patron responsible for the production of these items. Gabriel briefly glimpses the luxurious decorations and furnishings in Godoy's offices, becomes inhibited, and doubts his ability to express himself in front of Godoy:

> ¡Qué bellos tapices, qué lindos cuadros, qué hermosas estatuas de mármol y bronce, qué vasos tan elegantes, qué candelabros tan vistosos, qué muebles tan finos, qué cortinajes tan espléndidos, qué alfombras tan muelles! No pude detenerme en la contemplación de tan bonitos objetos porque el ujier nos llevaba a toda prisa, y yo me sentía atacado de una cortedad tal, que se disipó mi anterior envalentonamiento, y empecé a comprender que me faltarían ideas y saliva para expresar ante el príncipe mis anhelos (391).

> [What beautiful tapestries, what pretty paintings, what lovely bronze and marble statues, what elegant glasses, what colorful candelabras, what fine furniture, what splendid draperies, what soft carpets! I was unable to stop to contemplate such pretty objects because the usher led us at top speed, and I was afflicted with such shyness, that my earlier bravery disappeared, and I began to realize that I would lack the ideas and saliva necessary to express my desires to the prince.]

Gabriel reads these works of art as signs of power linked to Godoy's patronage system in a reaction similar to that of the Spanish people to the historical Godoy.[24] Just as such riches must have intimidated the minister's real-life subjects, the art patronized by the fictional Godoy subdues Gabriel, and contradicts his confident determination to seek a "destinillo" despite his lack of education.

However, since Godoy is now a character in Gabriel's memoirs, the older Gabriel—defender of his younger self—is able to use art to "contain" the once-powerful minister, just as he reduced Moratín's stature for posterity. Gabriel begins this deflationary process by giving a physical description of Godoy that makes him seem a paragon of conventionality. In appearance he is more agreeable than handsome, with a large, turned-up nose that gives him an expression of sincerity and communicativeness. He seems to Gabriel to be about forty-five years old—pleasant to look at, with lively eyes, fine manners, a graceful head, and a body smaller rather than larger (391). With the wisdom provided by the years that have passed between this event and the time in which he writes, Gabriel then offers an assessment of Godoy's role in Spanish history, which again contextualizes him as unable to rise above the misconceptions of his age: "en su cabeza bullían el desvanecimiento, la torpeza, los extravíos y falsas ideas acerca de los hombres y las cosas de su tiempo" (391–92). [in his head there seethed complacency, clumsiness, errors, and mistaken ideas about the people and things of his period.] In other instances the text is sympathetic to Godoy, but here we have a deflationary description that counters any argument that the *Episodios* serve as an uncomplicated apology for his role in history. If Gabriel sees Godoy as a competitor—a rival patron of the arts—his memoirs successfully reduce the minister to the level of the commonplace.

Nevertheless, like the protective gesture in *La corte de Carlos IV* to salvage Gabriel from association with the *antimoratinistas* at the premiere of *El sí de las niñas,* this textual reduction of Godoy is merely a temporary solution. In the rest of *El 19 de marzo y el 2 de mayo,* Gabriel is constantly thrown into and absorbed by menacing, uncultured crowds. At times he resists, but throughout this third *episodio* he struggles to free himself completely from the association with hordes of cultural barbarians. Crowds begin to appear immediately after this visit to Godoy. As Gabriel and Celestino return home, the older man laments the presence in Aranjuez of large numbers of outsiders, who form a mob. The crowd frightens Gabriel-author because of its potential to be uncontrolled cultural critics.[25] Fittingly, the threatening mob figures in the text just as (young) Gabriel's legitimacy is called into question by his lack of culture. Celestino expresses his hatred for the crowd, and indeed, the large numbers of unfamiliar people inspire fear in the entire town. Gabriel observes that groups of ominous strangers argue riotously, and explains that general opinion held that there had never been so many people in Aranjuez. Celestino asks his sacristan Santurrias why this "gentuza" (rabble) has come to Aranjuez, and what this "canalla" (mob) could possibly want (393). When Celestino sends Gabriel out to investigate, the young man sees that all over the city the numbers of people are growing. Gabriel contextualizes the crowd's enthusiastic support of their rulers the king and queen within their misreadings of Godoy, so that his description of them as generous seems ironic (394–95). When Gabriel's friend Lopito explains that people are being paid to acclaim the king and queen and to call for Godoy's death, Gabriel questions this practice, imagining that the king will wish to quell an incipient rebellion of this sort with the troops he has at his command, and arguing that the king should in fact control the people (396). His concern for order and the people's acceptance of the king's authority recalls again the parallel between the unruly mob in the streets and the undisciplined public confronting would-be authors—preoccupations particularly of the older narrator of the *Episodios.*

Continuing with his portrayal of the people as undiscriminating, the narrator even condemns the characters associated with culture, poetry, and rhetoric—that is, people of the word. In a tavern where Gabriel and Lopito converse together many people have gathered, including the inferior poet who led the protest of *El sí de las niñas*. Using the perspective of his older self, Gabriel mocks the poet and his companion as poor excuses for artists. Lopito explains that these last characters have come to Aranjuez from Madrid, sponsored by the conspirators, so that the rebellion would seem to have the support of educated men ("científicos") (398). Again we see that, drawing on the historical perspective that allows him to distinguish authors of classics from perpetrators of literary fads, and proposing by implication that he is a better judge of national intellectual life than these inferior poets, the older Gabriel does not hesitate to scorn official representatives of cultured society.

Gabriel attends an organizational meeting in which an uncultured crowd listens to their leader, Pujitos. The text connects this figure to literature by comparing him to "regular guy" characters from the work of Ramón de la Cruz, although Pujitos himself does not know how to read (399). He is blessed, nevertheless, with his own "Spanish" style of interpreting material others read to him: "Tenía su poco de imaginación . . . Tenía ese don particular, también español neto, que consiste en asimilarse fácilmente lo que se oye, pero exagerando o trastornando de tal manera las ideas, que las repudiara el mismo que por primera vez las echó al mundo" (399). [He had his own sort of imagination . . . He had that particular gift, also characteristically Spanish, which consists of assimilating easily all that one hears, but exaggerating and distorting ideas in such a way that they would be rejected even by their progenitors.] Gabriel, aware of the political events of the seventy years following the incidents in Aranjuez, projects Pujitos into his own present, making him literate, and arguing that his political influence would still be considerable. In the older Gabriel's day, Pujitos would have been a shoemaker who subscribed to two or three newspapers, and would have incorporated revolutionary vocabulary into the harangues he delivered to his audiences (399–400).

Pujitos, then, is the man who leads the poets. Here, the novel pokes fun at Pujitos's pedestrian nature by comparing this scene to one that might take place on Mount Olympus:

Mientras limpia el sudor de su frente coronada con los laureles oratorios, la moza de la taberna se acerca a escanciarle vino. ¿Es Hebe, la gallarda copera de los dioses, que vierte el néctar de Chipre en el vaso de oro del joven de los rubios cabellos, al regresar de la diurnal carrera? No: es Mariminguilla, la ninfa de Perales de Tajuña, a quien trajo desde las riberas de aquel florido río el señor

Malayerba, dándole el cargo de escanciadora mayor, que desempeña entre pellizcos y requiebro (400).

[As he wipes the sweat from his brow crowned with laurels in recognition of his bravery, the barmaid draws near, in order to serve him wine. Is it Hebe, the lovely cupbearer of the gods, who pours the nectar of Cyprus into the golden glass of the blond-haired young man after he returns from his daily run? No: it is Mariminguilla, the nymph of Perales de Tajuña, brought from the banks of that flowered river by Mister Malayerba, who gave her the job of head pourer, which she carries out amidst pinches and flattery.]

Pujitos incites the crowd to take up arms against Godoy, which they do. Lopito is unable to explain to Gabriel exactly what the mob is going to do at Godoy's mansion, but still happily follows his leaders, anticipating an error in judgment that Gabriel will also make (401). There is a shot, followed by some confusion, and the mob tears down the door to the palace belonging to the Prince of Peace, inspiring Gabriel's disapproval of their blind rage (401–2). He explains that lukewarm supporters, salaried servants, and even the eternally beholden always desert their fallen idols, exhibiting base ingratitude along with their hatred (402).

Here, though, as witness to the brutality, Gabriel also becomes a participant, and calls into question his alleged superiority to the mob. Gabriel is shocked by the anger and savagery of the crowd, which has broken down the door to the mansion, and has thrown itself inside, "bramando de coraje" (bellowing with rage). The mob's savage panting ("salvaje resoplido") provokes in him terror and indignation, particularly because the people were going to quench their thirst ("saciar su sed") with the body of a defenseless man (402). Gabriel then doubts the crowd's ability to make fair judgments, as they play a role in deciding the fate of political figures that recalls their control over literary texts: "Era aquélla la primera vez que veía yo al pueblo haciendo justicia por sí mismo, y desde entonces le aborrezco como juez" (402). [That was the first time I saw the public taking justice into its own hands, and from that time I have hated the public as judge.] The passage ostensibly refers to the *pueblo*'s act of vengeance perpetrated on Godoy's body and possessions, but the reference to the people as "juez" connects the event to the expression of public opinion in the cultural arena, particularly if we remember Godoy's fame as patron of the arts and education.[26] When Gabriel recognizes the public's potential for vile conduct, he problematizes his earlier admonition to authors and artists to accept the will of the public. When describing the public's good judgment at the time of the premiere of Moratín's play, Gabriel said: "Si alguien no pudo jamás tenerle propicio, culpa suya fue" (281). [If anyone was unable to win them over, it was his own fault.]

At this point, Gabriel's memoirs begin to focus on the precise nature of the crowd's destructive acts. First, they attack the furniture of the mansion, which responds with anthropomorphized cries as it breaks under "las garras de la fiera" (the beast's talons), and the mob seems less human than its victims, the art objects. Although he claims no sympathy with the cause, and wishes to disavow himself of responsibility for his actions, Gabriel is dragged into the crowd by his alter ego Lopito, whom he refers to as an adolescent devil. Gabriel passes through the same rooms he visited two days earlier, where the costly furniture that intimidated him before now receives cruel treatment at the hands of the mob. As Gabriel explains, the crowd is unable to express its "hambre de destrucción" (hunger for destruction) toward the "objeto humano" (human object) of its anger, so it avenges itself on the "bodies" of Godoy's innocent furniture (402). Gabriel describes the scene in the following way, highlighting the mob's stupidity, brutality, ignorance, and animality:

La multitud subía y bajaba, abría alacenas, rompía tapices, volcaba sofas y sillones . . . hacía trizas a puntapiés los biombos pintados; desahogaba su indignación en inocentes vasos de China; esparcía lujosos uniformes por el suelo; desgarraba ropas; miraba con estúpido asombro su espantosa faz en los espejos y después los rompía . . . se arrojaba sobre los finos muebles para quebrarlos; escupía los cuadros de Goya; golpeaba todo por el simple placer de descargar sus puños en alguna parte; tenía la voluptuosidad de la destrucción, el brutal instinto tan propio de los niños por la edad como de los que lo son por la ignorancia; rompía con fruición los objetos de arte, como rompe el rapaz en su despecho la cartilla que no entiende; y en esta tarea de exterminio, la terrible fiera empleaba a la vez y en espantosa coalición todas sus herramientas: las manos, las patas, las garras, las uñas y los dientes, repartiendo puñetazos, patadas, coces, rasguños, dentelladas, testarazos y mordiscos. (402)

[The crowd ascended and descended—it opened cupboards, ripped tapestries, turned over couches and chairs . . . smashed to pieces the painted screens; it vented its indignation on innocent Chinese glasses; it scattered luxurious uniforms over the floor; it tore clothes; it looked with stupid surprise at its terrifying face in the mirrors and then broke them . . . it hurled itself on top of the fine furniture in order to break it; it spat on paintings by Goya; it beat upon everything for the simple pleasure of discharging its fists somewhere; it had the voluptuosity of destruction, the brutal instinct typical of children, whether children because of age or ignorance; it broke with pleasure objects of art as does the youngster who rips with resentment the page he does not understand, and in this task of extermination, the terrible beast employed at the same time and in frightening unison all of its tools: hands, feet [of an animal], claws, nails, and teeth, doling out punches, kicks, buckings, scratches, snaps of the jaw, headbutts and bites.]

Over and over, the animalistic crowd confronts art without understanding it, and turns this incomprehension to violence, like a frustrated reader who rips up a difficult piece of writing. In this passage, Gabriel links the public's rage directly to the act of reading—the invaders are unable to understand the works of art they handle, so they act with anger to destroy their victims. The crowd celebrates the substitution of one victim for another, throwing out the window the paintings, tapestries, china, clothing, and furniture which they see as Godoy's accomplices (403). Thus, because the people are unable to discriminate and correctly value the works of art, this *episodio* connects riotous destruction with the loss of critical judgment.[27]

At this point, we begin to see revealed the continuing lack of judgment of the young Gabriel, and the reasons why his distinction from this mob is ultimately problematic. Gabriel now takes an even more active role, although he excuses his actions by saying that he was merely trying to escape suspicion. He refers to himself and his accomplices as monsters— the Cyclopes of an immense forge—and emphasizes that he too participated in the violence, which he claims he did in order to avoid drawing attention to himself as a dissenter (403). Gabriel knows that these deeds are politically pointless, yet at the end of the chapter that narrates the *motín de Aranjuez,* Gabriel commits an act that further degrades him, so that he is in no way superior to his brutal compatriots. He picks up a bronze clock, senses it as a living being, animates the object in his imagination, and emphasizes its integration into human life (403–4). Incredibly, Gabriel then chooses to be the specific human being who destroys the clock, throwing it so that it smashes into a thousand pieces. In destroying the clock, Gabriel attacks the anthropomorphized artistic representation of Godoy's arbitrary power. Young Gabriel then proceeds to damage other valuable articles, including luxuriously bound books, in a deliberate rejection of the cultural education Godoy represents, and as confirmation of his status as just one more participant in a brutal mob (404).

The next day, Gabriel finds his degraded double, Lopito, celebrating. The king has relieved Godoy of his position, and the government will be reconstituted, so Lopito expects employment with the new administration. Highlighting the parallels between the two uncultured upstarts, Gabriel reminds him that his writing skills may not be sufficient (407). Here, Lopito parallels Gabriel's own ambition, ridiculing by implication the idea of forming part of the government staff without any training—indeed, without being literate. Soon after this discussion, Lopito and Gabriel mingle with the inferior poet from the protest of *El sí de las niñas,* the poet and Lopito compete for the same woman: "Lopito trabó cierta pendencia con el poeta, porque a éste se le antojó requebrar a Mariminguilla, llamándola *ninfa* de no sé qué aguas o poéticos charcos" (407). [Lopito struck up a fight with the poet, because the poet had decided to flatter Mariminguilla, calling her a nymph of who knows what bodies of water or poetic puddles.] In this way, the text further degrades literary expression as practiced by the novel's characters, until there is little left to distinguish an illiterate kitchen boy from an established poet.

When Godoy finally comes out of hiding to turn himself over to the police, the people crowd toward him. Gabriel is disgusted, and describes the scene as that of a cat toying with its prey. Although Gabriel has no respect for this beast, he configures it as a domestic cat, unthreatening to all but its helpless prey. In fact, the next sentence confirms this subordination of the people, explaining that the troops ended up restraining them (408). The crowd has no compassion for the captured Godoy, and as Gabriel suggests, their anger shifts to pleasure when they see that the former minister is now one of them. Gabriel believes that the "martyr" Godoy suffered more because he was not executed but merely humiliated (409). Here, though, this denigration of the mob must be contextualized by the fact that Gabriel participated in their violent acts, and thus cannot legitimately maintain that he is superior to them.

Gabriel next travels to Madrid, where his battle to distinguish himself from the crowd continues. Inés now lives in the capital with her adoptive mother's cousins. They have all but enslaved her, and, as Gabriel soon learns, they expect her to marry her cousin don Mauro Requejo. Gabriel offers himself as a servant, and thus penetrates the Requejos' oppressive home. Upon entering their service, Gabriel meets another person, the reliable store clerk Juan de Dios, who has begrudgingly become engaged to doña Restituta, according to the wishes of her brother don Mauro. At this point, French troops have arrived in Madrid, Fernando VII is officially crowned king, and on March 24 the new monarch makes his triumphant entry into the city.

When the two Requejos venture outdoors on that day, they allow Gabriel and Inés to accompany them. Gabriel observes another crowd, similar to that of Aranjuez in its animality. The mob incorporates Gabriel, even as he attempts to maintain his superiority by dehumanizing them. All have left their quotidian occupations, and diverse citizens gather as a bestial body that tramples any member who dares to separate from the rest: "La muchedumbre, obligada por su colosal corpulencia a estarse quieta, se arremolinaba y estremecía como un monstruo atado . . . el retroceso (era) tan peligroso que había riesgo de ser hollado por las mil patas de la bestia" (426). [The crowd, obligated because of its colossal stoutness to be still, milled about and shook like a restrained monster . . . pulling back (was) so dangerous that one ran the risk of being trampled by the thousand feet of the beast.] Distracting attention from the new monarch to themselves, the French unfortunately anger the Spanish crowd, and the crowd responds. When the French occupy the small plaza, the Spanish observers are displaced, and they react as one body. Then the audience protests with a storm of whistles, reproaches, and insults directed at the French invaders (428). In an echo of the disruption of the premiere of *El sí de las niñas,* which was also identified for the Spanish audience with France, now the public whistles disapprovingly at the French soldiers. As in the earlier incidents of *El sí de las niñas* and the riot of Aranjuez, the masses erase Gabriel's independence. Captivated by the arrival of their chosen king, the single body of Madrid absorbs even Gabriel, throwing him together with Inés. The unification of their two bodies mirrors that of the entire society, apparently according to the will of that larger group (429).

Thus, the crowd of May 24 calls into question Gabriel's individuality, inciting him to attempt to prove at least to Inés that he retains some degree of creative autonomy. Fortuitously, the masses of people do allow the two lovers to escape from the Requejos, and this is when Gabriel begins his campaign for individuality and creativity. While they are alone Gabriel tells Inés that he possesses important information about her, representing himself as a storyteller: "Tú no sabes un cuento que yo te voy a contar" (429). [You don't know a certain story I'm going to tell you.] However, before they are recaptured by the Requejos, Gabriel is only able to tell her that she is not doña Juana's daughter, and to beg her to swear to always love him even when she is a great lady.

Over the next several weeks at the Requejos', Gabriel struggles to prove himself a creative individual. He gradually wins over doña Restituta, and acquires the trust of both his hosts. Nevertheless, the custody of Inés remains in the hands of his immediate rival, Juan de Dios. At this point, we begin to see that there are several parallels between these two men. Both are nominally accepted in a house whose owners guard jealously, both maintain some connection to Restituta, and as we discover with Juan de Dios's revelation in this chapter, both love Inés and plan to rescue her. Gabriel learns that Juan does not in fact have the key to Inés's room, but intends to have a locksmith make a copy from a wax mold. Because Gabriel appears to encourage him, Juan requests that Gabriel act as a go-between, so that he may ascertain if Inés loves him in return. Juan asks Gabriel to give Inés some violets, and to explain to her that they are from a person who loves her. He also intimates that sometime soon Gabriel might pass to Inés a letter that he (Juan) is composing, which already consists of eight written pages, and which—according to its author—is beautifully written (433).

Here, then, are two significant differences between the two men. Inés actually loves Gabriel, whereas she merely pities Juan de Dios. At the same time, Juan de Dios is able to write her a long love letter, but Gabriel cannot. This potential for written communication with Inés threatens even Gabriel, who has consistently lost himself in the uncultured, animalistic mob, precisely when he is attempting to assert his creative individuality. As an additional challenge to Gabriel's primacy, Juan establishes himself in a specular relationship with Gabriel, relating his fantasies in nearly the same words Gabriel has just used in the previous chapter to describe his intimacy and isolation with Inés: "Tiene que ser, tiene que amarme: yo me la llevaré a una parte del mundo donde no haya gente, y allí, solitos los dos, ¿no es verdad que tendrá que quererme?" (433–34). [It has to be, she has to love me: I will take her to a place where there are no people, and there, with just the two of us all alone, isn't it true that she will have to love me?] Gabriel recognizes that Juan's love for Inés could be of assistance to his own projects, but the competition could also be an obstacle (434). In an attempt to eclipse his rival he gives Inés the flowers, but claims they are from him, rather than stating enigmatically—as Juan wished him to do— that they are a gift from someone who loves her (433–34).

Continuing in this effort to efface Juan and prove himself a special individual, Gabriel convinces Restituta to leave the house, and informs Juan that it is time to give Inés the letter, expecting then to receive from Juan the copy of the key to Inés's room. Juan is proud of the letter, and lords it over the less literarily able Gabriel: "¿Qué te parece este trabajo? ¿Has visto alguna vez letra como ésta? Repara bien esa eme y esa hache mayúsculas. ¡Qué rasgos tan finos! Y esas letras con que pongo su nombre, ¿qué te parecen?" (439). [What do you think of this piece of writing? Have you ever seen penmanship like this? Look closely at this capital "m" and this capital "h." What fine strokes! And these letters I use to write her name, what do you think of them?] Juan then hands the letter to Gabriel, but refuses to give him the key to the room. Juan seems to retain complete control of Inés's fate, revealing that he plans to rescue her that evening. When don Mauro returns, Juan delivers to him a different letter that he has composed, and the store owner sends his clerk on an errand. Out of desperation, Gabriel breaks through Inés's door, but they do not go far before being apprehended by the character Lobo.

With Juan's greater literacy mocking his powerlessness, young Gabriel is then subjected to punishment by the Requejos for his attempt to escape with Inés, and by Lobo for the favors he allegedly received from Godoy, after "his" gift of Celestino's Latin verses. Confident that he will not escape, the two misers shut Gabriel in the cellar, where he feels humiliated by his impotence and lack of culture. In his jail, Gabriel discovers upon meditation that his own war for independence will be textual and linguistic. First he recognizes that his reality is not that of the novelists, when he touches hard bricks (442). He resigns himself, and voluntarily encloses himself within his own thoughts, explaining that his prison seemed to him an extension of his brain. Trapped in the prison of his own mind, he invents a text that is mathematical in its logic. He dreams of geometric shapes, fixating on one syllogism that indicates for him his and Inés's future victory. With renewed confidence sparked by his rational creativity, Gabriel welcomes the "light" provided when Juan de Dios unexpectedly descends the stairs. Juan, in contrast, shows that he is plagued by irrationality, staring at Gabriel as if he had appeared by black magic (443). Despite his surprise, Juan trusts Gabriel, asking him if he gave the love letter to Inés, because if so, she should be prepared for their escape that night. Gabriel says that he did, and offers to periodically check on Restituta as Juan raids the coffers. When Juan agrees, Gabriel promptly betrays him to Restituta, showing her the letter he wrote to Inés, and when she rushes to him in the basement, he traps them both below. A newly empowered Gabriel rescues Inés, and as they flee, both notice the blood-red color of the sky. It seems, at least temporarily, that he has defeated his rival, and proved himself the more enlightened lover.

When Gabriel leaves their shelter and ventures out into the street, he is again threatened with absorption by a menacing crowd. Gabriel sees "un gran gentío" (a great crowd)—an immense human surf against which he cannot fight (447). Hostilities begin as Gabriel is carried by his own curiosity to immerse himself in the group. However, the older Gabriel now comes to his younger self's rescue, and prevents the mob from absorbing Gabriel. The narrator comments: "Aquel fue uno de los cuadros más terribles que he presenciado en mi vida" (449). [That was one of the worst scenes I have ever in my life witnessed.] Here he is, alluding to both his historical perspective and his talents as the creator of a "cuadro"—the framed tale of May 2. Gabriel describes the crowd as less than human— living perhaps, but as animals instead of human beings. He explains that the foreign invaders did not count on the arms that wrapped around them from all sides, "como rejos de un inmenso pulpo" (450). [like tentacles of a giant octopus.]

Here Gabriel will be different from the masses, separating himself from the mob because he is an author. At this point, Pacorro Chinitas, illiterate alter ego of Gabriel, interrupts Gabriel's observations and meditations, reminding him of the tool he holds, and asking if he simply plans to pick his teeth with it (451). Gabriel now raises the rifle as if it were a pen, and adopts a more active role as chronicler of the rebellion. When la Primorosa, Chinitas's aggressive wife, takes the weapon from him, she leaves him with pen alone. Navigating the space between his younger self (participant in the uprising of May 2) and his older self (author of the *Episodios*), and possessed of only a pen and of history, Gabriel rescues himself and salvages his authority.

Because Gabriel configures the scene as a *cuadro* we think immediately of Goya's painting of May 2, a connection confirmed later when the *mamelucos* engage the Spanish citizens: "Los manolos los atacaban navaja en mano, y las mujeres clavaban sus dedos en la cabeza del caballo" (452). [The *manolos* attacked the *mamelucos* with knives in their hands, and the women drove their fingers into the horse's head.] As Gabriel explains, in this conflict "se formaba una confusión, una mescolanza horrible y sangrienta que no se puede pintar" (452). [a confusion formed, a horrible bloody jumble that cannot be painted (described).] Suddenly switching to the present tense ("que no se puede pintar"), the text suggests that the real drama takes place in the narrator's present. He says the scene cannot be painted, yet he attempts to describe it in words. The frustration of the attempt to paint the scene enhances the authority of the narrative—if the scene cannot be represented visually, perhaps Gabriel's words are the closest representation left to students of May 2. In this way, the text suggests its ability to supplant Goya's famous painting as the authoritative representation of that eventful day. Paradoxically, the horror is more than can be painted, but it must be painted in a new world in which all scenes are *cuadros,* a form associated as much with writing and verbal representation as with painting. Repeatedly, Gabriel describes scenes that cannot be portrayed, yet then appropriates the decision of what to include in the literary history of the event for himself: "Oyóse un tiro; después, una de las muchachas lanzó un grito espantoso y desgarrador. Lo que allí debió de ocurrir no es para contado" (453). [A shot was heard; afterwards, one of the girls let out a frightening and heartrending scream. What occurred there should not be told.] In this way, the (old) narrator decides what of this story to preserve, just as he does when later he states that it is no longer possible to narrate the events, but then continues his account (460).

Thus, thanks to his older incarnation, Gabriel successfully recovers some degree of authority. Nevertheless, the end of the novel marks a crisis in which, when he is outmaneuvered by Juan de Dios, the young Gabriel must face his own inferiority as a writer. When all are briefly reunited, Celestino convinces Gabriel and Juan de Dios to join him in the fight. Neither wants to leave Inés, but both do. In the street, Gabriel is separated from the others, and witnesses the death of Chinitas (his former alter ego), along with much other violence. He is eventually reunited with Juan de Dios, who cries that Inés and Celestino have been taken. Juan and Gabriel cooperate to save their friends, and decide to split up to be able to search for them in two places. Gabriel, however, loses consciousness, and groggily imagines that he and Inés are together again in Aranjuez. He is then distracted from this unproductive fantasizing when Juan de Dios informs him that Inés is not where they expected her to be, in the Retiro or in the Buen Suceso. Gabriel begs to be taken prisoner also, and ends up in the same group of prisoners as Inés and Celestino. He pleads with the French to save Inés, but he is unable to convince them. Juan de Dios, on the other hand, does not give up his independence. He intercedes with the French and manages to free the girl that both young men love. Young Gabriel then becomes confused, and as the older narrator explains, loses his mental faculties and his grasp on sanity when he sees that Juan has recovered Inés (469). Gabriel then faints again, believing himself close to death.

In this way, young Gabriel's ineffectiveness at this crucial point—the historical moment designated the beginning of the Spanish War for Independence—indicates that his struggle to establish himself as a competent reader and author has just begun. He must pass through numerous tests of his critical abilities before he reaches the level of sophistication of his older self, author of his memoirs. What we have seen in this chapter—particularly in the discussion of the novels *La corte de Carlos IV* and *El 19 de marzo y el 2 de mayo*—is that over the course of his long life, Gabriel does become culturally literate. He then uses his expertise in critical reading to help his younger self compete with other authors. Nevertheless, the young Gabriel who narrowly escapes the seductions of the quixotic Godoy story reveals himself to be still quite vulnerable to romance narratives of all sorts. At times Gabriel chooses a realistic approach in contrast to other characters, but in other instances he is as irrational and even animalistic as the mob. The young narrator seems at the end of *El 19 de marzo y el 2 de mayo* to come close to the realization that he needs to channel his creative imagination through practical skills of literacy and a realist worldview, but he is ultimately eclipsed by a more experienced writer. The next group of novels, however, begins with Gabriel's "rebirth," and his chance to again confront the dilemmas of his authorial apprenticeship.

2

The Nation Fights Back:
Quixotism Challenges a Novice Author in *Bailén,*
Napoleón en Chamartín, Zaragoza, and *Gerona*

IN THE NEXT FOUR NOVELS GABRIEL CONTINUES TO DISCOVER THE RIGHTS
and responsibilities of authorship, relying less on the direct assistance of
his older self as his younger self develops a heightened sense of his own
identity by confronting his animalistic nature. Gabriel defines for us what
it means to be an author, revealing the selfishness (as he puts it) implicit in
the authorial function. (Although Gabriel does not make the connection
explicitly, this authorial selfishness is a form of quixotism.) Along with the
romanticism recalled by the focus on the self, Gabriel must confront in
these novels the links to romanticism of heroism, patriotism, and bravery.
Predominantly a realist, Gabriel successfully competes with other authors,
but he also begins to recognize the romanticism within himself, and in the
others who are war heroes. At times the text suggests the following question: if the heroes of the war stories are romantic Quijotes, will the author-
character who figures as hero of the "rest of the story" not need to be
something of a romantic hero as well?

BAILÉN

I look now at the first of these novels. The fourth *episodio, Bailén,* continues with the topic of animalization, which was important throughout the
third *episodio.* In *Bailén,* Gabriel returns to the topic of his own inhu-
manity, as he did when analyzing his participation in the revolt at Aranjuez. He also confronts texts authored by others, and these belittling influ-

ences drive him to reassert himself as superior at least to his alter ego don Diego. In *El 19 de marzo y el 2 de mayo,* animalization was manifested on a large scale as the conversion of the human crowd into a huge beast in the Madrid of May 2. One striking feature of this earlier animalization was its association with the characters' loss of individuality, and this dehumanization of groups continues in *Bailén* in the portrayal of the French and Spanish armies. Although cohesive action seemed necessary for the patriotic defense of Madrid on May 2, the *Episodios'* narrator still appeared concerned with the eclipse of the human subject by the crowd, and *Bailén* also features this preoccupation. Furthermore, in this novel, Gabriel participates more fully in the reduction to animal status, so that this metamorphosis has an impact on his status as both reader and author. The association of Gabriel with animals begins early in *Bailén.* When he first recovers consciousness in the home of doña Gregoria and her husband Santiago Fernández, Gabriel learns that a veterinarian has treated the injuries he sustained on May 3 (479).[1] Being attended to by a veterinarian in an episode that serves as a sort of unwritten prologue to the novel *Bailén* echoes the animalization of groups of people that we have seen in *El 19 de marzo y el 2 de mayo,* and will continue to observe in the later *episodios.* These incidents related to Gabriel's literary competition and to his animalization anticipate the text's juxtaposition of his experiences with those of the other characters, suggesting that Gabriel may be as much an animal as others are. In a struggle as vital to him as the war in which he participates, Gabriel fights to distinguish himself from the characters he views as inferior readers.

Another significant instance of the animalization of Gabriel occurs during the actual battle of Bailén, after Gabriel has established the animal nature of all participants in the struggle. In some descriptions of the army—the dwarf that eventually becomes a giant—Gabriel's text reconfigures individual soldiers as grotesque distortions of normal (individual) human forms: "Removido el seno de la patria, echó fuera cuanto habían engendrado en él los gloriosos y los degenerados siglos, y no alcanzando a defenderse con un solo brazo, trabajó con el derecho y el izquierdo, blandiendo con aquél la espada histórica y con éste la navaja" (513). [With the homeland's breast shaken, it threw forth all that glorious and degenerate centuries had engendered, and unable to defend itself with one arm, worked with the right and the left, brandishing with the right the historical sword and with the left the knife.]

When the Spanish encounter the French, such images of animalization and quasi-humanity continue to predominate, as the text represents the Spanish as swarms of insects, and the French as their bulky opponent—the eagle the vermin were devouring (525). At times the two armies are monsters, as what were originally individuals form a single body that is then reconstituted as animalistic: "El ejército todo se estremeció desde su cabeza hasta su cola" (533). [The entire army shuddered from its head to its tail.] At one point, Gabriel remarks on the specific dehumanization caused by the blending of rider and horse, in an unlikely harmonization that inspires ridicule. Gabriel characterizes the army as a body with one heart, experiencing the emotion transmitted to its single hand and rifle (536).

The narrator also comments on his study of what he refers to as the "individualization" of the army, defined as the composition of one individual from many. This process comprises each soldier's loss of identity, as well as the reconstitution of the men into a massive being endowed with human qualities (536–37). In the final pages of the novel, after the French defeat at Bailén, Gabriel again uses the image of a giant animal or grotesque human to represent the effect of the loss on the French empire, which continued walking, but always with a limp (558).

During the battle, Gabriel is forced to come to terms with the animalization of his own consciousness, and here we see the impact of generalized brutishness on the narrator as an individual. Gabriel has an experience similar to that he had during the riot, the *motín de Aranjuez,* at Godoy's mansion: he is absorbed by the dehumanized mass, and this incorporation into the savage collectivity ultimately impairs his ability to read. Gabriel participates directly in the redefinition and undermining of humanity when he, and many other soldiers, suffer from intense thirst. The water they so intensely desire and need, possessed by the army only in small quantities, "era para otros sedientos, cuyas bocas necesitaban refrescar antes que las nuestras, si el combate había de tener buen éxito" (539). [was designated for other thirsty ones, whose mouths needed to be refreshed before ours, if the battle was going to be successful.] The water is destined for the cannons. The thirsty troops lose their opportunity to drink, then, when they are supplanted by their nonhuman (yet anthropomorphized) competitors. Reduced to the status of machines in competition with other machines, the soldiers discover a *noria,* or waterwheel, but must fight the French for access to the turbid water (540). This struggle, Gabriel notes, changes the men into beasts: "Por un momento dejamos de ser soldados, dejamos de ser hombres, para no ser sino animales" (540). [For a moment we stopped being soldiers, stopped being men, and were only animals.]

Here, Gabriel is disturbed to find that he forms part of an animalistic group when he is driven to satisfy his basic physical needs. During the narration of the battle scenes, Gabriel's shocked recognition of his own animalization in response to the distortion of all soldiers' humanity mirrors a process that centers on the interpretation of texts. On two occasions in *Bailén,* Gabriel reads letters written by other people, and then becomes preoccupied with the relative insignificance of his public role in Inés's life.

His helpless reading of others' letters and the insecurity he feels as a result of these readings motivates Gabriel to bear witness to the secondary characters' processing of literature and art, and then to attempt to set himself apart from these "inferior" readers, even if he is not distinct from them. In this sense, Gabriel's recognition of others' skillful use of the written word complements his shocked realization of his animal nature, and both discoveries spur Gabriel on to establish and defend his authorial selfhood.

Gabriel's efforts to present himself as superior to other readers, despite the doubts he himself feels as a result of his own animalization, continue to be important in this novel. There is a shift in Bailén from one alter ego for Gabriel to another, after Gabriel triumphs over the previously threatening Juan de Dios. Juan, who also boards at the home of Gregoria and Santiago, is in bad shape. He explains that he flagellates himself every night, since he has lost Inés, whom the lawyer Lobo claims to have returned to her true parents, who are "some of the most important people in Spain" (478). Although Juan repeats this explanation, he believes the story to be a lie, but Gabriel surmises it is true. In this way, although Gabriel initially fears his rival in textual production, he proves himself to be a better "reader" of Inés's story. Juan de Dios follows the same example that led Don Quijote to dream up his ridiculous penitence in imitation of Beltenebros. Gabriel learns that Inés has been faithful to him, which confirms his victory over his competitor. Nevertheless, Gabriel has a new rival for Inés. Paralleling the struggle of Juan de Dios and Gabriel for Inés, the competition between Gabriel and the new character don Diego becomes a literary contest, with the winner defined as the one who best handles the texts available to him. Gabriel is disturbed by the way in which the *afrancesado* Santorcaz manipulates Diego, and suggests that his alter ego Diego is vulnerable to Santorcaz because he does not read critically. In this way, Gabriel assesses Diego's seduction as a cautionary tale about authorship as well as reading.

Gabriel meets this young man when he travels south in search of Inés, accompanied by Santorcaz and the young servant Andrés Marijuán.[2] Eventually, the three travelers arrive in Bailén, and lodge in the mansion of *la condesa de Rumblar,* the countess that Andrés serves. It is here that we encounter Gabriel's new rival, the countess's son and dangerously pliable reader don Diego. Diego is being educated by the pedantic tutor don Paco, who claims to know Latin and modern history, but exhibits no such competence in these fields (495). Diego, being uncultured, young, and officially engaged to Inés, mirrors Gabriel. Gabriel learns that Amaranta's family has settled an inheritance dispute with the Rumblars by obtaining a royal authorization of Inés's legitimate status, and arranging her marriage to Diego. The family has agreed to Inés's engagement to don Diego, but she still loves Gabriel, and does not wish to marry don Diego. Because Diego mirrors Gabriel it is difficult for Gabriel to witness Diego's degradation by Santorcaz, even though this debasement separates Diego from the more capable and astute Gabriel. When Santorcaz joins the same band of soldiers as Gabriel, Andrés, and don Diego, he quickly learns to manipulate the young nobleman "con la desenvoltura subyugadora de su conversación" (511). [with the subjugating grace of his conversation.] Santorcaz fabricates stories specifically to win over Diego, exercising his creativity and imagination in fabricating narrations against which the unlearned Diego has no chance to defend himself. Santorcaz quickly captivates the will of the boy by stimulating his naive imagination with fantastic stories (512).

In addition to convincing Diego to believe political ideas contrary to his own advantage (Santorcaz teaches Diego to argue for the abolition of primogeniture), the *afrancesado* rewrites for the vulnerable Diego the documents of Diego's own family's heritage. When the countess, motivated by family pride, decides to send her son off to war, she gives Diego several items—a sword with an inscription, and letters for the relatives who will soon be his in-laws. The countess intends to marry Diego to the daughter of richer relatives in order to bolster the family's fortune, but the wedding is delayed by the war. He remains engaged to his young relative, however, and we soon discover that his betrothed is Inés. After meeting the man who becomes his new "tutor," Diego allows Santorcaz to define the texts that signify his family, saying to Santorcaz: "Pero ya que me enseña usted lo que ignoro, contésteme a una duda: ¿por qué tenemos nosotros en nuestras casas tantos papelotes llenos de garabatos, y por qué usamos esos escudos con sapos y culebras?" (522). [But since you are teaching me what I don't know, resolve a doubt for me: Why do we have in our houses so many scraps of paper full of scribbles, and why do we use this coat of arms with toads and snakes?] Santorcaz explains that these signs and painted images ("signos" and "pinturas") no longer mean anything, and suggests that any significance one might read into them was only relevant in the distant past, when long-dead ancestors acted in the name of the family (522). In this way Santorcaz undermines Diego's confidence in his studies and in the signs of his family as interpreted (read) by his mother. With Santorcaz's help, Diego decides to begin learning to "read" again, starting with the most basic signs of his world, those that represent his identity. Motivated by his own interests as Inés's father, Santorcaz influences Diego so that he replaces his own family's coat of arms—a sign the older man refers to as empty—with the new text of revolution. Diego accepts the substitution gladly, claiming to have had the same thoughts, but has lacked the vocabulary (text) to conceptualize them (523). Liberated by Santorcaz from his linguistic prison, Diego celebrates Santorcaz's ideas, confessing that these conversations with the *afrancesado* have won his heart and filled his previously empty mind (524).

Diego revels in his newly acquired knowledge, but Gabriel is less sanguine, painting a picture of the corruption incubating in his young master's mind—a description tinged with the realist's scorn for romanticism:

Así, aquella fantasía, encerrada en el capullo de una educación mezquina, agujereaba con entusiasmo su encierro, porque había vislumbrado fuera alguna cosa que tenía la fascinación de lo nuevo. Así, aquel germen de pasión y de inteligencia, guardado en un huevo, se reconocía con vida, se reconocía con fuerza, y empezaba a dar picotazos en su cárcel, anhelando respirar fuera de ella otros aires, y calentarse con calores más enérgicos. Así, aquella ceguera abría sus párpados, gozándose en la desconocida luz. (524)

[In that way, that fantasy, trapped in the cocoon of a meager education, poked holes in its cell with enthusiasm, because it had glimpsed something outside that held the fascination of the new. Thus, that germ of passion and intelligence, reserved in an egg, recognized that it was alive, that it was strong, and it began to chip away at its prison, desiring to breathe fresh air outside, and to warm itself with more energetic heat. In that way, that blindness raised its eyelids, enjoying the unknown light.]

As others drift off to sleep, a feverishly alert Diego participates in an animated dialogue with Santorcaz, and Gabriel observes them uneasily (524). Gabriel confirms as the novel progresses that he is concerned about the role of Santorcaz in Diego's readings of various texts and ideas. When the characters briefly visit Diego's family, the young heir shocks them all by espousing revolutionary theories, refusing to acknowledge his heritage as determining his character, and renouncing his tutor don Paco. He states that he wants to stay in the army, go to Madrid and meet philosophers and people who "know things," to read the *Encyclopedia,* to see the secret societies, and to learn things beyond the foolishness he has learned from don Paco (527). He brags that he has changed swords, giving up for a new saber the ineffective blade his mother gave him when he left. The ancient sword was covered with a virtual family story—the emblems of his noble heritage. He explains his choice: "Era una hoja mellada, llena de garabatos, letreros, sapos por aquí, culebras por allí y cubierta de moho desde la punta a la empuñadura. ¿Para qué me servía?" (528). [It was a dented blade, full of scribblings, signs, toads here, snakes there, and covered with rust from the point to the handle. What good was it doing me?]

Gabriel notes the lack of control and logic in Diego's ideation, and in no way celebrates his egalitarian sentiments, which issue forth in confusion (527). Indeed, after this visit to his family home, Diego remains under the control of Santorcaz, still enthralled by his entertaining stories. When Diego reveals the facts of his engagement to Inés to Santorcaz, not realizing of course that he is speaking to the girl's father, Santorcaz takes advantage of this new information to entangle Diego in a plot. Once again, the old soldier entreats Diego to leave his old way of life and start off on "a wonderful adventure." Utterly captivated, Diego asks for details. Believing the girl to still be in the convent, they imagine scaling the walls of the building to steal her for Diego. Diego confesses that he is seduced by the narrative—the unfolding, unresolved mystery of what they discuss—and he begs Santorcaz to continue as storyteller (531). Shocked by this undiscriminating consumer of tales, Gabriel laments the weakness in Diego that allows him to be manipulated, and associates Diego's faults with what we recognize as a predisposition to romanticism. Exhibiting nervous enthusiasm, Diego is ready to commit atrocities, and carry out abominable plans, "con viva imaginación, arrebatado temperamento y ningún criterio, igualmente fascinado por las ideas buenas y las malas" (532). [with a lively imagination, and impetuous temperament, and no sense of judgment, convinced as much by good ideas as bad.] Don Diego's final adventures in this novel are scandalous; he is taken prisoner by the French, and displays his new ideas and his artistic "talents" for this audience, who degrade him. Adding to Diego's humiliation, he later narrates this escapade willingly, in front of Gabriel, his own family, and Inés's, explaining to them that he had self-righteously disparaged Spain and the Spanish aristocracy for his French audience (556).

It is this model that Gabriel rejects, then. He feels threatened by the other characters—Juan de Dios, Amaranta, and Santorcaz—who are able to create texts and control others with their narratives, and he sees that Diego is vulnerable to the author Santorcaz because of the young man's irrationality and attraction to quixotic ideas. Indeed, Santorcaz succeeds in erasing, along with his family's code, Diego's identity as a member of the Spanish nobility. Observing Diego betray his country as well as his social class, Gabriel determines that his own ignorance will not get him into such trouble. In most of the novel his reading is similar to that of the other characters, but when he discovers certain important letters in Santorcaz's saddlebags, he appears motivated to distinguish himself from the others, describing this drive as selfishness. In the heat of battle, Gabriel jumps on a riderless horse, and, suffering from intense hunger, searches the saddlebags for food. He realizes that the horse is Santorcaz's when he finds a portrait of Inés, along with three letters—one addressed to Santorcaz from Amaranta, one from Santorcaz to her, and one to Santorcaz from Amaranta's butler Román. Reading all of these texts, Gabriel confirms that Santorcaz and Amaranta are Inés's parents, and discovers that Santorcaz has asked Amaranta to marry him so that they can recognize Inés as their legitimate daughter, although Amaranta has refused him.

Having learned what loss of self means for Diego, Gabriel thinks only of the letters, Inés's fate, and his own role in her life, as others defend Spain from the French. Gabriel's personal struggle—the fight to be important, and literally to have an identity—is what concerns the young man, much more than the war itself (544). He knows that his readers might find him selfish ("Decid que yo era un estúpido egoísta" [Tell me that I was a stupid egoist]), and accepts the consequences of this judgment: "Si es egoísmo, confieso mi egoísmo" (544). [If that is selfishness, I confess my selfishness.] In reality, what Gabriel labels selfishness is the desire to be a self, to think and read differently from the crowd, and ultimately, to be an author. This overwhelming desire colors his presentation of the battle scene, in which individuals formed a unified, undifferentiated patriotic community, with the exception of one rebel: "El único que se conservaba aislado y podía llamarse hombre era el egoísta Gabriel, grano de arena no conglomerado con la montaña" (546). [The only one who remained isolated and who could call himself a single man was the selfish Gabriel, grain of sand not incorporated by the mountain.] With this conception of egoism, Gabriel stakes his claim to independence in reading and in authorship. Earlier Gabriel was absorbed by the animalistic crowd, now he separates himself precisely by associating with texts and the written word.

Significantly, the *episodio Bailén* links the concepts of egoism (the necessary selfishness of authorship) and quixotism, as a first step in Gabriel's realization that the quixotic impulse cannot be simply dismissed, for it lies at the heart of the authorial project. The linkage of authorial selfishness and quixotism comes about in the following way. Although Gabriel views condescendingly Diego's seduction by Santorcaz's narrative, he also associates with quixotism as he develops his authorial sensibilities. If we return to the voyage to Córdoba undertaken by Gabriel, Santorcaz, and Andrés Marijuán, we note that the trip is a stage in Gabriel's development as a creator of literature. The three travelers cross La Mancha, familiar to all, as Gabriel says, ever since the whole world became accustomed to the image of the plains crossed by Don Quijote. For Gabriel, the area's beauty lies precisely in its monotony, which frees the imagination by presenting no distractions to it. This expansiveness of imagination has given birth to the character Don Quijote, who is now firmly tied to the region (487). In Gabriel's opinion, Don Quijote could never have existed in a fertile land, since he depended to such an extent on the barrenness of La Mancha, and on the lack of the common sense that would be "cortapisas de la imaginación, que la detendrían en su insensato vuelo" (487). [an impediment to the imagination, which would detain fancy in its illogical flight.] In this way, Gabriel contextualizes his physical experience (crossing La Mancha) as an encounter with the quixotic mentality, and grounds himself in the region that inspired Cervantes's novel. As they cross La Mancha, Gabriel continues to think of *Don Quijote,* the reading of which remains fresh in his memory (487).

With the *Quijote* (Don Quijote) on Gabriel's mind, when the travelers require entertainment, Santorcaz tells them stories of France. As a Quijote himself, inundated with nineteenth-century history instead of *novelas de caballerías,* Santorcaz confuses everything he sees with the battle of Austerlitz (Moravia, December 2, 1805), during which Napoleon defeated an Austrian and Russian alliance.[3] Santorcaz is unable to determine whether his imagination has constructed a replica of the battleground, or they have been magically transported to Austerlitz. Santorcaz interprets the Manchegan landscape as the site of the 1805 battle while, acting as his skeptical Sanchos, Gabriel and Andrés laugh at him (488).

Here, Santorcaz plays the role of the storyteller who cannot convince his audience to enter his imaginary world, and who finally gives up the battle with his readers and retreats into fantasy alone. Gabriel at first seems unaffected by this "author's" struggle, resisting and laughing as much as Andrés, but the tension eventually unsettles him. The sentiments the older man expresses are precisely those of a frustrated author, and Gabriel is perhaps anxious about the proximity of his own battle to Santorcaz's, that of interesting his readers in Spanish history.[4] As much as he regrets Santorcaz's manipulation of don Diego, Gabriel identifies with the older man as fellow Quijote (that is, fellow author), and joins him in promoting the quixotic vision of La Mancha. Featuring episodes of "selfishness" as testimony to his individuality and status as novice author, Gabriel's participation in the battle also involves the contamination of his acts as a new author by the persistence of quixotism. During an early skirmish, Gabriel is unable to fight with the vanguard, and instead engages in a quixote battle with shrubbery, pretending the bushes are French soldiers (518). Afterwards, Gabriel and the others exaggerate and fictionalize the conflict for the uninformed audience, who were even further from seeing action than they were (519). Clearly, Gabriel still fights with the ghost of Don Quijote, alternatively attracted and repelled by the knight-errant's vision of the world.

Gabriel recalls Don Quijote, enters into his own meditation on the Knight of La Mancha, and begins to see images in the clouds as he remembers Cervantes's protagonist (490). He visualizes squadrons and battles also, then an enormous hat and face belonging to Napoleon, who gestures toward the horizon. Santorcaz observes the same vision, and asks the boys if they see it too. In this way, Gabriel is first an unwilling reader, but then as writer himself, suspends his disbelief in solidarity with Santorcaz. It is only when Andrés Marijuán processes the same images that the illusion is destroyed. Andrés laughs heartily, and describes the vision with sarcasm. When Andrés defies the storytellers once more, the clouds shift from the precarious balance between caricature and greatness noted by Gabriel, and the scene loses its magic in the face of a defiant reader (491).

Still, this incident cements the identification of Santorcaz and Gabriel. For all intents and purposes these two characters are rivals, but in this instance they share the plight of the misunderstood author.

We see here, then, that *Bailén* marks an important stage in Gabriel's reevaluation of quixotism. With his parallel relationship to Santorcaz, Gabriel realizes that the newfound egoism that discomfits him is a feature of authorship, and that all authors are, at least in some sense, Quijotes. In the next novel of the series Gabriel pursues this reassessment of quixotism, and realizes that the quixotic impulse is not merely inherent in the authorial process, but is also a fundamental component of patriotism.

NAPOLEÓN EN CHAMARTÍN

If the Quijotes Diego and Santorcaz have been of doubtful loyalty to Spain in *Bailén,* the next novel, *Napoleón en Chamartín,* suggests that an excess of fancy is precisely what leads to Spanish success in the war against the French. On the one hand, Gabriel observes the inability of various characters to engage in critical reading, and sets himself apart from them and their failures. At the same time, the climax of the novel comes when the text makes evident that the skills required for responsible reading are not the same abilities the characters need in their struggle against the French. As capable readers fall by the wayside in the political and military battles, the heroic obstinacy of the secondary character Santiago Fernández anticipates Spain's dogged, ultimately successful resistance against the French. Even if Fernández is as crazy as Napoleon in taking up a quixotic campaign, both men succeed gloriously for a brief period. Soon after Gabriel recognizes the distinction between the skills required for competent reading and those needed for patriotic action, he slips from an attitude of superiority and qualifies his rejection of inferior fictions. This moment of self-doubt makes Gabriel vulnerable to an antagonistic audience, over which he then loses control. Near the end of the novel, Gabriel allows others to fictionalize him, and to relegate him to the band of outcasts (poets, readers, and actors) who must leave Spain, even—as in Gabriel's case—physically chained.

Still, before Gabriel's fall, examples abound of the inferior readings carried out by secondary characters. In the first chapters of *Napoleón en Chamartín,* Gabriel follows Diego de Rumblar, his faithful foil and erstwhile rival for Inés, on his nightly visits to primitive Masonic lodges, degraded debates hosted by notorious women such as Diego's love-object Zaina, and farcical *tertulias* in bookstores. These meetings involve, in addition to the pantomimes the order was known for, the reading of verses and the delivery of speeches. One of the lodges, the *Rosa-Cruz,* which seems to Gabriel a cage for humorous lunatics, features a pensive skeleton which listens to debates and analyses of texts, and threatens to cause Gabriel to explode with laughter (562). Gabriel further asserts his superiority over these gatherings by animalizing them as well as their progeny: "De la larva de aquellas logias no es aventurado afirmar que salió al poco tiempo la crisálida de los clubs, los cuales, a su vez, andando el voluble siglo, dieron de sí la mariposa de los comités" (562). [It is safe to say that from the larvae of those lodges there emerged shortly the chrysalis of the clubs, which in their turn, as the changeable century advanced, gave birth to the butterfly of the committees.]

As for the *salones,* this degraded environment is Diego's school, and he presents himself there faithfully. As Gabriel observes, his punctual attendance, if it had been to a real institution of learning, would have made him a second Aristotle (563). This is the site for political discussion, led by the familiar Pujitos, described by Gabriel ironically as "joven instruidísimo y de gran erudición, pues no dejaba de saber leer" (563). [a highly educated, erudite young man, since he was not unable to read.] With the strange expression "no dejaba de saber leer," Gabriel calls attention to the tenuousness of Pujitos's grasp on the written word, and to the continual presentation of his acts of reading as a series of proofs of his hard-won battle with literacy. As does the naivete of Diego, Pujitos's partial knowledge elicits scorn from Gabriel.

At the *tertulias* in the bookstores, where politics were most discussed, writers and would-be authors take the stage, profaning and dishonoring the engagement in critical commentary (565). Here, Gabriel effectively conveys the proximity of these characters to the literary world, as well as their failure to make contributions of any value to literature. He also connects their pseudoliterary activity to patriotism—a link that, as we have seen in *El 19 de marzo y el 2 de mayo,* suggests that whereas such characters may argue unwaveringly for the rights of the Spanish nation, this commitment does not in any way mean that they are critical readers or thinkers. In this environment, even Gabriel toys with the association of verbal production, ignorance, and patriotism, and contributes to the vacuity of political discourse: "También me daba una vuelta por las librerías, bien acompañando a don Diego, bien solo, echándomelas de gran patriota, y en la de las Veneras me acuerdo que dije una noche muy estupendas cosas, que me valieron calurosos aplausos" (565). [I also visited the bookstores, either accompanied by don Diego or alone, playing the great patriot, and in the Veneras bookstore I remember that one night I said stupendous things, which earned me warm applause.]

As well as the sham *tertulias,* another scene of inferior reading is the home of Santiago Fernández, where Gabriel lodges, and which we have visited in the *episodio Bailén.* The participants in a contest for the audience's attention are Fernández himself, and the aficionado of the popular press, don Roque. Fernández is the faithful patriot, proud of his ignorance, who exhibits blind faith in his country's superiority even in the face of numerous defeats by France. Believing that the trusting Spaniards are the victims of a duplicitous press, Santiago recommends censorship (566). Don Roque—quintessential nineteenth-century Quijote (his sacred text is a newspaper)—opposes Santiago Fernández. Roque is utterly faithful to the *Semanario Patriótico,* a newspaper around which his entire week revolves. As he explains, he often goes without food in order to afford his subscription. Reading the newspaper is as vital to him as is the sustenance of his body. He dreams of the paper and imagines its contents the night before it comes out, forgetting food, drink, and all his sorrows on the day it is issued.[5] As we have seen Gabriel do in the case of the *tertulia* participants, Roque counters Fernández by associating patriotism with ignorance, saying that the "patriots" distort the truth, and questioning the validity of news acquired by word of mouth instead of from the newspaper (567). Fernández, in turn, strikes at the source of Roque's information, and challenges his manner of reading by explicitly associating his adversary with Don Quijote: "¿Qué saca usted en limpio, señor don Roque, de todas esas hojas que lee día y noche, y que le van a volver loco, como al bueno de Don Quijote los libros de caballería?" (567). [Mr. don Roque, what do you get out of all of those sheets you read day and night, and which are going to drive you crazy, just like Don Quijote with the chivalric novels?] When Roque defends his newspaper, he exalts the periodical: it is as if the paper speaks with the mouths of Aristotle and Plato, he says, but then reconfigures it as a sacred text he proposes as the new Spanish Bible, which would resolve all the nation's problems if all citizens were faithful readers (567–68). In hopes of carrying out this program, he commits to memory long passages of this more ephemeral text, just as the religiously faithful might treat biblical excerpts (568).

Gabriel, whose memoirs ridicule Roque, appears to disdain him for his populist views. A silly man in love with a periodical, Roque embodies Gabriel's fear of the power of the public that reads uncritically. Although Gabriel refers to Roque the solitary individual as harmless, the text raises the question of what the ultimate result of such irresponsible readings would be if they were carried out by the masses this series of novels animalizes and degrades. At one point in the novel, the character Father Salmón discusses exactly this issue with Amaranta. When Amaranta states that at this time Spaniards do not concern themselves with the future, Father Castillo corrects her, basing his judgment on textual production. He explains that the nation's printed matter speaks for itself—Spain is fraught with internal divisions, which will become even more apparent when the country's citizens attempt to establish new laws (582). In this way, for

Father Castillo, printed texts are the best measure of public opinion, but these same writings indicate that when this public is free to produce its own texts (laws), divisions will threaten any authority over such people. By anticipating the moment in which the public will become authors themselves, Castillo suggests that even though authors appear to write for a public who looks to them as authority figures, they do not so much lead their readers as they are controlled by the readers who make the ultimate decisions.

Perhaps the most disturbing portrayal of the people as cultural consumers out of control is Gabriel's description of the *madrileños*' defense of Madrid from the invading French. When the Quijote figure Santiago Fernández persists in his determination that Madrid will not surrender, Gabriel suggests that they follow a crowd. He describes the Puerta del Sol as a heart toward which all blood flows in times of extreme emotion. This organ beats, and the people who fill it compose a mass of humanity, while the most restless, crazed, and excited masses seethe at the Post Office (612). In a now-familiar evolution, this crowd that at times appears as one giant body loses its connection to humanness, and becomes a monster: "Después el pueblo empezó a arremolinarse y a culebrear como dragón de mil colas que se dispone a emprender movimientos" (613). [Afterwards the people began to mill about and to slither like a thousand-tailed dragon readying itself for action.]

Instead of taking up any mail (texts), this crowd is committed to reading stories of treason in the actions around them. When they find cartridges filled with sand instead of gunpowder, the crowd searches for a scapegoat, just as they did in the case of Godoy. They turn now against Juan de Mañara, a character who appeared in *La corte de Carlos IV* as Lesbia's lover and rival to the actor Isidoro Máiquez. The mob breaks down the door of Mañara's home in an act of violence that does not surprise Gabriel, since "the people" had already trampled the royal crown in Aranjuez (615). Gabriel condemns without hesitation Mañara's murder: "¡Pobre y desgraciado Mañara! Ayer ídolo, ayer amigo, ayer compañero de la vil plebe, cuyo traje, y costumbres, y hablar y modos imitaba; hoy inmolado por ella con barbarie inaudita, con esa cruel presteza que ella emplea, ¡la infame furia!, en todas sus cosas" (615). [Poor, unfortunate Mañara! Yesterday an idol, a friend, a companion of the vile masses, whose clothing, habits, speech, and behavior he imitated, today was immolated by them with unheard-of savagery, with that cruel speed that they use—evil fury!—in all that they do.] Gabriel concludes that it was Mañara's formerly close association with the people that now intensifies their wrath when avenging themselves, and inspires them to drag his body through the streets. Gabriel controls his readers' view of this scene ("Pero apartemos los ojos: no miremos, no" [But let us turn away our eyes; let us not look, no]), hiding the details of actions by monsters who are no longer human (615). At the same time, however, the narrator instructs us to contemplate the significance of these acts: "Meditemos sobre las mudanzas mundanas, y especialmente sobre las cosas populares, las más dignas de meditación y estudio" (615). [Let us meditate on the evolution of worldly things, and especially about what relates to the people, which is most worthy of meditation and study.]

Here Gabriel arrives at the core of the problem he addresses—the various manifestations of the "cosas populares," and specifically, the corruption of the public's ability to process texts. In the words of Santiago Fernández, ostensibly applied to the military situation of the people who lack leaders, but clearly related also to the dilemmas of authorship and audience, the people are "esta inmunda canalla motinesca, díscola y bullanguera, que en circunstancias tan críticas se vuelve contra sus jefes" (612). [this foul, riotous rabble, noisy and ungovernable, which at such crucial junctures turns against its leaders.] Synthesizing these comments and events, Gabriel's *Episodios* appear to suggest that authors (leaders) who attempt to court the public run the risk of that same audience turning against them, if not with violent results, then certainly with defiant readings. At the close of this chapter, by borrowing the words of Cervantes to describe the public that displays such bad judgment, Gabriel establishes that the crowd he refers to are readers: "Nada hay más repugnante que la justicia popular, la cual tiene sobre sí el anatema de no acertar nunca, pues toda ella se funda en lo que llamaba Cervantes 'el vano discurso del vulgo, siempre engañado'" (616). [There is nothing more disgusting than popular justice, which is stigmatized by the fact that it is never correct, since it is all based on what Cervantes called "the empty discourse of the masses, who are always wrong."] This, then, is the culminating example of the public as readers run amok, and Gabriel concludes his account of the people's barbarity not with a reference to the extravagant Don Quijote, but to Cervantes as the original crusader against fantasy.[6]

While he criticizes the public's misreadings, in this *episodio* Gabriel is generally successful in keeping himself above such uncritical processing of texts. Again with a nod to Cervantes and the book scrutiny in *Don Quijote,* Gabriel's text celebrates the protagonist's good sense. Early in the novel, Gabriel watches as the characters Father Castillo, Father Salmón, and Amaranta engage in an evaluation of books reminiscent of Cervantes's "Del donoso escrutinio que el cura y el barbero hicieron en la librería de nuestro ingenioso hidalgo" (of the pleasant and grand scrutiny made by the priest and barber in our ingenious gentleman's library) in the *Quijote.*[7] Gabriel enters the room, physically overexposed because of the transparency of his summer clothing. (Gabriel's only suit is for summer wear, and he has been soaked by a downpour on the way to see Amaranta.)

Salmón presents him to the others as a great Latin scholar, again referring to Celestino's poetry. Although he tries, Gabriel is unable to free himself from this unwelcome and undeserved fame, because when he denies his authorship, Castillo interprets his statement as provoked by excessive modesty.[8] However, over the course of the book scrutiny, the text subtly creates a new image for Gabriel—or rather, because he produces the *Episodios,* Gabriel is able to redefine himself as a writer.

The books the characters examine are an assortment of poetic works published in the previous three months, and most are defenses of Fernando VII or attacks on Napoleon. Castillo, Salmón, and Amaranta debate the merits of humorous, satirical, and unceremonious works. Castillo defends the rights of the people to address the national crisis in ways familiar to them, and acknowledges that while they are ignorant, one should not demand of the public a decency and composure they do not have. When Salmón laments the particularly irreverent title of a work of history, Castillo insists that unrefined provincial people sometimes evince better judgment than the educated, because studies have not made them complacent (580). This defense of the common, uneducated author in the production of historical texts goes to the heart of Gabriel's enterprise, and validates not only the writing of his memoirs, but also his development—even as a young, unread participant—as potential historian. If the *Episodios* address a young reader, as Gabriel seems to have in mind, Castillo offers another defense of Gabriel's project when he comments that anything that sparks the interest of the young is worthy of celebration (581). Finally, Castillo again praises Gabriel's memoirs when he comments that "este afán de tratar en malos versos lo que está pidiendo a gritos clara y valiente prosa me indigna y pone fuera de mí" (581). [this desire to portray in bad verse what is begging for clear, brave prose makes me indignant and beside myself.] As an old man, Gabriel provides the brave prose for which his history cries.

Castillo also argues the merits of Gabriel's *Episodios* because of their art—their use of the devices of fiction in historical representation. Castillo finds himself captivated by an author whose political beliefs threaten people and institutions vital to Castillo's livelihood as a friar, and explains that his partiality to such texts is testimony to the power of art, because good writing charms with its form even those it cannot win over with its ideas. The characters pursue this topic when they assess a historical study based on an analogy with the game *tresillo,* and Castillo finds charming the use of the *tresillo* image instead of "plain Spanish." Salmón confirms this judgment, saying that the elaborateness of the text is its merit, because simple prose is nothing special (582). With such comments, the two friars reclothe Gabriel's nearly naked figure of the impostor poet, creating him anew as a valiant author of useful, yet always captivating and novelesque prose history.

Although Gabriel's stature as cultural authority increases, the quality of his potential readers seems low. With the French now in Madrid, Gabriel focuses on the unfortunate uses of literary arts by the entire nation. As the disorganized army gathers, Gabriel witnesses a lack of control, and perhaps more important, the people's inability to correctly read the "signs" around them. The people are represented by much movement of tongues and legs, and a constant coming and going, accompanied always by shouts, threats, and mutual distrust—with this conglomeration topped off by the pennants, banderoles, symbols, signs, and emblems which, for Gabriel, "so mesmerize the people of Madrid" ("que tanto emboban al pueblo de Madrid") (605).

In response to these various challenges by uncontrolled reading, Gabriel promotes himself as author, using a technique similar to that he employed in the narration of the events of May 2. Explaining that the cloister hosting the enlistment of volunteer soldiers would be "digno de ser eternizado por los más diestros pinceles" [worthy of being immortalized by the most able of paintbrushes], he then offers his own pen in replacement for the paintbrush: "¡Dichoso yo si con la pluma pudiera dar efímera existencia a uno de ellos!" (605). [Would that I could be so lucky as to give with the pen ephemeral existence to one of them!] He is not sure which to represent, but then proceeds to describe the cloister of the Trinidad Calzada (605). In this way, just as he does with the representation of May 2nd, Gabriel calls attention to the impossibility of painting the scenes he narrates, and then supplants the act of painting with his own written word.

At still another point in the text, Gabriel rejects the idea of mixing fantasy into his life, demonstrating a turn away from quixotism. Gabriel explains to Amaranta, who earlier tempted him with fictions of personal advancement and glory, that he has renounced his extravagant projects (586). Amaranta, however, still favors theatrical constructs as models for behavior, and imagines a drama for Gabriel to represent at her home, for the purpose of disenchanting Inés. Gabriel should, according to Amaranta, pretend to come to the house in order to serve her, and then act in absolutely vile and evil ways, until Inés gives up her fascination with him (587). Gabriel refuses to engage in this charade, and gains an advantage in the struggle with Amaranta when he gives her the letters he has found in Santorcaz's saddlebags. Although he uses texts written by other authors, Gabriel nevertheless creates a new script in which Amaranta must recognize that he has protected her from scandal by not disseminating the letters, and must forego any plans to seduce him into playing theatrical roles. Before learning that he had read the letters revealing that she and Santorcaz are Inés's parents, Amaranta had attempted to seduce Gabriel with the old narrative of the family romance: "¿Tienes alguna noticia de tus padres?

. . . A veces suele acontecer que el que se creía humilde . . ." (588). [Do you know anything about your parents? . . . Sometimes it tends to happen that one who believes himself to be humble . . .] Now that Gabriel has the upper hand, Amaranta dutifully gives up her plans to engage Gabriel in theatrics, so that he appears to have met her challenge successfully.

With these examples, we see that the text presents Gabriel as a skilled, nonquixotic reader and a legitimate author, in opposition to a number of inferior (mis)readers. As one of the most egregious of those who cannot process information accurately, I turn back now to the brave but irrational Santiago Fernández, whose end is fundamental to Gabriel's evolving confrontation with the quixotic mindset prevalent in his nation. As Gabriel observes, Santiago Fernández finally recognizes Napoleon's presence in Madrid, but imagines a miraculous victory for the doomed forces of resistance, who lack rifles and gunpowder (603). When the disorganized troops Fernández leads—a group that includes Gabriel—gather and begin their march, however, they conclude that an advance of cavalry presses in upon them, and decide that especially under the cover of darkness they cannot fight an unidentified and probably numerous enemy. In this way, the quixotic impulse of the group carries Gabriel along as part of a crowd action that threatens to degenerate into the monstrous behavior the protagonist often condemns, but then distills itself into the solitary (Quijote) Santiago Fernández, the only one who argues for continuing the advance (617).

The next morning confirms Santiago's role as a Quijote figure, as he refuses to eat, and instead regales his companions with a speech similar to that Don Quijote delivered to the shepherds on the topic of the Golden Age (620). The characters soon hear that Madrid will capitulate, but this simply inspires the old man to more radical action. He rejects his wife's pleas to give up the fight, and sneaks home to write his will while she sleeps unaware. For now, Gabriel appears to disagree with Santiago's irrational bravery. Nevertheless, Gabriel later learns that Santiago Fernández—the quintessential martyred patriot—was able to temporarily resist the French in one area of the city, even though the city ultimately surrendered.

Before explaining the relevance of the quixotic Fernández to Gabriel's campaign to distinguish himself from misreaders, we must glance again at another of the characters the *episodio* sets up in opposition to Fernández— an astute reader, but of doubtful "patriotism." After the battle, Gabriel reads the articles of the capitulation of Madrid along with the friars in the monastery where he has taken refuge. In this scene we see Father Castillo as an example of a good critic of texts, in contrast to the extravagant Santiago Fernández. When one of the brothers suggests that they should at least argue their case with the French, since Napoleon plans to reduce the number of monasteries and regular clergy by two-thirds, the erudite Castillo produces two seventeenth-century Spanish texts that argue for the same reform. He then challenges his audience to examine their own consciences by asking themselves if they are really necessary to society, presumably because he is convinced by the arguments of the Spanish texts (636). The next day, the residents of the monastery, including Gabriel (who has taken refuge through fear of persecution by Santorcaz), discover that Napoleon is not obeying the articles of the surrender. They read together a second text—Napoleon's decrees for Spain—and discover that he does indeed plan to close two-thirds of Spain's convents and monasteries. Although these decrees indicate radical change and significant hardship for the religious orders, Father Castillo admits that he agrees with all but the most anticlerical of Napoleon's ideas (640–41). Even in his self-sacrifice, Gabriel's text portrays Father Castillo as a sensible reader.

With these two contrasting characters, Fernández and Castillo, we see the issue of patriotism and the War for Independence played out as textual interpretation. At first glance, Gabriel seems to respect Father Castillo, who is such a careful, judicious reader, over Santiago Fernández, who is fundamentally irrational. At the close of the novel, however, we are made to doubt this facile conclusion, as seen by Gabriel's own behavior. When Gabriel's protectors in the monastery begin to fear Napoleon's persecution, they decide that the young man must leave them. Gabriel's only chance for escape from persecution by Santorcaz is to rely on the assistance of his powerful friends, the marqués and the rest of Amaranta's family. To reach their home safely, Gabriel allows himself to be dressed as a novice. Whereas this may seem like an insignificant choice, the use of a disguise means several things: Gabriel now plays a theatrical role, just as Amaranta had wished. Also, for the earlier visit to Inés's mother he wore his own clothing, which in its diaphanousness ended up revealing him exactly as he was, with no ruses, whereas this costume deceives. Moreover, even though in the earlier visit to Amaranta he was transformed from an impostor poet to a dignified writer of captivating prose whose realist mentality enabled him to reject his hostess's fantasies, he now willingly disguises himself, adopting for his protection the fiction of his commitment to enter the monastery.

We might ask why Gabriel makes this change. Perhaps the answer lies in the contrast between the two examples of "reading" that he has just witnessed. Santiago Fernández, a quixotic old man—in other words, a "bad" reader—has accomplished a memorable feat of heroism for the glory of his country. Father Castillo, on the other hand, reads very well, but his competent analysis of texts only brings suspicion of his patriotism, as he applauds much of what the French enemy represents. In the final chapters of *Napoleón en Chamartín,* Gabriel travels in disguise to Amaranta, borrows the identity of Amaranta's cousin (and another potential suitor for Inés) the duke of Arión, and plans to leave Madrid by pretending to be the duke. When he changes his escape scheme in order to warn Amaranta that Diego intends to abduct Inés, the servants of the house eventually discover who he really is, and he endures a torture that parallels that experienced by Godoy and by Mañara. He requests that his reader imagine his martyrdom when the lowly servants attack him, the person they had believed to be a duke. They trample his supposed nobility and chivalry, and he is unable to defend himself from the small mob, who avenge the fiction of exalted rank created by Gabriel (663).

In this way, when Gabriel surrenders to Amaranta's urging that he play a theatrical role, and takes part in the fabrication of the nonrealist fiction of posing as an aristocrat, the feared public attacks him. When Gabriel chooses to fictionalize himself, and takes up a story of immediate social ascent as his disguise, his punishment at the hands of the (small) mob fits with the representation of the plight of the author, patron of the arts, or artist in the *Episodios* (recall the fates of Godoy and Mañara, along with the many examples of storytellers being rejected by unreceptive audiences). The final passages of *Napoleón in Chamartín* continue to focus on disrespect for authors; Gabriel is sent into exile along with the poet Cienfuegos, and both are accompanied and "profaned" by the inferior reader Roque, the worshipper of newspapers (the actor Isidoro Máiquez and the poet Sánchez Barbero would follow later) (666). At the same time these authors are sent away, Gabriel learns the whole story of the idealistic reader Fernández's last stand. Even Roque, who in life squabbled bitterly with Fernández, approves of his heroic death for the honor of Spain, and compares Santiago's "locura" to that of the other great Quijote of this novel, Napoleon (667).

The discussion of Fernández's heroism prepares for the idea that surfaces in the *Episodios* (and in Baroja's trilogy), that for all its pitfalls, quixotic reading lays the groundwork for brave self-sacrifice. It is this romantic vision of heroism that draws the attention of even the most critical readers, who glimpse alluring promises of a lost glorious destiny in the rejected narratives of quixotism. This examination of the illogical, irrational side of the bravery that permitted Spain's victory in the War for Independence is crucial to the *Episodios*' complex study of romanticism, realism, patriotism, and the mechanisms of imagining the modern Spanish nation. Humiliated at the end of this novel, Gabriel, in the next two *episodios,* allows other characters to protagonize and even narrate the battles of Zaragoza and Gerona. This gesture of self-effacement, however, is then erased in its turn, when Gabriel reclaims control of the narrative and reasserts his authority.

ZARAGOZA

The *episodio Zaragoza* begins with the arrival of the exiles of *Napoleón en Chamartín* in the city of Zaragoza. Gabriel and company reach the besieged city in mid-December of 1808, to the chiming of the clock in the "torre inclinada" (leaning tower), or Torre Nueva (669). Zaragoza has already weathered one attack during the summer of 1808, and now prepares for another French invasion. Although Gabriel takes an active role in the battle, much of this *episodio* focuses on the family and love interest of Gabriel's alter ego, the young Zaragozan Agustín de Montoria. Before meeting the Montorias, however, Gabriel spends his first night in the city in the monastery of Santa Engracia. At the church, he reads the destruction caused by the French during an earlier siege of Zaragoza as representing incompleteness and potentiality:

> En el interior vimos arcos incompletos, machones colosales, irguiéndose aún entre los escombros, y que, al destacarse negros y deformes sobre la claridad del espacio, semejaban criaturas absurdas, engendradas por una imaginación en delirio . . . Había hasta pequeñas estancias abiertas entre los pedazos de la pared con un arte semejante al de las grutas en la Naturaleza . . . Al ver semejante aglomeración de escombros, tal multitud de trozos caídos sin perder completamente su antigua forma, las masas de ladrillo enyesado que se desmoronaban como objetos de azúcar, creeríase que los despojos del edificio no habían encontrado posición definitiva. (669–70)

> [Inside we saw unfinished arches, colossal buttresses still raised up among the ruins, which, standing out black and deformed against the brightness of the space, seemed like absurd creatures, engendered by a feverish imagination. There were even small rooms open between the pieces of the wall with an art similar to that of natural caves . . . Seeing such a conglomeration of ruins, such a number of pieces that had fallen without losing completely their earlier form, the masses of plastered brick which collapsed like objects made of sugar, one would think that the rubble of the bulding had not yet found its definitive position.]

With this description of the ruined church Gabriel introduces several concepts crucial to the rest of the *episodio,* and demonstrates that he will be lead reader of the city's defense. The delirious imagination ("imaginación en delirio"), for example, issues forth in the poetic excesses of Agustín de Montoria, Manuela Sancho, and, indeed, all the Zaragozans. Just as the handiwork of men—destructive as well as creative—competes with Nature's caves, Agustín will return to the topic of human artists' competition with natural creation. Finally, the inconclusiveness of the scene mirrors the ongoing struggle between the two discourses of poetry and prose as expressions of romanticism and realism, respectively.[9] Gabriel identifies with the latter, but, as in *Napoleón en Chamartín,* recognizes the association of poetic heroism with patriotism and the defense of Spain. Although Gabriel allows Agustín to take over as "protagonist" of this *episodio,* he retains control of the reading of Zaragoza's struggle, as evidenced by his interpretation of the church's ruins for his audience. He also argues that he understands Zaragoza's spirit better than the French invaders do. At the same time, his prowess in reading the city hinges on his appreciation of poetry in Zaragoza. For this reason, Gabriel must simultaneously assert his aptitude for understanding the poetic mentality and demonstrate his imperviousness to the seductions of this same poetry. As Gabriel fights for the legitimacy of his particular prose history of Zaragoza's participation in the War for Independence, Gabriel's text nevertheless acknowledges the compelling nature of its competitor—the poetry based on the love, heroism, and patriotism that motivates the other characters and sustains the besieged citizens in the defense of their homeland.

In this literary battle—mirror image of the siege of Zaragoza—Gabriel the realist prose historian suffers an initial disadvantage when Roque, the newspaper worshipper exiled along with Gabriel in *Napoleón en Chamartín,* romanticizes his past. Roque presents Gabriel to the Montoria family as a son of nobility, participant in the battle of Trafalgar, recipient of a government assignment to Perú, hero of the Puerta de Pozos in Madrid, and feared enemy of the French (674). With a halo stolen from Santiago Fernández (the legitimate martyr of the Puerta de Pozos), and wearing the tattered remains of the suit belonging to the duke of Arión, Gabriel will have to fight to escape associations with fantasy and unearned glory.

Gabriel begins this struggle with a poetry that draws near to his own heart when he meets a young man who, in many ways, mirrors himself. Agustín de Montoria is desperately in love, and is unable to acknowledge his beloved because of social restrictions, just as is Gabriel. Gabriel notices their commonalities immediately, and although Agustín's "brilliant imagination" inclines him to poetry, Gabriel does not dismiss the young Zaragozan, but instead, admires him for his extensive study of theological "science," which he has learned even though he is a poet by nature (677). It is this poetic drive of Agustín's that Gabriel both celebrates and regrets, recognizing its power and seductiveness, but also its tragedy. The poetry of Agustín is most visible when he describes his beloved Mariquilla. Agustín and Mariquilla must love each other in secret, because animosity between their fathers plagues their Romeo-and-Juliet-style relationship. José de Montoria is a respected leader of the city; however, Andrés describes Mariquilla's father *tío* Candiola as a heartless miser who has revealed himself as antipatriotic in the previous siege of Zaragoza (678–79).

As Agustín explains to Gabriel, he has been plagued by this hopeless passion for Candiola's daughter ever since he encountered her during his lessons on love poetry. Augistín, who has no vocation, is studying for the priesthood (677). One day, his teacher Father Rincón, with whom he often spent afternoons reading and learning the poetry of Horace, distracted him from reading *Quis multa gracilis te puer in rosa* by taking him on a visit to his relative Candiola. When the man's daughter emerged instead, Rincón asked her to give peaches to Agustín, then grasped her face, turning it toward Agustín and asking him if he had ever in his life seen a prettier face (679). Commanded by his teacher, and influenced by his reading, Agustín agreed. He recounts for Gabriel this pivotal experience, relating his teacher's requirement, that he critically assess Mariquilla, to Rincón's earlier requests that he compare literary texts, and characterizing his reaction as obedient submission: "Esto me dijo mi maestro, y yo, mudo y atónito, no cesaba de contemplar aquella obra maestra, que era sin disputa mejor que la *Eneida*" (680). [My teacher told me this, and I, mute and astonished, did not stop contemplating that masterpiece, which was without a doubt better than the *Aeneid*.] Gabriel interrupts to ask prosaically about the peaches, but Agustín continues his story, explaining that from that day on he has preferred Virgil to Horace, and has welcomed the increase in freedom provided by the war. He lives at home instead of at the seminary, and visits Mariquilla nightly, in her garden, where they have developed a new sort of poetry together (681). Agustín, then, is the romantic alter ego Gabriel confronts in *Zaragoza*.

As additional opponents, the French appear in the city, and Gabriel must defend his patriotism by taking sides with the Zaragozans, which he does by claiming to appreciate their poetic nature better than do the French. When Gabriel describes the conflict, he emphasizes the French loss of control and perspective. While Gabriel has already started his mission of "reading" the Zaragozan character by studying Agustín's poetry, the French soldiers fight frenetically, and Gabriel believes it is this lack of purpose that causes them to lose that day's contest. He suggests that they should have remained calm, and that they should have taken a lesson from Napoleon, who, because he studied the human heart, could have understood the Zaragozans (683). This reasoning concurs with *Napoleón en Chamartín*'s equation of Napoleon with Santiago Fernández, because the Zaragozan quality that Napoleon would have understood is precisely that poetic heroism that drove the martyr of the Puerta de los Pozos to his self-sacrifice. It is this idealistic passion that the common French soldiers are unable to comprehend in their opponents.

In the next chapter of the novel, Gabriel proceeds to distinguish himself from this limitation demonstrated by the French soldiers by proving his ability to understand Zaragoza on its own terms. After the successful defense of December 21, the Zaragozans worship the Virgen del Pilar, and Gabriel and Agustín run to the church where the people are gathered.

Gabriel assesses this surprising scene, saying that he recognized the Zara-gozans' incoherent exclamations as the attempts of the people to com-municate with their beloved saint. As the crowd expresses its love, Gabriel recognizes that there are no authorities to restrain the people, giving his readers another glimpse of an uncontrolled public, this time processing the texts of prayer (684). In this way, eventually the familiar image of the untamed crowd comes into play here—the delirious language of the faith-ful is both remarkable and perfectly comprehensible to Gabriel.

He is also able to "read" the poetry of Zaragoza's virgin "saints," the Virgen del Pilar and Agustín's beloved Mariquilla. First Gabriel draws close to the statue of the saint, and describes her clothing, jewelry, and eyes in detail. Then Agustín distracts Gabriel from his examination of the statue, and instructs him to gaze at Mariquilla, just as Augustín's tutor had done earlier with him. Gabriel turns from the "carita morena" (little brown face) of the Virgen del Pilar to the "tez morena" (brown complexion) of Mariquilla, shifting his scrutinizing eye to examine the new "virgin" in the same manner—complexion, facial features, clothing—and imagines that she will be "poco habladora, falta de coquetería y pobre de artificios" (quiet, lacking in flirtatiousness, and without artifice), much like the statue he has just studied (684–85).[10]While other women might be soft like wax, Mariquilla seems to him to be made of hard metal (685), again, similar to the statue.[11] Reading both of these Zaragozan idols, Gabriel proves that he is able to participate in a Napoleonic appreciation of the heart of the Zaragozan people who seem to be his allies, but with whose poetry he must also compete as champion of the prosaic reading of life. In this scene, Gabriel also meets Candiola, describes him with unappealing detail, and consigns him to a literary world in a way that further calls attention to his own skill at reading Zaragoza as text(s): "Si don Jerónimo hubiera tenido barbas, le compararía por su figura a cierto mercader veneciano que conocí mucho después, viajando por el vastísimo continente de los libros" (685). [If don Jerónimo had worn a beard, I would compare his figure to a certain merchant of Venice I became acquainted with much later, when traveling the vast continent of books.]

As part of Gabriel's saga of Zaragozan heroism, female characters such as these two adored women play a significant role.[12] But here, on the subject of women, Gabriel begins his assertion of his superiority as a reader, by portraying the Zaragozans as victims of their own romanticism. The first stage in Gabriel's self-promotion is the association of all of the heroic, inspiring female figures with each other. Once Gabriel has com-pared the three important women and highlighted their similarities, we begin to see a pattern of difficulties linked to the romanticization of women in war. The third female character who takes a prominent part in this account of the siege of Zaragoza is Manuela Sancho. Manuela learns to fire a gun as Gabriel watches, then acts as a brave participant in subsequent encounters with the French. The novel links this valiant highlander who fought to defend her city with Mariquilla, when Mariquilla wishes for arms to defend her father from his enemy José de Montoria, and swears that if he invaded her home she would kill him (707–8, 710). Manuela is similar to Mariquilla, but the Zaragozans also recognize Manuela's parallels with the patron saint, because both inspire the men to greater heroic acts. When Manuela first takes up a gun, her lover Pirli encourages her by shouting "¡Viva la segunda artillera Manuela Sancho y la Virgen del Pilar!" (692). [Long live the second artillery woman Manuela Sancho and the Virgen del Pilar!] These three female figures, then—"feminine" in their beauty and "masculine" in their grim determination—form part of the poetry of hopeless resistance and martyrdom that the Zaragozans encourage, and that Gabriel reacts to with sympathy, but ultimately incorporates into his cautionary tale.[13]

For her part, Manuela proves central to the Zaragozan defense. When the French reach the small fort of San José, entering through a breach, the Zaragozan company (including Gabriel) panics. Each soldier thinks only of saving his own life, and they flee, plagued by cowardice, toward the bridge. Although their leaders order them back to the redoubt, they remain paralyzed, until they see among the ruins behind them a courageous female figure (694). This lone soldier is Manuela Sancho, and she marches majestically toward the "horrible breach" (694). As they watch her, suddenly the soldiers turn back, "azuzados por los jefes" (incited by the leaders), but also inspired by her bravery to help her. Gabriel comments that it was a sudden change, and that he can no more explain why they followed her than why they were cowardly just seconds earlier (695). Still unsure why or how, Gabriel recounts that the men threw themselves into the breach after her, and that, inexplicably, "aplastamos, arrojándolos en lo profundo del foso, a aquellos hombres de algodón que antes nos parecieron de acero" (695). [throwing ourselves into the depths of the pit, we flattened those straw men who had before seemed to us made of steel.] Just as if they were Don Quijote fighting Maese Pedro's puppets, formerly armies but now just cotton figurines, the soldiers imitate not only Manuela's physical movements, but her romantic narrative of heroism, however quixotic. Although the Zaragozans eventually surrender to the French, they enjoy a temporary victory. Again, as in the case of Santiago Fernández's hopeless resistance, Gabriel is forced to recognize that although following this sort of irrational "plot" is an inferior reading of reality, such an approach also leads to military success in desperate times.

At the same time, however, beyond the association with quixotism, Gabriel's text offers a critique of this brand of patriotism, in the sense that the leaders of the Zaragozan resistance use Manuela's heroism as a means of controlling the men who fight. In other words, the Zaragozans are victims of their own Quijote narrative. If we reexamine the feats of Manuela, we notice that when she begins to participate in the battle, the male soldiers lose control of their own contributions to the resistance, as heroism's quixotic illusion becomes a discourse used by those in power to control the soldiers. In fact, the myth of heroism continues to seduce the men even after Manuela falls injured, as when the friars employ the Virgen del Pilar in their manipulation of the soldiers. As the Zaragozans march toward the church of San Agustín to engage in a hopeless defense of the shrine the French already possess, the friars penetrate their ranks, promising them food and wine, and exhorting them to remember the Virgin (728). After they are forced to concede the church to the French, Gabriel notes that the promised wine is nowhere in sight, and calls attention also to the manipulative nature of the friars' comments related to the Virgin (730).

Gabriel is aware that it is the Zaragozans' vivid imagination and inability to critically read the texts of war that makes them vulnerable to this coercion by their leaders. As another example of Zaragozan lack of judgment, the citizens' assessment of Capitán General Palafox is a cause for Gabriel's concern. Gabriel includes in his narration of the siege of *Zaragoza* a description of Palafox, whose fame was in part due to his valor, but also resulted from the awe inspired by his lineage, apart from any of his own accomplishments. What made Palafox most attractive, Gabriel explains, was his youthful bravery in pursuit of an ideal (733). Because he lacks the necessary intellectual faculties, he surrounds himself with men who take care of these details, and appears as a figurehead: "Estos lo hacían todo, y Palafox quedábase tan sólo con lo teatral" (733). [Those other men did everything, and Palafox was left only with the theatrical.] Gabriel then summarizes the mechanisms of Palafox's power over his subjects, rooted not only in his own idealistic bent, but in the qualities of the poetically minded people: "Sobre un pueblo en que tanto prevalece la imaginación, no podía menos de ejercer subyugador dominio aquel general joven" (732). [Over a people in whom the imagination prevails to such a degree, that young general could not help but exert a subjugating control.] In a reverse of their construction of Godoy as demoniacal scapegoat, the public reads bravery into Palafox, "symbolizing" in him their virtues, their constancy, their ideal, mystical patriotism, and their warrior fervor. It is this (mis)reading of Palafox's vacuousness that allows him free rein over the people who project idealism onto him, and they believe he can do no wrong (733). As Gabriel notes, Palafox is supremely aware of this mechanism, and exploits it as needed. He realizes his success is due more to his abilities as an actor than to his abilities as a general: "Siempre se presentaba con todos sus arreos de gala, entorchados, plumas y veneras, y la atronadora música de los aplausos y los vivas le halagaban en extremo" (733). [He always showed up bedecked with all his gear, braids, feathers, and insignia, and the thundering music of the applauses and hurrahs flattered him in the extreme.] Our narrator concludes that this interrelationship between a *caudillo* (leader) and his followers—one based on the elaboration and projection of poetic fantasies—is always necessary in the expression of this particular sort of authority (733). When Gabriel allows us to see Palafox at work with his public, we observe the leader's absolute domination of his followers, barely concealed by the rhetoric of patriotism. The Capitán General shares with the Zaragozans a willing identification with the discourse of patriotic bravery, but he also combines inspiration with coercion in his addresses to his subjects, threatening them with death and confiscation of property in the same speech in which he tries to raise their spirits with respect to the battle (733).

Throughout the text Gabriel notes other examples of the Zaragozans' weakness as readers, and observes the unfortunate consequences of this debility. In the eleventh chapter, the besieged citizens shift from dejection to happy excitement when news circulates of the imminent arrival of additional troops (696). The people throng to receive the newspaper *Gaceta,* and Gabriel comments that he is not sure whether such news actually arrived in Zaragoza from outside, or whether the Zaragozan editor doctored the information. He is certain, however, that the story appeared in print, along with other fantastically encouraging news of Spanish victories and advances, and of promised reinforcements for Zaragoza (696). Gabriel mocks his own credulity, admitting that he was swept up by the crowd's uncritical reception of the news: "Con ser tantas y gordas, nos las tragamos" (696). [Even with the news being so amazingly unbelievable, we swallowed it all.] There is one audience, however—the French opponents—who ignore the apocryphal news, and continue to look to reality instead of fancy. As Gabriel explains, the French seem to mock the printed news by bombing with twice the intensity: "Aquellos condenados parecían querer mofarse de las noticias de nuestra *Gaceta,* repitiendo la dosis" (696). [Those wretches seemed to wish to mock the reports of our *Gazette* by doubling the dose.]

Bolstered by their fictions, the Zaragozans attempt to impose their version of reality on the French by running to the wall and singing in unison, with musical accompaniment, that the Virgin of Pilar does not want to be French (696). This poetic obstinacy merely invites additional bombs, which fall more heavily in that two-hour period than in the rest of the day (696–97). Even in the face of such evidence, the injured Zaragozans who take refuge in the church that houses the Virgen del Pilar continue to insist on their reading of the saint's face, and find there words that are much more romantic than the text Gabriel read earlier in the same countenance. The Zaragozans believe that the Virgin speaks ceaselessly, "with the language of her shining eyes" ("con el lenguaje de sus brillantes ojos"), that she does not want to be French (697). Although Gabriel often uses the first person plural in this episode, thereby including himself with the Zaragozans, here he keeps his distance from the faithful—the unquestioning readers and sufferers.

In addition to his critique of the Zaragozan people, Gabriel continues to question Agustín's poetic excesses, when the two young men visit Mariquilla after her father has engaged in a confrontation with Agustín's father. The interchange is fraught with Agustín's lies and fantasies, as he distracts Mariquilla from her desire for vengeance first by imagining that they will be united by a miracle, then by countering her earlier statement—that she will love him until the Torre Nueva straightens—with a declaration that he will love her until the giant rock Moncayo moves from its location outside the city and reduces Zaragoza to dust. Agustín explains that his claim to eternal love is more substantial than hers, because the works of nature are less changeable than those of humanity (708). Gabriel then comments on this interchange, noting the participation of the two lovers in a poetic pact that relies on the feverish imagination of both: "De este modo hiperbólico y con este naturalismo poético expresaba mi amigo su gran amor, correspondiendo y halagando así la imaginación de la hermosa Candiola, que propendía con impulso ingénito al mismo sistema" (708). [In that exaggerated way and with that poetic naturalism my friend expressed his great love, responding to and flattering the imagination of the beautiful Candiola girl, who was inclined with an innate drive toward the same system.] Just as the crowd possesses a mentality receptive to the theatrical leadership of Palafox, Mariquilla welcomes Agustín's flights of fancy, eager to conceptualize their love as represented by romantic words, and to retreat from the reality of the lovers' environment.

In this way, Gabriel sets himself apart from various uncritical readers. And yet, there is one reader who approximates Gabriel's own approach to the use of texts. Candiola, the selfish villain of Zaragoza, dares to doubt the utility of the city's sacrifice (737). By explicitly and implicitly interrogating the rhetoric of quixotic struggle and the critical capacities of the Zaragozan poetic imagination, Gabriel raises the same questions. Near the middle of the novel, Candiola is in despair. He believes his daughter has lost her virtue with a number of soldiers. (He has seen her with Agustín and Gabriel together, and imagines that she must have even more "suitors".) He issues forth his lament:

¿En dónde está mi hija? . . . ¡Ah! Esa loca no sabe permanecer al lado de su padre en desgracia. La vergüenza la hace huir de mí. ¡Maldita esa su liviandad y el momento en que la descubrí! Señor, Jesús Nazareno, y tú, mi patrono Santo Dominguito del Val, decidme: ¿qué he hecho yo para merecer tantas desgracias

en un mismo día? ¿No soy bueno, no hago todo el bien que puedo, no favorezco
a mis semejantes, prestándoles dinero con un interés módico, pongo por caso,
la miseria de tres o cuatro reales por peso fuerte al mes? Pues si soy un hombre
bueno a carta cabal, ¿a qué llueven sobre mí tantas desventuras? Y gracias que
no pierdo lo poco que a fuerza de trabajos he reunido, porque está en paraje
adonde no pueden llegar las bombas; pero ¿y la casa, los muebles, los recibos y
lo que aún queda en el almacén? Maldito sea yo, y cómanme los demonios, si
cuando esto se acabe y cobre los piquillos que por ahí tengo no me marcho de
Zaragoza para no volver más . . . Mi hija se ha envilecido. No sé cómo no la
maté esta mañana. Hasta aquí, yo había supuesto a María un modelo de vir-
tudes, de honestidad; me deleitaba su compañía y de todos los buenos negocios
destinaba un real para comprarle regalitos. ¡Mal empleado dinero! ¡Dios mío,
tú me castigas por haber despilfarrado un gran capital en cosas supérfluas,
cuando a interés compuesto hubiérase ya triplicado! Yo tenía confianza en mi
hija. (720–21)

[Where is my daughter? Oh! That crazy girl does not know how to stay at her
father's side when he is disgraced. Shame makes her run from me. Damn her
frivolousness and the moment I found her out. Lord Jesus of Nazareth, and you,
my patron saint Dominguito del Val, tell me: What have I done to deserve so
many misfortunes in one single day? Am I not good, do I not do all the good I
can, do I not favor my fellow men, lending them money at a moderate interest
rate, for example, the small sum of three or four *reales* to the *peso fuerte* per
month? Well, if I am a man who represents goodness itself, for what reason
does so much bad luck rain down on me? Luckily I cannot lose the little I have
been able to acquire by working, because it's in a spot the bombs can't get to;
but the house? The furniture, the receipts and what's still left in the warehouse?
Let me be damned, and let devils eat me, if when this ends and I recover the
small sums owed me I don't leave Zaragoza and never come back. My daughter
has turned evil. I don't know how I didn't kill her this morning. Up to now, I
had always supposed María a model of virtue, of honesty; I enjoyed her
company and from all my good business deals I took a *real* to buy her little
presents. Wasted money! My God, you punish me for having wasted a great
capital on superfluous things, when at compound interest it would have tripled!
I trusted my daughter.]

Candiola's lament is reminiscent of that of *La Celestina*'s Pleberio upon
his own daughter's death. The two girls are about the same age. Pleberio
knows his daughter is dead, and his lament reveals greater anguish and
generosity of spirit than Candiola's; nevertheless, Candiola echoes many
of Pleberio's comments. Pleberio:

Oh duro corazón de padre, ¿cómo no te quiebras de dolor, que ya quedas sin tu
amada heredera? ¿Para quién edifiqué torres; para quién adquirí honras; para
quién planté árboles; para quién fabriqué navíos? . . . ¡Oh vida de congojas
llena, de miserias acompañada; oh mundo, mundo! . . . Cébasnos, mundo

falso, con el manjar de tus deleites; al mejor sabor nos descubres el anzuelo: no lo podemos huir, que nos tiene ya cazadas las voluntades. Prometes mucho, nada nos cumples; échasnos de ti, porque no te podamos pedir que mantengas tus vanos prometimientos . . . ¿Por qué te mostraste tan cruel con tu viejo padre? ¿Por qué me dejaste, cuando yo te había de dejar? ¿Por qué me dejaste penado? ¿Por qué me dejaste triste y solo in hac lachrymarum valle?"[14]

[Oh, father's hard heart, why do you not break with pain, since you now are left without your beloved heir? For whom did I build towers; for whom did I acquire honors; for whom did I plant trees; for whom did I build ships? Oh life full of woes, accompanied by miseries, oh world, world! You feed us, false world, the dish of your delights; with the best flavor you hook us: we cannot escape from it, because it holds our will captive. You promise much, you deliver nothing; you shun us, so that we cannot ask that you keep your vain promises. Why were you so cruel to your old father? Why did you leave me, when I should have left you? Why did you leave me in sorrow? Why did you leave me sad and alone in this valley of tears?]

In the end of this *episodio,* Candiola and Mariquilla die, Agustín escapes to the seminary, José de Montoria suffers humiliation by the French, and Zaragoza falls to the invaders. Gabriel's text appears to be the one survivor of the struggle, proving that Agustín was correct in his assessment of the impermanence of such human creations as the poetic love he had earlier imagined. However, we must remember that Candiola (Gabriel) revives Pleberio, showing that this ultrarealist text does in fact survive, and forming of his Golden Age model an even more crass and materialistic father. Once again, Gabriel rewrites a canonical work of Spanish literature, updating *La Celestina* and outdoing Fernando de Rojas. When faced with the choice between the quixotic poetry of an illusory patriotism and the prose model suggested by Candiola, Gabriel opts for the latter, and ensures that realism remains as the textual survivor of the Zaragozan holocaust. In the final chapter of *Zaragoza,* Gabriel raises the issue of the epic poem as he recalls the moment in which the French finally took possession of the city: "Inmensas, espantosas ruinas la formaban. Era la ciudad de la desolación, de la epopeya digna de que la llorara Jeremías y de que la cantara Homero" (760). [Immense, frightful ruins formed it. It was the city of desolation, of the epic poem worthy of Jeremiah's tears and Homer's song.] In this way, Gabriel identifies the text that would narrate the epic saga of Zaragoza in all its glory as something other than what he himself produces.[15] He leaves the task to Homer, and takes up his own pen with another goal in mind. In the penultimate chapter of the novel, Gabriel explains that 1808 marks the definitive establishment of Spanish nationality, and that Spain's destiny is "poder vivir en la agitación como la salamandra en el fuego" (759). [to be able to live amidst unrest like a salamander in fire.] Clearly, Gabriel's text argues that the true survivor of the conflicts of the nineteenth century is its own salamander-like realism—the heritage of Pleberio as articulated by Candiola. Still, Gabriel is far from resolving realism's separation from (poetic) romanticism, largely because he continues to sympathize with quixotic ideations, just as he did when reading Zaragozan poetry.

GERONA

Whereas most of the next *episodio* is narrated by Gabriel's alter ego Andrés Marijuán, *Gerona* is another story about Gabriel's struggles with reading and authorship. Like Gabriel, Andrés is a young man attracted to romantic quixotism and concerned by the author's stigma of "selfishness." Andrés is evidently an alter ego of Gabriel, yet his narration of *Gerona* allows Gabriel to temporarily remove himself from the dilemmas and difficulties he had faced in the earlier *episodios*. Paradoxically, turning the narration of *Gerona* over to someone else provides Gabriel with a superior vantage point, as he is able to watch someone else vacillate between realist and romantic worldviews, and worry about his audience rejecting him.

Before allowing Andrés to narrate, Gabriel meditates once again on the fickleness and instability of the reading public, presenting himself as authoritative analyst of national culture. In the first chapter, Gabriel returns to his preoccupation with the control of the masses—potential readership, but also immanent threat. He explains that during the winter of 1809–1810, the Junta Central consolidated all the regional councils, and formed the Consejo de Castilla (763). The competition for power, however, threatened the integrity of this organization. The Consejo denied the legitimacy of the Junta that had empowered it, and began to manipulate some of the people: "En Sevilla azuzaron a lo que un gran historiador llama con enérgico estilo *la bozal muchedumbre,* y hubo frecuentes serenatas de berridos y patadas por la calle, mas no pasó de aquí" (764, italics in original). [In Sevilla they incited what a great historian calls with energetic style *the untamed crowd,* and there were frequent serenades of bellowing and stamping, but it didn't go beyond that.] Here, Gabriel asserts that whereas the corrupt leaders were able to take advantage of a portion of the public, and to dictate in this manner the production of some aspects of the national epic poem of the war, there was a larger public untainted by these particular fictions, which retained a certain savage innocence "cierta inocencia salvaje" (764).[16] In this way, Gabriel sets the stage for his continued treatment of the fight by authors for control of a readership, and suggests that a significant component of the public remained available to the storyteller who could establish primacy over other narrators. At the same time, the savagery of this untutored and unreclaimed audience reminds us of the vulnerable position of the author who would attempt such a conquest. Later Gabriel returns to the corruption of the Junta, explaining that these leaders who profaned the trust of the people were nothing more than "inquietos y vividores reptiles" (restless and lively reptiles) who disappeared from the accounts of "la Historia"—a "vulgo," "gentezuela sin ideal, que se perdería en la muchedumbre . . . si la vituperable neutralidad política de la mayoría honrada, decente, entendida y patriota, no les permitiera actuar en la vida política" (767). [a common people, riffraff with no ideal, who would be lost in the crowd . . . if the reprehensible political neutrality of the honest, decent, sensible, and patriotic majority did not let them take part in political life.] Gabriel concludes his meditation on the availability of a public of good sense with an analysis of how the people, despite the perspicacity of its majority, can be corrupted by unscrupulous leaders (or, we could read, narrators).

With these introductory statements, Gabriel frames Andrés's account of the siege of Gerona. Gabriel confesses that although his intention had been to recount his own adventures in Cádiz, his patriotic duty requires him to temporarily suppress his desire to tell his story, "dando la preferencia a algunos hechos del sitio de Gerona, que contaré también, si bien los contaré de oídas" (767). [letting events from the siege of Gerona take precedence—events that I will narrate, even though I heard them from someone else.] Thus, whereas he appears to concede primacy to another narrator, his self-effacement is merely an illusion, because he is the one who will tell this story.[17] Indeed, he even confesses to having altered the narration, taking advantage of the authorial skills he has acquired since the events took place:

> He modificado un tanto la relación de Andresillo Marijuán, respetando, por supuesto, todo lo esencial, pues su rudo lenguaje me causaba cierto estorbo al tratar de asociar su historia a las mías . . . Tampoco yo me hubiera expresado así en aquellos tiempos; pero téngase presente que, en la época en que hablo, cuento algo más de ochenta años, vida suficiente, a mi juicio, para aprender alguna cosa, adquiriendo asimismo un poco de lustre en el modo de decir (767).

> [Although I have left intact everything essential, I have modified slightly the story told by Andrés Marijuán, since his crude language caused me certain difficulties when I tried to link his story with mine. I would not have expressed myself like this at that time either; but keep in mind that, at the time in which I am speaking now, I am more than eighty years old, having lived long enough, in my judgment, to learn a few things, acquiring in addition a bit of polish in my storytelling.]

By calling attention to the improvements he has made, Gabriel establishes the fact that he sees Andrés as a competitor in the struggle to be the primary author of *Gerona,* although his age and experience at the time he writes the novel convince him of his superiority over Andrés. Still, one component of their competition is the confusion of the two young soldier-narrators, as when (cited above) Gabriel confesses that he would have written just as crudely as a young man, and later, when he explains that his adversities have forced him to question his own identity: "Conservo cierta duda de si seré yo mismo el que en aquellos fieros combates se halló, o si, después de muerto, me habré trocado en otro sujeto" (764). [I continue to have a certain doubt about whether it was really me in those ferocious battles or whether, after death, I might have become a different person.] Andrés is aggressive in his attempts to usurp Gabriel's position as domi-nant narrator, as he tries to force his story on his listeners ("nos había venido aturdiendo con el perenne contar de sus privaciones y hambres en Gerona" [Andrés had been going along dizzying us with his perpetual story of his deprivations and hunger in Gerona], as Gabriel comments), offering to read them the diary of don Pablo Nomdedéu, and singing a song about the valor of Gerona "Marijuán repetía la canción con que nos aporre-aba los oídos desde que le encontramos" (765). [Marijuán was repeating the song with which he had been drumming our ears since we found him.]

Although Gabriel views Andrés as vying for the job of narrator, this prologue of sorts to Andrés's narration of the siege of Gerona leaves no doubt as to the primacy of Gabriel as head *raconteur.* As he explains, when they spend the night in Bailén in the now deserted palace of the Rumblars, Gabriel revisits alone the sites and stories of the mansion: "Solo, y mientras Marijuán dormía, recorrí varias habitaciones altas de la casa, iluminadas no más que por la luna, y una dulce, inexplicable claridad llenaba mi alma durante aquella muda y solitaria exploración. No hubo mueble que no me dijese alguna cosa, y mi imaginación iba poblando de seres conocidos las desiertas salas" (766). [Alone, and while Marijuán was sleeping, I walked through several upper rooms of the house, which were illuminated only by the moon, and a sweet, inexplicable clarity filled my soul during that mute and solitary exploration. There wasn't a single piece of furniture that didn't say something to me, and my imagination continued filling the empty rooms with the people I knew.] In this way, Gabriel argues that he has an exclusive connection to the palace in Bailén, just as he is intimately linked to the stories of the *Episodios nacionales,* in a manner that precludes other narrators' infringement on his status as primary author. Nevertheless, he does temporarily cede control to Andrés. After Gabriel asserts his power over this novel, as well as the entire series of *episodios,* he awakens the next morning to Andrés's insistent refrain—the same song that annoyed him during the journey—and allows this other young man to tell the story of Gerona.

As Andrés's narration begins, he has become a substitute father for three orphaned children who share his home. Andrés plans to marry their older sister, who has cared for them since their father's death, and he has taken on a parental role with respect to the boys Gasparó, Manalet, and Badoret. When his girlfriend, Siseta, becomes discouraged about the family's lack of resources, Andrés attempts to boost her spirits with fantasies about their life after the war, in the setting of lower Aragón, which he describes as a sort of utopia (769). Humble though it is, the brief narrative that Andrés constructs to anticipate their emancipation from the misery of Gerona and their establishment in a postwar paradise shows Andrés as an author of fictions, just as we have seen Gabriel portrayed throughout the series. Moreover, Andrés's beloved's name provides another connection to Gabriel's dilemmas of authorship. Although she is called Siseta, her true name is Narcisita, which anticipates a concern in this *episodio* with selfishness. As in the scene at the battle of Bailén, when Gabriel the storyteller acknowledges the conflict of his "selfishness" with a commitment to patriotism, in *Gerona* the drive to author stories is again at odds with patriotic participation in the War for Independence, as that loyalty to the nation is defined by many characters in the *episodios*. Clearly, authorship poses problems for simple visions of patriotism and national conflict; in this *episodio* storytelling is associated with the narrator's turn from the battle (the nation) toward the inner circle of his family (his chosen audience). Patriotism, in its turn, requires a submerging of the author's individual subjectivity within the collectivity of the struggling country. By incorporating narrators and author-characters other than Gabriel, the *Episodios* permit an extensive exploration of this tension. Whereas Gabriel retains ultimate control of the narrative of *Gerona,* Andrés's account of the siege reveals other characters who wish to tell stories, and who must negotiate their participation in the "patriotic" efforts of the city under siege.

We have already noted the pattern of Gabriel being paired with more openly quixotic alter egos, such as don Diego and Agustín Montoria. Here in *Gerona,* a similar dynamic sets up an alter ego for Andrés—a double of Gabriel's double, in other words. As a "father" of his young charges and of the fictions that sustain them, Andrés matches don Pablo Nomdedéu, mentioned earlier as author of a diary of the siege. Nomdedéu and his invalid daughter Josefina live above Siseta and her brothers, and as Andrés's story begins, the young man pays the older a visit, and presents his neighbor to his readers. In the constitution of this prematurely aged doctor, all is weakness and decline, except for his penetrating glance, which reveals his energetic soul and active mind. When "patriotism" does not require his presence at the hospital, Nomdedéu spends his time using his active imagination to create fantasies for his daughter

(770). He realizes that his need not to be designated cowardly and un-patriotic by the other citizens of Gerona distracts from the attention he might pay to his daughter—his audience—and acknowledges his dilemma with tears (773). Because Nomdedéu is diverted by his daughter from the practice of medicine and from helping the other citizens of Gerona, Andrés would like to present himself as more rational and altruistic than Nom-dedéu. Nevertheless, under the pressure of the battle, the two fictionalizers share a common (quixotic) purpose, as in one of the first scenes of the novel's action.

As Andrés informs Nomdedéu about the state of Gerona and the pro-gress of the French, both men become agitated, and Josefina, although she is deaf, senses that they are speaking about the war that she dreads. Nom-dedéu responds to her terror by "mintiendo como un histrión" (lying like an actor)—telling her that the war is over and that they will soon retire to their house in the country (771). When Josefina persists in her fear that they are talking of battles, Andrés comes to her father's aid in his fantasiz-ing, denying the facts and giving Nomdedéu the opportunity to pretend that as the war is over, the young man is no longer needed as a soldier. In this way, the two fabricators of fantasy join forces to deceive their audience, and Nomdedéu concludes their joint effort by placing the First Part of the *Quijote* in Josefina's hands and encouraging her to read.

Andrés and Nomdedéu are thus established within the larger frame of Gabriel's novel and series as a pair of fictionalizers in competition with the primary narrator, Gabriel. Curiously, this tripartite construction of author-ship is reflected in the novel by the presence of several triads. When Andrés returns home Siseta's cat *Pichota* has just given birth to three kittens. Although Gasparó, Manalet, and Badoret (another group of three) love *Pichota,* Andrés insists that they must drown two of the kittens for lack of available food. Siseta dissuades him, and the three kittens continue to struggle for life, just as the three authors of *Gerona* continue to produce texts. However, in the case of Nomdedéu, the drive for authorship—the campaign to be a storytelling "self"—leads this character to a cannibalis-tic extreme, as he plans to use his own body as fuel for his fictions. Nomdedéu vows to employ all his strength to continue to deceive Josefina with fictions of peace and plenty. His most serious problem is that the scarcity and inferior quality of food threatens the believability of his idyllic stories, so that, as his servant Sumta reports to Andrés, Nomdedéu has resolved to make a fiction of his own body in order to convince his beloved reader: "Capaz es mi señor don Pablo de cortarse un brazo y aderezar un guisote con él, haciendo creer a la enferma que tenemos aquel día pierna de carnero" (775). [My master don Pablo is capable of cutting off his arm and making a stew of it, convincing the sick girl that we have leg of lamb to eat that day.]

With the outrageous passion of his co-author suggesting cannibalism, Andrés distinguishes himself from Nomdedéu's madness. Looking at the kittens he exclaims that the three princes and princesses of Spain should be saved, and that if the family becomes desperate, they can eat cat meat (775). Here, then, Andrés recalls the three authors of *Gerona,* links their plight to that of the Spanish royal family and the state of the nation, and attempts to exchange the flesh of one triad for that of another—the kittens for the authors—implicitly protecting himself as he shifts attention from the potential cannibalism of Nomdedéu. However, even Andrés must fight for his fictions, decrying the war and begging God to allow him to lead the family to the utopian scene he has imagined for them (775). In this way, all groups of three—kittens, Siseta's brothers, Spanish princes and prin-cesses, and the authors of and in the *Episodios*—share a common father in the War for Independence which brings them into prominence. The omni-presence of the triad suggests the inevitability of the threesome, meaning that the pattern of three dictates that Gabriel cannot escape from Andrés, just as Andrés cannot completely disassociate from his degraded double, Nomdedéu.

In the context of the battle for Gerona, the character don Mariano Álvarez de Castro forms a contrast to Andrés, Nomdedéu, and even Gabriel. Don Mariano leads Gerona's defense, but the servant Sumta finds him to be "poca cosa" (not much). Sumta believes he should have more presence, like the woman who leads the squadron of female soldiers, inspiring all to kill the French (774). Rather than constructing visions of glory for the troops, don Mariano wages war on disorder in their ranks (782–83). Andrés recounts that when don Mariano passed by him during the battle, he did not speak of any of the ideals for which they were fighting, but instead informed the soldiers that retreat was not an option; they would be shot by the troops behind them if they tried to retreat (784).

Andrés establishes that don Mariano's rule-by-terror is effective, and that there was never another leader like him (785), but he also suggests that his leadership is a sort of prison (793). As the privations and suffering of Gerona intensify, don Mariano refuses to consider surrendering the city. When Nomdedéu complains of the lack of medicine to treat the growing numbers of wounded and ill citizens, don Mariano responds, "empléense las que hay, y después se hará lo que convenga" (799). [use what there is, and then whatever's best will be done.] As Andrés explains, this phrase is don Mariano's trademark, and indicates his absolute refusal to imagine a story line for his compatriots to follow—he reduces all to "se hará lo que se convenga" (799). [whatever's best will be done.] In this way, don Mariano cuts short any attempts to imagine a continuing story for the besieged city. The soldiers and citizens seem more dissatisfied by their leader's inability to dream than by their sickness and unsatisfied hunger.

If don Mariano refuses to fictionalize, and perhaps hinders his leadership with his lack of poetic idealism, Andrés and Nomdedéu stand in
contrast to him, turning the material of their own bodies into food for
fictions. Because their narratives of hope depend on the physical nourish-
ment of their starving audience, both "fathers" resort to more desperate
measures to feed their families. As the hunger in the blockaded Gerona
intensifies, the efforts of these two authors become a competition, with
Nomdedéu as dominant. He forces Andrés, Siseta, and the boys to dance
for Josefina's entertainment, although Andrés engages in an interior battle
with himself "para contraer y esforzar mi espíritu en la horrible comedia
que estaba representando" (792). [in order to contract and exert my spirit in
the horrible play that I was acting in.] Exhausted and reluctant to participate in the "farsa lúgubre" (lugubrious farce) dreamed up by Nomdedéu,
Andrés informs the stagemaster of the grotesque scene that he would like
to stop pretending. Nomdedéu counters with "¿Qué cuesta representar esta
farsa? Nada: la pobrecita se deja engañar fácilmente" [What does it cost to
stage this farce? Nothing: the poor girl allows herself to be deceived
easily], and continues to dance, all the while worrying about the possible
calamities of the next day, but trusting in God to inspire him with new
ideas: "¿qué comedia representaremos? Dios me favorezca y me inspire"
(792–93). [What play will we put on? May God help and inspire me.] As
Andrés leaves, he turns to witness the degradation of Nomdedéu in his
desperation to sustain his fiction. The older man jumps around, dislocates
his joints, trips over himself, and displays a thousand grotesque attitudes,
provoking Andrés's comment that he never saw a spectacle that made him
sadder (793).

Andrés thus records the humiliating conduct of his competitor, which
increases as the search for food continues, and Nomdedéu sinks to an
animalistic state that threatens any view of him as a better author of fiction
than Andrés. Soon after, when Nomdedéu and his family have consumed
the bodies of the kittens, the decrepit father is forced to fight Andrés for
possession of *Pichota* herself. After Andrés kills her, Nomdedéu refuses to
share the meat, and they struggle, with Andrés noting the influence of
"egoísmo" (selfishness) in both of them, and Nomdedéu firing a shotgun at
Andrés. Finally, the young man concedes the cat to his older adversary,
acknowledging that his furious enemy is as much an animal as his prey,
and recalling Nomdedéu's earlier association with cannibalism by referring to him as a tiger (who wishes to consume the cat) (797). Nomdedéu
will now ingest even the mother of the three kittens that mirrored the three
authors of the text, seeming to highlight his position of power in the novel.
Nevertheless, as Andrés reminds us, Nomdedéu has had to become a beast
to win this struggle, and his animalization threatens his control of the text,
in that the creation of narratives remains a human occupation. Confirming

this degradation, Nomdedéu then threatens to eat Siseta's family, saying that his daughter will not die, because when there is nothing left, she and her father will eat Andrés and Siseta's family, "y después se resolverá lo que más convenga" (805). [and afterwards whatever's best will be worked out.] Although he still hopes to procure the food that will allow him to continue fictionalizing for his daughter, here Nomdedéu recognizes that his days as a creative author are numbered, and he uses the favored expression ("lo que más convenga" [what's best will be done]) of don Mariano, the patriot who cannot inspire with idealism.

Although Nomdedéu now seems inferior to Andrés as a storyteller, at this stage of the novel Andrés begins to withdraw from the production of narrative as well. In one of the more memorable passages of the novel, he comes face to face with an unruly mob of indiscriminating readers. In this scene, Andrés has gone to look for Siseta's brothers at the home of the cathedral's canon, and he finds the canon's collection of rare books being assaulted by "un verdadero ejército, una nación entera, masa imponente que en otras circunstancias me habría hecho retroceder con espanto" (806). [a true army, a whole nation, an imposing mass that in other circumstances would have made me turn back in terror.] Terrified, Andrés feels himself bitten, and refers to what the reader now recognizes as rats as a "turba insolente" (insolent hoard) able to consume art works—in theaters, museums, and rare book shops "se traga los libros" (808). [it swallows up books.] Andrés, fighting to maintain his integrity as a creator of narrative in the face of the dehumanizing influences of the siege, feels the insult of these predators on not only his physical strength, but also his intellectual skills: "Era realmente una vergüenza para mí el rendir mi superioridad de fuerza y de inteligencia ante aquella chusma de los bodegones" (808). [It was truly shameful for me to surrender my superiority in strength and intelligence in the face of that rabble from cheap restaurants.] He survives the attack, but confesses that if the rats return, they will beat him. When he finds Manalet, the boy tells Andrés that he and Badoret were awakened during the night by a buzzing of teeth and nails: "Eran esos pillos que se estaban cenando la biblioteca" (809). [It was those scoundrels who were dining on the library.] With these images of the undiscriminating rodent consumers of texts as centerpiece of the novel, the concern with the uncontrolled audience causes Andrés's testimony of the siege to hark back to Gabriel's introduction to the novel. If the initial chapter of *Gerona* begins with the preoccupation with the *bozal muchedumbre,* turns to Gabriel's skills as reader and author, and then concludes with the topic of the corruption of the *populacho,* Andrés's narrative mirrors Gabriel's frame, and acknowledges Gabriel as primary author and cultural critic.

Andrés completes his subordination to Gabriel by transforming into the same sort of animal as Nomdedéu. In the marketplace, the two characters fight over the giant rat Napoleon and an almond paste image of Jesus. Now it is Andrés's turn to become an animal, and he compares himself to the other barbaric mammals he has just encountered, stating that he was a rabid beast lacking the judgment even to recognize its own stupidity (815). Believing that he has killed Nomdedéu, Andrés stares at the immobile figure, and the rat Napoleon escapes with the baby Jesus. In this way, the animal who represents the unwieldy audience escapes the author's control, at the same time the author loses the last vestige of humanity marking him as a creative individual. As if to confirm his renunciation of "selfish" authorship for selfless patriotism, Andrés next rushes to participate suicidally in the battle. The selfishness—indeed the selfhood—that allowed him special status ebbs away as Andrés submits to "una fuerza superior, colectiva," "un abandono a la general corriente, una fuerza pasiva" (816–17) [a superior collective strength, an abandonment to the general current, a passive force.]

Although he is injured in battle, Andrés musters the strength to visit Nomdedéu when he hears the older man is dying. At this point, both characters emphasize their renunciation of authorship, leaving the position of primacy to Gabriel alone. In the case of Nomdedéu, his daughter has recovered on her own, and he acknowledges his ignorance and lack of good judgment, reflecting specifically on his ineptitude as an author (fictions were the medicine he prescribed for Josefina), and it turned out that rather than being an expert, he knew absolutely nothing (823). As for Andrés, he is unable to convince Nomdedéu to believe in his happy fictions of life after the war. Nomdedéu refuses to accept from Andrés the tall tale that he will get well, and explains that the evolution of self involved in the campaign for authorship has exhausted him. He has become completely transformed in a matter of days, and has felt as if a series of different men had developed within him (830). In this way, both men relinquish control of the narratives they had earlier been fabricating.

Nomdedéu, in fact, returns in a sort of last confession specifically to the linkage of egoism and authorship. He explains that when he threatened to eat Siseta and her brothers he was motivated by a selfishness that drove him to wish to be with his daughter in isolation from the rest of humanity: "Era una aspiración brutal a aislarme en el centro del planeta devastado, arrojando a todos los demás seres al abismo, para quedarme solo con mi hija" (831). [It was a brutal aspiring to isolate myself in the center of a devastated planet, throwing all other beings into the abyss, in order to remain alone with my daughter.] As Nomdedéu explains his attack of selfishness, and Andrés recounts the event for Gabriel and for us, we realize that Nomdedéu's was not a desire merely for self-preservation, because his fantasy had as its center his relationship with his daughter. For this reason, we might suggest that here again he describes the egoism of the author who craves the unfailing attention of a reader. The food Nomdedéu covets is not only sustenance for his daughter's body, but the tool he uses to assert his authority through the texts he produces for her. On his death-bed, Nomdedéu gives up these trappings of authorship. He makes one more attempt to tell his daughter a story, but fails to convince her of his vision: "Paseemos por nuestra huerta viendo cómo van saliendo los pepinos, y no nos cuidemos de lo que pasa en Gerona. Mira qué tomates, hija, y observa cómo van tomando color esos pimientos" (833). [Let us walk around our garden, observing how the cucumbers are growing, and we will not worry about what is happening in Gerona. Look at what tomatoes we have, daughter, and see how the peppers are developing their color.] He concludes the lengthy and complicated idyll by asking her if she sees what he describes, but he has lost his power as a storyteller, and so Josefina does not. Nomdedéu then dies, leaving Andrés his diary of the siege in an ultimate renunciation of authorship.

Andrés turns over this diary to Gabriel, and it is at this point, when Andrés himself has given up any intention of being an author, that Gabriel reclaims the story, immediately subordinating Andrés's account to his own: "Así acabó su relación Andresillo Marijuán. La he reproducido con toda fidelidad en su parte esencial, valiéndome como poderoso auxiliar del manuscrito de don Pablo Nomdedéu, que aquel mi buen amigo me regaló más tarde cuando asistí a su boda" (841). [Andrés Marijuán finished his story in that way. I have reproduced with precision the essential part of it, relying on the manuscript of Pablo Nomdedéu as a powerful assistant, which my good friend (Andrés) gave to me later, when I attended his wedding.] With this statement, Gabriel provides several important pieces of information. First, because he has married Siseta, Andrés has been able to live out at least the first part of his ideal narrative for the future. Also, Gabriel has reproduced his text, allowing him a certain degree of author-ship, but then altering the document in some unspecified but supposedly minor way. Finally, in his (the *Episodios'*) version of the siege of Gerona, Gabriel has returned to Nomdedéu the older man's portion of authority, compiling his own narrative from both available accounts. Nevertheless, these "happy endings" are narrated by Gabriel, from a vantage point of unquestioned authority over the text, in that the two other author/narrators are no longer active. They have become characters in Gabriel's tale.

As he closes his frame for Andrés's story of Gerona, Gabriel emphasizes his own prominence and power over whatever narrative Andrés has en-trusted to him: "Repito lo que dije al comenzar el libro, y es que las modificaciones introducidas en esta relación afectan sólo a la superficie de la misma, y la forma de expresión es enteramente mía" (841). [I repeat what I said at the beginning of the book, and that is that the modifications introduced into this story affect only its surface, and the form of the expression is entirely mine.] With this oddly contradictory statement, Gabriel testifies to the eyewitness accuracy of Andrés's tale, but then takes possession of this original narrative for himself as superior author. Gabriel recognizes the possible loss of Andrés's individuality as an author (the word "lose" or "loss" appears twice in the same clause), but then justifies this suppression as necessary for the correct telling of his (Gabriel's) story: "Tal vez haya perdido mucho la leyenda de Andrés al perder la sencillez de su tosco estilo; pero yo tenía empeño en uniformar todas las partes de esta historia de mi vida, de modo que en su vasta longitud se hallase el trazo de una sola pluma" (842). [Perhaps Andrés's legend has lost much in losing the simplicity of its crude style; but I was determined to make uniform all the parts of this story of my life, so that in all of its vast extension there would be found the strokes of only one pen.] A stronger claim to authorship could hardly be imagined. Not only are the *Episodios* now the story of Gabriel's life, rather than an account of the initial years of the nineteenth century including the War for Independence, but they are identified with the traces of a single pen.

The final two chapters of the novel reveal Gabriel still in the process of reclaiming his authority over his story. He is in the heart of Andalucía, in Cádiz, a city that assumed at that point in history "toda la poesía del mar" [all the poetry of the sea], since its poetic glory multiplied as its white walls contained the whole of nationhood (843–44). This focal point of all poetry of the sea and of Spanish nationality grounds the next stage of Gabriel's narrative, which he begins authoritatively: "Estadme atentos, y dejadme que ponga orden en tantos y tan variados sucesos, así particulares como históricos" (844). [Pay attention to me, and allow me to put in order so many and such varied events, private as well as historical.] In handling "fecund History," he explains that he will address both his own adventures and the nation's, but that he privileges his own, in a continuation of his usual narrative procedure (844). Here, Gabriel calls attention to himself, reminding us of the issue of the selfishness of authorship in conflict with the selflessness of patriotism, which Andrés and Nomdedéu have illustrated so compellingly. Gabriel insists on his own presence, despite the problematic association of authorship with lack of patriotism.

In this way, Gabriel appears secure in his rejection of idealistic narratives, and in his authorial status as well. As proof of his strength, Amaranta, the woman who earlier dominated him, has grown old and now begs his assistance. Gabriel's commanding treatment of his story forms a backdrop for a reencounter with Amaranta. His former mistress welcomes him back, surprising him with her generosity when she promises that he will see Inés, and recognizing that he has incrased in status. As she recalls their earlier adventures together, she continues to acknowledge his power by emphasizing how desperately she needs his help (846). In the next novels,

Gabriel enjoys many such victories in his struggle for authority. Nevertheless, Gabriel also suffers setbacks that cause him to recognize the extirpation of his quixotism as incomplete. The final three *Episodios* of the First Series ultimately reveal a cautious and self-effacing Gabriel, unsure even whether he has authored his own life.

3

The Internal Author's Continuing War for Independence in *Cádiz, Juan Martín el Empecinado,* and *La batalla de los Arapiles*

IN THIS CHAPTER, WE SEE THAT GABRIEL "STARTS OVER," RETURNING TO his natal city of Cádiz just as Spain is defining itself as a modern nation with a new constitution.[1] In the three novels *Cádiz, Juan Martín el Empecinado,* and *La batalla de los Arapiles,* Gabriel confronts romanticism and quixotism, and attempts to project this idealist mentality he sees as unhealthy onto the foreigners Lord Gray and Miss Fly. At the same time, he realizes that these romantic patterns of thought are fundamentally autochthonous. It is in these final novels of the series that Gabriel comes face to face with national and personal quixotism at both its most problematic and its most heroic, embodied by his degraded double don Pedro, and by the animalistic *guerrilleros* of *Juan Martín el Empecinado.* As Gabriel blends with the militia of General Juan Martín, inhabiting the border between humanity and savagery, he finds that he has become just one more of the barbaric Quijotes natural to his country. He beats the *guerrilleros* at their own game, but only by descending to their level, thereby calling into question his literacy. After this crisis undermines Gabriel's image as cultural authority, the series comes to a climactic end in the internal author's encounter with an ultraromantic, foreign, and female alter ego in *La batalla de los Arapiles.* As we will see, Gabriel sustains a dubious victory, not over this woman herself, but over the aspects of his own nature that she mirrors. Gabriel's final act of the series is to turn over his story and his destiny to two other women: his wife, Inés, and his mother-in-law, Amaranta. This last group of novels in the series contains the most dramatic examples of realism as resistance. On one hand, the three novels feature Gabriel's desperate projection of romanticism onto foreigners instead of other Spaniards, but at the same time they also include the author-protagonist's compelling examination of the inextinguishable romanticism within him and within his nation.

CÁDIZ

In the first chapter of *Cádiz*, Gabriel returns as a soldier to his birthplace. When he arrives at the house of doña Flora de Cisniega—the older woman who pursued him in *Trafalgar*—both his hostess and Amaranta, who is staying with doña Flora, perhaps fittingly, treat him as a child. Doña Flora calls him "caballerito," "hijo mío," "jovenzuelo," "picarillo" (little gentleman, my son, youngster, little rascal)—lamenting, "¡Qué sería de ti . . . tierna criatura, lanzada en edad tan temprana a los torbellinos del mundo, si nosotras, compadecidas de tu orfandad, no te agasajáramos y cuidáramos, fortaleciéndote a la vez el cuerpecito con sanos y gustosos platos, el alma, con sabios consejos! ¡Desgraciado niño!" (849). [What would become of you, tender child, thrown at such a young age into the world's whirlpools, if we, taking pity on your orphanhood, didn't take care of you and shower attention on you, strengthening your little body with nutritious, appetizing dishes, and at the same time, your soul with wise advice. Unfortunate boy!] When Flora scolds him for associating with various notorious women of the city, Amaranta agrees: "El señor Gabriel es un chiquilicuatro sin fundamento, y mi amiga haría muy bien en ponerle una calza al pie" (850). [Señor Gabriel is an unreliable whippersnapper, and my friend would do well to rein him in.]

To review earlier events, in the middle novels of the First Series, Gabriel has advocated realism and authorial responsibility, and has successfully competed with other potential authors. Nevertheless, he has also realized the power of romanticism as a basis for patriotism and the "self"ishness of authorship, even if these two manifestations are at times in conflict. Clearly, as *Cádiz* begins, Gabriel has not fully resolved the realism—romanticism dichotomy, just as Galdós, the implied author, remains attached to romanticism as an essential part of both the novelization of history and the construction of the author-character. In Cádiz, Gabriel is reborn to his original dilemma of competing literary styles, as he continues to struggle with the quixotism he has deflected onto others in *Bailén*, *Napoleón en Chamartín, Zaragoza,* and *Gerona*. This eighth novel of the series pairs Gabriel with two other characters, the Spaniard don Pedro and the Englishman Lord Gray. Cádiz is also the setting for another rebirth, in addition to that of Gabriel: the protagonist arrives at the city just as the form of the modern Spanish nation is being decided at the Cortes de Cádiz.

For this reason, the Cortes—and indeed, the new version of Spain itself—are a third alter ego for Gabriel. The Cádiz of the Cortes hosts Gabriel's battle for realism and "good judgment" in reading. The call for rational reading meets with several obstacles, including an untutored audience, don Pedro's anachronistic extravagances, Lord Gray's exaggerated romanticization of Spain, and Gabriel's own nostalgia for the romanticism that might make him an author in the heroic mode.

With *Cádiz* set in 1810, Gabriel's memoirs associate the childhood of self and nation at various points in the *episodio,* and highlight the importance of reading, writing, and texts for the formation of both. If we look at the moments in which each of these entities (the new government, the Cortes, and the Constitution) writes itself, we note that in the meantime, Gabriel is forced to define himself, confront his youth, and come face to face in textual contests with his alter egos. For this reason, the Cortes and their participants are equated with Gabriel, as evidenced by the comparisons of Gabriel and the "actors" at the Cortes to children. His attendance at the political convocation contextualizes an extensive meditation on the public's reception of texts, within an analysis of his own plight as author dependent on audiences.

When Gabriel attends the Cortes, held in a theater, he records the comments made by the various characters who accompany him in the audience. Amaranta raises the issue of youth, comparing the delegates (one of whom is a "little angel who should still be nursing") to the young Gabriel, since they are of the same age (875). Continuing with such images of birth and renovation, Gabriel informs his readers that he was able to hear the speech—that of don Diego Muñoz Torrero—which ends the eighteenth century and begins the nineteenth for Spain (876). Because he identifies with the new government which sponsors the birth of modern Spain, and because this birth takes place in a theater, it is not surprising that Gabriel also worries about the reception of these innovations by the people, and exhibits his now familiar concern for the judgment of the public.

Gabriel questions the imposition of the power of the people when he explains that the Regents were being forced by popular pressure to swear loyalty to the Constitution: "Era el primer golpe de orgullo de la recién nacida soberanía, anhelosa de que se le hincaran delante los que se conceptuaban reflejo del mismo rey" (877). [It was the first prideful blow given by the recently born sovereignty, desirous that those who thought of themselves as reflections of the king himself would kneel before them.] There in the theater, then, the people demand a function to suit their taste, and Gabriel notes this domination of the political process by a public he has consistently described as captivated by theatrics. He elaborates on Amaranta's observation that the people in the "paraíso" seats of the theater believe that they are watching a skit and wish to take part, by adding that this new actor (the public) who imposes himself where he's not wanted will cause trouble for the Cortes (877). The people divide into two groups, consisting of those who believe that by swearing loyalty to the Cortes, the Regents debase themselves, and those who disagree. Observing these factions, Gabriel synthesizes the imagery of childhood and the concern with the public's judgment: "Los dos bandos, que habían nacido años antes y crecían lentamente, aunque todavía débiles, torpes y sin bríos, iban sacudiendo los andadores, soltaban el pecho y la papilla y se llevaban las manos a la boca, sintiendo que les nacían los dientes" (878). [The two bands, which had been born years before and were growing slowly, although they were still weak, clumsy, and unspirited, were now getting rid of their crutches, renouncing breast and baby food, and touching their mouths with their hands, feeling that their teeth were coming in.] Thus, Gabriel endows these neophyte political participants with the teeth that might seem the harmless dentition of babies, but are also the menacing tools that will grasp and tear any work of art or political discourse offered them.

In another examination of the mechanisms that form public opinion, Gabriel visits the Calle Ancha of 1811, the "heart of Spain" in its role as source of information for the people (900). As Gabriel explains, news is disseminated here in the form of written texts, specifically the newly hatched periodicals that announce the birth of modern Spain and mark his own youth. According to Gabriel, Calle Ancha produced the printed material on which public opinion fed, reading accounts of the quarrels of literary men and politicians in the little newspaper butterflies that hatched into the bright light of publicity (900–901).[2] With the words of his memoirs revealing his preoccupation with youth and inexperience in reading, Gabriel meets doña Flora in the Calle Ancha. Flora mentions the new freedom of the press and the headaches it has caused her because of printed attacks on her liberal *tertulias*. She resists petty vengeance, but ultimately affirms that she now sees freedom of the press in the same way that don Pedro Congosto does—as a scourge from God and a punishment for sins (903).

I read this conversation, set against the backdrop of Gabriel's recognition of the proliferations of the youthful free press, as part of Gabriel's self-definition and as preparation for his return to realism. When doña Flora praises the overblown don Pedro, Gabriel counters with an oblique defense of Flora's enemy, doña Francisca Larrea, which then becomes an indirect proposal of a literary project for the future. Gabriel explains that doña Francisca was the enlightened wife of the wise Böhl de Faber, and mother of the (woman) writer Cecilia Böhl, also known as Fernán Caballero, "novelista sin igual de fama tan grande como merecida dentro y fuera de España" (903). [unequalled novelist, of a fame as great as it is deserved, both within and outside Spain.]

Just after this defense of Fernán Caballero, often considered the founder of the Spanish realist novel, Gabriel learns that his beloved Inés is at the Cortes, without doña María's supervision, and possibly exposed to the seductions of Lord Gray. In this scene, then, he has recognized the infancy of freedom of the press in his country using the same imagery of youth that other characters have employed to characterize Gabriel himself. When doña Flora refers to the authority of the chivalric ideas of don Pedro, Gabriel suggests an alternative reigning discourse, that of literary realism. Now, with this reminder that his textual agenda is as much threatened by the mentality represented by don Pedro as his love life is by the actions of Lord Gray, Gabriel rushes to witness the development of another of his alter egos, the newborn Cortes.

When he returns to the Cortes, Gabriel is able to watch the effect of the proceedings on the young Presentación, sister of don Diego. He listens to her comments, observing carefully the naive girl's reactions to the speeches and debates of the delegates, and associating her by implication with an ingenuous public, receiving the "texts" of democratic politics for the first time. Presentación compares the function to a bullfight (905–6), and to the theater, with a stage curtain from behind which actors emerge periodically (906). Gabriel contemplates and analyzes her reaction to the spectacle:

> A cada nueva conquista hecha por su inteligencia en el conocmiento de las cosas parlamentarias más sorpresa mostraba la niña, y no distraía su atención del Congreso sino para hacerme preguntas, tan originales a veces y a veces tan inocentes, que me era muy difícil contestarle. Carecía en absoluto de toda idea exacta respecto a lo que estaba presenciando; y aquel espectáculo la conmovía hondamente, sin que las ideas políticas tuviesen ni aun parte mínima en tal emoción, hija sólo de la fuerte impresionabilidad de una criatura educada en estrechos encierros y con ligaduras y cadenas, mas con poderosas alas para volar, si alguna vez rompía su esclavitud.
>
> Era tierna, sensible, voluble, traviesa y, por efecto de la educación, disimuladora y comedianta como pocas; pero en ocasiones tan ingenua, que no había pliegue de su corazón que ocultase ni escondrijo de su alma que no descubriese. Por eso, que era, sin duda, efecto de un anhelo irresistible de libertad, aparecía a veces descomedida y desenvuelta con exceso. Poseía en alto grado el don de la fantasía; la falta de instrucción profana, unida a aquella cualidad, haciále incurrir en desatinos encantadores. (906)

[At each new conquest her intelligence made in acquiring knowledge of parliament, the girl showed surprise, and did not take her attention away from the Congress, except to ask me questions, so original and so innocent sometimes that it was difficult to answer her. She lacked completely any exact idea of what she was witnessing; and that spectacle moved her deeply, without political ideas taking even the least part in such emotion, which was a product only of the intense impressionability of a girl raised in close confinement and with bonds and chains, but with strong wings to fly, if at some point she broke out of her slavery.

She was tender, sensitive, emotional, mischievous, and, because of her training, able to put on an act like few girls could; but at times she was so naive that there was no fold of her heart that she would hide nor secret in her soul that she wouldn't discover. Therefore, because of this irresistible desire for freedom, she appeared at times immoderate and brazen. She possessed a well-developed imagination; the lack of secular teaching, together with her imagination, led her to incur charming absurdities.]

Observing all of this in his innocent companion, Gabriel is struck by the vulnerability of an unguided audience, while his readers glimpse parallels between the situation of the young Presentación and Gabriel himself. Presentación loves watching the debate, but continues to expect the political event to share features of the theater ("¿Se anunciará por carteles en las esquinas?" [907; Will it be announced on posters at the streetcorners?]. Presentación celebrates the liberty the Cortes promise, because she imagines that such a principle represents freedom from the tyranny of the domineering and reactionary doña María (909). The innocent figure of Presentación thus distills all of Gabriel's authorial concern for acquiring the favor of the naive reader.

Late in the novel, Gabriel again faces an untutored audience, and here he weaves his preoccupations with the ingenuous public and the politics of the nascent national consciousness together with his tactic of projecting the quixotic mentality onto an alter ego, in this case the familiar don Diego. When Diego and Gabriel attend a liberal political gathering, once again images of infancy and baby animals predominate in the narration of political events, as the more progressive opponents of the reactionary clerics show themselves to be no more mature or clear-minded than their adversaries. As Gabriel explains, passions boil in the cake that had just been put into the oven, and new, ingenuous life emerges: "Los huevecillos que depositaba la mariposa para dar vida al gusano no se abren, no echan fuera la diminuta criatura, ni ésta se desarrolla con más presteza al calor de la primavera que aquellos inocentes embriones de gente política" (924). [The eggs laid by a butterfly in order to give life to a caterpillar do not open, do not send forth the tiny creature, nor does the creature grow in the warmth of spring any more quickly than those naive embryos of political people.]

Gabriel focuses on a certain frenetic, anticlerical Gallardo, and laments his unfortunate influence on the young, whom he stupefies into thinking that liberty means killing priests (925). Gabriel recognizes all of this as "puerilidades" (childishness), and convinces Diego to leave, although they merely carry the discussion to another venue (Poenco's tavern), where the degradation of political discourse is even more pronounced (926). Diego leads the discussion, championing the sovereignty of the same ignorant people who then celebrate him, calling him a little angel with their garbled slogans and uneducated speech (927–28). After thus planting the seeds of doubt as to the public's capacity for good and fair judgment, Gabriel happily escapes this profaning atmosphere when don Diego passes out from drinking. Whereas don Diego remains an infantile "angelito," Gabriel takes a different path, and orchestrates many of the events of this *episodio* with confidence and authority. Nevertheless, he also does battle with two other rivals of sorts, and his apparent victory over both of them is anything but decisive. We must now examine the role of Gabriel's two alter egos in defining Gabriel's favored (albeit not without conflict and contradiction) discourse of realism.

Gabriel first hears of his "rival" don Pedro when he arrives at doña Flora's home at the beginning of the novel. While Amaranta spends her time making uniforms for the regular soldiers, doña Flora is sewing elaborate costumes for the followers of don Pedro. The uniforms for don Pedro's *Cruzada del Obispado de Cádiz* (Crusade of the Bishopric of Cádiz) seem to Gabriel "garments of a theater company," and while Flora compares the idealizing attentions of her suitor to those of Don Quijote for Dulcinea, Amaranta suggests that she consider finding herself a younger lover, such as the tender little puppy Gabriel. Curiously, although Gabriel shrank from Flora's advances in *Trafalgar,* he is quite willing in *Cádiz* to accept her flirtations (850). Flora, on the other hand, discourages Amaranta and Gabriel in their endeavors, and tells Amaranta not to teach the "poor little boy" such things. Children should be in school, presumably where they learn to be good and quiet, without getting excited, and, in Gabriel's case, to follow the example of don Pedro's seriousness, his respectability, and his impassive, undisturbed "Platonism" (851). In this way, although she mischaracterizes don Pedro, who is anything but circumspect, doña Flora confirms his pairing with Gabriel not just as rival suitor for her attentions, but as a model he must either accept or reject.

When characters anticipate the meeting of the Cortes, comparing it to a theatrical production, they wonder how the "actors" will behave. Amaranta fears that don Pedro's extravagances will deflate the seriousness of the convocation; as she says, some people change everything they touch into a farce (863). As if to confirm this fear, just after a group of liberal poets arrive, don Pedro makes his showy entrance, causing Gabriel to beg his readers' indulgence as he represents this character, because don Pedro will seem like a figment of Gabriel's imagination, even though he actually appears in history books as an even more striking figure than the one Gabriel "paints" (describes) in his memoirs. When don Pedro asserts that all of Spain's problems are the result of imitating French customs (864), and that an effective remedy would be to return to earlier styles of clothing (865), the other characters attack his ignorance. As he mocks the modernization he reduces to anticlericalism ("en vez de padres de la Iglesia tenemos periodistas" [866; instead of church fathers we have journalists], the poet Quintana replies by ridiculing don Pedro's reactionary simplicity, saying that of course all the world's evils are caused by books, and that all ills will be cured if Spaniards just dress in costume (866).

Amaranta confirms the association of Gabriel with the grotesque don Pedro when she suggests that the young man join don Pedro's Order of the *Cruzada.* Amaranta mocks Gabriel's ambitions by observing that this company is composed of men who invent their own ranks, and for this reason, he would fit in well with them (867). As she explains to don Pedro, however, she is concerned that Gabriel's passionate love affair might interfere with his participation in the Order, and she invents for the benefit of the would-be warrior don Pedro a secret relationship between his "Dulcinea," doña Flora, and Gabriel (868). Again, Gabriel does nothing to disabuse don Pedro, who becomes irate. His devotion to Flora has always been respectful and pure, and now an audacious rival threatens him. After his departure, doña Flora blames Amaranta for inciting Gabriel, who promises to be from then on as respectful, reserved, and circumspect as don Pedro. In response to this, doña Flora gives him candy, again reminding all of his youth, which is relevant to the question of the model he chooses to imitate (869).

When the Regency government is installed in the Palacio de la Aduana on the 29th of May, 1810, Gabriel witnesses hordes of squealing children announcing don Pedro's triumphant entrance at the head of one hundred men on horseback, all wearing the same ridiculous uniform. Don Pedro leads them triumphantly, wearing a commander's sash over a harlequin suit, and Gabriel remarks that the antics of his pseudorival would be more appropriate for a Carnival celebration (871). The narrator thinks that don Pedro's company is quite out of place at the solemn birth of a new political entity, and would indeed have embarrassed the nation if the French had seen the spectacle. Although the crowd enjoys the show, the soldiers try to prevent don Pedro and his men from entering the palace grounds. However, upon being informed of the nature of the contingent, the government still accepts the *Cruzada,* as Gabriel explains, "temiendo despopularizarse si no lo hacía" (871). [fearing the loss of popular support if it did not.]

In a now familiar association, Gabriel suggests here that political actors can be degraded by indulging popular desires, and by extension, that authors and artists can be profaned via the same mechanism. Later in the text, however, Gabriel confronts himself with an exaggerated version of this viewpoint, as if to temper his conservative opinions. At doña María's *tertulia,* Gabriel hears from the reactionary Ostolaza views quite similar— though in vastly overstated form—to the cautionary comments Gabriel has just made about the Cortes. According to Ostolaza, "La tropa . . . ha

cometido la falta de inclinarse al populacho . . . Yo he dicho que la soberanía de la nación por un lado y la libertad de la Imprenta por otro son
dos obuses cargados de horrorosos proyectiles que nos harán más daño que
los que ha inventado Villantroys" (880). [The troops have committed the
mistake of inclining toward the crowd. I have said that national sovereignty on one hand and freedom of the press on the other are two
cannons loaded with horrible projectiles that will do more damage than
those invented by Villantroys.] The baby teeth Gabriel described at the
opening meeting of the Cortes have now become cannons, but the threat is
the same, and both will wreak havoc on—and by way of—printed texts.
Perhaps uncomfortable with the boldly ungenerous restatement of his idea,
Gabriel agrees with Ostolaza, but at the same time, recognizes the cowardice implicit in their shared apprehensions about the (reading) public, and
calls himself effeminate: "Caballero—observé yo afeminadamente—esa
comparacioncita es exacta, y procuraré retenerla en la memoria" (880).
[Sir—I exclaimed effeminately—that little comparison is perfect, and I
will try to remember it.]

Don Pedro begins his presentation, unexpectedly extracting from his
silly costume a pair of reading glasses, and greeting the members of the
Regency, who alternate between anger and laughter. He surprises his audience once again, when he takes out a paper that Gabriel evaluates at first
by its length: it measures at least a yard. Instead of the political speech that
many expect, don Pedro then proceeds to read bad poetry, as inferior as
one would expect, considering it was composed by the man reading it
aloud. Gabriel cannot recall the exact words, but the message was that
everyone should return to the old styles of dress, in order to resuscitate the
heroism of days gone by (871).

The culmination of don Pedro's theatrical production is his procession
through the streets of Cádiz, met by the people's great joy, although they
were not dressed in the old style, as he had recommended. Thus, as Gabriel
explains, the crowd celebrates don Pedro, but as a laughingstock, like Don
Quijote in Barcelona, and the narrator even wonders if youngsters had
applied the famous shrubs to certain parts of the horse, because he believes
they might have (872). In this way, children continue to have an important
presence in this mockery of political participation—children like the suddenly young Gabriel who plays at identifying with, then ridiculing don
Pedro.

Despite the text's (Gabriel's) consistent mockery of don Pedro, the
narrator finds himself mirroring the conduct of the would-be knight-errant.
Soon after don Pedro's unseemly adventure with the Regency government—in fact, in the same chapter—Gabriel participates in an enterprise
that approximates the one he has just condemned. His company is led by a

commander who has acquired his position merely by publishing a proclamation with an engraving lampooning José Bonaparte (we recall that we
have just seen don Pedro celebrating a similar satire of the "intruder king"
[867]). The expedition to the north, commanded by this inexperienced,
untutored, crazy warrior don Mariano de Renovales, fails utterly, prompt-
ing Gabriel to make the comparison directly, because he and his companions in that endeavor matched don Pedro and his "crusaders" in lack of
common sense (872). These troops are also welcomed with much fanfare
into Cádiz, as was don Pedro, and the reception of Gabriel's company is
similarly tainted by hypocrisy, but this time the "patriotic" crowd itself is
dishonest, since they do not admit that Renovales was a fool (873).

Gabriel also imitates don Pedro by engaging in theatrics at the *tertulia*
hosted by the reactionary doña María, mother of don Diego. Because Inés
is staying with the family, Gabriel infiltrates the ultraconservative home of
doña María, urged by his own desire and by Amaranta, who is prevented
by her relatives from seeing her daughter. In order to be accepted by the
group that gathers at doña María's *tertulias,* Gabriel must feign religious
fanaticism, which he does surprisingly well (878–79). However, Gabriel
begins to express discomfort with his own hypocrisy, and his unhappiness
and impatience increase when he cannot elicit a commitment of continued
love from Inés, who fears doña María's vigilance. He confronts her with
his disgust at the dishonesty of this pretentious environment: "Pero, ¿hay
que ser cómico para entrar aquí?" [But, does one have to be an actor to be
admitted here?] Inés answers sincerely: "Sí; es preciso estar siempre sobre
las tablas, Gabriel, fingiendo y enredando" (885). [Yes, it is necessary to
always be on stage, pretending and scheming.] Gabriel comes to despise
doña María's deceptive practices, which make of her *tertulias* a theatrical
representation (887).

Gabriel comes to a breaking point in his association with don Pedro
when at doña María's *tertulia,* the two characters shift from being polite
competitors to being angry rivals. Don Pedro suspects Gabriel's friendship
with María's daughters Asunción and Presentación, and he proceeds to
destroy Gabriel's reputation for doña María's benefit, calling him a monster and a corruptor of families (914). After don Pedro has insulted him,
Gabriel enjoys a sort of revenge when don Pedro takes part in the expedition to the Condado de Niebla and is badly beaten. Gabriel makes a point
of telling the story of don Pedro's humiliation, adding that the French
laughed heartily at his entire company, and that when he was carried "todo
molido y quebrantado" (all broken and beaten) back to Cádiz, he blamed
his defeat on the loss of a horseshoe (916). At this point, it appears that the
division between don Pedro and Gabriel is definitive, and that there can be
no more parallelism of their characters, especially given Gabriel's textual

revenge on the unfortunate *estrafalario* (eccentric). Nevertheless, we will return to the rivalry of don Pedro and Gabriel at the end of the novel, in the context of Gabriel's duel with Lord Gray, another of his alter egos.

Gabriel first hears of Lord Gray from Amaranta, when the same Amaranta who appeared so dependent on Gabriel at the end of *Gerona* devastates him with the news that Inés loves this infamous Englishman. Amaranta praises Lord Gray, focusing on his artistic talents: "Tiene un gran libro lleno de dibujos, representando paisajes, ruinas, trajes, tipos, edificios, que ha pintado en esas lejanas tierras; y en varias hojas ha escrito en verso y prosa mil hermosos pensamientos, observaciones y descripciones llenas de grandiosa y elocuente poesía" (853). [He has a great book full of drawings, representing landscapes, ruins, uniforms, characters, and buildings, which he has drawn in those distant lands; and in several pages he had written in verse and prose a thousand beautiful thoughts, observations and descriptions full of grandiose and eloquent poetry.] According to Amaranta, Lord Gray seduces many women with these works of art and with his tales of distant lands. She further tortures Gabriel by declaring that she approves of Lord Gray's relationship with Inés (855).

When Gabriel meets his rival, he finds Lord Gray exasperatingly perfect (856). Even when Gabriel attempts to argue with him about the advisability of England's intervention in the war, Lord Gray merely agrees with him, praising Spain, denigrating England, and proclaiming his desire for Gabriel's friendship. Although Gabriel questions his loyalty when he insults his native land, Gray's response to this criticism is much like Gabriel's own commentary on the complexity of patriotism when he observes the fraternization of Spanish and English sailors in *Trafalgar* (858, compare to 227–32).[3] Lord Gray confesses that he would love to fight with the *guerrilleros* ("esos generales que no saben leer ni escribir y que eran ayer arrieros, taberneros y mozos de la labranza" [858; those generals that don't know how to read or write and that yesterday were muledrivers, bartenders, and farmhands]), anticipating Gabriel's actions in the next *episodio,* in which he joins the *guerrillero* band led by Juan Martín, el Empecinado. Wherein the two men have much in common, then, the extremes of Lord Gray's character repel as well as attract Gabriel (859).

Later in the novel, when he believes that he has received confirmation of Lord Gray's love for Inés and of her reciprocation, Gabriel resolves that he must kill his rival (894). (Lord Gray is actually attempting to seduce Asunción, not Inés, but Gabriel does not learn this until later.) Thus, the discovery of Inés's supposed perfidy, Gabriel's misinterpretation of a letter (he reads the note as confirming her choice of Lord Gray), and Gabriel's subsequent resolution to murder his competitor mark a turn away from the text's initial suggestions that Gabriel's primary adversary is the histrionic don Pedro. Now, Gabriel focuses on Lord Gray as a threat to his integrity and his power over the text. Of course, in their extravagance, anachronism, and cult of individuality, don Pedro and Lord Gray have much in common, and Gabriel's new attention to Lord Gray is in many ways merely a shift in the way he approaches the same adversary he vied with before, as we will continue to see.

When Gabriel is ultimately unable to prevent Lord Gray from abducting Asunción, he competes with don Pedro for the honor of defending doña María's family's honor in a duel with Lord Gray. Gabriel offers his services, but this conversation is interrupted by the extravagant, tragicomic gesture of don Pedro, who vows to María that he will fight Lord Gray. Gabriel makes no statement about his plans, even though he probably still intends to kill Lord Gray. Because of Gabriel's silence, it seems at this point that the only defender of the family's honor is don Pedro, who will duel with Lord Gray that night. The old eccentric receives the blessings and gratitude of doña María. María welcomes his assistance, even though the marquesa de Leiva tells her that she should expect nothing but "ridiculeces" (ridiculous things) and a "función quijotesca" (quixotic production) from don Pedro (951).

When Gabriel finds Lord Gray, he learns that the sexual encounter with Asunción was a grave disappointment for the Englishman. Both men relate Lord Gray's tryst with Asunción to international and domestic politics: Lord Gray declares that to fight with her is to fight with a whole nation, while Gabriel explains that his defense of the girl, an intervention Lord Gray calls "quijotismo, puro quijotismo" (quijotism, pure quijotism), was inspired in part by love for his society, and a desire to protect it from Lord Gray, "una peligrosa, aunque gallarda, bestia, a quien es preciso perseguir y castigar" (953). [a dangerous, although lovely animal, which must be persecuted and punished.] In this way, Gabriel turns against Lord Gray, prepares to risk his life in a duel with his rival, and configures this struggle as related to national self-definition.

Just before Gabriel and Lord Gray fight to the death, they witness a strange simulacrum of a duel, in which the bands of supporters of Lord Gray and of don Pedro deceive don Pedro. This is the bar owner Poenco, dressed up as a dummy of Lord Gray, wearing feathers on his head and fully armed, and who obligingly falls to the sword of don Pedro. At this point, those in attendance at the sham duel first pretend to celebrate don Pedro, calling him the bravest "caballero" (knight or gentleman) of Spain, but then begin to beat him. When they have abused him thoroughly, the crowd raises him to their shoulders and carries him in a procession through the city (955). In this way, don Pedro is thoroughly and publicly humiliated.

With don Pedro removed from the scene, Gabriel is then left to kill Lord Gray, which he does with ease, because he is able to remain calm whereas his rival becomes agitated. A certain dark figure the duellists glimpsed before the match reveals herself to be doña María, on a mission to congratulate Gabriel, to thank him for his defense of her family's honor, and to recognize that she was wrong to trust don Pedro over him. Even for doña María, then, the primary advocate of living lies rather than truth, Gabriel has replaced don Pedro. Gabriel does not welcome her praise, however, and tells her that the pride of his deed does nothing but burn his heart like a flame (956). Uncomfortable in his presence but overcome first with compassion and then with deep pain, Gabriel leans over Lord Gray and hears the words he reveals to his readers only in the final paragraphs of the novel.

When he leaves the scene of the duel, doña María continues to compliment Gabriel, but he does not respond (957). She explains her desperate faith in don Pedro, when no one else would defend her honor, and champions the lofty, extravagant ideals that shape her vision of society. She knows that people say don Pedro is ridiculous, but she wonders if this is simply because his heroism is not the social norm: "Como la hidalguía, la nobleza y la elevación de sentimientos son una excepción en esta sociedad, las gentes llaman ridículo al que discrepa de su vulgaridad nauseabunda" (957). [Because chivalry, nobility, and elevation of feeling are an exception in this society, people call ridiculous anyone who disagrees with their nauseating vulgarity.] When Gabriel tries to change the topic, possibly embarrassed at doña María's associating him with these chimeras, and trying to lift the weight from his soul, he is unable to articulate his suggestion that María's repressive treatment of her daughters might have caused the problem. María cuts him off, unwilling to examine her conscience, but also disturbed by the noise of those who clamor at the reading of the new Constitution at the Cortes. Gabriel's explanation to doña María of the significance of the "ruido de esa canalla" (noise of that rabble) prompts her to recognize her own figurative passing, even as a new Spain is born. She declares that she is already dead, and that from now on, she will keep her house closed like a tomb (957).

As we have seen before, the renaissance represented by the Cortes matches images of Gabriel's rebirth and youth, but whereas other scenes held promises of undetermined choices he might make in the future, here Gabriel's new life is marred by his degradation at being associated with don Pedro. María may forecast her own death, Lord Gray may be gone, and don Pedro has certainly suffered a beating, but in the same way that he came back from the humiliation of the battle of the Condado de Niebla, "todo lleno de bizmas y parches" (all covered with plasters and poultices) (935), he will fight again, as has his quixotic spirit through the actions of Gabriel. Just as he slips in *Napoleón en Chamartín,* allowing Amaranta to script him a new, extravagant identity, here Gabriel again falls into a trap which, despite its association with the imaginative tradition of the Spanish nation, is not the realist model he would like to follow. As if to confirm his fall, doña María offers him Inés's hand, a prize he has sought for years, but then destroys any satisfaction he might derive from such a victory by degrading his "Dulcinea" as frivolous, unfortunate, and illegitimate (957–58).

Of course, Gabriel does not need María's insults to understand his dilemma. As he and Inés flee from Doña María's domain, he remembers and records for his readers Lord Gray's final words: "¿Crees que he muerto? ¡Ilusión! . . . Yo no muero . . . , yo no puedo morir . . . , yo soy inmortal . . ." (958). [You think I have died. Illusion! . . . I do not die . . . , I cannot die . . . , I am immortal . . .] When Inés asks for clarification, wondering if in fact the Englishman did not die, Gabriel fears for his own sanity, believing that Lord Gray is the figure who passes in front of them at that very moment. In this way we see that Gabriel, divided throughout this episode between the seductions of quixotic alter egos and the images of rebirth promised by modernity and the realist mentality, has experienced a setback. Lord Gray is not dead, but lives on as don Pedro and as Gabriel himself.[4]

JUAN MARTÍN EL EMPECINADO

The ninth novel of the series, *Juan Martín el Empecinado,* turns to an aspect of the war that Gabriel has ostensibly ignored up to this point. Although he has informed his readers about the accomplishments of the armies, the struggles of the politicians, and the heroic acts of the people within the cities, he explains that this is not sufficient for understanding the war in its entirety. He must now deal with the true national war—the uprising of improvised armies of people from the countryside, born from the earth like native grass (959). Gabriel declares that he will now speak of the regimented anarchy of the *guerrilla* war, which he has not yet addressed (988). Despite this claim, we must question whether Gabriel's focus of study on the *guerrilla* is truly unprecedented in the series. In the previous eight novels the narrator has examined and indeed has highlighted the people's participation, particularly in anarchic or untutored forms, in the War for Independence and in the coterminous construction of the new nation as cultural entity.

Fittingly, as *Cádiz* ends with the danger of don Pedro on the loose in the very birthplace of modern Spain, *Juan Martín el Empecinado* takes up the ghost of don Pedro, the national scourge that Gabriel could not eliminate by fighting Lord Gray.[5] If don Pedro is the ridiculous exaggeration of heroism, scandalous in appearance and uncontrolled in behavior, the *guerrilla* warfare that characterized Spain's resistance to the French invasion is the national embodiment of the tendencies of don Pedro. Just as Gabriel essentially becomes don Pedro in the duel with the Englishman, he now turns to the analysis of another problematic phenomenon endemic to Spain, one in which he himself takes part. Gabriel refuses to say whether the *guerrilleros* are bad or good, particularly as he praises their leader Juan Martín. According to Gabriel, Juan Martín is a renowned *guerrillero*—impartial, noble in his impulses, generous, and without a direct connection to ruffians and troublemakers, although in his effort to free Spain from France, he inadvertently taught this criminal element the tools of what would be their trade (976). In this way, Gabriel defends the individual leader Juan Martín, while at the same time questioning the way of life and the sort of war to which he gave rise. Gabriel is aware that the rough, disorganized troops were at least partly responsible for his country's success against the French, but the nature of these forces seems to him a national embarrassment as well as a source of pride. It is the entity of the *guerrilla,* then, as heritage of the tenacious don Pedro absorbed by Cádiz, that Gabriel confronts in *Juan Martín el Empecinado.*

Thus, according to Gabriel, "caudillaje" (bossism or tyranny) is a national problem, exemplified by three main figures: the *guerrilla* soldier, the contrabandist, and the highway robber (975). The "lepra" (leprosy) of "caudillaje" started with Spain's earliest history, played a role in the unification of the country during the medieval period, and extended itself into foreign wars under the absolutist rulers (976). Eventually, the country was exhausted by its international efforts and the soldiers came home to unemployment and inactivity, causing the problem that Gabriel describes in the following way: "España volvió a España, donde se aburría, como el aventurero retirado antes de tiempo a la paz del fastidioso hogar, o como Don Quijote, lleno de bizmas y parches, en el lecho de su casa y ante la tapiada puerta de su biblioteca sin libros" (976). [Spain went back to Spain, where it got bored, like the adventurer who returns before his time to his tedious home, or like Don Quijote, full of plasters and poultices, in his bed at his house and in the presence of the blocked door of his library without books.] This boredom then made Spain vulnerable to the spirit of the *guerrilla,* manifested in the country's response to Napoleon. Gabriel does not condemn the *guerrilleros,* and indeed speculates that without them the French might have remained in Spain much longer than they did, yet at the same time, he calls the War for Independence the "gran academia del desorden" (great academy of disorder), as well as the "gran escuela" (great school) of "caudillaje" (976).

These passages reveal several things. Using the precise words with which he described don Pedro ("lleno de bizmas y parches" [935; "all carved with plasters and poultices."]), by associating the disease with Don Quijote and with Spain, Gabriel now acknowledges the inherent "Spanishness" of the national infection he temporarily projected onto Lord Gray. He also calls attention to the *guerrilla*'s replacement of traditional institutions of learning ("academia" and "escuela") with corruptions, as in the case of the *guerrillero* leader Vicente Sardina's attempt to profane formal military actions and writing as "pura farsa" (utter theatrics) (962). Gabriel emphasizes the impossibility of remedying these abominations through education and reading, because along with the protection from *libros de caballería* provided by the enclosure of the library comes a prohibition of access to all books. The library is not only walled off; it is empty.

Here, Gabriel includes his agenda for the novel along with his examination of the "lepra del caudillaje." He explains that in the *guerrilla,* there are no real battles, since nothing is planned (975). Instead, the *guerrilla* is based on surprise—with one faction unaware of the presence of the other ("es preciso que una de las dos partes ignore la proximidad de la otra") (975). ["it is necessary that one of the two parties be unaware of the proximity of the other."] The *guerrilleros*' most important quality is a good gait ("buena andadura"), because they almost always win by running: they escape rather than retreat, and escaping is not shameful for them (975). These, then, are exactly the tactics that Gabriel uses in his "war" on the figures whose features he shares in *Juan Martín el Empecinado.* We will now observe the parallels first between the former priest Mosén Antón Trijueque and Gabriel, and then between the *guerrillero* commander Juan Martín and Gabriel. These characters do not recognize Gabriel as a threat ("es preciso que una de las dos partes ignore la proximidad de la otra" ["it is necessary that one of the two parties be unaware of the proximity of the other"]), and Gabriel is infinitely accomplished in retreats and surprise attacks.

In fact, what this episode features is not so much a definitive separation of the secondary characters into categories of good and evil, but rather a competition between Gabriel and two doubles who are at times adversaries. Gabriel has consistently recognized—here and in earlier novels such as *Napoleón en Chamartín*—the power of the quixotic impulse as linked with various notions of patriotism. In *Juan Martín el Empecinado,* Gabriel acknowledges the contributions of the intrepid *guerrilleros,* but then questions their rhetorical excesses. Although he testifies to the power of the men he portrays, he fights a sustained, linguistic *guerrilla* against them, undermining them at every turn with the ultimate weapon, the text of *Juan Martín el Empecinado.*

To begin with, in this story of dubious heroism, Gabriel has definite favorites—the general Juan Martín, and his subordinate Vicente Sardina, who take up arms with reluctance, because they see their traditional way of life threatened by the French. Gabriel consistently criticizes characters such as Mosén Antón, called to the *guerrilla* by his desire for fame and power, the *guerrillero* Saturnino Albuín, who is motivated purely by greed, and the students Viriato and Pelayo, who revel in the disorder and duplicitousness of life in the *guerra chica*. Gabriel ultimately competes with and defeats Mosén Antón Trijueque, one of these less respected characters.

Having referred to himself as a "bestia" (beast, animal) in his involvement in savage behavior in a town that has been sacked (960), Gabriel prepares for his temporary parallelism with Mosén Antón, the warrior priest. Snorting like a mule at the lack of drive exhibited by the rest of the men, Mosén Antón rises, and Gabriel observes: "Era un gigante, un coloso, la bestia heroica de la guerra, de fuerte espíritu y fortísimo cuerpo, de musculatura ciclópea, de energía salvaje, de brutal entereza" (964). [He was a giant, a colossus, the heroic beast of war, of strong spirit and body, of cyclopean musculature, of savage energy, of brutal integrity.] Gabriel himself has been a cyclops in *El 19 de marzo y el 2 de mayo,* and an animal in this same episode, but this character far exceeds Gabriel in crossing the boundaries between humanity and animality. With his efforts in the war, Mosén Antón has literally ripped the seam between his identity as priest and as fighting man, and now walks with his cassock open from the waist down, revealing his "fornidas piernas" (robust legs) (964). Both this chapter and the next end with images of Mosén Antón as a beast, attempting to catch the scent of the French (966), and forming a grotesque unit with his horse, which Gabriel refers to as an apocalyptic monster (969).

Gabriel first outshines Mosén Antón when he acquires the death sentence for which the older man has been clamoring. To understand the significance of Gabriel's accomplishment, we must note that in their confrontations with each other the brave *guerrilleros* often ask their opponents to kill them, implying that martyrdom would be the ultimate act of heroism. At one point, Juan Martín confronts Mosén Antón, who by rights should defer to Martín, his commander. Although Trijueque has led his men to victory in Calcena, he has done so by disregarding Martín's assignment and deserting his post in Borja, risking the troops stationed there by not coming to their aid. When the general refers to him as a savage hyena, Mosén Antón counters by charging Juan Martín to shoot him for winning a battle without his leader's consent (991). Realizing Mosén Antón's worth as a warrior, his commander refuses to comply with Trijueque's wishes. However, Juan Martín's authority is then further undermined by the greedy Saturnino Albuín, who has stolen money from a villager and refuses to return it, also daring the general to fire on him immediately (995). Juan Martín is able to restore order only after sacrificing several of Albuín's henchmen, and fighting rather ignobly with Albuín, called *el Manco* (the One-armed) because of his physical disability. At the height of his embarrassment in this scene, Juan Martín cries, "Que venga todo mi ejército a atropellar a su general . . . pisad el cadáver de vuestro general" (997). [Let my whole army come to trample their general . . . step on the cadaver of your general.] Although the men approach him, Juan Martín fights them off, so that he too is denied fulfillment of the suicidal wish. However, the *guerrillero* general continues to suffer such humiliations at the hands of the proud and rebellious Mosén Antón. Martín again turns to his own death as solution when he becomes convinced that the ex-priest has joined the French. He orders his men to pursue the French, shouting that he wants the invaders to kill him: "Si quiero que me maten esos condenados . . . ¡Si quiero morir!" (1007). (I want those wretches to kill me . . . . I want to die!) Rather than escaping a hopeless battle as is the custom of the *guerrilleros*, when he has confirmed Mosén Antón's betrayal Juan Martín rushes desperately, even self-destructively, at the French, and many of his men— including Gabriel—are caught (1010). At this point, one of Gabriel's companions in his small band of prisoners stabs a French sergeant, and Gabriel is condemned to be executed along with the rest of the group. The French soldiers escort him to the cell where he will enjoy the death sentence so coveted by the *guerrilleros,* foremost among them Mosén Antón.

Gabriel has thus superseded the *guerrilleros* in heroism as they define it. He then also supplants Mosén Antón as a priest, succeeding in stealing his original occupation from him. As Gabriel is in the cell awaiting the fulfillment of his death sentence, several characters visit him, and offer "confessions" of sorts. After Gabriel learns officially of his condemnation, he prepares mentally for death. When he has achieved the peaceful state of his new priestly identity, Santorcaz first agitates him with news of Inés, but then decides to confide in him the story of his life, explaining that one may confess anything to a person condemned to death, and he would like to clear his name (1015). In this way, Santorcaz appeals to Gabriel as a sort of confessor, but also as his judge, in an act that highlights the older man's vulnerability. Having usurped Mosén Antón's role as spiritual leader, Gabriel continues in a position of superiority to his various interlocutors, having achieved a new respectability by being sentenced to death.

When Mosén Antón enters the cell, he acknowledges that he envies Gabriel his honorable death, and confesses that he joined the French because they promised him the command of three thousand men. Gabriel senses that Trijueque is ashamed of having defied his leader, and recommends a penance of begging the forgiveness of his former general (1020– 21). He tells his anxious visitor that the only other option is to hang himself, like Judas after betraying Jesus (1020). When Gabriel then tries to dismiss Mosén Antón, Trijueque reminds him that the French sent him so that Gabriel could make a last confession. To this Gabriel replies that if anyone heard them, it would seem he was the chaplain and Mosén Antón the condemned man (1021). This sensible observation of the reversal of

their roles inspires Trijueque to give a full account of his "conversion"—
away from the church congregation to which he was in the act of preach-
ing, and towards the office of *guerrillero*, guided by his "savior" Juan
Martín. This passage reads:

> Yo no sabía lo que predicaba. El pueblo y los guerrilleros se volvieron locos, y
> con sus patadas y gritos, atronaron la iglesia. Seguí mi misa . . . ¡Ay!, cuando
> consumí no supe lo que hice: no respondo de haber tratado con miramiento al
> santo Cuerpo y a la santa Sangre de Nuestro Señor . . . El cáliz se me volcó.
> Durante el lavatorio, el monaguillo, entusiasmado, se puso a dar brincos
> delante del altar . . . Yo no cabía en mí, y los pies se me levantaban del suelo.
> Todo cuanto tocaba ardía, y hasta dentro de mí creí sentir las llamas de un
> volcán. Cuando me volví al pueblo para decir *Dominus vosbiscum*, alcé los
> brazos y grité con toda la fuerza de mis pulmones: '¡Viva Fernando Séptimo,
> muera Napoleón!' Juan Martín, subiendo precipitadamente al presbiterio, me
> abrazó, y yo, por primera y única vez en mi vida, me eché a llorar. El pueblo
> aplaudía, llorando también (1021–22).

> [I didn't know what I was preaching. The people and the *guerrilla* soldiers went
> crazy, and with their kicks and screams, they stunned the church. I continued to
> say mass. Oh! When I took communion I didn't know what I was doing: I am
> not sure I treated appropriately the holy Body and Blood of our Lord. I spilled
> the chalice. During the lavatory, the excited acolyte began to jump around in
> front of the altar. I was beside myself, and my feet lost touch with the ground.
> Everything I touched was burning, and even inside me I thought I felt the
> flames of a volcano. When I turned back to the people to say *Dominus vos-
> biscum*, I raised my arms and screamed with all the power of my lungs: "Long
> live Fernando VII, death to Napoleon!" Juan Martín, climbing quickly up to the
> presbytery, embraced me, and I, for the first and only time in my life, began to
> cry. The people applauded, crying along with me.]

With the role of the priest thus left unoccupied, Gabriel has now assumed
it.

When Gabriel escapes from prison thanks to a trick of the *guerrilleros*,
he begins the last stage of his eclipse of the ultimate *guerrillero*, Mosén
Antón. He wanders in the cold, attempting to reach Inés before Santorcaz
does, only to be rescued from freezing by Trijueque himself, who in his
resentment has deserted the Spanish for the French. As Gabriel recovers in
an inn under French control, he learns from his rescuer that Santorcaz is at
the same place, with the captive Inés. Her cries from below have the effect
of completing his transformation into a new Mosén Antón, just as the other
is incapacitated by humiliation and remorse. As Gabriel explains, he had
become an imbecile—suddenly as crazy as Mosén Antón, when asked by
the French what he would do if they freed him, he responds that he would
kill. He admits to having murdered several Frenchmen in order to acquire

their horses, and states that he desires to be shot (1041). Just as Mosén Antón earlier guessed the location and plans of his French adversaries, now Gabriel is able to intuit that Juan Martín has reformed his army. He uses information given to him by Mosén Antón, but when asked how he knows where the *Empecinado*'s army is located he states that he is divining the army's position, just as did Mosén Antón (1042). When his comrades arrive and attack the French, Gabriel is able to reunite with Juan Martín in Cifuentes, officially becoming his new Mosén Antón.

Gabriel's final triumph over Mosén Antón comes with the former priest's death, under circumstances orchestrated by Gabriel himself. When the captured Mosén Antón will not ask forgiveness for his treason of his *guerrillero* comrades, Juan Martín refuses to grant his wish that he be executed, because he knows that Trijueque does not fear death and realizes that this would not be a severe punishment. Instead, he sends his former ally home to his church, saying that he forgives him, but that now he must return to the village to say Mass, which is his true occupation (1048). Juan Martín thus imposes the most humiliating punishment possible for Mosén Antón. Even as he still begs to be shot, the "multitud" (crowd) led by the unscrupulous former students Viriato and Pelayo fashion a paper miter and cape for Trijueque, insulting him and mocking his ambition. Remembering that Mosén Antón saved his life, Gabriel acts as his escort when the renegade priest makes his way on a calvary out of the village. As we have seen, Mosén Antón has conceded this identity—that of priest—to Gabriel. He now has no role other than that of the degraded Christ figure, with Gabriel as his apostle, but also as his executioner, in that Gabriel originally suggested the penance of suicide. The final paragraphs of the novel tell of Gabriel's discovery that Mosén Antón has taken his advice, perhaps because it was imposed in the setting of the improvised confessional, and has hanged himself (1050). In this way, Gabriel definitively eclipses this misguided, yet valiant *guerrillero*.

As he eliminates the animalistic Mosén Antón, Gabriel also competes with the *guerrillero* leader Juan Martín, in order to establish himself as unquestioned hero of the novel. When introducing Juan Martín, the narrator explains that most people imagine him as a hero from the old days, resuscitated in the present age as proof of the protection Heaven was providing in the war against the French (974). Gabriel describes him as a Hercules who possessed great genius for *guerrilla* war, but also observes that in the general this natural talent was accompanied by a rejection of cultivation and erudition: "En el hablar era tardo y torpe, pero expresivo, y a cada instante demostraba no haber cursado en academias militares ni civiles. Tenía empeño en despreciar las formas cultas, suponiendo condición frívola y adamada en todos los que no eran modelo de rudeza primitiva" (975). [When speaking he was slow and clumsy, but expressive, and at every moment he demonstrated that he had never studied at either civilian or military academies. He made a point of disdaining fine manners, assuming that all who were not the very model of crude primitivism were instead frivolous and effeminate.] Juan Martín combines this lack of literacy with a drive for conflict. For Gabriel this aggression is both innately Spanish and reminiscent of Don Quijote, since Juan Martín's spirit is formed from the typical Spanish stock that feeds on continual struggles, and because he set out at the start of the war like Don Quijote with his Sancho (975).

Juan Martín, then, is a Quijote similar to Santiago Fernández of *Bailén* and *Napoleón en Chamartín.* Generally, the Quijotes of the series are learned people who have developed monomanias—for example, Godoy, Celestino, Santorcaz, Nomdedéu, and even don Pedro, because he composes poetry. Juan Martín, on the other hand, is a sort of "natural" or even illiterate Quijote, again like Santiago Fernández or, more important, like (young) Gabriel.[6] Indeed, is the general's tendency to combativeness much different from Gabriel's own sustained dialectic with an untutored public? Despite the evident parallel between the two "natural" heroes, however, *Juan Martín el Empecinado* contextualizes the *guerrillero* general so that Gabriel is able to suggest his superiority to this foil just as he does with Mosén Antón and the former students Viriato and Pelayo.

Before meeting Juan Martín, Gabriel encounters someone who prepares for the introduction to the *guerrillero* general. When he suddenly hears the unexpected cry of a toddler, Gabriel notices that Santurrias, former sacristan of Inés's uncle Celestino and now part of Sardina's band, carries a two-year-old who cries for a mother's milk (968). The former student turned *guerrillero* Viriato explains to Gabriel that they recovered this baby they call *Empecinadillo* from a home destroyed by the French. Santurrias has given the baby a name derivative of Juan Martín's nickname; moreover, he now uses the baby to more effectively beg for food. Consequently, the band is obligated to find temporary wet nurses wherever they lodge. Santurrias enjoys comparing the toddler to the famous general, and admonishes him not to cry: "Un general pidiendo teta . . . Calla hombre, no toques diana, que nos vuelves sordos . . . Vamos, es preciso ir dejando esas mañas . . . Los hombres no maman" (968). [A general crying for the breast . . . Quiet, man, don't sound the reveille, because you're deafening us . . . Hey, you have to give up these bad habits. Men don't nurse.] The appearance of this child, because it precedes that of Juan Martín, colors the portrayal of the general by subtly mocking and infantilizing him.

Thus, the initial debasing gesture in the portrayal of Juan Martín is his presentation as a postscript to the diminutive *Empecinadillo.* Still, in order to appreciate the full significance of the baby's mirroring of the general, we must jump ahead to the conclusion of the novel. The primary tension of this novel is between Juan Martín and the man who should be his subordinate, Mosén Antón. The former priest Trijueque cannot accept his inferior rank, explaining in his final confrontation with Juan Martín that in his soul there is more than just ferocity—he wishes to be second to none, and to take orders from no one (1047). Evidently, with these central passions, Mosén Antón is unable to accept Juan Martín's command, and in fact characterizes his superior as his foe. He declares that he fled the countryside to tame Juan Martín's terrible pride, and to free himself from an authority figure intolerable to him (1047). We must keep in mind the intensity of this passion as we assess the tensions between the two men. Gabriel addresses the topics of Mosén Antón's brilliance in battle, uncontrolled pride, and desire for vengeance, just before the first appearance of Juan Martín. The narrator's suggestion, thus, is that Mosén Antón's power and refusal to be dominated threaten Juan Martín's stature, converting him from *Empecinado* to *Empecinadillo*. Moreover, later in the text, Gabriel turns back to the baby at the same time that Mosén Antón breaks with Juan Martín, and the general realizes the extent of the betrayal. Again, Trijueque's challenges to his authority reduce Juan Martín to a specular image of the toddler.

There is more to say as well about the way the baby represents the general's endangered supremacy. If we return to the two instances of textual attention to the *Empecinadillo,* we note that Gabriel includes descriptions of the baby's role as sentimental distraction from the stress of battle. In the first case (chapter 4), his innocent pleasure in nursing inspires the soldiers to cheer him on, while later (chapters 13 and 14), the *Empecinadillo*'s deformation of certain words and his fear of Mosén Antón prompt Gabriel's extensive meditation on the toddler's antics with the men. Of course, this treatment of the baby could be a spoof on the general's illiteracy and his conflicts with the former priest. In any case, for this digression Gabriel asks for his audience's indulgence, explaining that although he agrees with his listeners that this infant subject is less important than the man whose name gives a title to the *episodio,* he wishes for small things to accompany the great, as they do in Nature ("yo quiero que aquí, como en la Naturaleza, las pequeñas cosas vayan al lado de las grandes") (1006). ["I want that here, as they do in Nature, for small things to accompany great one."] In saying this, Gabriel undermines the status of Juan Martín; and his frequent contrasting of the *guerrillero* with more famous commanders suggests that el *Empecinado* himself could be a "pequeña cosa" (small thing). If we look back to the initial presentation of Juan Martín, Gabriel ambitiously compares him to Napoleon in the devotion he inspires in his followers (974). However, while doing so Gabriel also suggests that Napoleon sets an unbroken standard. The *Episodios*' narrator declares that Martín possesses genius in war, but ranks only third place, to

Mina's second and Napoleon's first (975). In this way, even as he praises his skill Gabriel subordinates Juan Martín to both of these generals in a gesture that culminates at the end of this chapter (5) with a long list of "pequeños grandes hombres" (small, great men), of which Juan Martín is just one of many (976).[7]

If we wonder by what mechanism Gabriel has been able to successfully compete with the two *guerrilla* leaders, we find a clue in his first conversation with his immediate supervisor, veteran *guerrillero* Vicente Sardina. In fact, Sardina initially dismisses Gabriel's earlier experiences as part of the official army, reducing these activities to linguistic games symbolized by the "ripio" (padding) of military braid: "¿Batallitas, eh? . . . Y mandadas por generales de entorchado . . . Me parece que las veo . . . Mucha escritura, parte acá, parte allá, oficios en papel amarillo con sello y mucho de: 'Excelentísimo señor, participo a vuecencia que habiéndose presentado el enemigo . . .' Farsa, pura farsa" (962). [Little battles, eh? And commanded by generals designated by their braiding . . . I can see them now . . . A lot of writing, a report here, a report there, communiqués on yellow paper with a seal and a lot of: "Most Excellent Sir, I submit to you that, the enemy having presented himself . . ." Theatrics, pure theatrics.] Although Sardina downplays the importance of verbal expression, this mechanism is Gabriel's most powerful weapon. In a protracted competition, Gabriel initially draws near to and blends with his opponents, to eventually rise above them, but also to realize his parallels with them. Also, there is an element of truth in Sardina's statement, in that Gabriel has fought up to this point against foreign enemies—the French, or the English Lord Gray—but now must renounce such farces, and confront the true enemy within Spain and within himself.

One of his first opportunities to compete with Juan Martín comes just after the introduction of the general and the meditation on the significance of the *guerrilla*. This is the first time Gabriel's readers encounter Juan Martín speaking and acting, as he is engaged in the composition of an official letter. The general struggles with the language of the report, and rejects most of the polite suggestions of his scribe. Juan Martín's virtual illiteracy as well as his comical arguments with his more tutored assistant form the basis for the funniest scene in the novel. Gabriel includes passages from the laughable epistle, ensuring that his readers are fully aware of the multiplicity of errors in Juan Martín's text.

Soon after (chapter 8), Gabriel has the opportunity to write letters of his own to Amaranta, but in typical *guerrilla* style—he has learned well from his new "leaders"—Gabriel does not reproduce his letters. He leaves his readers the responsibility of assuming that his written product is superior to that of Martín's, but protects himself from critical scrutiny with a textual absence—the standard retreat of the *guerrillero*. In the twelfth chapter,

Gabriel again writes to Amaranta, who is now lodged with Inés in her family's castle in the town of Cifuentes. Although he promises to show part of his correspondence with Amaranta, the letters included are entirely hers, and again we are unable to judge his writing. In not revealing his own writing, Gabriel also makes a *guerrilla*-style attack on the former student Viriato, who, while Gabriel writes the undisclosed letters to Amaranta, develops the national malady of quixotism: "el señor Viriato contaba . . . las más estupendas mentiras que he oído en mi vida, todas referentes a fabulosas batallas, encuentros y escaramuzas, que harían olvidar los libros de caballería si pasaran de la palabra a la pluma y de la pluma a la imprenta" (982). [Señor Viriato told the most stupendous lies that I have ever heard in my life, all referring to fabulous battles, encounters and skirmishes, which would cause novels of chivalry to be forgotten, if they (Viriato's lies) went from spoken to written word, and then to the printing press.] Again, Gabriel competes with this rival narrator by hiding the texts he composes and attacking his adversary's efforts, free from the exposure that would make his own work vulnerable. Of course, with the production of his memoirs, Gabriel wins the textual war and has no more need for such indirection, because he has ultimate control of every narrative framed by the *Episodios*. Until that time, however, his engagement in a linguistic *guerra chica* functions as a means of paying tribute to, as well as subjugating, the other *guerrilleros* of this novel.

Gabriel's ultimate success in his competition with the *guerrilleros* is anticipated by his reencounter with Amaranta, who, because Gabriel is her only protection, now acknowledges her dependence on him (1046). From the beginning of the antepenultimate chapter, Gabriel notices how the war, the trials with her family, and now the loss of Inés have diminished Amaranta's beauty (1043). This triumph of Gabriel over the woman who often manipulated him in the past precedes the climax of the novel, in which Mosén Antón and Juan Martín are both eliminated or contained by Gabriel's text. Thus, Gabriel beats the *guerrilleros* at their own game when he replaces Mosén Antón and belittles Juan Martín, but he does so with a verbal sneak attack, in which the only text of his we see is that of the finished *Episodios*. In this way, he is once again rescued by his older self, author of the *Episodios,* while his younger self blends in perfectly with the "heroes" the text associates with the national malady of the *guerrilla*. Consequently, we return to the same issues: Gabriel can be a hero, but to do it he must be a (*guerrillero*) Quijote. Also, as soon as he authors a text, he sets himself apart—selfishly—in a mirroring of one of the central concerns of the *Episodios'* treatment of the *guerrilla*. Mosén Antón's crime is that he wants to be the hero, the leader, and the author of the war, and he does not accept Juan Martín's authority over him. When Gabriel supplants Mosén Antón, this penultimate novel of the series explores another aspect of the author's romantic self, struggling for control and legitimacy, for he is ultimately able to surpass these rivals only by becoming as savagely "selfish" as they are.

LA BATALLA DE LOS ARAPILES

The tenth novel of the series, *La batalla de los Arapiles,* reveals that Gabriel has achieved a certain status in the regular army, and that he is now serving a Spanish division cooperating with the English Lord Wellington. The Spanish collaboration with the English is a reversal of the allegiances we saw in the first novel of the series, when Spain fought at Trafalgar together with France and against England, and the new alliance brings Gabriel into contact with a second English alter ego. The character in question is romantic, like Lord Gray, but this time Gabriel's partner is a woman, Athenais Fly. *La batalla de los Arapiles,* then, is the story of Gabriel's continuing confrontation with his romantic temptations, particularly as they are reflected by Miss Fly. Although many passages throughout the text reveal a Gabriel who acts with confidence and authority in rejecting romantic extravagance, the end of the novel shows him as passive, having conceded control of his destiny to others, and having taken up the same—albeit, parodic—discourses he has ostensibly discarded.

Gabriel begins the novel by referring to his ongoing confrontation with the spirit of don Pedro (the Quijote within him and within Spain), and insisting that his text will be realistic. When they stop for the night in a village near Salamanca, Gabriel reports that he goes to bed without anything poetic happening to him: "sin que nada extraordinario ni con asomos de poesía me ocurriese en aquel acto vulgar de la vida" (1057). [without anything extraordinary or anything with even a hint of poetry happening to me during that everyday act.] It is also true, he says, although equally "prosaic," that he fell asleep, aware only vaguely of his assistant singing a ballad in the next room (1057). The song is not loud enough to prevent him from sleeping, which he does "prosaically." Still, just as Andrés's songs of Gerona punctuate Gabriel's sleep in Bailén, this ballad prepares him to recognize the presence of other—in both cases, romantic and poetic— stories. Initially, however, Gabriel denies the presence of any such romance, recalling both the *Quijote* and the models that inspired it in a long commentary about the pedestrian nature of his experience and account:

> Me dormí, y no se crea que ahora van a salir fantasmas, ni que los rotos artesonados o vetustas paredes de la histórica casa, antaño palacio y hoy venta, se moverán para dar entrada a un deforme vestiglo, ni mucho menos a una alta doncella de acabada hermosura que venga a suplicar me tome el trabajo de desencantarla o prestarle cualquier otro servicio, ora del dominio de la fábula,

ora del de las bajas realidades. Ni esperen que dueña barbuda, ni enano enteco, ni fiero gigante vengan de súbito a hacerme reverencia y mandarme los siga por luengos y oscuros corredores que conducen a maravillosos subterráneos llenos de sepulturas o tesoros. Nada de esto hallarán en mi relato los que lo escuchan. (1057)

[I fell asleep, and don't think that now ghosts are going to come out, nor that the broken coffered ceilings or ancient walls of the historic house, years earlier a palace and nowadays an inn, will move to allow a deformed monster to enter, much less a high-born maiden of consummate beauty who might come to beg me to take on the task of disenchanting her or of servicing her in whatever other way, whether in the realm of fantasy or in that of lowly reality. Don't expect a bearded duenna, nor a puny dwarf, nor a fierce giant to come suddenly to bow to me and to command me to follow them down long, dark corridors that lead to marvelous underground passages full of tombs or treasures. Those who listen to my story will find none of this in it.]

Thus, Gabriel insists repeatedly on the lack of fantastic elements in his story. Nevertheless, despite Gabriel's resistant realism, the discourses he attempts to eliminate soon insinuate themselves into his consciousness. After a period of profound quiet, the memory of the song or some other unidentified influence work together with the drama of Gabriel's interiority and force him to become aware of his divided nature. He awakens suddenly in response to a strange sensation that he cannot decipher, believing that someone is in the room with him. He calls to his servant to bring light, but in that same instant realizes that he has been deceived by his own spirit. He explains the incident in the following words: "Comprendí mi engaño. Estaba enteramente solo. No había ocurrido otra cosa sino que mi espíritu, en una de sus caprichosas travesuras (pues esto son indudablemente las fantasmagorías del sueño), había hecho la más común de todas, que consiste en fingirse dos, con ilusoria y mantenida división, alterando por un instante su eternal unidad. Este misterioso *yo* y *tú* suele presentarse también cuando estamos despiertos" (1058). [I understood my mistake. I was completely alone. The only thing that had happened was that my spirit, in one of its capricious acts of mischief (since this is undoubtedly what the fantastic illusions of dreams are), had done the most common of all such acts, which consists of pretending to be two, with imaginary yet distinct division, altering for one instant its eternal unity. This mysterious "I" and "you" tend to present themselves also when we are awake.] I suggest that the "you" and "I" that appear even when Gabriel is awake are realism and romanticism in dialogue, forming the basic nature of a narrator who cannot simply will the elimination of half of his dual self. Although this doubling resolves itself here with no further consequences, Gabriel's confused perceptions both confirm that he carries with him an alter ego—perhaps the don Pedro alter ego from which he tried to escape—and foreshadows the encounters that he will have in *La batalla de los Arapiles* with a more seductive version of his romantic, alternative nature. We will soon meet Gabriel's unwelcome other half, the last of the major characters of the series.

Although he hopes to recover Inés from her father, Santorcaz, who has taken her with him against her will, Gabriel ends up rescuing a different woman, the English maiden called Miss Fly (1070). Gabriel is first impressed by her when she addresses him with the ceremonious and old-fashioned "vos," and when he notices her physical appearance. He describes her as beautiful, and as exemplifying the model for the particular beauty used by poets (1071). Indeed, Miss Fly's function in this novel is to intensify and accelerate Gabriel's confrontation with quixotic idealism, by tantalizing him with the possibility that such romanticism is an alien influence, but then simultaneously revealing that melodramatic sentimentality is lodged in the core of his own being. One of his first interactions with her is indicative of his internal division: Gabriel responds to Miss Fly's poetic inspiration by serving her, gallantly procuring the tea that other Spaniards seem unable to provide. With this gesture Gabriel imitates the chivalry of the literature he has difficulty eradicating entirely, but then situates his heroism in the unpoetic locus of the kitchen, as if imposing his own realist note in the discursive competition.

From the moment he meets her, Gabriel reacts to Miss Fly both by rejection and by imitation. At many points in the novel he challenges her romanticism, suggesting that a more realistic mentality is unquestionably superior. I turn first to these instances of Gabriel's defiance of Miss Fly's idealism. When Gabriel accepts a dangerous assignment—the penetration of French-occupied Salamanca—he initially refuses to take Miss Fly with him, even though she would like to engage in what she has imagined to be a thrilling adventure. Because her horse can no longer walk she makes an effort to catch up to him on the road to Salamanca, but again he leaves her (1085). Relieved by the others who come to her aid and by the intervention of the prosaic reality (the horse's exhaustion) he champions, Gabriel is able to escape from his obligation to her and to the romanticism she represents.

This incident with the horse is an excellent example of Miss Fly's offering a romantic interpretation of her adventures with Gabriel, and his reconfiguring of such a vision into more pedestrian form. When she catches up to him, Miss Fly explains that their mission to Salamanca should be guided by the model of the *romances,* and informs Gabriel that she is an avid reader of this literature. She tells him she knows all of these *romances* by heart, and delivers an elaborate discourse on the subject of the romantic eclipse of conventional history:

> Parece que resucitan los tiempos . . . parece que salen de su sepultura los hombres revistiendo forma antigua, o que el tiempo y el mundo dan un paso

atrás para aliviar su tristeza, renovando por un momento las maravillas pasadas
. . . La Naturaleza, aburrida de la vulgaridad presente, se viste con las galas de
su juventud, como una vieja que no quiere serlo . . . Retrocede la Historia,
cansada de hacer tonterías, y con pueril entusiasmo hojea las páginas de su
propio diario, y luego busca la espada en el cajón de los olvidados y sublimes
juguetes . . . Pero ¿no veis esto, Araceli, no lo veis? (1085).

[It seems like past ages are resuscitating; it seems that men dressed in old-
fashioned styles are emerging from the tomb, or that time and the world are
taking a step back in order to alleviate their sadness, renewing for a moment
past wonders. Nature, bored with present vulgarity, is dressing herself with
youthful finery, like an old woman who does not want to be aged . . . History
takes a step back, tired of doing stupid things, and with childlike enthusiasm
looks through the pages of its own diary, and then searches for the sword in the
box of forgotten and sublime toys . . . But, don't you see this, Araceli, don't
you see it?]

Because Miss Fly asks him directly if he sees what she sees, Gabriel
must either commit to or reject her vision. Suddenly he is saved from
making this decision by Miss Fly's horse. As reality intrudes, Gabriel
makes the connection to Athenais's earlier comment about the retreat of
history, poking fun at her sublimity: "El caballo que arrastraba, no sin
trabajo, el carricoche de la poética Athenais, empezó a cojear, sin duda
porque no podía reverdecer, como la Historia, las lozanas robusteces y
agilidades de su juventud" (1085). [The horse that dragged, with much
effort, the coach of the poetical Athenais began to limp, without a doubt
because it couldn't rejuvenate like History, the lovely healthiness and
agility of its youth.]
Later, as the armies prepare for battle, Gabriel is jarred by two contrasting visions, and again prosaic reality protects him from the romantic
idealization of Miss Fly's charms. Near the burning village Villorio
Gabriel sees a figure, "tan distinta de las comunes imágenes terrestres
como lo son de la vulgar vida las admirables creaciones de la poesía del
Norte; una mujer ideal" (1128). [as different from common earthly images
as the admirable creations of the poetry of the North are from those of
everyday life.] He greets Miss Fly ecstatically, but as he draws near to
her—coming physically closer to reality—his view of her changes consid-
erably: "Cuando la vi de cerca, no pude menos de advertir la diferencia que
existe entre las imágenes transfiguradas y embellecidas por el pensamiento
y la triste realidad" (1128). [When I saw her up close, I could not help but
notice the difference that exists between unhappy reality and images that
are altered and made more beautiful by our mind.] Gabriel's critique
extends beyond the simple recognition that her physical appearance is not
what he imagined it to be from a distance, and his disappointment reaches
into the more abstract realm of ideas, in that he finds her less "interesting"

(1128). It is not her beauty that he finds lacking, but rather, her ability to seduce him psychically, perhaps because he realizes what indulging and responding to her will cost him.

As if to confirm his rejection of Miss Fly and her romanticism, Gabriel defends Inés when Miss Fly insults her, calling her a "joven de miras poco elevadas, de corazón pequeño" (young woman without lofty vision, and with a small heart), who lacks imagination and drive—an "ave doméstica" (domestic bird) who would answer Gabriel's passionate declarations "cacareando en su corral" (clucking in her poultry yard) (1130). Earlier he did not respond one way or the other to Athenais's questioning of Inés's value (1122); now he champions Inés, albeit continuing with the pedestrian hen imagery when he says that hens are useful, caring, sensitive, and disposed to self-sacrifice (1130). Gabriel even goes so far as to contrast the trusty hen with the eagle he identifies with the exalted Miss Fly. The "hen" gives man her children, her feathers, and finally her life, "mientras que un águila . . ." (while an eagle . . .) (1130). Gabriel does not complete his thought, but it is clear that he would like to renounce Miss Fly and content himself with the hen, Inés.

In fact, it seems that Gabriel successfully negotiates this choice, as his reputation is restored.[8] The commander Carlos España leaves Gabriel in charge in his absence, and the young man takes to his new role easily, giving orders right and left (1131). Gabriel is also in control when he next faces Santorcaz, whom the French have accused of spying and have taken prisoner, and who is now with Inés. Santorcaz realizes that he is Gabriel's captive, and is forced to beg him to allow Inés to stay (1133). In addition, Gabriel and Inés are able to speak openly, and she informs him that she has entertained Miss Fly with exaggerations of Gabriel's heroic deeds, laughing at the English maiden, but also admitting her own jealousy (1135). Gabriel calls Miss Fly "loca," renouncing her romantic fantasies and situating his relationship with Inés firmly in the carnal, realistic realm. When he threatens to eat her if she does not embrace him, she says he must be hungry ("hambriento estás"), and he declares his desire for a relationship with her in which she is a physical reality instead of a figment: "Hambriento de quererte, esposa mía. ¿Te parece? . . . Seis meses amando a una sombra . . ." (1135). [Hungry to love you, my bride. Don't you think so? . . Six months loving a shadow.]

He observes to Inés that if Miss Fly could see them, she would appreciate the difference between a true, concrete love and the fantasies she pursues. At this point, however, his description of his love for Inés verges into idealism, and we begin to see the weakness in his position. He muses that if Miss Fly could see the two of them, she would understand the difference between her poetic sparks, and "esta luz divina en que se gozan nuestras almas, y se gozarán por los siglos de los siglos" (1135). [this divine light in which our souls rejoice, and will continue to do so forever more.] He also accepts Inés's loyalty to Santorcaz, admiring her constancy, and only wishes that he could be miserable and unfortunate, in order to receive the same loving treatment from her (1139). When he realizes that Inés is laughing at his excesses, he demands death ("Yo quiero morir!"), and explains that his love for her inspires his extravagance. He feels that the pure and exaggerated affection brought to his mind a thousand strange subtleties and silly scruples, and to his heart incomprehensible and ridiculous desires (1140). In this way, Gabriel seems to have made his commitment to realism and to Inés, but he articulates this very choice using Miss Fly's language.[9]

Thus, we must also read an opposing conclusion. Despite his ostensible choice of Inés over Miss Fly, throughout the text Gabriel gives indications that he also identifies strongly with Miss Fly, as in this culminating example. He pretends that he is indulging her crazy (foreign) fantasies, but acknowledges nearly from his first encounters with her that her visions appeal to him because of his own innate romantic nature. I now explore the moments in which Gabriel imitates Miss Fly, acknowledging his susceptibility to her way of thinking even as he struggles to espouse realism.

For example, soon after they meet, Gabriel and Miss Fly take a walk together, and Gabriel indulges her extravagant notions of Spain. When she flatters him by declaring that he must be of noble birth, he claims to be descended from Hercules, confirms that he is in love—by definition he must be, after all, he is a young Spanish soldier—and acknowledges that he has decided to participate in the fantasies of his new friend (1074). She explains that her interest in his personal life is the curiosity of an Englishwoman—she would almost say of an artist—and that she is engaged in a program of study of the customs and characters of Spain. When Miss Fly asks if his lady lives in a nearby castle, Gabriel confirms his assessment of the young woman as possessing an exalted, novelesque imagination (1075). At this point Gabriel describes his attitude toward Miss Fly's extravagances in a contradictory manner. On one hand, he dismisses his playing along with her fantasies by referring to what he does as mocking her, but at the same time, he admits that her poetic vision appeals to his own subjectivity: "Todos somos algo poetas, y es muy dulce embellecer la propia vida, y muy natural regocijarnos con este embellecimiento, aun sabiendo que la transformación es obra nuestra" (1075). [We are all poets of sorts, and it is very agreeable to make one's own life beautiful and very natural for us to rejoice in this beautification, even knowing that we accomplished the transformation ourselves.] Evidently, Gabriel concedes to the young woman mastery over their shared discourse, only to insist that his own choices guide his behavior. In this way, Gabriel atttempts the difficult task of convincing his readers that the false idealism proceeds from Miss Fly, and that although his own nature responds to this poetry and indeed contains some of it, he maintains control over his participation in the fantasy.

Gabriel then demonstrates this creative ownership of the same models he purports to reject by casting his story in chivalric terms. He speaks to Miss Fly of Inés's perfection, but then asks of what use is her perfection, when an enchanter has transformed her into a common actress, and she is held captive by a group of traveling players? When he mentions enchanters, even Miss Fly has trouble accepting that there could "still" be enchantments in Spain. Although Gabriel qualifies his statement, saying that so-called enchantments might be instead "devil's artifices, evilness and trickery by perverse men," she identifies him as a reader of chivalric novels (1075). In response, Gabriel defends the *libros de caballerías*, calling such novels the most beautiful books ever written: "Suspenden el ánimo, despiertan la sensibilidad, avivan el valor, infunden entusiasmo por las grandes acciones, engrandecen la gloria y achican el peligro en todos los momentos de la vida" (1075). [They astonish the soul, awaken sensibilities, arouse bravery, create enthusiasm for great acts, magnify glory and make danger seem small all through life.]

At this point, Miss Fly celebrates Gabriel's idealistic sentiments, calling him worthy of having been born in another age (1076). However, when Gabriel confesses that he plans to rescue Inés from Santorcaz even before the Spanish forces reclaim Salamanca from the French, Miss Fly denies the validity of everything he has told her, assuming that he is mocking her. She accuses him of inventing a chivalric tale, claiming to protagonize it, and adorning his fiction with a Dulcinea and some enchanters, who only exist in his imagination (1076). She then asks Gabriel to accompany her to her room, but quickly locks the door behind her (1077).

After losing his audience by not being credible as a romantic hero, Gabriel seems desperate to prove to her his appetite for "real" adventure, and requests in her presence the mission to infiltrate Salamanca. Gabriel's acceptance of this assignment just hours after his rejection by Miss Fly raises doubts about the impetus for his actions. Is he a brave soldier and devoted lover, or a slave to Miss Fly's manipulations, responding only to her implicit challenge that he prove himself as a "noble" (poetic) soul? It is during this trip to Salamanca that Gabriel struggles hardest to resist Miss Fly's temptations, all the while realizing the internal divisions that make him susceptible to quixotism. When Miss Fly suggests accompanying him to Salamanca, Gabriel refuses her offer, citing the grave danger he will soon face and the possible damage to her honor she would incur if she traveled alone with a male acquaintance. However, she then admonishes him with an observation that touches the sore point of Gabriel's desire to stand out from the crowd. She deduces that either his accomplishments are fabricated, or his character is far inferior to his deeds, and warns him: "Por Dios, no os arrastréis al nivel de la muchedumbre, porque conseguiréis que os aborrezca" (1082). [By God, do not allow yourself to be dragged down to the level of the crowd, because you will succeed in earning my hatred.] This challenge sets the tone for Gabriel's behavior in the rest of the novel, and explains much of his indulgence of Miss Fly's fantasies: he must evidence poetic idealism to convince her (and perhaps himself) of his distinctiveness. He would like to reject definitively the quixotic mentality, and throughout the series he associates this problematic way of thinking with a plurality of characters he believes are his inferiors. At the same time, Athenais's insinuation that in so doing he might in fact sink to the level of the "muchedumbre" (crowd) spurs him to attempt to prove to her his superiority, and this must be accomplished by adopting the conventions of the discarded romantic discourse. Again, the problem that plagues Gabriel is the continued split in his being—the division we have seen since the beginning of the series between Gabriel as both champion of realism, and romantic throwback.

In the next passages, Gabriel confirms his paradoxical nature by first donning a costume just as complicated as the one he described and mocked for Miss Fly, in order to change from army officer to "the most uncouth peasant who has ever appeared in the fields of Salamanca" ("el más rústico charro que ha parecido en campos salmantinos") (1082). He then plans to evade Miss Fly, but does so by imitating her favorite literary model: "bonitamente y sin decir nada a nadie, como Don Quijote en la primera salida, eché a correr" (1082). [craftily and without saying anything to anyone, like Don Quijote in the first sally, I set out.] In this way, Gabriel appears to reject her poetic ideas, but then creates for himself a fanciful adventure—complete with costume and the faithful following of a novelistic example.

Miss Fly is just as good a reader of the *Quijote* as he is, and surprises him by catching up with him. She brings him a letter from Amaranta, which he allows her to read, knowing the effect it will have on her. Amaranta writes that Gabriel is the angel on whom her happiness depends, that she owes him her life, and that she would give everything she owns for the nobility of his heart and the trueness of his lofty sentiments. When she reads the emotionally charged letter the effect on Miss Fly is instantaneous. Gabriel describes her transformation, as her face becomes inflamed with sweet confusion, and her brilliant fantasy springs to life, magnifying the adventure before her. She is now converted to his extravagant plan, but insists on associating it with the *romances* she loves and knows by heart. When he hears this, Gabriel has a curious reaction, acknowledging to himself that Miss Fly suffers from a literary monomania, but addressing her as "señora mía e insigne maestra" (my señora and distinguished teacher) (1084). Indeed, although he may conceive of her as addled, he defers to her as his teacher, accepting easily her encouragement and articulation of his romantic adventure. Miss Fly then declares that she reads the *romances* with passion, but cannot find them in real life, at which point Gabriel explains that those times have passed, and that there are no more of these romantic characters around (1084). Miss Fly responds to this dismissal, however, by forcing Gabriel to admit that he has not read the *romances* of Bernardo del Carpio. With this recognition, Gabriel further subjugates himself to her tutelage, saying "he descuidado mucho mi instrucción, miss Fly" (1085). [I have seriously neglected my studies, Miss Fly.]

Confirming that he is in thrall to Miss Fly, as he approaches Salamanca and while in the city, Gabriel does nothing but elaborate and represent extravagant fictions. Although he acts this way to gain access to Inés, he has clearly not relinquished the poetry of Miss Fly. Disguised with a load of vegetables and a donkey, he learns from the villagers that the French are not permitting the entry into Salamanca of anyone who does not hold a French pass. Gabriel realizes that he will have to borrow the identity of Baltasar Cipérez, son of the peasant Cipérez, "the rich" (1086). After playing this role as long as he can, feigning stupidity and inventing prior relationships with some of the French soldiers he meets, he takes up the identity of a lovelorn nobleman when the earlier disguise is no longer effective (1094).

Later, after the bitter disappointment of Inés's rejection of his offer to take her from her father, Gabriel finds himself in the street, face to face with the French soldiers who had attempted to apprehend him earlier.[10] Mentally incapacitated by his conflict with Santorcaz, Gabriel is unable to invent a trick or artifice to evade capture (1106). Suddenly trapped in the realist mode he would like to favor, but which provides him no escape, Gabriel is at a loss to rescue himself. Fortunately for him, Miss Fly suddenly approaches on the arm of a French colonel. Ready to repay Gabriel for saving her life, Athenais is quick to improvise a fiction that will provide him a new identity, when she refers to him as her servant. Gabriel happily accepts the role, and placidly tolerates her calling him an idiot (1106). Gabriel further debases himself by begging her forgiveness for leaving her earlier, and she responds by referring to him as "señor aldeano" (señor villager) (1107).

As they converse at the inn where they are lodging, Gabriel tries to point out to Miss Fly the flaw in her method of assessing reality—she believes that all love affairs and adventures in the real world mirror those about which she has read in novels—but he also recognizes that he is no match for her creative imagination: "Yo hacía esfuerzos de ingenio por sostener de algún modo un coloquio en que Miss Fly, con su ardoroso sentimiento poético, me llevaba ventaja, y a cada palabra mía su atrevida imaginación se inflamaba más" (1109). [I made efforts of wit to continue a dialogue with Miss Fly, a dialogue in which with her burning poetic sentiment she had an advantage over me, and with every word of mine her daring imagination became more inflamed.] Miss Fly believes he should battle the entire French army if necessary. Not seeing this as feasible, Gabriel assumes that she has acquired her plan of action from a literary text, and asks her from which one, so that he can read it too. When she explains that she has extracted the plot from the book of her heart and her fancy, he concedes that her soul is superior to his (1110).

Gabriel attempts to reject her plan, but ultimately she wins him over thanks to qualities inherent in him. He outlines this reaction in the following way: "Su inflamado semblante, sus brillantes ojos, el timbre de su patética voz, ejercían extraño poder sobre mí y despertaban no sé qué vagas sensaciones de grandeza, dormidas en el fondo de mi corazón, tan dormidas, que yo no creía que existiesen" (1110). [Her inflamed countenance, her shining eyes, the timbre of her voice full of emotion—all exerted a strange power over me and awoke in me who knows what strange sensations of greatness, asleep in the depths of my heart, so fast asleep that I didn't realize they existed.] Thus, Gabriel concedes that Athenais controls him because of a "flaw" in his own nature. When Jean-Jean arrives to report that Santorcaz and company will leave that night after midnight, Gabriel and Miss Fly prepare for what he refers to, quoting the *Quijote,* as "aquel estupendo y nunca visto suceso, que verá el lector en los siguientes capítulos" (1111). [that stupendous and unheard-of event, which the reader will see in the following chapters.]

Gabriel begins the next chapter with a qualification, expressing his disbelief that it was actually he that attempted the daring feats, spurred by the influence of the Englishwoman. Again, he imagines the agent of the deeds as a second self. Perhaps, he writes, "en vez de ser mi propia persona la que a tales empeños se lanzara, fue otro yo quien supo interpretar los fogosos sentimientos y caballerescas ideas de la hechicera Athenais" (1111). [Instead of being my own person who threw himself into such adventures, it was a different "I" who was able to interpret the impassioned sentiments and chivalrous ideas of the bewitching Athenais.] Using this image of the divided self, Gabriel again calls attention to the divergences within him: he is controlled by Miss Fly, but only because he is previously disposed to such manipulation.

As they walk through the city, Miss Fly encourages Gabriel to read Salamanca as she does. Although Gabriel is anxious to complete their mission so that he can arrive on time for a meeting with Lord Wellington, she is captivated by the beauty of the city. Athenais calls attention to the features of Salamanca, preceding each observation by expressing incredulity that such sights do not signify in the same way for Gabriel, and challenging him to prove his romantic sensitivities by allowing the city to speak to him (1112). When they knock on Santorcaz's door Gabriel reflects on his actions, thinking that he remembers reading about an unarmed lover rescuing his beloved from a castle where she was imprisoned by "el más barbudo y zafio moro o gigante de aquellos agrestes confines" [the most bearded and uncouth Moor or giant in those rustic confines], and he is happy to be imitating such legendary behavior (1113). He acknowledges again that Athenais has a powerful influence over him, and resorts to a literary phrase to convey his situation: "No puedo expresar aquel dominio suyo y la esclavitud mía sino empleando una palabra muy usada en las novelas . . . Miss Fly me fascinaba" (1114). [I cannot express her dominion over me and my enslavement to her except by using a word common in novels . . . Miss Fly bewitched me.] As he did earlier, he describes her control over him as dependent on a feature of his own being: "Aquella grandeza de espíritu; aquel sentimiento alambicado y sin mezcla de egoísmo que había en sus palabras . . . hallaban secreta simpatía en un rincón de mi ser" (1114). [That greatness of spirit; that subtle and completely unselfish feeling that there was in her words . . . found a secret sympathy in one corner of my being.] He is torn as to how he should respond to her, and reacts in the most contradictory ways, laughing at her but also admiring her, and obeying her even when she speaks nonsense, because he does not want to appear a coward (1114).

Gabriel's indulgence and imitation of Miss Fly while they are in Salamanca is clear; he also responds to Miss Fly's temptations when he is incapacitated after the battle—the actual "batalla de Arapiles." Gabriel is wounded when capturing the French flag, and while he lies recovering in the hospital, Miss Fly visits him frequently. Although Gabriel is unable to answer her declarations of love, she informs him that when he was delirious and unable to impose the control of his rational faculties, his spirit confirmed that he feels the same: "El alma, cuando se ve libre del imperio de la razón, se presenta desnuda y sin mordaza: enseña todas sus bellezas y dice lo que sabe" (1160). [The soul, when it finds itself free from the dominion of reason, exhibits itself naked and unbound: it shows all its beauties and it says what it knows.] Thus, Gabriel's second self has betrayed him, and he is unable in his disadvantaged physical state to silence Miss Fly or to defend Inés when his visitor insults her (1161). He feels the same internal cry ("arriba, arriba todo" [up, all the way up]) he felt during the battle on the hill, but he cannot articulate a response, and merely screams incoherently (1162).

After Juan de Dios reduces Gabriel's relationship with Inés to a fantasy similar to his own, predicting that Gabriel will also lose his mind (1162), Gabriel is left alone with Miss Fly.[11] When he musters the strength to confess to her that he still loves Inés, Miss Fly seems to give up on him, despite her love. She characterizes Gabriel as a divided person: "Estáis compuesto de grandeza y pequeñez" (1163). [You are made up of greatness as well as meanness.] Although he has deliberately discouraged her, when she actually prepares to leave, Gabriel wishes that she would stay, and promises that he will believe any fictions she requires: "Pues bien, señora: deliraré, deliraré, y diré todas las majaderías que usted quiera, con tal que me acompañe" (1164). [Well then, señora: I will talk nonsense—I will talk nonsense and I will say all the foolish things you want, provided that you accompany me.] For Miss Fly, however, the enchantment is over. She waits until Gabriel is asleep, then cuts a lock of his hair (1164).

The significance of this act appears to be that Miss Fly has renounced her fantasies about Gabriel, and is taking the hair as a souvenir of an illusion that no longer captivates her. She then disappears from his life forever, having been for Gabriel a beautiful insect of a thousand colors, which flew in circles around him for a few days (1174). His vision of her as a butterfly prepares us for Gabriel's final comments about Miss Fly. He insists that he has proved his trustworthiness to his readers, and that such a faithful narrator could never "oscurecer su reputación con ficciones absurdas, con fábricas de la imaginación que no tengan por base y fundamento la misma verdad, hija de Dios" (1174). [tarnish his reputation with absurd fictions, with manufactures of the imagination that don't have for a base and foundation truth itself, daughter of God.] And yet, he allows that many people who have heard him tell this story have doubted the existence of Miss Fly, and have insinuated that the episode with her is his own invention (1174).

Putting all of these comments together, it seems that despite Gabriel's insistence on his commitment to the truth in his narration, the butterfly of fancy hovers around him until his narrative is utterly contaminated with this fantastic figure. And yet, at the same time, the permeation by romanticism may also be read as an inherent feature of Gabriel's story: it is all his invention, and part of the fiction is romantic. In fact, it appears that Miss Fly is as real as Gabriel's second (romantic) self. For this reason, he cannot completely reject her, just as he cannot escape from that component of himself. The absent lock of hair indicates that Miss Fly recognizes that the fantastic stories she loved were as much a part of Gabriel as his hair. However, losing this hair does not mean the elimination of Gabriel's romantic tendencies. The absence merely recalls the poetry that remains within him, ready to sprout again, in the same way that he will regrow his forelock. Miss Fly cannot take this aspect of his character with her because it is part of Gabriel—indeed, the same Gabriel who writes the *Episodios,* that blending of *caballería* and realism.

Although Gabriel ostensibly chooses Inés over Miss Fly, or the hen over the eagle, in no way does he extirpate his romanticism. When he is alone with Inés, and at the same time that he swears he has no love for the English maiden, he speaks the language he spoke with Miss Fly, telling Inés that he will never leave her: "Me has enamorado, porque eres una criatura de otros tiempos, porque vuestra alma, señora (me gusta tratar de vos a las personas), de la mano a la mía y ambas suben a las alturas, donde jamás llega la vulgaridad y bajeza de los nacidos. Por vos, señora, seré Bernardo del Carpio, el Cid, y Lanzarote del Lago" (1171). [You have made me fall in love with you, because you are a creature from another age, because your soul, Señora (I like to use "vos" with people), hand in hand with mine, rises to the heights, where the vulgarity and lowliness of mortals never reaches. Because of you, Señora, I will be Bernardo del Carpio, el Cid, and Lancelot of the Lake.] Inés begins to laugh at him, and refers to his excesses as "tonterías," (sillinesses) but Gabriel insists on continuing (1171). In returning to the comparison of the hen and the eagle, he confuses his readers as to what (whom) he is really choosing: "Vos sois el imán de mi existencia, la única pareja digna de mi alma; adoro las águilas que vuelan mirando cara a cara al sol, y no las gallinas, que sólo saben poner huevos, criar pollos, cacarear en los corrales y morir por el hombre" (1171). [You are the magnet of my existence, the only partner worthy of my soul; I adore eagles that fly facing down the sun, and not hens, which only know how to lay eggs, raise chicks, cluck in poultry yards and die for humans.] However, in the next passage, Gabriel's use of this rhetoric is so excessive that it is clear that he mocks Miss Fly's language, reassuring Inés that he is happy with the prosaic love she represents: "De veras sois tonta; os habéis empeñado en amarme con cariño dulce y tranquilo, propio de costureras . . . ¡Oh, amadme con exaltación, con frenesí, con delirio, como amaba Bernardo del Carpio a doña Estela" (1172). [You are truly foolish; you have tried to love me with sweet, calm affection, appropriate to seamstresses . . . Oh, love me with exaltation, with frenzy, with delirium, like Bernardo del Carpio loved doña Estela.] In this way, Gabriel proves to Inés that he does not take such extravagances seriously, and her anger and jealousy turn to happiness. Of course, he also displays his facility for this language, clinging to it even when he purports to reject it, just as in several instances he attempts to retain Miss Fly when she leaves him. In the end, though, Gabriel and Inés are ostensibly reconciled. Miss Fly publicly dismisses any claims to Gabriel, and so he and Inés are free to start their life together, with Gabriel's reputation restored. Amaranta welcomes Gabriel into the family, as does Santorcaz, and Inés's estranged parents even make amends to each other.

Nevertheless, even though all Gabriel's problems are solved, it is curious that the text in its final stage effaces him as hero. Indeed, the last two chapters of the novel and of the series present Gabriel as passive, standing back while Inés informs Santorcaz that she is getting married and that she and her husband are leaving him for life in Madrid (1175). Furthermore, Inés manipulates Santorcaz—lying to him that Amaranta has left when she is actually still there and available for a reconciliation—so that she becomes the hero(ine) of her parents' rapprochement. In the final chapter, Gabriel concludes his story with the tale of his military advancement—a meteoric rise, but due to Amaranta's intervention (1180). He even concedes responsibility for the communication of any other details of his life to other, hypothetical texts, writing, "[L]os que quieran saber cómo y cuando me casé, con otras particularidades tan preciosas como ignoradas acerca de mi casi inalterable tranquilidad durante tantos años, lean, si para ellos tienen paciencia, lo que otras lenguas menos cansadas que la mía narrarán en lo sucesivo" (1180). [Those who might want to know how and when I got married, along with other details, as lovely as they are unknown, related to my nearly undisturbed peace of so many years, should read, if they have the patience, what other tongues less tired than mine will narrate henceforth.] Here, Gabriel highlights his passivity by consigning his remaining years to oblivion. Even the last sentence of the novel is ambiguous: Gabriel instructs his young readers, if any of them are disadvantaged, to remember him who "nació sin nada y lo tuvo todo" (1180). [was born with nothing at all and had it all.] With this statement, Gabriel leaves unclear the stage of his life in which he "had it all"—was it at the end of his life, or did he at one point have it all, only to subsequently give up some of what he had?

But perhaps the defining gesture of this renunciation of control of his life and his story is when Gabriel allows Inés to speak for him to Santorcaz, because of the irony implicit in the situation. Inés tells her father that she and Gabriel hate the "populacho" (the masses), and for that reason they will leave Santorcaz's revolutionary society, and take refuge in the court (1175). In this way, Gabriel, who so often insisted on the villainy and monstrosity of the mob—inferior readers and bad judges all—has conceded even his battle against interpretive insensibility to another warrior who now fights in his stead. Having striven to distinguish himself, he now falls completely mute, and retreats into the textual background instead of standing out in any way. In earlier stages of the *episodios* Gabriel demanded that his readers differentiate the special case of his own responsible reading from readings done by his uncritical or quixotic alter egos and adversaries. Here, though, he erases himself from the picture, ultimately unable to defeat the Miss Fly, Mosén Antón, don Pedro, Santiago Fernández, and perhaps even don Diego within him. With this gesture of self-effacement, Gabriel acknowledges that he cannot dictate the distinctions between "bad" and "good" readings, any more than he can extinguish his internalized romanticism, as reflected by Miss Fly. Gabriel has presented himself as champion of realism, but at every stage has indicated as well the pull of romanticism. He may well be a model for readers to follow in their confrontation with the texts of their culture and history, but as testimony to the seductions of fiction just as much as hero of rationality and dispassionate analysis.

Galdós's First Series of *Episodios* chronicles the founding moment of modern Spain, when the romanticism—realism dichotomy was crucial for the establishment of the nation's self-image, just as it is for Gabriel's persona. After fighting the temptations of romanticism or quixotism throughout this ten-novel series, Gabriel arrives at the ambiguous end of his story. Having followed him through his examination of romanticist and realist mentalities, we have seen that although romanticism is associated with immaturity, excessive passion, and distorted thinking, it is also the mode of heroism. Heroism, in turn, is the essential ingredient in any patriotic endeavor, such as the War for Independence, the focus of the First Series of *Episodios*. Whereas reading realistically protects the thinking subject from extravagant ideations, the greater degree of control thus achieved comes at the expense of strong emotions and forceful personality. Gabriel witnesses this vacillation between controlled realism and adventuresome quixotism within himself, and as a feature of various audiences' reactions to the "texts" they confront. In this way, Gabriel, as ultimate master of the narrative and author of the *Episodios,* ends his story with a bow not just to his readers, as he places himself at the mercy of their interpretation, but more important, to Inés and Amaranta. Of course he has the last word—he is, after all, the internal author of the *Episodios*—but his final act as "author" is to point out that his destiny was decided and his life was lived by these two women. This conclusion to his adventures begs the question of how his submission to Inés and Amaranta relates to his continuing vacillation between realism and romanticism. I pursue this issue through readings of two more texts that feature author-characters who struggle with the same internal divisions.

4

Escape from Romanticism in *La lucha por la vida*

Pío Baroja's novels have a very different flavor from those of Galdós, in that Galdós's study of groups is displaced by Bajora's concern for the internal struggles of the individual. Whereas the First Series of the *Episodios* is narrated in first person by Gabriel Araceli, in *La lucha por la vida,* Baroja's protagonist does not tell his own tale, and he is not at all a conventional hero.[1] Still, Manuel Alcázar presents a number of intriguing parallels with Galdós's realist romantic Gabriel Araceli. The trilogy *La lucha por la vida* (*The Struggle for Life*) follows the development of the young Manuel into adulthood, as he vacillates between living on the margins of society and striving for greater economic and emotional security. Gradually, with periodic slips even into criminal behavior, Manuel renounces the unconventional activities he finds exciting, and comes to terms with the tranquility of life as a married property owner. If Galdós's Gabriel Araceli engages in a permanent struggle with romanticism, revealing his most basic (authorial) self as dependent on and inseparable from romantic structures of thought, Manuel Alcázar appears to eventually escape for good from the temptations of romanticism. In this chapter, I trace the process of Manuel's departure from romanticism, and examine the final stage of his experience, in which his renunciation parallels Gabriel's. Even more so than Gabriel, Manuel eliminates his nonrealistic ideations by becoming a nonentity at the end of the three novels. He erases his authorial "I" when he gives up romanticism, and this authorial self is, in some senses, the self itself.

LA BUSCA

In *La busca* (*The Search*), the first novel of Baroja's trilogy, Manuel arrives in Madrid and is exposed to fantasy and romantic readings, but

quickly allies himself with the rational, realistic mentality of his friend
Roberto. As he ventures out into the world beyond the boardinghouse
where he stays with his mother, he encounters realities that are stranger
than fiction, and begins to doubt the possibility of clearly differentiating
fiction from fact. Still, he remains committed to realism and objectivity,
and rejects the romanticism of his co-worker, Karl, a baker. Manuel's
defenses against idealism are undermined, though, when he falls ill, and as
he recovers he is fascinated by the romantic novels he has been reading
while convalescing. He ends up homeless, however, when he tries to put
such arts into practice in the seduction of his landlady's niece. At this
point, Manuel again meets Roberto, who presents himself as a Christ
figure by claiming that Manuel will deny him three times before the cock
crows. The rest of *La busca,* as well as the next novel, *Mala hierba*
(*Weeds*), chronicles Manuel's three renunciations of Roberto. By the third
novel, Manuel has stopped defying Roberto with romantic fantasy, and has
become an unwavering convert to realism, property ownership, and famil-
ial stability. At the same time, the end of *Aurora roja* (*Red Dawn*) is sad.
We are prepared for this sadness, because we have seen the persistent
linkage of self and romanticism, so that elimination of one implies loss of
the other. Even when Gabriel Araceli concedes control of his story and life
to Inés and Amaranta, he retains some of his status as hero of his narrative.
Manuel, on the other hand, literally disappears, overshadowed by his flam-
boyant brother Juan. He has thoroughly extirpated his romanticism, but he
has also erased himself. More important, he has abdicated his subjectivity
in favor of other characters, to an even greater degree than does Gabriel. I
turn now to the novels of the trilogy, in order to explore this process in
more detail, and to characterize the new "heroes" who take over from
Manuel.

At the boardinghouse where his mother works, Manuel is exposed to a
number of romantic texts, but he ultimately commits to the realism represented by Roberto. Although Manuel has established himself as a weak
student, he now joins an environment at the boardinghouse that privileges
reading.[2] Along with several female characters, Manuel meets a newspaper man, a bookkeeper ("un tenedor de libros"), and the student Roberto.
He also encounters the texts read by the landlady, doña Casiana, whose
only consolations are "unos cuantos tomos de novelas por entregas, dos o
tres folletines y un líquido turbio fabricado misteriosamente por ella
misma con agua azucarada y alcohol" (269). [several volumes of serial
novels, two or three *folletines,* and a murky liquid she made mysteriously
herself, with sugar water and alcohol.] Casiana even gives Manuel a name
from a theatrical work, so his identity in the house is tinged by fiction and
fantasy.[3] Manuel's main occupations have to do with the transmission of

written items on behalf of the boarders: he carries the journalist Super-hombre's work to the printing press, as well as letters from the women, Celia and Irene, to their friends (269). Texts are also part of his mother's discipline; she combines blows with orders to read prayer books (270). Thus, Manuel is surrounded by a variety of texts, and his central adventure in this first part of *La busca* encompasses his increasing awareness of the various styles of reading and his competing attraction to divergent means of understanding the written word.

In an environment primarily of nostalgia and fantasy, dancing and sing-ing, the student Roberto—blond, and with eyes of steel—refuses to par-ticipate in the merrymaking (271). He disdainfully rejects Celia's invita-tion to dance, and from this early point in the text forms a contrast to the anti-realistic attitudes of the others. He also serves as an alternative model for Manuel, who is drawn to Roberto's resolve, and conversely, to ro-mance. Whereas Roberto speaks with the baroness's daughter, Kate, and develops a friendship with her, Manuel idealizes the seamstress's appren-tice who sews for the same mother and daughter (Part I).[4] Although Roberto suffers from melancholy related to the difficulties of his relation-ship with Kate, he maintains his "habitual frialdad" (customary coldness) even while courting the girl (272). Too shy to speak to the apprentice, Manuel imagines her, like Don Quijote's Dulcinea in a different, poetic way, particularly after her work with the baroness and Kate is finished. The memory of her is for Manuel "una música encantadora, fantasía, base de otras fantasías" [a lovely music, a fantasy that led to other fantasies], and often he imagines stories in which he acts as hero and she as heroine (272). Here, we note that although Manuel admires Roberto, his concep-tions of love adhere to quixotic models.

Still residing with his mother at the boardinghouse, however, Manuel learns to be skeptical of unrestrained fancy. When the occupants develop a prurient interest in the celebrated crime of Malasaña Street, they imagine—much like the narrator of Galdós's "La novela en el tranvía"—that their fellow boarder don Telmo must be the old lame man mentioned in the newspaper chronicles of the criminal investigation (273). The house rapidly divides into those who read the news and fantasize about their housemates, and those who disavow such nonsensical procedures, thereby incurring suspicion from the first group. The "sensatos" (sensible ones), as the narrator terms them, are Roberto, don Telmo, and a Basque lady, and the "insensatos" (foolish ones) assign all three of them roles in the horrific crime: "Indudablemente—dijo el Superhombre—don Telmo mató a Doña Celsa Nebot; la vizcaína fue la que regó el cadáver con petróleo y le pegó fuego, y Roberto el que guardó las alhajas en la casa de la calle de Amaniel" (273). [Undoubtedly—said Superhombre—don Telmo killed doña Celsa Nebot; the Basque woman was the one who poured gasoline over the body and set it on fire, and Roberto was the one who stashed the jewels in the house on Amaniel Street.]

The irrationality of the other boarders provides the basis for the friendship of Roberto and don Telmo, whereas Manuel is drawn to this pair of characters by their intriguing discusions of Roberto's attempts to claim an inheritance. Even at this early stage, we see that Manuel is processing this mysterious story of Roberto's background differently than would the naive readers who surround him. Although he succeeds in eavesdropping merely on portions of Roberto and don Telmo's discussions, he records exactly what he hears and makes no attempt to embellish or complete the narrative with invented detail (273–75). Furthermore, when the curious boarders interrogate him about what he might have heard while serving coffee to the two men, Manuel refuses to tell them anything, implicitly confirming his loyalty to the cause of rationality: "Se había decidido por el bando de los sensatos" (275). [He had sided with the sensible group.] Manuel makes definitive his identification with this rational approach and with Roberto when don Telmo and the Basque lady quit the house, leaving Manuel and Roberto at the mercy of the rest of the boarders. Manuel defends himself (and by extension, Roberto) from the insults and blows of the commission agent by kicking the man in the stomach and causing him to vomit.

Here, the narrator makes a choice parallel to Manuel's siding with the realist "sensatos," in spite of his interest in romanticism and idealism. The next chapter—the first of Part II of *La busca*—begins with a first-person intervention by the narrator:

El madrileño que alguna vez, por casualidad, se encuentra en los barrios pobres próximos al Manzanares, hállase sorprendido ante el espectáculo de miseria y sordidez, de tristeza e incultura que ofrecen las alturas de Madrid con sus rondas miserables, llenas de polvo en verano y de lodo en invierno. La corte es ciudad de contrastes; presenta luz fuerte al lado de sombra oscura; vida refinada, casi europea, en el centro, vida africana, de aduar, en los suburbios. Hace unos años, no muchos, cerca de la ronda de Segovia y del Campillo de Gil Imón, existía una casa de sospechoso aspecto y de no muy buena fama, a juzgar por el rumor público. El observador . . .
     En este y otros párrafos de la misma calaña tenía yo alguna esperanza, porque daban a mi novela cierto aspecto fantasmagórico y misterioso; pero mis amigos me han convencido de que suprima tales párrafos, porque dicen que en una novela parisiense estarán bien, pero en una madrileña, no; y añaden, además, que aquí nadie extravía, ni aun queriendo; ni hay observadores, ni casas de sospechoso aspecto, ni nada. Yo, resignado, he suprimido esos párrafos, por los cuales esperaba llegar algún día a la Academia Española, y sigo con mi cuento en un lenguaje más chabacano. (277).

[The *madrileño* who at some point finds himself by accident in the poor neighborhoods close to the Manzanares river, will be surprised by the spectacle of misery and squalor, of sadness and ignorance the heights of Madrid offer with their miserable streets, full of dust in the summer and mud in the winter. The capital is a city of contrasts; it offers strong light alongside dark shadows— sophisticated, almost European life downtown, and wild, gypsy-style life in the outskirts. Some years ago, but not many, near Segovia Circle and the Campillo of Gil Imón, there was a suspicious-looking house with a bad reputation, judging by the people's comments. The observer . . .

I was hopeful about this and other paragraphs of the same nature, because they gave my novel a certain phantasmagoric, mysterious quality; but my friends convinced me to suppress such paragraphs, because they said that in a Parisian novel they might be acceptable, but in one from Madrid, no; and they add, also, that here no one gets lost, not even on purpose; nor are there observers, nor suspicious-looking houses, or anything like that. Resigned, I suppressed those paragraphs, which I had hoped would earn me a place someday in the Spanish Academy, and I continue with my story in more common, vulgar language.]

In this way, the narrator's rejection of rhetoric departing from objective observation mirrors Manuel's decision to ally with Roberto. The narrator laments the loss of the hopes and dreams he associated with the use of such idealistic language, and his reluctant renunciation prefigures Manuel's ambivalence about his choice to join the sensible band, and indeed encapsulates the primary action of the trilogy. Influenced by his friends—"el bando de los sensatos"—just as is the narrator, Manuel gives up the romanticism that attracts him. The narrator mourns his lost words, even as he accepts his friends' judgment that they are out of place in the type of novel he wishes to produce; and Manuel chooses rationality in spite of his competing affiliation with the narratives that inspired his dreams of the seamstress's apprentice.[5] Roberto acknowledges Manuel's choice, siding with him against the others, and promising to maintain contact with him even when he is expelled from the house (277).

In the next stage of the novel, Manuel ventures out of the boardinghouse and into Madrid society, where he confronts more romantic extravagance, at times in the form of real-life situations that are stranger than fiction. While he is living with relatives in another part of Madrid, Manuel's cousins Vidal and Leandro introduce him to life as a street urchin. He also maintains contact with Roberto. Manuel meets a new character, Alonso Guzmán Calderón y Téllez ("El Hombre-Boa" [the Boa-Man]), who plays a recurring role from this point on in the trilogy.[6] With a name reminiscent of Spain's great authors and playwrights, don Alonso is a storyteller himself. He has directed a circus in America and loves to amaze his listeners with tall tales of life in the New World, the best example of which is his acrobatic escape from a giant screaming crab (322).

At times Manuel's imagination turns to don Alonso's stories (310), but he is also absorbed by the romance playing itself out in his own family. His cousin Leandro is involved in a stormy relationship with his neighbor Milagros, who treats the young man badly, and then rejects him in favor of the flashier "Lechuguino" (the Dandy). Leandro attempts to ignore this new relationship, and indeed is the last to know of the engagement of his former girlfriend to "el Lechuguino" (314), although Manuel finally confirms his suspicions. As foreshadowed by Leandro's regular encounters with the ghastly woman nicknamed "la Muerte" (Death), and the specter's repeated use of verses to refer to his cuckolding (314), Leandro kills Milagros and then takes his own life. Just before he stabs a knife into his side, he steps back and again runs into "la Muerte," who has begun to insult him (323). Adding a final melodramatic touch, when a doctor performs an autopsy on Milagros he finds that she still wears a tiny medallion with Leandro's portrait (324). Engulfed by this world in which real life appears as unreal and impossible as the stories of don Alonso, Manuel doubts the distinctions between fiction and reality that he earlier imagined to be so clear.

Still, at his job in a bakery, Manuel champions the pedestrian in conversations with the German baker Karl Schneider, an alcoholic aficionado of Balzac's *Lost Illusions* and "a collection of German poetry" (328). Manuel finds this man odd, and ascribes his strangeness to his readings: "Estos dos libros, constantemente leídos, comentados y anotados por él, le llenaban la cabeza de preocupaciones y de sueños. Entre los razonamientos amargos y desesperados de Balzac, pero en el fondo llenos de romanticismo, y las idealidades de Goethe y de Heine, el pobre hornero vivía en el más irreal de los mundos" (328). [These two books, which he constantly read, commented on, and annotated, filled his head with worries and dreams. Between the bitter, desperate logic of Balzac, which was at heart full of romanticism, and the idealism of Goethe and of Heine, the poor baker lived in the most unreal of worlds.][7] Nevertheless, Manuel strikes up a friendship with Karl, and the latter shares his obsessions with his new friend, recounting the novels he reads, explaining the characters' conflicts, and asking Manuel to offer solutions for their problems. Manuel invariably finds unromantic, practical solutions, so that Karl is impressed by his rationality, but remains convinced that such simple answers are not appropriate for his extravagant texts: "Veía que la tal solución no podía tener valor para sus personajes quintaesenciados, porque el conflicto mismo de la novela no hubiera llegado a existir entre gente de pensamientos vulgares" (328). [He saw that such a solution could not be viable for his idealized characters, because the basic conflict of the novel could not have existed among people of vulgar thoughts.]

Although Manuel is initially at odds with Karl's sentimentality, a sudden illness brought on by grueling work at the bakery lands him again at doña Casiana's, and just as it will in the third volume of the trilogy, weak health coincides for Manuel with a breach in his defenses against romantic readings and sensibility (see pp. 545–47). After two weeks of delirium and high fever Manuel rises from his sickbed. He has grown, and has become emotionally susceptible, so that his body is physically weak, and any strong word makes him want to cry (329). Manuel pleases doña Casiana with a gift, and she allows him to recover at her boardinghouse, where he spends the most agreeable days of his life, engaged in copying for the journalist Superhombre in exchange for "novelas de Paúl de Kock y de Pigaul-Lebrún, algunas de un verde muy subido, como *Monjas y corsarios y Gustavo el calavera*" (329). [novels by Paul de Kock and Pigault-Lebrun, some quite off-color, such as *Nuns and Pirates* and *Gustavo, the Shameless One*.][8] These readings transform Manuel into a romantic lover, seducing him to such an extent that he wishes to put the two authors' theories of love into practice with the landlady's niece (329). Influenced by the author of *Monjas y corsarios,* Manuel convinces the girl to meet with him alone, but a neighbor frustrates their tryst, and Casiana beats her niece and again expels Manuel from her house (330). Alone in the streets of Madrid, Manuel confirms his new romantic sensibility by lodging with Karl for the night (330). In this way, the romantic mentality is associated for Manuel with adverse fortune, and it is after his rejection by his customary society that he arrives at a most desperate state, and again encounters Roberto and his doctrine of rationality.

Manuel lives on the margins of society in the company of his cousin Vidal, and at times with the brutal "Bizco" (Cross-Eyed One), a violent and fearsome acquaintance of Vidal's. When his mother dies, Manuel begins to rely on communal meals provided by charity. At one of these gatherings of mendicants Manuel encounters Roberto, who is also temporarily dependent on public aid, although he maintains his faith that he will recover his inheritance, which leads Manuel to think he must be crazy (339). They discuss Roberto's future wealth, and Roberto presents himself as a Christ figure, in an association featured in the rest of the trilogy. When Manuel expresses skepticism about Roberto's inheritance, Roberto answers by imitating Christ's words to Peter: "Me parece que eres de los que no tienen fe . . . Antes de que cantara el gallo me negarías tres veces" (340). [It seems to me that you are one of those who lacks faith. Before the rooster crows you will deny me three times.]

However, it is important to specify, as does Roberto, that the faith he requires for belief in his prosperous future is allegiance to a life model that shuns extravagant ideations of heroism. Roberto explains that he has realized that in order to avoid a sterile life, he must cultivate his will, because one requires a strong will to work patiently and live productively, as opposed to hoping for intelligence (or imagination) to achieve miraculous feats. Roberto has thus resolved to follow the more difficult course of unromantic, sustained effort, as he elaborates in the following passage:

> "Se necesita más voluntad . . . para vencer los detalles que aparecen a cada instante que no para hacer un gran sacrificio o para tener un momento de abnegación. Los momentos sublimes, los actos heroicos, son más bien actos de exaltación de la inteligencia que de voluntad; yo me he sentido siempre capaz de hacer una gran cosa, de tomar una trinchera, de defender una barricada, de ir al Polo Norte; pero ¿sería capaz de llevar a cabo una obra diaria, de pequeñas molestias y de fastidios cotidianos?" (341–42).

> [More will is needed to conquer the everyday obstacles than to make a great sacrifice or to act in abnegation. Sublime moments and heroic acts are the product more of intelligence than of the will. I have always felt myself capable of doing something great, of taking the trench, of defending a barricade, of going to the North Pole. But would I be capable of carrying out a work requiring daily effort, small annoyances, and everyday bothers?]

As soon as Roberto asks himself this question, he begins to labor constantly, dedicating himself to archival work and to the preparation of a solid foundation for the "tower" he will eventually climb: "He plantado durante estos dos años los cimientos para levantar la torre a la que he de subir" (342). [For these last two years I have been laying the foundation in order to then erect the tower I am going to climb.] For Roberto, the achievement of success is preceded by years of gruelling, or even boring, preparatory work. Whereas the quixotic reader imagines superiority as preordained personal excellence, in Roberto's model exaltation is the result of a rationally planned, minutely elaborated, and certainly unglamorous course of action.

This, then, is the way of thinking that Manuel initially dismisses, in his first of three betrayals of Roberto. Manuel continues in his thievery, and is eventually rescued by the ragpicker "el señor Custodio." Manuel views this man as having followed Roberto's plan for success, even though Custodio lives on the margins of society. At don Custodio's, however, Manuel idealizes and romanticizes the ragpicker's life, setting himself up for his first rebellion against Roberto. Under the influence of romanticism, Manuel colors his new environment with a good degree of lyrical imagination:

> Aquella tierra, formada por el aluvión diario de los vertederos; aquella tierra, cuyos únicos productos eran latas viejas de sardinas, conchas de ostras, peines

rotos y cacharros desportillados; aquella tierra, árida y negra, constituida por detritus de la civilización, por trozos de cal y de mortero y escorias de fábricas, por todo lo arrojado del pueblo como inservible, le parecía a Manuel un lugar a propósito para él, residuo también desechado de la vida urbana" (359).

[That land, formed by the daily flood of the spillways; that land, whose only products are old sardine cans, oyster shells, broken combs and chipped utensils; that land, arid and black, made up of civilization's detritus, by pieces of lime, mortar, and factory waste, by everything cast off by the people as useless; that land seemed to Manuel as appropriate place for him, also a cast-off residue of city life.]

When Manuel is first left alone by his host and his wife, he imagines himself as lord of such a manor, thrown there as a cast-off from society instead of achieving respectability as a result of work:

Aquella vida tosca y humilde, sustentada con los detritus del vivir refinado y vicioso; aquella existencia casi salvaje en el suburbio de una capital, entusiasmaba a Manuel. Le parecía que todo lo arrojado allí de la urbe, con desprecio, escombros y barreños rotos, tiestos viejos y peines sin púas, botones y latas de sardinas, todo lo desechado y menospreciado por la ciudad, se dignificaba y se purificaba al contacto de la tierra.

Manuel pensó que si con el tiempo llegaba a tener una casucha igual a la del señor Custodio, y su carro, y sus borricos, y sus gallinas, y su perro, y además una mujer que le quisiera, sería uno de los hombres casi felices de este mundo. (361)

[That rough and humble life, maintained by the detritus of refined, pampered life; that almost savage existence in the outskirts of a capital excited Manuel. It seemed to him that everything the city threw there with disdain—debris, broken clay bowls, old flowerpots, combs missing teeth, buttons, and sardine cans—everything that was thrown away and scorned by the city—was dignified and purified when it came into contact with the earth.

Manuel thought that if in time he could have a hovel like señor Custodio's, and his cart, and his donkeys, and his hens, and his dogs, in addition to a woman who loved him, he would be one of the men who are almost happy in this world.]

Confirming that he is not actually in agreement with Roberto, Manuel attempts to inject his romanticism into the lives of the ragpicker and his wife by reading to them. Although Custodio would like to become literate, the act of learning to read seems to him vaguely suspect. Instead, he asks Manuel to read to him the newspapers and illustrated magazines that he collects in the streets—and the ragpicker and his wife listen intently as Manuel reads (361). Custodio's daughter has left him several volumes of serial novels, and as they read all of these texts together, Manuel replicates with his listener the attitude Karl the baker took with him, and thus further defies Roberto's advice. When Custodio suggests the same sort of practical solutions that once appealed to Manuel himself, Manuel becomes as frustrated as Karl with his audience's prosaism: "Las observaciones del trapero, el cual tomaba por historia la ficción novelesca, eran siempre atinadas y justas, reveladoras de un instinto de sensatez y de buen sentido. El criterio sensato del trapero a Manuel no siempre le agradaba, y a veces se atrevía a defender una tesis romántica e inmoral; pero el señor Custodio le atajaba en seguida, sin permitirle que siguiera adelante" (361). [The observations of the ragpicker, who mistook novelesque fiction for true history, were always sound and fair, revealing an instinct for good sense. The sensible criterion of the ragpicker did not always please Manuel, and sometimes he dared to defend a romantic or immoral theory, but señor Custodio always cut him off immediately, and did not permit him to continue.]

When Manuel discovers that the seamstress of his early fantasies is Custodio's daughter Justa, he continues to idealize this girl, evidence of his commitment to the role of romantic lover. Justa accommodates his fantasies with furtive looks, so that Manuel's imaginary relationship with her blossoms in her absence. When she departs after her first contact with Manuel in Custodio's home, Manuel feels that he has been left in the dark, with only the memory of her fiery glances to sustain him for two or three weeks (363). On subsequent visits, Justa entertains herself by inciting Manuel with flirtatious comments charged with double meanings (364). Unfortunately, Justa soon develops a formal relationship with the son of a butcher, who beguiles the young woman as well as her parents. Manuel is suspicious, particularly after he overhears "el Carnicerín" (the young butcher) speaking disrespectfully of Justa (366). Although Custodio's practicality, which is reminiscent of the teachings of Roberto, has had some impact on him, Manuel reveals his continuing allegiance to the spirit of adventure and chivalry, in both his dedication to the protection of Justa's honor (369), and his vague plans for the future: "Sus instintos aventureros le persistían, pensaba marcharse a América, en hacerse marinero, en alguna cosa por el estilo" (367). [His instincts for adventure remained with him. He thought of moving to America, or becoming a sailor—of things like that.][9] Here, Manuel displays his quixotic spirit in the defense of the maiden entrusted to his care, and in his enduring drive to imitate the adventuresome storyteller, "el Hombre-Boa." Manuel's romantic sensibility brings him embarrassment not only when Justa rejects him, but also in his excessive sensitivity at a bullfight. Because of his distress at the violence of the spectacle, he is now the laughingstock of Custodio's entire family, as well as of el Carnicerín (368).

Manuel's misadventures in the society of don Custodio, caused by his imposition of a romantic, idealistic vision onto a prosaic environment, constitute the first of three denials of Roberto. The novel ends with Manuel wishing to redefine himself as part of the "Madrid trabajador y honrado" (honest, hard-working Madrid) that works by day, rather than the "Madrid parásito, holgazán, alegre" (gay, parasitic, lazy Madrid) that lives by night (373). Manuel the knight-errant, or adventurer, is at odds with Manuel the practical thinker, and he must choose between these two alternatives. The struggle of Baroja's "pícaro" to extinguish his quixotic passions continues in the next novel of the trilogy.

MALA HIERBA

Mala hierba begins with Roberto giving Manuel a second chance. Roberto is hard at work at his desk, and when Manuel asks about his inheritance, he (Manuel) is able to watch the taming of imagination as if on display for his edification. He sees that Roberto gets more and more excited as he speaks about the fortune he is going to have—his imagination paints for him pictures of wealth, luxury, and marvelous voyages ("su imaginación le hacía ver perspectivas admirables de riqueza, de lujo, de viajes maravillosos"), but then there is a sudden change. In the midst of all his enthusiasm and his illusions, the practical man ("el hombre práctico") appears, as Roberto looks at his watch, recovers his calm, and begins writing again (380). In addition to exemplifying diligence, Roberto also articulates for Manuel a critique of the errors of artists who work only by inspiration, rather than by expecting to expend some amount of plodding effort. Roberto's roommate Alex is a sculptor, and Manuel serves as his model. In the artistic world of Alex and his companions, rather than unrestrained genius, Manuel finds judgmentalism, envy, and hatred. Whereas Manuel suspects Alex of inventing elaborate artistic theories to excuse his lack of focus, Roberto succinctly diagnoses the malady of Alex and his fellow artists: they might have sparks of genius, but they are unable to carry out their ideas with daily, consistent work (384). Roberto also criticizes the would-be photographer Bernardo Santín, who calls himself an artist but who knows nothing about the practical questions of photography. With his frustrated artist friends as examples, Roberto attempts to teach Manuel that material success depends on sustained effort and the gradual acquisition of knowledge and expertise.

When Manuel expresses amazement at Roberto's constancy in work, Roberto explains that he does nothing more than what Manuel himself should be doing: staying active, searching, running from place to place, and asking around (382). As Manuel settles into the bohemian lifestyle of the envious artists, he notes that Roberto seems displeased. Roberto speaks severely to Manuel when he raises the issue of his inability to find substantive work. He tells Manuel that there is always work if Manuel is really looking, but if he starts out shiftless and lazy, he will end up a good-for-nothing scoundrel. When Roberto tells Manuel he should develop a will ("voluntad") and change his "static" life into a "dynamic" one, Manuel observes that the two of them speak different languages (384).

This incomprehension turns to indignation and even hatred for Roberto, because Manuel is unable to imagine how he will acquire a will if he does not possess one innately (385). Manuel avoids his scorned mentor, and one day he is given the opportunity to replace Roberto in the family of which "el estudiante" would most like to be a part: the baroness's and Kate's. Manuel's involvement with this family and their schemes is his second betrayal of Roberto. The baroness hires Manuel to pretend to be her son so that she can swindle her ex-lover into supporting the education of the boy she claims is his. In this one move Manuel defies Roberto's challenge to apply himself to job-hunting, continues living in a fantasy world of play-acting and drama, and physically replaces Roberto, the would-be sustenance of this troubled mother and daughter. Moreover, melodramatic texts figure prominently in Manuel's new life from his first interview with the baroness, when he entertains her by embellishing his autobiography with fantasy (396). Living this elaborate fiction, then, is Manuel's second betrayal of Roberto.

Just as he was surrounded by figurative and literal *novelas por entrega* in doña Casiana's largely female realm, Manuel again finds himself in such a house, cushioned by fantastic narratives such as the lie that creates his apocryphal identity, and hosted by the baroness who links the two residences by having lived in both places. The baroness herself becomes the heroine of the serial novel recounted by her servant "niña Chucha," who tells the story of her mistress "en varios folletines" [in several *folletines*] (397). When Manuel feels nostalgia for his bohemian life, his readings fill the gap. Niña Chucha lends him volumes of long serial novels, and these texts reduce his desire to loiter in the streets, transporting him instead, in the company of Fernández y González and Tárrago y Mateos to life in the eighteenth century, "con sus caballeros bravucones y damas enamoradas" [with its swaggering gentlemen and passionate ladies] (397). The act of reading is also an integral part of the farce they stage for the baroness's victim, don Sergio. In preparation for a visit from her unsuspecting former lover, the baroness poses with a book and orders Manuel to install himself in another room and study (405). When Sergio asks where Manuel is, niña Chucha says that he is studying, and she directs his attention to Manuel, who is reading with his elbows on the dining room table and his head in his hands. In fact, Manuel is actually not studying, but rather is absorbed in a serial novel by Tárrago y Mateos (408).

The presence of the literary in Manuel's life increases when Kate comes home from school at Christmastime. At this point Manuel's infringement on Roberto's place in the baroness's family is exacerbated, while his appropriation and creative use of narratives increases. Manuel accompanies mother and daughter to a theatrical production, and Roberto is excluded from the group: "Notó Manuel que Roberto Hasting iba a alguna distancia detrás de ellos" [Manuel noticed that Roberto Hasting was walking some distance behind them], but Kate does not acknowledge him (409). Roberto's courtship of Kate eventually progresses, only because of the courier service Manuel performs for them, controlling the texts the lovers send to each other (409). Manuel occupies the powerful position of confidant to both (410), but also enjoys a relationship of special intimacy with Kate, based on their sharing of stories: "Manuel tenía cierta gracia para contar sus impresiones; exageraba y rellenaba con fantasías imaginadas los vacíos dejados por la realidad. La Nena le solía escuchar muy intrigada" (410). [Manuel had a certain ability when recounting his impressions. He exaggerated and filled with fantasy the emptiness left by reality. The girl listened to him with great interest.]

The undoing of the baroness's successful scheme comes when she falls for her cousin Horacio, a fan of the English sociologist Herbert Spencer. Horacio's extravagant theories coincide well with Manuel's imaginative tendencies. Horacio reinforces Manuel's turn toward reading and away from Roberto's practicality with his discourse on brain lobes. Horacio explains that each brain lobe has its appropriate function, with one dedicated to the activities of reading and writing (415). Because in Spain nearly thirteen million people do not possess these skills, their brain activity is channeled in different, problematic directions—toward barbarous instinct instead of reading, criticism, and discourse (415). Horacio accentuates the irrationality of this idea in spite of himself, when he draws further conclusions: "Consecuencia de esto, el crimen aumenta, aumenta el apetito sexual, y al aumentar éste, crece el consumo de alimentos y encarece el pan" (415). [As a consequence of this, crime is on the rise, as is sexual appetite, and as that increases, so does the consumption of food, and the price of bread goes up.] Ultimately, for all his pretenses to science, Horacio demonstrates that his material is as wildly creative and speculative as any romantic *novela por entrega* read by Manuel and niña Chucha, and reveals the permeation of Manuel's environment by fantasy, even in aspects that purport to be scientific.

For her part, the romanticism kept alive by her readings predisposes the baroness to an unhappy attraction to her cousin, and when don Sergio objects to and ends Horacio's constant presence in the home he himself is furnishing, the baroness turns to epistolary arts to reconquer her cousin: "Ella, que padecía el último brote de romanticismo de la juventud de la vejez, se desesperó, escribió cartas al galán" (417). [She suffered from the last gasp of that romanticism common to the first stage of old age. She became desperate and wrote letters to her beau.] Despite her efforts and the family's brief country idyll financed by the last support they receive from don Sergio, the first part of *Mala hierba* and Manuel's second defiance of Roberto end with Manuel's tearful good-bye to Kate and the baroness, and to his last thoroughly lyrical environment.

The second part of the novel begins with Roberto and Manuel discussing, once again, Manuel's prospects for work, and with Roberto giving Manuel yet another chance to follow his advice. This time, Manuel does embark on an utterly new life, which coincides with his definitive break with the quixotic reading of *folletines*. Ironically, from now on in the trilogy, Manuel remains closer to the mechanical production of writing and texts than he has been so far, even in his days as an avid reader of serial novels. At the same time, he severs himself from the romantic departures from practicality represented by his earlier encounters with texts. Manuel accomplishes this feat with Roberto's help, by acquiring a job at a printing press, and eventually the skills of a typesetter.[10]

Nevertheless, while Manuel renounces attempts at living romantic texts in favor of employment as a mechanic of the printed word, this change leads to his third and final deviation from Roberto's model. Once Roberto leaves Manuel at the press on his first day as an apprentice, Manuel requires help to learn basic procedures. The typesetter Jesús shows Manuel where the letters are, and explains to him exactly how he is to use these essential elements to compose new texts (426). From the first day that he instructs Manuel how to "create" words, the character Jesús plays an important role, eclipsing for the rest of this novel all other mentors and models that Manuel has had. This young man befriends Manuel, spends periods of time living with him, and encourages and incites him in his amorous and political adventures. Curiously, just as the apparently docile Manuel eliminates the last buds of literary romanticism from his psyche, and might be seen as finally loyal to Roberto in that he has acquired conventional employment, he establishes an emotional connection to a new sort of messiah in the barbaric Jesús. If Roberto represents the taming of Manuel, Jesús acts as an outlet for Manuel's rebelliousness, or a refocusing of the energies once directed to his quixotic readings. We must now examine Jesús's entry into Manuel's life, and the renegotiation of Manuel's relationships entailed by the new character's appearance.

Within a few months, Manuel is composing with ease, and sharing lodgings with Jesús (432). Despite his intimacy with Jesús, however, Manuel immediately identifies reasons for his repugnance toward the conduct of his friend. Jesús is frequently drunk, and lives with his two sisters, the pretty, provocative Sinforosa and the sickly, skinny, malformed, and scrofulous Fea. When Jesús announces coldly to Manuel that Fea is pregnant, Manuel notes his friend's selfishness with an astonishment that increases when he discovers how Jesús and Sinforosa continue to overwork their sister, even in her vulnerable state (433). On the day Fea gives birth to a child, fated to survive only a week, Manuel's shock reaches its zenith when he hears from the neighbors that Jesús and Sinforosa have been carrying on an incestuous relationship, spending all of Fea's money on alcohol and making their pregnant sister sleep on the floor so that they could enjoy the family's one bed together (435).

Although Manuel is disgusted with Jesús, the ties between him and and his housemate are strong, as evidenced by the continuing parallelism of the two characters in the plot line of the novel. When Jesús's sister-lover Sinforosa disappears, her place in the home is quickly filled by the orphan girl Salvadora (437), a sort of adopted sister who eventually marries not Jesús, but Manuel. Here, again, we see evidence of parallelism. In character, the two women could not be more different, but their sisterly roles, the similarity of their nine-letter names beginning with "S" and ending with "a," and the replacement of one by the other all suggest a parallelism.

Dissatisfied with conventional work, both Jesús and Manuel soon tire of the frugal practicality of Jesús's sister Fea and of Salvadora. In a pattern that plays itself out several times in the trilogy, the two men rebel as Jesús "seduces" Manuel into disobedience. Significantly, this particular escapade (chapter 5 of the second part of *Mala hierba*) involves Manuel's initiation into sexual activity, and it is fitting that his deflowering takes place under the authority of Jesús. Of note is that this chapter, which deals with "la iniciación del amor" (initiation into love), is preceded by an isolated, chapter-long update on the status of Bernardo Santín, the failed photographer friend of Roberto's, and his unhappy bride, Esther. Roberto takes pity on Esther, kissing her fervently even though he has just maintained that he is inflexible and will not stray from the course he has planned for his life (444). The text is ambiguous as to whether this kiss leads to a consummated seduction of the resolute Roberto, but in any case, Roberto's passionate reaction to Esther mirrors Manuel's positive response to the carnal temptations represented by Jesús. At this point, Jesús's dominance in the novel is such that the eroticism he embodies unsettles even Manuel's alternate leader and role model, Roberto.

In the next period of his life, Manuel drifts along with Jesús, away from their jobs at the printing press and into life in the streets. Jesús eventually replaces another of Manuel's mentors, don Alonso, el Hombre-Boa. In makeshift lodgings, don Alonso regales the two young men with his typically fantastic stories, but it is at this point that Jesús and Manuel—

"hartos de narraciones americanas" (sick of American tales)—reject the tales by pretending to be asleep, so that don Alonso is left to tell the tales to himself and to recognize Jesús's ascendancy over Manuel (452). Furthermore, just before don Alonso disappears from their society, Jesús definitively betters the old man with a political statement that prefigures the rise of anarchist theory and narratives as the hegemonic discourse of the third novel of the trilogy. If the romanticism that had earlier tempted Manuel was literary, now he is seduced by political idealism. One morning, Alonso, Manuel, and Jesús observe the people of the neighborhood Injurias on their way to degrading jobs in the center of Madrid—the human waste, "envuelta en guiñapos, entumecida por el frío y la humedad, la que vomitaba aquel barrio infecto" (453). [wrapped in rags, stiffened by the cold and the dampness vomited up by that infected neighborhood.] Don Alonso suggests that if rich Spaniards could see this site, they might remedy the misery. Jesús disagrees, arguing that the wealthy would do nothing, because half of the rich man's good fortune is knowing that others suffer from hunger and cold (453). Don Alonso expresses incredulity at this cynicism, but Jesús merely adds that they should not even concern themselves with the rich, because while the three refugees from society search for lodgings, the rich sleep peacefully (453). Later, don Alonso again argues with Jesús, this time about the value of civilization, and again Jesús sustains that advances are designed for those who have money, because they are the only ones who benefit from material progress. As Jesús explains, modernity has changed the habits of the rich, but the poor continue with their primitive ways: the rich man uses electricity while the poor man still relies on the candle, the poor man walks while the rich man—who used to ride a horse—now travels by car, the poor and rich used to live side by side, but now the rich surround themselves with walls, so they do not hear the cries of the poor (459). In this way, Jesús the vagabond wins a narrative contest by using parables that can be seen as extensions of the biblical stories told first by Jesus Christ. Soon after, don Alonso disappears, his "narraciones americanas" (American tales) replaced for Manuel by a much more compelling narrative of class struggle.

In the third part of *Mala hierba,* Manuel continues to follow Jesús by demonstrating his solidarity with society's marginalized and disadvantaged. He reconnects with his cousin Vidal, supports himself as does Vidal with gambling scams, and has a brief relationship with Justa, Custodio's daughter, who has been dishonored by el Carnicerín and is now a prostitute. This relatively easy life comes to a tragic end when Vidal is murdered by the savage character el Bizco, and Manuel is taken into custody and forced to hunt for his cousin's killer. Manuel is unable to engage in honest work at any printing press, because the police require his services and prevent him from working regular hours. Finally, it is Jesús, who led him away from working life in the first place, who challenges Manuel to stand up for himself and refuse to pursue el Bizco. Manuel demands the help of the ringleaders of the gambling racket where he was earlier employed, threatens to expose them, and with their assistance rapidly rids himself of his obligation to the police.

The novel concludes with Manuel free to decide his own destiny, yet afflicted by a hatred for society. Jesús listens supportively to his raging, and when Manuel fantasizes about eight days of dynamite raining on the earth, Jesús identifies Manuel as an anarchist, explaining that he shares these sentiments himself (507). Confirming his role as a degraded messiah, Jesús then furnishes the vision of the earthly paradise that will come after such destruction: "Luego habló con una voz serena de un sueño de humanidad idílica, un sueño dulce y piadoso, noble y pueril" (507). [Then he spoke with a calm voice of a dream of idyllic humanity; a sweet, pious dream, noble and childlike.] Humanity, guided by a new idea, would reach a superior state, without hatred or rancor: "La ley del amor ha sustituido a la ley del deber, y el horizonte de la Humanidad se ensancha cada vez más extenso, cada vez más azul" (507). [The law of love has replaced the law of duty, and the horizon of Humanity continues to expand, and to become more blue.] As Jesús speaks, his words fall "como bálsamo consolador sobre el corazón ulcerado de Manuel" (507). [onto Manuel's ulcerated heart like a soothing balm.] Together, they contemplate the sky, and "la vaga sensación de la inmensidad del espacio, lo infinito de los mundos imponderables, llevaba a sus corazones una deliciosa calma" (507). [the vague sensation of the immensity of space, and the infinity of inconceivable words brought to their hearts a delicious tranquility.] *Mala hierba* ends, then, with Manuel clearly identifying with Jesús as his leader and model. He is captivated by all that Roberto is not: idealism, revolutionary political action, and poetic imagery. In the trilogy's third novel, however, Manuel seems finally, definitively changed, as if since his third betrayal of Roberto he has truly "seen the light" and settled down into conventionality.

AURORA ROJA

This third novel, *Aurora roja* [Red Dawn], differs from the previous two by beginning with a prologue. *Aurora roja* also marks a thematic shift. Manuel, while remaining a focalizing character whose views shape the narrative, is less a true hero of the novel than is his brother, Juan. I suggest that Manuel's passivity and lack of protagonism in this novel are almost eery, and prepare the reader for the conclusion that Manuel has lost his original spirit and even his identity. In fact, although this new protagonist seems unfamiliar, we have heard of Juan before *Aurora roja:* when Manuel first comes to Madrid in *La busca,* and he remembers his former school-master's favorable opinion of his younger brother and his dismissal of Manuel himself (265). The prologue to *Aurora roja* reveals that Juan has continued in his academic success, and has been studying at a seminary. Now, however, as the novel begins, Juan informs his companion Martín that he has lost his faith and does not intend to return to the seminary (512). The rest of the novel follows Juan's journey to the Spanish capital, his establishment of contact with Manuel, his involvement with the anarchists in Madrid, and his death from tuberculosis.[11]

To explain this shift in the protagonism of the trilogy, we note the many parallels between Juan and Manuel. Although Juan is in some ways a new character, he is also an alter ego of Manuel, and his adventures mirror and are intimately connected to Manuel's. The prologue features Juan's discussion of his romantic readings, and his identification of their drama with the intense experience he has decided to seek from life (512–13). He meets the village doctor's daughter, Margarita, and as a courtly lover with the lady he worships from afar (or as Don Quijote with Dulcinea), he respectfully dedicates his vague, altruistic mission to her. Thus, in his first appearances as an active character in the trilogy, Juan grapples with reading and reality just as Manuel does in his early undertakings. Moreover, as the action progresses and Juan takes up residence in Madrid, he turns to the anarchists, in the same way that Manuel does at the end of *Mala hierba.* In fact, after Manuel's conversation with Jesús about the dream of anarchism at the end of the second novel, Juan appears to appropriate Manuel's attraction to political radicalism, whereas Manuel himself breaks with such sentiments by becoming a property owner. Throughout *Aurora roja,* Manuel observes dispassionately as Juan replaces him in quixotic quests prefigured by romantic readings. Meanwhile, Manuel remains essentially committed to Roberto's practical way of life, although he does not comply with Roberto's advice that he develop a strong will. We might view this novel as the last stage of Manuel's confrontation with quixotism, as he steps back from his former "affliction" and watches his brother attempt to impose literary ideals on reality. At the same time, as we will observe, Manuel also makes a break with his earlier, often energetic self, paying this high price to avoid associations with romanticism.

I return to the beginning of the novel to examine this process in detail. Before joining his brother, Juan says his good-byes to his traveling companion Martín, then undertakes a long journey that culminates in Madrid. Juan reveals to Martín that he first became disillusioned with the seminary when he discovered the scandalous conduct of one of the priests, but that his reading subsequent to learning of the corruption was just as important to his decision to leave the priesthood.[12] Juan tells Martín details of the plot of Eugenio Sue's *Los misterios de París,* which he has memorized out of devotion to the author's ideals. Sue's strident and emphatic humanitarianism ("el humanitarismo declamador y enfático del autor") had found in Juan an enthusiastic propagandist ("un propagandista entusiasta") (513). After those by Sue, Juan recounts for Martín the novels of Victor Hugo, mentions the work of Marcus Aurelius and Caesar's *Commentaries,* and both young men conclude that in comparison to these characters and writers, they are not alive (513). Thus, Juan discloses at this early stage his belief that these fictional characters live a life more "real" than his own, and sets himself up for later disappointments when life outside the seminary does not offer the drama and passion of his readings. After this prologue, in which Juan encounters both cruel and sympathetic characters while making his rural trek, the text temporarily leaves Juan, the ex-priest and now artist-in-training, on a journey to Barcelona and points beyond.

Since the end of *Mala hierba* Manuel has achieved considerable stability, with a job at another printing press and a pacific family life. Manuel now resides with his widowed sister, Ignacia, the orphan Salvadora, and Salvadora's brother, Enrique. All cooperate in the "respectable" occupations of working diligently and saving money, and all engage in tranquil diversions like playing cards with their neighbors. Still, although Manuel has followed Roberto's instructions with regard to working steadily, he has not made progress in acquiring the will that Roberto found lacking in him. In *Mala hierba,* Manuel felt strong emotions—even hate—toward Roberto when the latter demanded that he develop strength of will, and often rebelled against Roberto's council by consorting with the messiah of carnality, Jesús. In effect, it seems that Manuel does have a will, but that it can only reveal itself when he is expressing his romantic, idealistic self. Manuel falls short in will when he tries to adapt to Roberto's system, and when Roberto judges his progress in that pursuit. In *Aurora roja,* Manuel, living according to Roberto's advice, has curtailed his drive to rebel, and has severely constrained his emotions.

One of the arenas in which we best see Manuel's deficiency of passion is his relationship with Salvadora. In some ways, Salvadora "replaces" Justa at the time of Vidal's death. Justa leaves Manuel, unable to adjust to the calm life of daily employment on which Manuel has embarked. When Manuel is detained by the police for questioning in connection with the murder, it is Salvadora who sends him food (495). Yet, she was adopted by the combined family of Jesús and Manuel as a young girl, and taken into their midst as a sister. In the new arrangement, she forms a pair and works in tandem with Ignacia, Manuel's biological sister. Indeed, even Manuel emphasizes the sisterly aspect of her relationship to him when he introduces her to Juan ("Es una amiga que vive con nosotros como una hermana") (528). [She is a friend who lives with us as a sister.] Again, the parallelism between Manuel and Jesús and their sister-lovers Salvadora

and Sinforosa comes to mind. Manuel further deflates any eroticism lurk-
ing between him and Salvadora by explaining to his neighbor Perico
Rebolledo that he is not sure if they love each other, and that Salvadora is
really more like his older sister, or even his mother: "Me impone como si
fuera una hermana mayor, casi como si fuera mi madre" (523). [She
commands me as if she were an older sister, almost as if she were my
mother.] Salvadora is described as a romantic woman ("La Salvadora,
como casi todas las mujeres enérgicas y algo románticas, era entusiasta de
los animales" [La Salvadora, like almost all energetic, somewhat romantic
women, loved animals]) (526), but she does not appear to express this
aspect of her character with Manuel, and temperance predominates in the
family, which lives "sin grandes satisfacciones; pero también sin grandes
dolores" (528). [without great fulfillment, but also without great pain.]
Manuel clearly does not feel any significant passion for this woman.

When Juan arrives at their home, his presence destabilizes the family.
Asserting the rules of the house he might threaten, Ignacia and Salvadora
refuse Juan's invitation to Manuel to go out, speaking for Manuel and
informing Juan that Manuel does not go anywhere at night (533). Again,
Manuel seems to have no will of his own, and allows his behavior to be
controlled by the women. Yet, despite their reserve toward him, Juan
embraces his recovered family with love, forming a contrast with the
colder Manuel. Even though his audience does not understand him, Juan
speaks effusively of his artistic goals. He tells his family that he wants to
produce "este arte nuevo, exuberante, lleno de vida, que ha modernizado la
escultura en las manos de dos artistas, uno francés y el otro belga" (529).
[this new art—exuberant, full of life—which has modernized sculpture
through the hands of two artists, one French and the other Belgian.] [13] Juan
wishes to free art from classical formulas, heating it with passion, and he
dreams of creating a social art for the masses, an art that would be useful
for all people, rather than a paltry thing available to only a minority (529).
Juan offers these ideas without hesitation—the absence of concern for his
audience's comprehension demonstrates his quixotic tendency to impose
imaginative creations on even the most unwilling public.

Salvadora, however, does not remain unreceptive. When Juan comes to
the house to sculpt a bust of her, the two characters' intimacy increases as
Salvadora models for Juan. He brings her a dog named "Kis" ("En inglés
quiere decir beso" [It means "kiss" in English], he tells her) and makes
direct references to her relationship with Manuel: "acabarán ustedes casán-
dose . . . Ya lo creo; Manuel no podría vivir sin usted" (533–34). [You two
will end up getting married. I'm convinced. Manuel couldn't live without
you.] At this point, though, Juan also comments on the change in Manuel,
and although he ascribes the alterations to the influence of Salvadora, he
does not hesitate to speak nostalgically of the old Manuel: "Está muy

cambiado y muy pacífico. De chico era muy valiente; tenía verdadera audacia, y yo le admiraba" (534). [Manuel has changed a lot, and he is very pacified. As a boy he was very brave; he was truly audacious, and I admired him.] Juan then recounts Manuel's defying an older boy in order to liberate a trapped butterfly, and his building a cart for a sickly child so the child could accompany Manuel and Juan (534). Clearly, Juan is sorry to see many of the changes in Manuel, and now aspires to cultivate himself the generous behavior he admired in his older brother. He also revives for the moment the idea of Manuel as romantic hero of the oppressed, further accentuating the parallels between the two brothers, but also calling attention to what Manuel has lost or given up. At this point, an incident occurs that confirms the lack of passion in Manuel's current existence. When Juan's artistic success gives the family reason to celebrate in a restaurant, Manuel sees the ex-lover with whom he had an intense relationship. Now, though, Manuel reveals that he feels nothing but repugnance toward Justa, who has taken on a repulsive, bestial appearance (540).[14]

Just as Manuel's spirit and passions are extinguished, Juan prepares to shift his interest from art to politics. Whereas Juan notices the overwhelming misery of the factory area (541), Manuel responds to the urgings of Salvadora and Ignacia, and asks Roberto to be his capitalist partner in the purchase of a printing press (544). Manuel blames the two women for hatching the plan: "Son cosas de mujeres. Ya sabe usted que soy cajista, y mi hermana y otra muchacha que vive conmigo están empeñadas en que me debo establecer . . . Y ahora se puede comprar una máquina nueva y tipos también nuevos . . .; y no tengo dinero bastante para eso . . .; y ellas me han empujado para que le pida a usted el dinero" (544). [It's a women's thing. You know that I'm a typesetter, and my sister and the other girl who lives with me are determined that I should establish myself in business. And now there is an opportunity to buy a new press and new types, and I don't have enough money for all of that, and the two of them have urged (pushed) me to ask you for the money.]

Thus is Manuel established as "un burgués, todo un señor burgués" [a bourgeois, a totally bourgeois gentleman] (544), even though Juan expressed disgust at Manuel's desire to be a property owner: for him, the instinct to own property is the most repugnant thing in the world (542). Of course, in reality, Manuel has no such desire, in that his actions are controlled by his sister and Salvadora, but he does make the purchase.

When Manuel visits Roberto he learns that Roberto is now married to Kate, and is established in his role as protector of her family. In this way, Roberto has effaced with Kate's family the earlier, romantic Manuel who lived with the baroness and her daughter. This erasure of imaginative, creative Manuel is another example of the shifting of Manuel's identity away from his quixotic roots.

Manuel then falls gravely ill. As before, when Manuel suffered a serious illness after coming into contact with the readings of Karl the German baker, his recovery is marked by sentimentality and a return of romanticism. While recuperating from the earlier illness, Manuel read serial novels and planned to use them as models to seduce a girl. During this second recovery, Manuel draws on the lyrics of the blind man who sings in the streets below, to whom he gives the nickname "el Romántico," to fabricate more intense feelings for Salvadora (546–47). While still ill, he dreams of her and begs her for a kiss, but as he improves, the distance between them increases, even though Manuel would have liked to feel that he was still special to her (547). Although he appears to wish for more intensity in his relationship with Salvadora, Manuel's return to the printing press is marked by a break with Jesús, embodiment of his passion, when Jesús accuses him of being a joyless "cochino burgués" [bourgeois pig] (548). In this way, sentimentality in Manuel is now present only as a feature of physical weakness, and does not persist as part of his natural state. He has changed significantly from the first novel of the trilogy, when his quixotism persisted beyond his physical illness.

In the second part of the novel, the adventures of the passionate Juan and the subdued Manuel continue. It is at this point that Juan discovers anarchism, giving us the opportunity to contrast his idealistic approach to his new mission with Manuel's staid vision of his own life. We recall Juan the seminarian when we read that as abruptly as he renounced his faith in Catholicism, Juan has relinquished his fervent views on art to idealize, equally quixotically, the worker (551). As soon as Juan and his new friend "el Libertario" plan to organize anarchist meetings on Sunday afternoons, Juan sees himself as the hero—in reality, the Don Quijote—of the imagined group: "En el cerebro del escultor comenzaba a germinar la idea de que había una misión social que cumplir, y que esta misión era él el encargado de llevarla a cabo" (551). [There began to germinate in the sculptor's brain the idea that there was a social mission to be accomplished, and that he was the one chosen to complete this mission.] At the first meeting, it is Juan who baptizes the group with the name "Aurora roja" (553).

For Manuel, life has become routine, uneventful, and devoid of the emotion that characterized the vicissitudes of his picaresque early years. He and Salvadora have come to a wordless understanding that they will discuss marriage only after they have begun to prosper economically, so that Manuel does not articulate even the sentimental experience of an engagement in passionate terms (551). In the evenings, he meditates as he pushes a wheelbarrow, delivering printed material to various destinations. Manuel muses that his early life was like a labyrinth of crossing alleys, and that now existence was more like the straight path he was walking down, with the wheelbarrow, and the constant preoccupation with getting ahead enough to settle down and assure himself a good living (552). Confirming the elimination of passion and adventure from his current experiences, the narrator refers to Manuel's forgetting Justa: "El recuerdo de la Justa [read: passionate love] había quedado ya borrado para siempre de su memoria" (552). [The memory of la Justa had been erased from his memory forever.]

Still, as a vestige of Manuel's muted spirit, Jesús continues to make appearances in the narrative. He lives in the attic of the house where Manuel and his family reside, and occasionally even puts in a day's work at the printing press (552). It is Jesús who invites Manuel to attend an anarchist meeting (552), and unexpectedly, Manuel finds the appeal in the group's "alegría de jugar a los revolucionarios" (554). [happiness at playing at being revolutionaries.] In their attraction to the anarchist "stories," the two brothers draw closer together, and it seems that even Manuel is captivated by the anarchist "idea," in spite of having "become bourgeois" (554).

At the same time, however, as we glimpse the possibility of the return of Manuel's romantic spirit as parallel to Juan's expansive nature, the text parodies Juan's idealistic anarchism with degraded doubles. These profanations of Juan's discourse seem to confirm the "good sense" Manuel demonstrates in rejecting such lyricism as Juan brings to the political conversation. The mocking phantasms make their appearance as soon as Juan associates anarchism with literature. Confirming his allegiance to quixotism, and bringing this idealism full circle to its literary origins, Juan articulates the importance of narrative to the anarchist endeavor. When the more individualist anarchists question the need to meet regularly, Juan argues this necessity by referring to the activities of reading and analysis of texts. He explains that the anarchists should meet to talk, to argue, to lend each other other books, and to spread propaganda (554). This preliminary activity would be the prelude to action, so that the communal reading would form the basis for individual feats. We also see the influence of the chosen texts in subsequent meetings, as the members' readings dictate their very language:

Cada domingo se iba haciendo el grupo más numeroso: se habían comprado folletos anarquistas de Kropotkin, de Reclus y Juan Grave, y pasaban de una mano a otra. Ya comenzaban a hablar todos con cierta terminología pedante, entre sociológica y revolucionaria, traducida del francés. (554)

[Every Sunday the group was growing: they had bought anarchist pamphlets by Kropotkin, Reclus, and Juan Grave, and were passing them around. All of them were beginning now to speak using a certain pedantic terminology, half sociological and half revolutionary, translated from the French.]

Juan's particular brand of anarchism, "entre humanitario y artístico" (between humanitarian and artistic), is utterly dependent on texts, primarily works of fiction: "No leía Juan casi nunca libros anarquistas; sus obras favoritas eran las de Tolstoi y las de Ibsen" (554). [Juan hardly ever read anarchist books. His favorite works were by Tolstoy and Ibsen.] As his physical condition worsens, Juan grows ever more extreme in his anarchist exaltation. His political passions are fed by a constant diet of reading and writing—he had acquired twenty to thirty anarchist books—and he defies doctor's orders and continues working for the sake of his "idea" (601). He renounces his career as a sculptor to finance the movement, using the money from the sale of Salvadora's bust and his other sculptures to pay for the promotion of anarchism (601). (I will return to Juan's basing his identity as an anarchist on profits from his artistic representation of la Salvadora.) As his strength declines further, his sole activity is producing (written) propaganda, and he keeps up a voluminous correspondence with anarchists in the provinces and in foreign countries (607).

Here in the text we see how this literary turn can be perverted by bad readers and unfortunate interpreters. The ultraindividualist anarchist Canuto appears at this point as a degraded version of Juan, and continues in this role through to the end of the novel, when he lies dying in a hospital as Juan also occupies a death bed. If Juan's anarchism is lofty and lyrical, the anarchism of Canuto is "un anarquismo de arroyo . . . la destrucción, sin idea filosófica fija (555). [a gutter anarchism—destruction without a definite philosophy.] Canuto also depends on vague memories of texts, recalling "una porción de frases extravagantes de Teobaldo Nieva, el autor de la *Química de la cuestión social"* [a selection of extravagant sentences from Teobaldo Nieva, author of *Chemistry of the Social Question*], and speaking of "cosas pasadas, de artículos de *El Condenado* y de *La Solidaridad,* y de las épocas en que él había tenido gran mano en las cuestiones de los anarquistas" (555). [things from the past, of articles from *The Condemned* and *Solidarity,* and of the age in which he had taken an important role in anarchist questions.] Canuto fancies himself a champion of the writings of the original anarchist leaders, and he rejects more recent tracts. Yet he ultimately reveals all of his claims to readings as farces designed to camouflage his ignorance: "Apenas estaba enterado de las corrientes modernas, y la fama de Kropotkin y Grave, cuyos libros no había leído, le parecía una usurpación cometida en contra de Fourier, Proudhon y otros. Es verdad que tampoco había leído las obras de éstos; pero sus nombres le sonaban" (555). [He knew barely anything about modern tendencies, and the fame of Kropotkin and Grave, whose books he hadn't read, seemed to him a usurpation of Fourier, Proudhon, and others. It is true that he hadn't read their work either, but their names sounded familiar to him.]

The French anarchist Caruty is another degraded double of Juan, and is also enamored of the literary uses of anarchism. Juan is a lyrical anarchist, and often when he speaks, Caruty echoes him. This strange character appears one Sunday at the meeting of the anarchist group "Aurora roja," and his description echoes the account of Juan's arrival at Manuel's house: "Se presentó dando apretones de mano y haciendo reverencias ceremoniosas a todos. Habló largamente de sus viajes de vagabundo. Él era el hombre de las carreteras; ninguno le entendía bien: parte porque hablaba incorrectamente el castellano, y parte porque sus teorías eran incomprensibles" (572). [He showed up shaking hands and making ceremonious bows to all of them. He spoke at length of his voyages as a vagabond. He was the traveling man; no one understood him: partly because he spoke Spanish incorrectly, and partly because his theories were incomprehensible.] In the same way that Juan first burst into Manuel's home, greeting and celebrating each family member, recounting his amazing adventures on his long road to Madrid, and expounding on artistic theories his listeners cannot understand, Caruty descends on the anarchists of "Aurora roja." He entertains the Spanish anarchists with French revolutionary songs, pretending to be the anarchist Ravachol insulting the bourgeoisie (573), and losing his own identity in the role he is playing, just as Juan refashions himself into an anarchist martyr. When four of the characters visit an executioner who demonstrates the action of the guillotine, Juan and Caruty react together— Juan, pale and in a cold sweat, and Caruty reciting poetry about the gallows (591). If Juan admires Sue, Hugo, Tolstoy, and Ibsen, Caruty speaks often of Verlaine (603). In addition, Caruty's discourse features a grotesque theatricality, which anticipates the more subtle, yet still manipulative histrionics Juan displays near the end of his life: "Caruty cantó una canción en *argot* campesino, en la que se llamaba ladrones y canallas a los propietarios. Después entonó la *Carmañola Anarquista:* 'Ça ira, ça ira, ça ira, tous les bourgeois á la lanterne; ça ira, ça ira, ça ira, tous les bourgeois on les prendra'; y saltaba el hombre, exagerando los movimientos de una manera grotesca" (606). [Caruty sung a song in rural slang, in which property owners were called thieves and riffraff. Then he intoned the *Anarchist Carmagnole:* "Ça ira, ça ira, ça ira, tous les bourgeois á la lanterne; ça ira, ça ira, ça ira, tous les bourgeois on les prendra"; and the man jumped around, exaggerating his movements in a grotesque way.]

This mirroring of Juan by the lunatic Caruty culminates with the anarchist gathering in the Barbieri theater. This meeting is a chaotic forum in which speakers with a range of abilities and ideas articulate plans and express opinions, with Juan speaking last. In his discourse, Juan equates anarchism with love and calls for all men to avail of reason in their struggle to shake off the yoke of authority (613). Affirming that people are naturally good and free, Juan uses a number of metaphors, contrasting clear with stagnant water, freed with caged birds, and new with decrepit boats, in order to captivate his audience with romanticized images of the unnecessary and unjust misery of the city's poor (613–14). Part of Juan's speech is as follows:

> "Sólo lo libre es hermoso," exclamó, y en una divagación pintoresca dijo, "El agua, que corre clara y espumosa en el torrente, es triste y negra en el pantano; al pájaro se le envidia en el aire y se le compadece en la jaula. Nada tan bello como un barco de vela, limpio y preparado para zarpar. Es pez en su casco y pájaro en su arboladura; tiene velas blancas, que parecen alas; un bauprés, que parece un pico; tiene una aleta larga, que se llama quilla, y una aleta caudal, que es el timón. Es una gaviota que navega, marcha y se le mira con envidia como a un amigo que se va. En cambio, ¡qué triste el barco viejo y desarbolado que ya no puede salir del puerto! Y es que la vejez también es una cadena." (613–14)

> ["Only that which is free is beautiful," he exclaimed, and in a picturesque digression he said, "Water, which runs clear and foamy in the torrent, is sad and black in the bog. The bird is envied when it's on the wing, and pitied when it's in the cage. There is nothing more beautiful than a ship, clean and ready to set sail. It is a fish in its hull, and a bird in its masts and spars. It has white sails that look like wings, a bowsprit that seems like a beak; it has a long fin called a keel, and a tail fin, which is the rudder. It is a seagull that sails, progresses and is looked at with envy as if at a departing friend. On the other hand, how sad is an old, broken-down boat that can no longer set sail! And really, old age is just another sort of chain."]

The narrator explains that the spellbound audience does not consider the possibility or impossibility of Juan's ideas, as all hearts beat in unison (614). Nevertheless, Caruty interrupts Juan's speech, profaning his elevated political ideas and associating them with poetic fantasy by shouting "¡Viva la anarquía! ¡Viva la literatura!" (614). [Long live anarchy! Long live literature!]

In response to Caruty's exclamations, Juan simply waves to him, leaves the platform, and the meeting soon adjourns (614).The audience is unsettled by Caruty's unwitting suggestion, and the people in attendance find themselves emotionally stimulated, but unsure of the boundary between fantasy and reality. They rise to their feet "as if awakened from a dream, and realizing its beauty" ("como despertado de un sueño y dándose cuenta de su belleza"), applaud furiously (614). The novel's narrator, however, is less confused about the significance of Juan's message, and explains that Caruty struts around excitedly, having arrived (although perhaps without understanding) at the heart of Juan's speech with his linking of anarchism and literature (614). Manuel asks whether Caruty meant to say that anarchism is just a question of literature. Juan dismisses the question, but Manuel himself is sure there is a connection. He muses to himself, sensing a relationship between the two terms, but is unable to determine exactly what the link is (615).[15]

Unsettled by anarchism's impracticality, Manuel remains aloof, doubting the attainability of anarchist visions of utopia (559). Even though he continues to attend the meetings, Manuel maintains his independence, his freedom from seduction by the anarchist idea. He works steadily at his press, and the narrator again compares his activity to following a straight path: "Comenzaba a encarrilarse la imprenta" (560). [The printing press was starting on the right track.] Thus, what Manuel has done, even in his ostensibly will-less state, is to negotiate his emancipation from the tyranny of quixotic narrative. He has achieved the model of success presented by Roberto, who dreamed of affluence but then took practical steps to attain his goal. In *Aurora roja,* Manuel even resists Jesús, who earlier tempted him away from Roberto's control. Jesús challenges Manuel to go out with him for a night of revelry, and they spend the evening in the company of a prostitute and a servant girl. Manuel appears to enjoy himself, even making a date with the maid, but then he returns to the waiting Salvadora and heads to work the next day, passing by Jesús, who lies drunk in the street (564–65). Manuel agrees to see the girl at her sister's house the following Sunday, accepts the address she gives him, kisses her good-bye, and even tries to embrace her, but oddly, the text gives no further information about his relationship with the maid or any subsequent meetings (564). It appears that we are to assume that Manuel either did not visit her at the appointed time, or that he did, but that nothing of consequence occurred. Manuel now resists relatively easily the appeal of dissolute activity represented by Jesús.

Accordingly, when Roberto articulates to Manuel the enlightened despotism he practices with him, Manuel does not question his mentor. Roberto explains to Manuel that he himself experienced a period of rebellion while in school, which manifested itself as an insistence on independent, critical reading. He tried to understand what he was reading, and to extract the meaning of things, but his professors accused him of laziness because he didn't memorize his lessons instead, and he protested in fury (565). The lesson that Roberto took from this experience is that whereas he might remain an anarchist "on the inside," it would behoove him to appear conformist. However, Roberto's ostensible conformism and conservativeness are merely vehicles for the attainment of power, and he fights to dominate (566). He believes that it is necessary to struggle, and that there will always be social inequality, in the sense that in society, one is either a creditor or a debtor (566). With this subtle reference to Manuel's debt and consequent subordination to him—we recall that Roberto has furnished the money that allowed Manuel to become a property owner—Roberto concludes the interview with his theory that for all southerners ("meridionales"), and for all half-African Mediterraneans ("mediterráneos medio africanos"), a strong dictatorship would be the best form of government, in order to tame excessive appetites and compensate for what society lacks in organization (566). Clearly, this political theory has relevance for Roberto's relationship with Manuel, who, like the wayward society Roberto describes, has gradually come into the sphere of the dictator's dominion. Roberto agrees when Manuel refers to his political system as despotism, but specifies that his ideal government would be enlightened and progressive despotism, which at this time he believes would be good for Spain—and by implication, for Manuel (567).

Roberto, then, is one of the characters who decides Manuel's fate for him. In the next chapter, Manuel concedes to others even more control over his life, just as he has submitted to Roberto. He hires a foreman for his press, Pepe Morales, and defers to this man in both business and political questions. Morales is a socialist, and Manuel often witnesses his debates with the anarchists, observing passively as his surrogate argues with the anarchists whom he used to confront himself (595–97). Also, Manuel dutifully follows his employee's orders that he find a bookbinder to set up shop next to the press, so that his business might prosper (594). Manuel also lacks initiative with Salvadora and allows his relationship with her to stagnate, making resolutions at night and abandoning them in the light of day, as the details of daily life got in his way and prevented him from advancing (569).

Although the extinguishing of Manuel's spirit makes him seem less human, his apathy coincides with a skepticism that protects him from being seduced by the anarchist's impossible dream. Manuel appears to reach new lows in his confidence in the anarchist idea when he is disturbed by the Aurora roja club members' glorification of the violent acts committed in the name of their program: "Manuel se sentía inquieto, profundamente disgustado en aquel ambiente" (578). [Manuel felt agitated and deeply disappointed in that environment.] Although he finds himself entranced by various histories of the French Revolution, Manuel is careful not to apply his readings to his daily life. When his foreman Morales argues for social discipline, Roberto remembers the French hero Danton, but holds his tongue because he now believes that procedures as quixotic as Danton's have no place in practical life: "Esto de la disciplina hacía torcer el gesto a Manuel; le parecía mejor aquella frase dantoniana: '¡Audacia! ¡Audacia! ¡Audacia!'; pero no decía nada, porque era burgués" (599). [This stuff about discipline was unpleasant to Manuel. He preferred that Dantonian expression: "Audacity! Audacity! Audacity!" But he said nothing, because he was a bourgeois.] Still later, Manuel listens to the anarchists argue about truth and fiction while punctuating their accounts of historical events with songs and verses. Manuel observes to himself, distinguishing his own good sense from the anarchists' insanity, that all of them were somewhat crazy, and he would have to separate from them (606).

It is at this point that Manuel attends the anarchist meeting at the Barbieri theater, hears Caruty equate anarchism with literature, and becomes convinced that there is in fact an inherent connection between the two. Manuel now begins to reap significant "rewards" for his commitment to rationality and to Roberto, as he links the anarchism that alternately attracts and repels him with the quixotic literature he definitively rejects. These benefits, because they come from Roberto, also speak to Manuel's continuing subordination to the "friend" who has always reminded Manuel of his inferiority and dependence, even while accommodating him with favors. While Juan deceives himself with plans to heroically redeem a group of brutal homeless people (617–19), and allows his desperation for definitive action to blind him to the suspicious conduct of police spies (625–31), Manuel receives from Roberto the full ownership of the printing press, as well as orders to marry Salvadora (636). Juan, in contrast, has his books confiscated by the police, losing his library as does Don Quijote (629).

Juan's pathetic vision for the homeless people in a park he visits is as follows:

> ¡Qué hermoso—pensaba Juan—sería sacar a estos hombres de las tinieblas de la brutalidad en que se encuentran y llevarlos a una esfera más alta, más pura! Seguramente, en el fondo de sus almas hay una bondad dormida; en medio del fango de sus maldades hay el oro escondido que nadie se ha tomado el trabajo de descubrir. Yo trataré de hacerlo . . . (617).

> [How beautiful, thought Juan. It would be so easy to rescue these men from the darkness of their brutality and to raise them to a higher, purer realm! Surely in the depths of their souls goodness sleeps. In the midst of the mire of their evilness there was a hidden gold that no one had taken the trouble to discover. I will try to do it.]

This chapter ends with the sentence: "El oro de las almas humanas no salía a la superficie" (619). [The gold in these human souls was not rising to the surface.]

Before bestowing on Manuel his "gifts," Roberto assures himself once again of his friend's loyalty, challenging and belittling him by saying to Salvadora, with respect to Manuel: "¿Ve usted? . . . Este chico no tiene soberbia. Luego es un romántico, se deja arrastrar por ideas generosas; quiere reformar la sociedad . . ." [Do you see? This boy has no pride. Then, of course, he's a romantic. He lets himself be carried away by ideas of generosity, and he wants to reform society.] To Manuel himself, Roberto says, "Eres un sentimental infecto" (632). [You are a disgusting sentimentalist.] Of course, Manuel is anything but a romantic, and could not possibly motivate himself to work for social reform. He protests Roberto's accusations, but still he is again forced to listen to his mentor's defense of enlightened despotism, to his exhortations to action, and finally to his lamentation that Manuel is lost because he does not feel "el egoísmo fiero" (savage egoism), all before Manuel can be commended for his obedience through the gifts of the printing press and Salvadora (635).

It would seem that Manuel's conversion to realism is now complete, as Juan's romantic visions of heroism fail, and he bids a final farewell to his anarchist comrades from his death bed. For some time before these final events, Juan's sole thought has been for the day of the coronation of the new king, and he becomes obsessed with taking some type of action during this public event. An agent provocateur deceives the anarchists with stories of a massive, international anarchist conspiracy organized to carry out the assassination of King Alfonso XIII on the day of his coronation in 1902. Although the plot was fabricated to catch anarchist subversives, Juan persists in dreaming of an imminent violent revolution, even one that will include his own death. He sees himself leading the charge in a dramatically staged event, and is willing to end his own life for the cause: "Juan estaba febril, deseando que llegar el momento; sus nervios, en constante tensión, no le dejaban reposar un instante. Estaba dispuesto a sacrificarse por la causa" (637). [Juan was feverish, wishing the moment would arrive. His nerves, in constant tension, would not let him rest even for a moment. He was ready to sacrifice himself for the cause.] Clearly, Juan sees himself as the new epic hero, and holds fast to his literary quixotism: "Esto le perdía, veía el acontecimiento en artista. Veía la brillante comitiva de reyes, de príncipes, de embajadores, de grandes damas, pasando por en medio de las bayonetas, y se veía a él avanzando, deteniendo la comitiva con el grito estridente de ¡Viva la Anarquía!" (637). [This was what did him in. He saw the event with an artist's eyes. He saw the spectacular procession of kings and queens, princes, ambassadors, and great ladies passing between the bayonets, and he saw himself advancing, stopping the procession with the strident cry of "Long live anarchy!"]

Just as Gabriel Araceli recognizes the significance of quixotic heroism in the War for Independence, here the utterly subdued Manuel Alcázar mourns the loss of an impossible fiction. On the surface, Manuel reveals the vestiges of his passions as jealousy of the intense feelings between Juan and Salvadora. He returns to this obsession throughout the novel (547, 601), even implicitly comparing Salvadora's passionate protection of her brother-in-law from an unwelcome priest (641–42) with the anticlimax of his own marriage: "No se varió nada en la casa con el matrimonio, que se celebró sin ceremonias de ninguna clase" (636). [Nothing changed in their home when they married in a ceremony with no fuss whatsoever.]

After Juan dies, however, Manuel discovers the full import of what he has given up and what Juan has retained despite his death. He marvels at the impact Juan has had on his life: "¡Quién le había de decir que aquel hermano a quien no había visto en tanto tiempo iba a dejar una huella tan profunda en su vida!" (643). [Who would have guessed that the brother he hadn't seen in so long would leave such a profound mark on his life!] He wonders if there is anything left in life "digna de ser deseada" (worthy of being desired), and directs a thought tinged with resentment toward Juan's corpse: "¡Te has ido al otro mundo con un hermoso sueño . . . con una bella ilusión!" (643). [You have departed for the other world with a beautiful dream, with a lovely illusion.] That night, after Salvadora orders him to bed, he dreams of the other anarchists, perhaps identifying with them himself as they denigrate the same ideals they once championed (643–44). When "la Filipina," a prostitute from Juan's seemingly fruitless days in the park with the homeless, comes to weep over Juan's body, Manuel is called by this contemporary Mary Magdalene to consider his lost brother as the third Christ figure of the text. As María Embeita argues, "Juan es el Cristo de la conciencia moderna, el consolador de los miserables y abandonados, el exponente de un anarquismo incorrupto, que aboga por la piedad y la protección de los débiles; es también el cruzado de los derechos de los desamparados; su paralelismo con la figura del Cristo de Renan es evidente" ("La lucha por la vida" 889–90) [Juan is the Christ of the modern conscience, the consoler of the destitute and abandoned, the promoter of an unadulterated anarchism, who argues for compassion and the protection of the weak. He is also the crusader for the rights of the neglected ones. His parallelism with the Christ of Renan is obvious.] After el Libertario's eulogy for Juan, in which he praises his fallen comrade's hope and love, the novel ends and the curtain falls on this final example of renounced romantic quixotism with the words "Había oscurecido" (Night had fallen) (645).

In preparation for my reading of *La Regenta,* I wish to look again at Manuel's elimination of his romantic self. Evidently, giving up literary and political idealism saddens Manuel, and yet for some compelling reason, he has no alternative. I believe that the key to Manuel's choice can be found in the close relationship of Juan and Salvadora. Although Manuel's obsession with their intimacy seems at first glance to be conventional jealousy felt by an insecure husband about the friendship between his dynamic brother and his own wife, the text does not sexualize in any way the bond between Juan and Salvadora. In fact, Juan is presented as lacking erotic interest in women, in a portrayal reinforced by his associations with Christ. For example, in the novel's prologue, when the guards he meets on his journey insinuate that he is leaving the priesthood because of an interest in women, Juan does not reply (517). At the same time, Juan has nothing that appears to be a homosexual relationship. I suggest, then, that we reexamine the linkage of Juan and Salvadora to make the suggestion that Juan is "feminized" by the text, largely because of his similarity to Salvadora. If Juan is a Christ figure, Salvadora is the savior who rescues him. He promotes himself by sculpting her bust, and they both are "siblings" of sorts to Manuel (recall Manuel's description of Salvadora as sisterly). In addition to these commonalities with a specific female character, Juan has stereotypically female traits: he is physically weak because of his illness, he is creative, artistic, social, but most of all, romantic (recall that the narrator refers to Salvadora as romantic as well [526]).

Since Juan—the embodiment of the quixotic mentality—is associated with the feminine, we might hazard a guess that Manuel is obligated to renounce those aspects of his nature that parallel Juan for fear of emasculation. In other words, he must reject romanticism, or he risks becoming as much a woman as his brother. Nevertheless, the text confirms that this is not an easy decision. Just as does Gabriel, but here perhaps to an even greater degree, Manuel can only escape his romantic self by erasing himself. The choice reveals itself to be: commit to realism and practicality at the expense of subjectivity, or, preserve the heroic, romantic self, and run the risk of effeminacy. In *La Regenta* this dilemma reaches its culmination.

This last novel we will examine—published roughly a decade after Galdós's First Series of *Episodios*—carries us to the later part of the nineteenth century and the beginning of the Bourbon Restoration. In *La Regenta,* protagonists Ana de Ozores, Fermín de Pas, and Álvaro Mesía all recall Gabriel Araceli and Manuel Alcázar, particularly in their divided allegiance to what they conceive of as poetry and prose. Clarín's three protagonists are anxious about the pull of romanticism at play in their own instincts for reading, and this insecurity drives them to compose new narratives. For this reason, *La Regenta* is a competition among three would-be authors, in a dynamic reminiscent of Gabriel's narratorial jousting with Andrés Marijuán, and Manuel's romantic resistance to Roberto's realism. I turn now to Clarín's novel, to explore the idealism that haunts the protagonists and motivates them to author stories.

5

La Regenta and the Hegemony
of the Female Author

In *La Regenta* (1884–85), Leopoldo Alas explores hypocrisy in the provinces during the Restoration period. The primary "story" of the novel is the struggle of the female protagonist, Ana de Ozores, to resist her would-be seducer, the popular Álvaro Mesía, while negotiating a satisfactory relationship with her confessor Fermín de Pas, who falls in love with her. In the description of these complex dynamics, the novel teems with references to the characters' previous readings, which structure the protagonists' conceptions of their relationships with each other. In general, Clarín's central characters are aware of the pitfalls of quixotism, and at least attempt to resist the idealism they associate with a "poetic" mentality and with immaturity.

At the same time, just as Gabriel Araceli and Manuel Alcázar are drawn to romanticism, Ana craves the excitement she experiences alternately as religious fervor and as worldly passion, while Fermín longs for romantic love with Ana, and Álvaro is affected in spite of himself by poetry and melodrama. Nevertheless, each character is aware that this romantic heritage is out of date—inappropriate for the "prosaic" world of the late nineteenth century. Much of the novel focuses on the characters' anxieties about their lingering "poetic" conceptions, and we must acknowledge these internal conflicts if we wish to understand the relationships they develop with each other. Recognizing that their idealistic habits of thought do not fit (Restoration) life, Fermín, Álvaro, and Ana all try to diffuse their responsibility for romanticism by projecting it onto a reader. The characters believe that if they can position themselves as authors with a reader dependent on them, even if what they produce are romantic texts, the authorial role accords them superiority and thus protection. In other words, because of the degree of control they enjoy over their narratives, as authors they are less vulnerable to a mentality they find problematic. Like Gabriel and Manuel, Clarín's protagonists raise in this way the issues of reading and authorship, with Ana as catalyst for a three-way textual contest that ultimately has grave consequences. We note that over the course of the novel, although she acknowledges the dangers inherent in such an attitude, Ana is more receptive to lingering romanticism than are her male counterparts. In the end I will argue that Ana's bravery in engaging quixotically idealistic discourse gives her an advantage, and enables her to display greater authorial power than her competitors, Fermín and Álvaro.

Ana accepts, and indeed celebrates the idea of living the forbidden narratives, provided she has a companion with whom to enact her idealistic fantasies, and as long as she is the primary author. Fermín exhibits a similar attitude, and agrees to play a role in the fantasies he shares with Ana, but his needs for authorial control appear greater than Ana's, so he is threatened by Ana's independence. In contrast, Ana welcomes Fermín's collaboration in her design of their shared "stories," requiring only that in time he defer to her. Álvaro demonstrates the strongest drive to separate from romanticism, and wishes to project entirely onto Ana the "poetic" attitudes and behaviors that threaten him. Álvaro would like to believe himself utterly impervious to the love story in which he participates, and imagines that, solely for the purpose of seducing her, he allows Ana to create for him a romantic image to which he has no allegiance whatsoever. Given that the shared goal of all three is to make others "read" what they are writing, we see in *La Regenta,* just as we did in the *Episodios* (and even in *La lucha por la vida*), a preoccupation with the unruly reader. Each of the three characters selects an ideal reader for the texts he or she composes, but that target reader is also competing to be an author, so he or she does not accept the alien reading with docility.

A brief glance at a traditional reading of this novel will allow us to appreciate the contrast between that and what I propose here. Critics have identified a see-saw motion in *La Regenta* at least since the time of Galdós's 1901 prologue to the second edition of the novel. In Galdós's words, "El lector verá cómo se desarrolla el proceso psicológico y por qué caminos corre a su desenlace el problema de doña Ana de Ozores, el cual no es otro que discernir si debe perderse por lo clerical o por lo laico" (89). [The reader will see how the psychological process develops and along which paths the unfolding of Ana de Ozores' problem takes us, a problem which is nothing other than deciding whether she will lose her virtue with a cleric or a layman.][1] The two options for Ana's perdition are represented by the two potential "suitors," one being Ana's confessor the magistral (canon theologian) Fermín de Pas, and the other the small-town Don Juan, Álvaro Mesía. I would add a third pole—Ana herself—to the traditional dichotomy. If we imagine that what is at stake here is not simply the control of Ana's will and sexual favors, but rather the identity of the text's primary internal author, we see that the see-saw, dialectic, or *turno pacífico*–type movement should be recharacterized as a battle among three contenders, in that Ana must be accorded as much agency as the other two competitors. Galdós describes the narrative as Ana's oscillation between two poles, and I will return to the significance of his reading. I would also like to study how Fermín de Pas and Álvaro Mesía struggle for control over their actions and thoughts, rather than asserting themselves automatically. I believe that Fermín's and Álvaro's dilemmas in the pursuit of authorship relate to Galdós's reading, as I will explain.

I begin my examination of Clarín's novel by discussing the ways in which the history or constitution of each protagonist predisposes him or her to resist idealism. Indeed, poetic readings influence Fermín and Álvaro just as much as they do Ana. All three protagonists uneasily recognize that as readers, they are still attracted to or dependent on romantic, melodramatic narratives, and they perceive this unsettling tie to "poetry" as a weakness.[2] As we will see after this initial discussion of the protagonists' anxieties, this "debility" then goads each character into demonstrating strength by flexing his or her authorial muscles. But first we must explore the preliminary phase of this process, in which vestiges of romanticism plague each character.

ANA

In Ana's case, she is traumatized at an early age because of her romantic leanings, although others' scorn in fact fortifies her spirit and increases her desire to compose poetry of some type. She spends much of her childhood in solitude, and while she is left alone, Ana develops her creative capacities, focusing her energies on the production of a poem that she carries with her into the present, not in written form, but as a phantasm in her imagination (I, 191). At first, Ana manufactures her own story from her surroundings, which often include elements of nature: "Volvía de sus correrías por el campo, como la abeja con el jugo de las flores, con material para su poema" (I, 190–91). [She returned from her trips to the countryside with material for her poem, like the bee with nectar from flowers.] These first poetic impulses, then, are associated with loneliness and parental absence, and Ana's composition fills the void of her unsatisfied emotional needs. Eventually, Ana learns to read, and establishes a pattern that will remain in effect throughout the novel. The narrator explains her technique for appropriating narratives in the following way: "Al fin supo leer. Pero los libros que llegaban a sus manos, no le hablaban de aquellas cosas con que soñaba. No importaba; ella les haría hablar de lo que quisiese" (I, 191). [Finally she learned to read. But the books she had access to did not speak to her of the things she dreamed about. That didn't matter though—she would make them speak about whatever she wished.] Thus, Ana begins early in her life to partially shield herself by reading texts that are not her own, and then asserting herself as an author by violating the alien text.

This behavior leads to the most serious trauma of Ana's childhood, when she adopts the model of the epic poem. She suffers public ridicule when her governess doña Camila mischaracterizes as indecent Ana's innocent childhood escapade with a male playmate, Germán, whom Ana has selected to be the hero of the epic she is composing for herself (I, 192). We note that while Ana is embarrassed by her governess for her extravagant imagination and allegedly sinful behavior, she also manifests at this point a strong drive to author texts in spite of obstacles. She continues to seek the cover of accepted readings, turning particularly to religious works. As an extension of her childhood reformulation of dry books when no more exciting readings were available, Ana later develops a technique for selective reading of canonical texts, which amounts to a reauthoring of these works to suit her agenda.[3] For example, she discovers Saint Augustine's *Confessions* in her father's library, and celebrates her find, but alters the text so that it conforms to her prereading. She reads the parts of the text she considers relevant to her, and skips the final chapters (I, 204). When she becomes acquainted with the poetry of San Juan de la Cruz and Fray Luis de León, she uses these texts as inspiration for her own creativity and authorship.

However, just as she was punished for creating her own epic poem, she also suffers when she asserts herself as an independent author of texts on this second model, even though her poetry is religious. Finding the reading of religious verse insufficient, she fabricates her own romantic, spiritual, and sensual poetry, but then experiences a sense of foreboding associated with her poetic composition, as represented by the presence of an ominous dark bird (I, 210). As she recovers from the subsequent protracted illness we could conceive of as punishment for her authorial audacity, Ana recalls for us a concern articulated by Gabriel Araceli, when she suspects that her creative impulses have some connection to selfishness (I, 221). Again, as in the *Episodios,* initiation into authorship is accompanied by feelings of guilt, in that the act of writing implies an excessive degree of self-focus. In Ana's case, there is a direct correlation between the act of composing poetry and her resulting anxiety and suffering.

Ana's aunts take her in and she moves to Vetusta, the primary setting of *La Regenta.* This unfriendly city holds in store another crushing blow for her romantic self-expression, as the public scandal of Ana's literary pursuits coincides with her difficulties in finding a husband. Vetustan society is scandalized when Anuncia, Ana's aunt, discovers the notebook in which

Ana records her poetry, and all condemn her as a "literata" [woman of letters (with a negative connotation)], and a "Jorge Sandio" [George Sand] (I, 232–33). Eventually, with her idealistic hopes dashed, she accepts the best match available, the "Regente" whose position as magistrate leads to Ana's being known as "la Regenta." With this choice, Ana reveals the will-to-realism we have seen so often in Gabriel's struggles. Manuel Alcázar also gravitates toward realism, but with the difference that this movement is allied specifically with the eclipse of his will (despite the irony of Roberto Hasting's challenges to him to acquire a will). As we have seen, in *La lucha por la vida*, the escape from romanticism comes at the cost of even more of the authorial self than was renounced by Gabriel Araceli.

Ana now appears to abandon the poetry that led her into the temptation to be an author, and she muses as she departs for her honeymoon, "¿Para qué engañarse a sí misma? No estaba en Vetusta, no podía estar en aquel pobre rincón la realidad del sueño, el héroe del poema, que primero se había llamado Germán, después San Agustín, obispo de Hipona, después Chateaubriand y después con cien nombres, todo grandeza, esplendor, dulzura delicada, rara y escogida" (I, 248). [Why should she deceive herself? The hero of her poem—who was first called Germán, then St. Augustine of Hippo, then Chateaubriand, and afterwards by a hundred names, who was all greatness, splendor, and delicate sweetness, rare and select—was not in Vetusta, nor could the dream-made-reality possibly be found in that pathetic place.][4]

Thus, Ana seems to have renounced her poetic ideals. Mocking her earlier dreams and reinforcing the "good sense" of her rejection of poetry, immediately at her side is the man who is now her husband, Víctor Quintanar, a parody of the Vetustan *literata*. Víctor is engrossed in his reading of Calderón's honor plays, and is absorbed by questions of marital fidelity and just punishment for adultery, even as he ignores his new bride (I, 248). In marrying Víctor, Ana has deliberately sought a reminder of the inanity of allowing poetry to contaminate life. Nevertheless, as we see in the passage cited above, Ana reveals that she still feels superior to the Vetustans that surround her. In her parting observations on her companions' inferiority, Ana gives evidence of both the pride that compels her to continue composing poetry, and the "selfishness" Gabriel thought characteristic of any author.

When she has lived several years as a married woman in the provincial environment of Vetusta, Ana confirms that being ridiculed or even just imagining that others disrespect her serves as impetus for her prideful impulses, many of which take the form of defiant, though indirect, authorship. The best example of Ana's contradictory attitude—first blaming herself for indulging in poetic excesses, then defending herself by condemning others—comes at the beginning of the second volume of *La*

Regenta. Ironically, one writer who worships Ana also implicitly mocks her idealism by writing romantic poetry. This is the untalented Trifón Cármenes, whose work Ana reads in Vetusta's newspaper *El Lábaro.* Cármenes's work disgusts and embarrasses Ana as she remembers her own days as a "literata": "¿Si habría sido ella una *Trifona?* . . . ¿Si en el fondo no sería ella más que una literata vergonzante, a pesar de no escribir ya versos ni prosa? ¡Sí, sí, le había quedado el espíritu falso, torcido de la poetisa, que por algo el buen sentido vulgar desprecia!" (II, 12). [What if she had been a Trifona? What if at heart she was nothing more than a shameful literary woman, despite the fact that she no longer wrote poetry or prose? Yes, yes, it remained with her! That false, twisted spirit of the poetess that common good sense disdained with good reason!] However, although Ana might renounce this poetic spirit that has done nothing but cause problems for her, the part of her that insists on her superiority to her surroundings always emerges, and she inevitably ends up blaming Vetusta for her problems (II, 13). The creative impulses Ana channels through her love affairs and religious quest—primarily a feature of the second volume of the novel—are the result of her embarrassment, and represent her subsequent, reactive insistence on her subjectivity in the form of authorship.

I believe that these passages establish a basic characterization of Ana. She is at once ashamed of her poetic leanings, and determined to stand out from the crowd. This need to be different—to affirm her selfhood—then issues forth as an authorial drive, as Ana attempts to distinguish herself by producing more of the same sorts of texts that caused the Vetustans to be suspicious of her. She continues to be drawn to idealistic, romantic narratives, and adapts, or even invents, these stories for herself and her alternating partners, Fermín and Álvaro. Whereas each takes his turn(s) as her companion, Ana's desire to write urges her not only into further intimacy with them, but into battles for authorship with the two men.

FERMÍN

The text's presentation of Fermín is similar to that of Ana, in the sense that we learn about his early intellectual development. As a grown man, Fermín vaguely remembers the goals of his adolescence as "recuerdos de un poema heroico leído en la juventud con entusiasmo" [memories of a heroic poem read with enthusiasm during his youth] (I, 106), in an articulation that recalls Ana's attraction to the epic genre. Fermín associates these impossible dreams with poetry and pictorial arts, sees them fade, and speculates that such poetic desires are unattainable in the present (I, 106). As a substitute, Fermín converts his desire for promotion—his poetically irrational adolescent fantasy—into a drive for more material ends and an ambition for power in the small world of Vetusta (I, 105–6). In this way, he ostensibly renounces the discourses he associates with poetic idealism. As we will see, however, Fermín is not averse to recovering such narratives and images for the purpose of recruiting Ana for his designs. Moreover, and perhaps more important, Fermín himself exhibits a continuing sensibility to the seductions of poetry.

To cite just one example of Fermín's persistently poetic thinking, when he learns that Ana has come without warning to confess with him for the first time, he imagines a romantic motive for her actions without any specific information on which to ground his interpretation: "¿Era que con una delicadeza y un buen gusto cristiano y no común en las damas de Vetusta, quería confundirse con la plebe, confesar de incógnito, ser una de tantas?" (I, 151–52). [Was it that with a tactfulness and a Christian good taste that was not common in Vetustan ladies, she wanted to mix with the commoners, to confess incognito, to be just one among many women?] This hypothesis, which he invents out of whole cloth for his own enjoyment, pleases the Magistral, who finds it "un rasgo poético y sinceramente religioso" [a poetic, sincerely romantic act] (I, 152). In the technique Clarín uses to ascribe thoughts to specific characters, the following commentaries appear in quotation marks. The statements represent Fermín's feelings about Ana in comparison to the other Vetustan women, and himself in opposition to the clerics he sees as undistinguished. For Fermín, Vetustan women are generally scandalous, and profane the confessional with indiscreet confidences, and inferior priests contribute to the degradation by feeling flattered by such imprudent attentions (I, 152). He, on the other hand, is different, and expects from his budding relationship with Ana something out of the ordinary: "Esperaba algo nuevo, algo más delicado, algo selecto" (I, 152). [He hoped for something new, something more exquisite, something superior.]

In these passages, Fermín indicates to *La Regenta*'s readers that his break with poetic idealism is not as definitive as he has earlier argued. In fact, he takes quite easily to idealistic discourse ("algo nuevo, algo más delicado, algo selecto" [something new, something more exquisite, something superior.]), especially as it is coupled with visions of superiority for himself and for the woman who has recently won his favor. There is a parallel here with Ana's imagining (creating) of texts before reading them, or after reading only parts of them: Fermín the romantic writes the story of Ana before knowing her. Of note is the specific way he expresses his own and Ana's distinctiveness by contrasting her and himself with other characters—in Ana's case with the lascivious widow Obdulia and the chatty gadfly Visitación; in his own, with the officious and scorned Custodio. These distinctions become increasingly difficult to sustain as the text progresses, but despite his disillusionment, Fermín still resorts to poetry when he envisions himself and Ana as an elect pair. Fermín clings to a romantic conception of his relationship with Ana far into the novel. Eventually, he adds notes of Platonism to his dream of Ana: "No, no caería en la tentación de convertir aquella dulcísima amistad naciente, que tantas sensaciones nuevas y exquisitas le prometía, en vulgar escándalo de las pasiones bajas de que sus enemigos le habían acusado otras veces" (II, 21). [No, he would not fall into the temptation of turning that very sweet, newborn friendship, which promised him so many exquisite new sensations, into the vulgar scandal of dirty passions of which his enemies had earlier accused him.] Instead of material pleasures, Fermín imagines finding in Ana, "empleo digno de la gran actividad de su corazón, de su voluntad que se destruía ocupándose con asunto tan miserable como era aquella lucha con los vetustenses indómitos. Sí, lo que él quería era una afición poderosa, viva, ardiente, eficaz para vencer la ambición" (II, 22). [a worthy enterprise for the great energy of his heart, of his will, which ruined itself worrying about such paltry subjects as the struggles of the unruly Vetustans. Yes, what he wanted was a powerful, lively, burning, efficient affective impulse in order to defeat his ambition.] He expects to have with Ana "una pasión noble, ideal, que un alma grande sabría comprender, y que sólo un vetustense miserable, ruin y malicioso podía considerar pecaminosa" (II, 22). [a noble, ideal passion, which a great soul would be able to understand, and that only a wretched, despicable, malicious Vetustan could consider sinful.] These poetic dreams of companionship with Ana are the texts Fermín naturally produces, when, like Ana, he is inspired to authorial "selfishness" by the need to stand out from the hordes as author and protagonist of a beautiful story.

Indeed, even when his relationship with Ana is presented to him in pedestrian terms, Fermín imposes a romantic reading on the same material. Just before he begins his relationship with Ana, Fermín's friend don Cayetano, Ana's original confessor, informs Fermín that Víctor Quintanar cannot relate to his wife, and that it is up to Fermín to satisfy the unhappy lady. Cayetano incites Fermín with the following statement about Ana: "Y como no hemos de buscarle un amante para que desahogue con él—aquí volvió a reír don Cayetano—lo mejor será que ustedes se entiendan" (I, 398). [And since we can't just look for a lover for her to pour out her heart to—here Cayetano laughed again—the best thing would be for the two of you to come to an understanding.] Although by using such expressions Cayetano "profanes" from the start Fermín's contact with Ana, Fermín is quick to poeticize their interactions. Even after their first meeting, he persists in the same romantic characterization of the relationship that he imagined before beginning his work with Ana ("algo más delicado, algo selecto" ["something more exquisite, something superior"]), insisting that

Ana promise him something new and pure: "Sí, sí, era aquello algo nuevo, algo nuevo para su espíritu, cansado de vivir nada más para su ambición propia y para la codicia ajena, la de su madre" (I, 401). [Yes, yes, that was something new, something new for his spirit, which was tired of living only for his own and for his mother's ambition.]

As in this expression of resentment of his mother's control, part of Fermín's spirit rebels against the humiliating extinction of his youthful enthusiasm—the vivid dreams of his adolescence that were converted to gluttony in the form of an appetite for Vetusta. He expresses this rebellion by returning to literature, as when he recalls his days as a Jesuit, and remembers the old epic poem that guided his early life: "¿No era algo por el estilo lo que creía sentir desde la tarde anterior? ¿No eran las mismas fibras las que vibraban entonces, allá en las orillas del Bernesga, y las que ahora se movían como una música plácida para el alma? . . . Aunque todo ello sea una ilusión, un sueño, ¿por qué no soñar?" (I, 401). [Wasn't it something like that that he believed he had felt since the previous afternoon? Weren't these the same fibers of his being that had vibrated then, there on the banks of the Bernesga River, and that now were moving as if to a placid music played for his soul? . . Although it might all be an illusion—a dream—why not dream?] (The Bernesga is the river in León that passes by the building where Fermín studied with the Jesuits.) He is motivated by the same poetic fervor that affects Ana, and although at heart he is often embarrassed to be a romantic—just as is Ana—he refocuses this potential shame as the self-assertion of authorship, specifically of the texts with which he plans to conquer Ana.

We read another example of Fermín's deep-rooted appreciation for poetry in his assessment of the bishop's talents. Ashamed of his own corruption, Fermín feels inferior to the bishop, the kind-hearted simpleton don Fortunato Camoirán. Fortunato delivers sermons that demonstrate his passionate love for the Virgin Mary, but Fermín is more reserved. The Vetustans appreciate his formality, and say approvingly of Fermín, "No le gustaba sacar el Cristo" (I, 449). [He didn't like to make a spectacle of his faith.] In fact, the figure of Christ in human form is exactly what Fermín finds inaccessible, so that any time he has to recite the line "And the Word was made flesh," he sees in his mind's eye, instead of the child Jesus in the manger, the red letters of the Gospel of John, painted over wood in the middle of an altar: *Et Verbum caro factum est* (I, 450). From the basic images of Jesus that he replaces with texts, to the contemporary novels he reads, and his sermons based on rationality and utility (I, 450–51), Fermín is committed to the Word, and to being an author of texts that defy his romantic leanings. Nevertheless, he feels that he alone recognizes the superiority of the Bishop Fortunato's brand of religion, and that this religious discourse is poetic to its core: "Él era la única persona que sabía comprender todo el valor de Fortunato. ¡Qué poéticas, qué nobles, qué espirituales le parecían ahora la virtud del otro, su elocuencia, su culto romántico de la Virgen! Y las propias habilidades ¡qué ruines, qué prosaicas!" (I, 459–60). [He was the only person able to appreciate Fortunato's worth. How poetic, how novel, how spiritual, the other man's virtue, eloquence, and romantic worship of Mary seemed to Fermín. And his own abilities—how base and prosaic!] In other words, although he masks his conflicted feelings with condescension, Fermín not only appreciates the poetry of Fortunato's sermons, but also believes he is the sole Vetustan who does so.

In another instance of Fermín's essence being tied to poetic preconceptions, the Magistral models his relationship with Ana on Renan's tale of a Nordic friar and his German admirer. For Fermín, these two chaste lovers are "dos almas que se amaban en Jesús" [two souls who loved each other in Jesus], and their love is "la verdad severa, noble, inmaculada del amor místico; amor anafrodítico, incapaz de mancharse con el lodo de la carne ni en sueños" (I, 409). [the strict, noble, immaculate truth of mystical love; chaste love, incapable of soiling itself with the dirt of the flesh, even in dreams.] Inevitably, his idealistic conception of this friendship shocks Fermín, and brings him back to realism—the undeniable reality of his own physical strength (he is studying himself, naked from the waist up, in a mirror), now called into action to repress his poetic drive.

Fermín's internal conflict eventually compels him to write his way out of his feelings of insecurity. In several instances in the novel, Fermín experiences a sense of insecurity due to his poetic leanings, then has a prideful reaction to this perception of his own weakness, and finally, expresses this forced arrogance by writing. For example, he turns defensively to textual composition in the same passages of La Regenta in which he recalls Ana's first confession with him. As he remembers their meeting, Fermín is at work at the writing of the one "official" text we see him produce: a defense of papal infallibility. He is attracted to the power and energy implicit in the doctrine, imagining papal infallibility as "el valor, la voluntad enérgica, la afirmación del imperio, una aventura teológica, parecida a las de Alejandro Magno en la guerra y las de Colón en el mar" (I, 402–3). [the valor, energetic will, the affirmation of the empire, a theological adventure similar to those of Alexander the Great in war and Columbus at sea.] Nevertheless, the novel makes it plain that Fermín is frustrated and distracted during the first period in which he attempts to work. Even with these ambitious ideas inspiring him, he does not feel satisfied with himself until he has dispensed with the distraction of his comely servant Teresa, and has engaged in the act of writing. After doing so, his outlook is more positive:

Miró al cielo. Estaba alegre, sin nubes. El buen tiempo en Vetusta vale más por lo raro. El Magistral se frotó las manos suavemente. Estaba contento. Mientras había escrito, casi por máquina, una defensa, *calamo currente,* de la Infalibilidad, con destino a cierta Revista Católica que leían católicos convencidos nada más, había estado madurando su plan de ataque. (I, 408)

[He looked at the sky. He was happy, with no worries. Good weather in Vetusta was all the more valuable because it was rare. The Magistral rubbed his hands together gently. He was happy. While he had written almost mechanically a defense, *calamo currente,* of Infallibility, destined for a certain Catholic Review read only by committed Catholics, he had been developing his plan of attack.]

Although *La Regenta*'s narrator is dismissive of Fermín as an author, here the quality of his writing is not as important as the desire his text embodies. As is evident from the cited passage, the potency he feels, which he acquires with writing, accompanies his fabrication of a "plan of attack" with respect to Ana.

Thus, this evidence points to a pattern. Fermín recognizes his unwelcome romanticism, becomes frustrated with his tendencies, and then reaffirms his power and control by authoring a text. He protects himself from associations with weakness by composing narratives for his new audience, Ana. If the first volume of the novel sets up the background of romantic anxiety that motivates Fermín's textual battle for Ana, the final chapter of Part I provides fitting closure for this initial stage. At home in his room, Fermín stares out the window at the moon, longing for romantic love just as Ana did several chapters earlier. Fermín guiltily remembers his youthful passions for Jesuit heroism, and associates such fantasies with what he feels while studying the moon: "Para él no era nuevo, no, sentir oprimido el pecho al mirar la luna, al escuchar los silencios de la noche; así había él empezado a ponerse enfermucho, allá en los Jesuitas: pero entonces sus anhelos eran vagos, y ahora no; ahora anhelaba . . . tampoco se atrevía a pedir claridad y precisión a sus deseos . . ." (I, 560). [It was not a new thing for him—no—to feel his chest tighten as he looked at the moon, as he listened to the silences of the night; this was how he had turned sickly, there with the Jesuits. But back then his desires were vague, and now they weren't; now he desired . . . but he didn't dare to demand clarity and precision of his desires.] He thinks of Ana, and remembers his readings, but still he resists poeticizing his feelings for her: "En los libros aquello se llamaba estar enamorado platónicamente; pero él no creía en palabras" (I, 560). [In books that was called being in love platonically, but he didn't believe in words.] Suddenly, he begins to hear a neighbor's violin playing the opera *Fausto,* and he intuits that the music "speaks" of love (I,

561). Like Ana, he gazes at the moon with tears in his eyes, until he recognizes that he is inadvertently imitating the behavior of Trifón Cármenes, according to the poet's testimony in the *folletín* of the conservative paper *El Lábaro*. The thought shames Fermín and he attempts to dismiss his sudden sentimentality by ascribing it to the brandy he has consumed that afternoon (I, 562). Although he is embarrassed by his mother's avarice and corruption, and by his own relationship with his servant girls, he is most uncomfortable with the presence of his other self, the hopelessly romantic one. Humiliated by his proximity to Trifón Cármenes, Fermín consoles himself with the idea that Ana will soon come to confess with him, because he knows he can soothe his pride by writing stories for her. As I suggest later, Álvaro Mesía is also goaded into the seduction of Ana when his insecurities are awakened by poetry, specifically by the mockery he perceives in the verses of the poet Trifón Cármenes.

ÁLVARO

The novel presents Álvaro differently, in the sense that we readers do not become acquainted with the events of his early life, as we do with Fermín and Ana. The "poetry" that still affects him in his jaded state is melodramatic, but is not at any point appealing to him. At no time does he articulate his goals as a program of recapturing poetry in order to live such extravagances. Usually, Álvaro dominates other characters precisely by being impervious to the stories he keeps at his command to use for the manipulation of others.

Álvaro Mesía is a set of stories, and he benefits from these fictions. He is repeatedly referred to as a *Tenorio,* or Don Juan, so that beginning with his name, his identity is linked to Zorrilla's powerful protagonist. When circumstances require, Álvaro knows how to present himself "como un personaje de novela sentimental e idealista" (I, 493). [like a character from a sentimental, idealistic novel.] Many of the secondary characters inflate Mesía's stature. Pepe Ronzal, for example, fictionalizes his idol by comparing him to El Cid: "Ante su fantasía el Presidente del Casino [Álvaro Mesía] era todo un hombre de novela y hasta de poema. Creíale más valiente que el Cid" (I, 278). [In his imagination the President of the Casino was a true character from novels and even poems. He believed him to be braver than El Cid.] Álvaro welcomes this treatment: "Le divertía y le convenía la inquina de Ronzal, gran propagandista de la leyenda de que era Mesía el héroe; y aquella leyenda era muy útil, para muchas cosas" (I, 281). [Ronzal's ill will entertained and favored Álvaro, since Ronzal was a great propagandist of the legend of Mesía as hero; and that legend was very useful for many things.] Álvaro does not simply accept literary tribute passively. He actively uses his proximity to literary models to his advantage, borrowing phrases from popular novels to encourage Paco Vegallana to idealize his love for Ana so that the "marquesito" (Paco) will facilitate Álvaro's meetings with Ana in his parents' home. The plan succeeds, and Paco sees Álvaro in a new light as a lovesick romantic. *La Regenta*'s narrator calls attention to the way in which Álvaro manipulates Paco using literary texts: "Si en vez de la *Historia de la prostitución* Paquito hubiese leído ciertas novelas de moda, hubiera sabido que don Álvaro no hacía más que imitar . . . a los héroes de aquellos libros elegantes" (I, 298). [If instead of the *History of Prostitution* Paco had read certain fashionable novels, he would have known that Álvaro did nothing but imitate the heroes of those elegant books.] Still, even with his limited readings Paco is able to make Mesía conform to a familiar literary model, and it is his parallel with a fictional character that convinces Paco to help Álvaro: "Algo encontraba Paco en sus lecturas parecido a Mesía; era éste una Margarita Gautier del sexo fuerte; un hombre capaz de redimirse por amor. Era necesario redimirle, ayudarle a toda costa" (I, 298). [In his readings, Paco found something similar to Mesía; Mesía was a male Margarita Gautier; a man capable of being redeemed by love. It was necessary to redeem him, to help him at all costs.] (Margarita Gautier is a character from *La dama de las camelias,* another of Paco's favorite readings). But most of all, Álvaro benefits from Ana's poeticization of him, as she consistently configures him as the hero that he is not. When she stays home from the theater pitying herself, Ana imagines vividly that if she had married don Frutos, Álvaro would have stolen her away and killed her husband (I, 371). Later, at the production of *Don Juan Tenorio,* Ana is thrilled with the oddly medieval dress of the lead actor. She imposes the costume on Mesía, and eventually confuses the actor and her future lover: "Desde aquel momento vistió a su adorador con los arreos del cómico, y a éste en cuanto volvió a la escena le dio el gesto y las facciones de Mesía, sin quitarle el propio andar, la voz dulce y melódica y demás cualidades artísticas" (II, 47). [From that moment on she dressed her admirer with the adornments of the actor, and when he returned to the stage, she projected onto the actor the expression and features of Mesía, without taking from him his own way of walking, his sweet, melodic voice and his other artistic qualities.]

In this way, Álvaro's stature grows for Ana, amplified by the fantasies she derives both from Zorrilla's play and from the anachronisms of Vetusta's staging of the work. In another example of this same phenomenon, late in the novel, Ana attends Midnight Mass at the cathedral, and again fictionalizes Álvaro. In these examples Álvaro benefits tremendously from others' creation of legends and literary fantasies about him.

However—and this is what I wish to explore here—on occasion such stories control Álvaro, and ultimately induce him to vie for the position of primary author of the novel's action, just as do Fermín and Ana. Still, Álvaro joins in the fray—the competition for authorship—much later than Fermín and Ana. Whereas the priest and his penitent pass directly from feeling humiliated by their continuing romanticism to self-defense through attempts at authorship, Álvaro stalls at the initial stage. He allows his insecurities to paralyze him, so that for most of the novel he figures in the main action (the seduction of Ana) only as material for Ana's creative endeavors. She fictionalizes him, and he does not author his own texts until very near the end of the novel. The Álvaro Mesía of the entire first part, and much of the second part of *La Regenta,* suffers tremendously from assaults by the last enemy he would like to recognize: his own romantic nature.

For Álvaro, the unwelcome melodramatic narrative that tortures him throughout nearly the entire novel is the story of Fermín's bond with Ana. Mesía is threatened by what he perceives as an exclusive, amorous relationship between the priest and his *hija de confesión.* Because Fermín is a cleric, Álvaro knows that her confessor enjoys access to Ana's private life, and the erotic intimacy that Álvaro himself fabricates between Fermín and Ana restricts his attempts at her seduction. Álvaro's cowardice in the face of this compelling (albeit, degraded) love story is constant and enduring, but there are many other examples of his self-limitation as a result of his poetic imagination.

We first read Álvaro's thoughts in chapter 7 of *La Regenta,* and here he seems confident that he will succeed in the seduction of any woman he desires. He insists to himself that he is irresistible, and meditates on how physical attraction brings him political gains, as he hopes will happen with the minister's wife he has courted in the resort Palomares. However, the Don Juan of Vetusta is forced to admit that he has futilely—and according to his well-wrought political plans, inexplicably and unjustifiably—pursued Ana for two years, with as much success as the ridiculous poet Trifón Cármenes, who is also in love with her, "lyrically" (I, 295). Although Ana takes no notice of Álvaro's supposed "rival," Mesía reads the verses Trifón Cármenes dedicates to her with care: "Entonces ya no le quedaba al poeta más testigo de su dolor que Mesía, la única persona del mundo que entendía el sentido oculto y hondo de los versos eróticos de Cármenes. Aquellas elegías parecían charadas, y sólo podía descifrarlas don Álvaro, dueño de la clave" (I, 295). [And then the only witness to the poet's pain was Mesía, the only person in the world who understood the hidden, deep meaning of the erotic verses of Cármenes. Those elegies seemed like tasteless jokes, and only don Álvaro—master of the key—could decipher them.] Thus, Álvaro is the only true reader of Cármenes's poetic drivel. Because Álvaro's identification with the verses is so intense, he imagines that others see the parallels between him and Trifón, and the absurdity of the situation as he envisions it through others' eyes disturbs him and urges him to act. Even though at times it makes him laugh, when he thinks he may be making a spectacle of himself in Vetusta—he, as rival of Trifón Cármenes—Mesía realizes it is time to make a move (I, 295–96). Despite his occasionally good-humored acceptance of the imagined comparison, we can read Álvaro Mesía's desire for Ana—the guiding force of much of his behavior in the second part of the novel—as having originated in Cármenes's challenge. Even so, Mesía's self-confidence is so undermined by his sense of his own romantic weakness that he only truly acts in this campaign in the last three chapters of the novel. Although Trifón's words incite Álvaro to desire, he is also incapacitated by a lingering shame related to his poetic nature.

There is a concrete example of Álvaro's paralysis by a literary image after Ana's first confession with Fermín. Ana finds herself at home alone that night, and she indulges the self-pity that prompts her desires to live "poetically." When she compares her fading youth to the moon slipping behind a cloud, something inside her rebels and reclaims her "derechos de hermosura" [the rights she had as a beautiful woman]. She runs outside with her hands outstretched, "como si quisiera volar y torcer el curso del astro eternamente romántico" (I, 377). [as if she wanted to fly and change the course of the eternally romantic star.] With Ana in this vulnerable state, Álvaro has the perfect opportunity to progress in his seduction, when strolling in the street a short distance from her. He recognizes her before she identifies him, but does not speak to her. Álvaro is restrained from communicating with Ana by her reputation, which he melds with a literary legend he allows to intimidate and shame him as did Cármenes's poetry: "La superstición vetustense respecto de la virtud de Ana la sintió él en sí; aquella virtud, como el Cid, ahuyentaba al enemigo después de muerta acaso" (I, 380). [He felt within himself the Vetustan superstition about Ana's virtue; that virtue, like el Cid, would scare off the enemy perhaps even after she was dead.] Imagining her deceased like the Cid, Álvaro effaces Ana, so that the only adversary here lies in his own (poetic) conscience—his reading of *El Cid*. He flees from Ana, then thinks again and rushes back, but when he tries to call for her, she is gone. In this way, although at first glance he appears more insensitive to poetry than Fermín and Ana, Álvaro confirms his association with the other two protagonists when he reveals his continued reliance on structures of thought dictated by the epic poem *El Cid*. The reader should recall here that as a child, Fermín imagined a "poema heroico," and Ana an epic poem, so that with his reference to *El Cid* as his mental construct for Ana, Álvaro joins their group as a third reader of epic heroism. In Álvaro's case, however, the uncomfortable remnant of the epic will delay in manifesting itself as reactive authorial drive.

This, then, is Álvaro's "romantic insecurity" as evidenced in the first part of the novel. As we have seen in the introductions of Fermín and Ana, Part I of *La Regenta* primarily features elaborations of the continuing hold of romanticism and "poetry" on the characters. In Part II the actual competition among the protagonists tends to predominate. To be more specific, early in the novel Fermín and Ana proceed to the second stage of authorial jousting, and this contest makes up some of Part I and most of Part II. But Álvaro remains unable to participate in the contest, spooked by his vestigial romanticism until nearly the end of Part II. For now, I will stay with the paralyzed Álvaro, tracing his continuing lack of action even as the novel progresses, and Ana acts in his stead, in a sense "seducing herself" when he does not take the initiative. Eventually he does act as an author, but only in the final chapters of *La Regenta.*

As we proceed to Part II, Álvaro's feelings of self-doubt when reminded of poetry surface when he observes Ana's love for nature. We read that Álvaro is one of the Vetustans who scorn romanticism and grow impatient with Ana's romantic leanings (II, 17). Still, he does not act to rouse her from her meditative ecstasies, because in a sense, he is enthralled by the same deities. The idea that Álvaro is impervious to romanticism seems suspect when we remember his reaction to Ana's poetic enjoyment of the outdoors. As he explains, Álvaro feels sure that he cannot compete with Nature, and imagines that Ana finds him lacking when she compares him to ancient oaktrees (II, 18). Clearly, if he did not in some sense sympathize with the romantic glorification of nature, Álvaro would not be cowed by Ana's reverence for the trees, and would not endow her admiration with validity. Again, the poetry that affects Álvaro in spite of himself holds him back in the struggle to control Ana.

Álvaro is similarly incapacitated when the characters attend the play *Don Juan Tenorio,* although he enters the theater with every advantage. Ana is primed for Álvaro to seduce her because of her impatience with her pseudoreligious life. Earlier that day, Álvaro dominated and manipulated romantic discourse for his purposes by appearing under Ana's balcony on a white stallion. Furthermore, he seemed comfortable with his control of literature when he intuited that despite his dislike for the play, praising Zorrilla's *Don Juan* might help him in his pursuit of Ana (II, 29). Nevertheless, at the theater, Álvaro's confidence is shaken when he realizes he has a rival for Ana's attention—*Don Juan* itself (II, 45). I quote this passage at length, because I believe it reveals more of Álvaro's point of view than is commonly acknowledged:

> Empezó el segundo acto y don Álvaro notó que por aquella noche tenía un poderoso rival: el drama. Anita comenzó a comprender y sentir el valor artístico del Don Juan emprendedor, loco, valiente y trapacero de Zorrilla; a ella

también la fascinaba como a la doncella de doña Ana de Pantoja, y a la Trotaconventos que ofrecía el amor de Sor Inés como una mercancía . . . La calle oscura, estrecha, la esquina, la reja de doña Ana . . . los desvelos de Ciutti, las trazas de Don Juan; la arrogancia de Mejía; la traición interina del Burlador, que no necesitaba, por una sola vez, dar pruebas de valor; los preparativos diabólicos de la gran aventura, del asalto del convento, llegaron al alma de la Regenta con todo el vigor y frescura dramáticos que tienen y que muchos no saben apreciar o porque conocen el drama desde antes de tener criterio para saborearle y ya no les impresiona, o porque tienen el gusto de madera de tinteros; Ana estaba admirada de la poesía que andaba por aquellas callejas de lienzo, que ella transformaba en sólidos edificios de otra edad . . . (II, 45–46)

[The second act had begun and Álvaro noticed that as far as that night was concerned, he had a powerful rival: the play. Anita began to understand and to appreciate the artistic value of the enterprising, crazy, brave, and deceitful Don Juan of Zorrilla. He fascinated her just like he did the servant of doña Ana de Pantoja, and the procuress who offered him the love of Sister Inés like merchandise. The dark, narrow street, the corner, the barred window of don Álvaro . . . Ciutti's vigils, Don Juan's plans, Mejía's arrogance; the initial betrayal by the seducer who didn't need, for once, to give proof of his bravery, the diabolical preparation for the great adventure, for the raid of the convent, touched la Regenta's soul with all the dramatic vigor and freshness they have and that many do not know how to appreciate either because they have been familiar with the play since before they had any criterion to appreciate it and it no longer impresses them, or because they have no taste. Ana was surprised by the poetry that moved through the narrow streets made of canvas, which she transformed into solid edifices of another age.]

What we notice immediately in this passage is the shift in point of view, which might almost be characterized as a vacillation. Ana de Ozores is usually called "Anita" by the narrator (particularly when he treats her condescendingly or sympathetically as in the early chapters about her childhood and adolescence), by her husband Víctor, or by Álvaro. Here, I suggest that in using the name Anita in the second sentence the narrator wishes to communicate that Ana is being observed by a male attuned to her thought processes. This could be the narrator, but it could also be Álvaro, mentioned in the first sentence. Several paragraphs earlier, a similar structure conveys Víctor's perception of Ana, and now here we read Álvaro's thoughts.[5] Whereas absolute certainty is out of the question, the passage suggests the blurring of Ana's perceptions into Álvaro's. With the use of the name Anita, we uneasily wonder: Who is listing the components of this play? If the first sentence conveys Álvaro's state of mind, and ends with the words "el drama," could the following sentences not be Mesía's description of Zorrilla's work? By the end of the passage, the heroine is "Ana" and we seem to drift further from Mesía's perceptions, but where exactly do we make the transition from the consciousness of one lover to the other? Of course it could be the narrator who laments the lack of taste of much of Zorrilla's audience, but it could also be Álvaro, having been seduced by the play into rethinking his earlier resistance and into distinguishing himself from the unfeeling, unromantic crowd.[6] In any case, the end result of Álvaro's self-restraint is that he does not initiate any advances on Ana's virtue. He is unable even to touch Ana, although his degraded copy Paco Vegallana fondles his cousin Edelmira.

As the novel proceeds, Álvaro remains paralyzed. Ana thinks of him often but still resists him, to the surprise of Álvaro's allies Visitación and Paco Vegallana. Paco remarks on Álvaro's lack of initiative, telling his idol Mesía, "Ella está enamorada, de eso estoy seguro . . . pero tú . . . tú no eres el de otras veces . . . parece que la temes" (II, 98). [She is in love—that I'm sure of. But you—you're not what you used to be. It seems like you're scared of her.] Perhaps Álvaro is not so much frightened by Ana as he is by his own nature, which is more similar to Ana's than he cares to admit. When he accompanies Ana on an excursion to the country, Álvaro remains mute instead of indulging Ana's enthusiasm for the rustic setting. Álvaro keeps silent, calculating that his cultivation of a friendship with Víctor will eventually aid him in his campaign to seduce Ana.

Mesía initiates this odd relationship with Víctor because he hopes that he might serve as a means of gaining access to, or even as a substitute for, Ana.[7] At the same time, this association with Víctor only serves to cement Álvaro's passivity, because Víctor humiliates Álvaro with reminders of extravagant literature. When he visits Víctor's museum of "cosas inútiles" (useless things), Álvaro routinely pets a stuffed peacock before the two men enter Víctor's office, where the host regales his guest with verses from Golden Age theater. Álvaro sits listening, waiting to see Ana, resigning himself to beer and the theater of Calderón and Lope (II, 132)—painfully unable to act as author himself. While Víctor throws literature in his face, Álvaro remains as mute as his peacock ally, unable to generate a story of seduction for Ana. At one point, when he does see Ana at home, she lies recovering from an illness, inaccessible to Álvaro not only because of Fermín's influence over her, but because Álvaro "reads" her as linked to the romanticism he fears within himself. Ana seems to Álvaro "[h]ermosísima, eso sí, hermosísima . . . pero a lo romántico" (II, 160). [very beautiful, certainly very beautiful. But in a romantic way.] Thus, Álvaro reveals that he sees romanticism as a barrier to Ana, and as something he must avoid, precisely because such romanticism is a mark of weakness in his character.

Rather than recognizing that it is his shame that holds him back from Ana, Álvaro decides to blame Fermín for his failures. In so doing, however, Mesía actually makes indirect progress in the seduction of Ana, because he begins to fabricate stories, choosing the path that will eventually allow him to conquer his beloved. To recruit Fermín's enemies for an organized assault, Mesía must prove himself a worthy leader of their band, and he does this by acting as expert teller of tales of seduction. At a dinner at the Casino, when the conversation degenerates into personal stories of past seductions, Álvaro, who usually does not stoop to such unseemly confidences, "sintió comezón de hablar, de contar sus hazañas" (II, 173). [felt the urge to speak, to recount his feats.] This desire is new to him ever since his embarrassment by Ana de Ozores, and shows that he has begun to realize that the creation of stories is central to his campaign. As the narrator observes, Álvaro's sudden offering of narrative recalls classical mythology, Renaissance art, and the legends of the Knights of the Round Table (II, 177). Álvaro appears as a degraded Christ figure whose "message" is a seemingly endless string of tales by means of which he seduces his listeners:

> Inclinó un poco la cabeza, con cierto misticismo báquico, y con los ojos levantados a la luz de la araña, con palabra suave, tibia, lenta, comenzó la confesión que oían sus amigos con silencio de iglesia. Los que estaban lejos se incorporaban para escuchar, apoyándose en la mesa o en el hombro del más cercano. Recordaba el cuadro, por modo miserable, la *Cena* de Leonardo de Vinci. (II, 173).

> [He leaned his head forward a bit, with a certain Bacchic mysticism, and with his eyes raised to the light of the chandelier, with soft, warm, slow words, he began the confession that his friends listened to silently, as if they were in church. Those who were farther away came closer to listen, leaning on the table or on the shoulder of the nearest man. The scene was an ignoble imitation of *The Last Supper* by Leonardo da Vinci.]

Although Álvaro's stories greatly please his audience, the elements of degradation in the scene relate to his having chosen the wrong audience. Álvaro is in fact telling tales of seductions, but he is speaking to the men of the Casino, instead of channeling his imaginative energies into the creation of fictions for Ana. (Again, we note the homoerotic subtext.) His adventures are "románticas, peligrosas, de audacia y fortuna" [romantic, dangerous, full of audacity and good fortune], and demonstrate conclusively "el arte del seductor" (II, 173–74). [the arts of the seducer.] Álvaro speaks effectively to his audience, even seducing himself, because his true objective is to prove his worth to himself, rather than to entertain his listeners (II, 174). In this insecure moment the man who might have been a creative author for an audience of one expends his imaginative energies on listeners who distract him from his monomania. Absorbed with recapturing his proud stance by proving himself author of stories instead of consumer of sentimental poetry, Mesía remains powerless with Ana because his fiction does not turn on her. Nevertheless, Álvaro has made some progress; he is generating stories. Now, all that remains is for him to create narratives for his essential audience, Ana. At this point in the novel, Álvaro departs from Vetusta for the summer, and although he is angry at Ana for her continuing unreceptivity (II, 186), their farewell scene reminds Álvaro (and us readers) of what he needs to do upon his return. As Álvaro leaves the Ana who at that moment appears to him cold and inaccessibly virtuous, he trips over the stuffed peacock that mocks his mute condition. With the memory of his incipient authorship at the simulacrum of the Last Supper, and the peacock to remind him of the consequences of wordlessness, Álvaro returns after the summer holiday to a new phase of greater activity in the discursive seduction of Ana.

His ultimate success does not immediately follow on his arrival in Vetusta, however, and it is not until Ana receives stories from and about Álvaro that he makes further progress. The first stage of this assault by new narratives is a conversation Ana has with her friend Visitación, who acts as Álvaro's proxy, but who also has her own petty motives for desiring Ana's seduction. Visita tells Ana that Álvaro has given up his summertime lover, the minister's wife, so that he could find true love that winter, because he is restricted by a beloved chain (II, 304). Visita completes her attack on Ana's resistance with the hypothesis that Álvaro had ended the conversation at that point so that Visita would not see him cry. Ana is greatly affected by Visita's revelation and her skillful storytelling, but she still waits for Álvaro to take part himself in the manufacture of their shared narrative. With Visita having plowed the soil for him, Álvaro, the latecomer to the textual competition, successfully begins his verbal assault on Ana's virtue at the Carnival ball held in the Casino.

From a large party that spills into all parts of the Casino, a select group of guests retires for dinner—to the "gabinete de lectura" (reading room). They clear away newspapers and other reading material so that they may dine, in a gesture that recalls the unwelcome texts of romanticism that haunt Ana and Álvaro. In this setting of discarded readings, perhaps heartened by the group's elimination of physical evidence of earlier readings, Álvaro at last begins his rhetorical seduction of Vetusta's most virtuous lady. With Víctor's poetic attempts at courting Visitación mirroring Ana and Álvaro from across the table,[8] and reminding Álvaro of the vestiges of romanticism that drive him to be an author, Mesía weaves for Ana the tapestry of his feelings for her. He tells Ana that since the summer, he has given up the favors of a desirable woman because love for him was no longer a casual hobby, ever since real love had fallen on his soul like a punishment (II, 310). Álvaro eases into physical terrain by dancing with Ana, but always offering words in addition to his body: "Don Álvaro habló de amor disimuladamente, con una melancolía bonachona, familiar, con una pasión dulce, suave, insinuante . . . Recordó mil incidentes sin importancia ostensible que Ana recordaba también. Ella no hablaba pero oía" (II, 311). [Don Álvaro spoke of love stealthily, with a good-natured, confiding melancholy, and with a sweet, soft, insistent passion . . . He recalled for her a thousand seemingly unimportant incidents that Ana remembered as well. She did not talk, but she did listen.] In not speaking, Ana recognizes Álvaro as the winner in this particular discursive battle. Thus, while Víctor courts Visitación with his overblown poetry, Álvaro is spurred to action, and he offers Ana first flowery, then familiar language. He reaps the ultimate rewards for his creation of a narrative of seduction when he and Ana dance, and she faints in his arms (II, 312).

After her traumatic experience at the Casino ball, Ana passes through another stage of resistance to Álvaro, participating in the Holy Week procession that provokes her unbreachable rift with Fermín, and then recovering in the country at the marqueses' residence at El Vivero. Álvaro visits her often here, and having established a relationship with Ana of increased intimacy in conversation, Álvaro demonstrates his commitment to verbal conquest of Ana by focusing on the debasement of Ana's earlier discursive relationship with Fermín. He tells Ana that mysticism is just nervous agitation, and denies that Fermín was ever a mystic (II, 420). It is significant that Álvaro attacks Fermín on these grounds, because proving to Ana that he is not a mystic strikes at the heart of his authorial endeavors, because, for Ana, a mystic is always a writer. Yet the true breakthrough occurs when Mesía turns his energies from the fabrication of a critical discourse—the undermining of Fermín—to creative expression—a poetics of love for Ana and himself. This finally happens while Ana and Víctor are still at El Vivero. Ana and Álvaro stand in a gallery above the rest of the guests who are entertaining themselves with particular abandon, running and shouting. As the others play a children's game below, Álvaro reveals to Ana the text he has waited so long to deliver. Ana hears "por la primera vez de su vida una declaración de amor apasionada pero respetuosa, discreta, toda idealismo, llena de salvedades y eufemismos que las circunstancias y el estado de Ana exigían, con lo cual crecía su encanto" (II, 423). [for the first time in her life a declaration of love that was passionate, but also respectful, discreet, completely idealistic, full of the reservations and euphemisms that the circumstances and Ana's nature required, and this indirectness increased the declaration's charm.]

Ana is overwhelmed with emotion by this speech, and wishes only that Álvaro would keep talking (II, 423). She contributes nothing to the conversation, and notices how passive she is able to be with Álvaro in command, in contrast to the great effort religious passion required from her: "En lo que estaba pasando ahora ella era pasiva, no había esfuerzo" (II, 424). [In what was happening now, she was passive, and did not need to make any effort.] Since Ana is proud, Mesía adds fuel to her narrative of exclusivity, realizing exactly which "story" will please her: "Él no pedía más que lástima, y la dicha de que le dejaran hablar, de hacerse oír y de no ser tenido por un libertino *vulgar*, necio, que era lo que el *vulgo estúpido* había querido hacer de él" (II, 424, italics in original). [He only asked for her pity, and to be allowed to speak, to be listened to, and not to be considered a *common*, foolish libertine, which is how the *stupid masses* would characterize him.] Now in a gallery above the people to whom she desperately needs to feel superior, Ana hears her uniqueness acknowledged. Álvaro calculates well that this tactic will please Ana, and as he anticipates, she reacts happily: "Siempre le había gustado mucho a Ana que llamasen al vulgo *estúpido;* para ella la señal de la *distinción* espiritual estaba en el desprecio del vulgo, de los vetustenses" (II, 424, italics in original). [Ana had always liked to hear the common people called *stupid*. For her, the mark of spiritual *distinction* was in the disdainful reaction of the ordinary ones—of the Vetustans.] Although this trait of Ana's has caught the reader's attention before, here for the first time *La Regenta*'s narrator stops to suggest an origin for her attraction to the idea of superiority: "Tenía la Regenta este defecto, tal vez heredado de su padre: que para distinguirse de la *masa de los creyentes,* necesitaba recurrir a la teoría hoy muy generalizada del *vulgo idiota,* de la *bestialidad humana,* etc., etc." (II, 424, italics in original). [The Regenta had this defect, perhaps inherited from her father: that in order to distinguish herself from the *masses of the faithful,* she needed to rely on the commonly accepted theory of the *idiotic commoners,* of *human bestiality,* etc., etc.] The analysis of Ana's habits of thought at this particular point in the novel highlights Álvaro's success in taking advantage of what is now referred to as Ana's "weakness," and luckily for him, Álvaro knows exactly how to manipulate this mechanism in Ana (II, 425).

Álvaro then proceeds to challenge Ana to actively pursue the exceptionality she craves, inciting her to scorn the "common" by indulging him:

¿Tenía él derecho para que Ana siguiera sus ideas y despreciase las maliciosas y groseras aprensiones del vulgo? Oh, no; ya sabía que la *letra* estaba contra él . . . Ya lo sabía, sí; no exigía que Ana se hiciese superior a tantas tradiciones, leyes y costumbres . . . ¿podía él pedir a Ana, educada por fanáticos, que había pasado su juventud en un pueblo como Vetusta, podía pedirla que se dignase siquiera alentar su pasión con una esperanza?" (II, 425, italics in original).

[Did he have the right to influence Ana so that she would follow him in despising the crude and malicious concerns of the common people? Oh, no; he already knew that the common understanding of morality ruled against him. He already knew, yes, and he was not demanding that Ana rise above so many traditions, laws, and customs . . . How could he ask of Ana, who had been raised by religious fanatics, who had spent her youth in a village like Vetusta, that she deign to encourage his passion with even a glimmer of hope?]

Here Álvaro catches Ana in her own trap. He pretends to ask nothing of her, but in reality requests that she sacrifice her honor to prove her superiority: if she is truly "above" Vetustan morality, she must now defy such conventions and become his love. She does not yet do this, but she does relinquish verbal control, recognizing Álvaro as the beloved opponent who has defeated her at her own rhetorical game. She reserves for herself the role of inarticulate animal. Ana moans with a deep, needy, guttural sound, "como un animal débil y mortaraz herido" (II, 426). [like a weak and injured wild animal.] Ana's moan might be seen as the long-awaited triumph of staring animals—the swallow, the toad, even the tiger that has become her tiger-skin rug—over the false virtue these creatures have mocked in Ana since the beginning of the novel. Fittingly, Álvaro concludes with respect to his recent verbal triumph over Ana that cunning is indeed more important than physical strength (II, 427). Now that he has learned this lesson, we will see if he can maintain his commitment to the narrative battleground.

The final stage of Álvaro's seduction of Ana comes when Álvaro is pressured into action by Víctor, after Víctor confesses to him that despite Ana's maid Petra's willingness to engage in an affair with him, he has never been able to follow through with her sexually. Álvaro thinks to himself: "Este idiota me está avergonzando, sin saberlo" (II, 441). [This idiot is putting me to shame, without realizing it.] He sees the parallels between his own hesitation and Víctor's as the romantic image of the chaste courtly lover mocks him in his inaction. Víctor has mirrored Álvaro at the Carnival dinner in the Casino, parodying his rhetorical successes with Ana by reciting poetry to Visita. Now, however, Víctor's impotence with Petra threatens Álvaro on a much deeper level. Humiliated like Ana and Fermín by his tendency to live in the clouds, Álvaro is driven to consummate the love stories he has told Ana. With memories of Trifón Cármenes and his poetry forming the background for Álvaro's entire pursuit of Ana, he is now forced to act. After Álvaro and Ana become lovers, in the final chapter of the novel, Álvaro loses all textual control. If his seduction of Ana is ultimately a defensive act of self-affirmation in the face of humiliation by his lingering romanticism, now Álvaro cannot even author realism as resistance. Of course, Álvaro also fears sexual impotence, and seeming "unmasculine" in front of Ana, but this "effeminacy" is precisely what I propose as the stigma of lingering romanticism. Álvaro attempts to manipulate Petra, but she responds by defying him with a *folletín* plot, so that the melodrama he tried to escape comes back to haunt him, as he is defeated by Petra, another female author.[9] After he leaves Ana, his final communication with her is a perfumed letter: a "pliego perfumado . . . que olía a mujerzuela" [perfumed sheet of paper . . . that smelled of hussy], in which Mesía writes "con frases románticas e incorrectas" (II, 521). [with romantic sentences full of mistakes.] This is his last act of authorship, and while he has the upper hand with Ana and now rejects her, he does so at the cost of having to reveal his true romantic, *cursi* (pretentious), and even grotesquely feminine nature. Álvaro reduces himself to this scented, effeminate letter, as his composition of a text can no longer protect him or act as a shield. Mesía is finally exposed for what he is, and he is what he most feared being.

FERMÍN

That, then, is the story of Álvaro's role as author of Ana's seduction. If we follow Fermín's advances in a similar campaign, we see that although he does not ultimately become Ana's lover, he is overall a much more proficient author. As I have explained, Fermín takes much less time than Álvaro to realize the textual nature of the competition with Ana. In fact, he engages in a verbal contest with Ana at her first confession, as Ana recalls on the walk she takes afterwards. Ana remembers Fermín's portrayal of her unrefined faith as a gold nugget she might find while swimming in a river, and she is happy with this image (I, 342). Fortunately for him, Fermín has discovered the perfect approach to Ana's imagination. He allows Ana to recover the poetry she thought was forbidden, justifying this recuperation by arguing for her special qualities. As Ana remembers excitedly, during her "confession," Fermín had referred to her "temperamento especial" (special temperament), and had implied that certain avenues were open to her but not to others (I, 345). For this reason, even activities she had before considered problematic might be appropriate, given her unusual nature: "Por ejemplo, la lectura de libros prohibidos, veneno para los débiles, era purga para los fuertes" (I, 345). [For example, the reading of forbidden books—poison for the weak—was a purgative for the strong.] This new vision of herself as superior and able to reincorporate her poetic imagination energizes Ana. She observes to herself, "¡Y qué *elevación!*" (I, 344, italics in original). [And what *elevation!*] Here again, Fermín's words conform to imagery significant to Ana, in that she identifies with rising, climbing, and superiority.

Her new confessor senses that these ideas appeal to her, and combines the notion of reading with that of Ana's exclusivity. Ana repeats Fermín's words: "Ella que había leído a San Agustín ¿no recordaba que el santo Obispo gustaba de la música religiosa, no por el deleite de los sentidos, sino porque elevaba el alma?" (I, 345). [She who had read St. Augustine, didn't she remember that the holy bishop enjoyed religious music, not for the pleasure of the senses, but because music elevates the soul?] This man, who as a youth loved to climb and dream, articulates to a woman who also participated in these activities when she was younger, a synthesis of reading and ascending which encompasses all arts: "Pues así todas las artes, así la contemplación de la naturaleza, la lectura de las obras históricas, y de las filosóficas, siendo puras, podían elevar el alma" (I, 345). [In that way, all art, the contemplation of nature, the reading of historical and philosophical works—if they were pure—could elevate the soul.] As noted, Fermín explains to Ana that if she aspires to perfection, "cuando se llegaba más arriba" [when she reaches higher levels], all "espectáculos" [entertainments and spectacles] will be open to her strong spirit (I, 345). She is overwhelmed by the contrast between the "devoción vulgar" [common worship] that she has always known and the "religión verdadera" [true religion] that Fermín offers (I, 345). Fermín also suggests to Ana that he will be her companion in this exalted realm, referring to himself as her older brother of the soul, with whom sorrows are alleviated and desires are shared (I, 343). To suit his purposes Fermín must convince Ana that although she is superior to the rest of Vetusta, she needs his companionship. Readings are a vital part of this effort, and Ana recognizes his success: "La había halagado mucho el notar que don Fermín le hablaba como a persona ilustrada, como a un hombre de letras: le había citado autores, dando por supuesto que los conocía" (I, 344). [It had flattered her a great deal to note that Fermín spoke to her as if to an educated person, as if to a man of letters: he had mentioned and quoted from authors, assuming that she was familiar with them.]

Fermín also distracts Ana from her contemplation of Álvaro's physical beauty when they meet at the marqueses', after Ana has sent him a letter saying that she wishes to make another confession. As her two "protectors" talk to each other, Ana is able to compare Fermín and Álvaro. She notes their physical differences, but when she looks at Fermín, she thinks mainly of the words they exchanged the day before in the context of her confession:

> Recordó todo lo que se habían dicho y que había hablado como con nadie en el mundo con aquel hombre que le había halagado el oído y el alma con palabras de esperanza y consuelo, con promesas de luz y de poesía, de vida importante, empleada en algo bueno, grande y digno de lo que ella sentía dentro de sí, como siendo el fondo del alma. En los libros algunas veces había leído algo así, pero ¿qué vetustense sabía hablar de aquel modo? Y era muy diferente leer tan buenas y bellas ideas, y oírlas de un hombre de carne y hueso, que tenía en la voz un calor suave y en las letras silbantes música, y miel en palabras y movimientos. (I, 491).

[She remembered everything they had said to each other and that she had spoken to him as she had to no one else in the world, to this man who had gratified her ear and her soul with words of hope and consolation, with promises of light and poetry, of an important life, spent in something good, great, and worthy of what she felt within her, as if it were the basis of her being. She had read things like that in books, but what Vetustan knew how to speak in that way? And in any case it was different to read such beautiful ideals than to hear them from a man of flesh and blood, who had a sweet warmth in his voice, music in his sibilants, and honey in his words and movements.]

Ana's interest in Fermín, then, is based on his connection to words. Ana does not ignore Fermín's body, but she subordinates it to the textual contact he offers her, and Fermín confirms the verbal basis of their relationship. When she seeks protection from Álvaro's gaze by turning to Fermín's, as long as they are talking Fermín meets her glance, with his eyes "un modo de puntuación de las palabras" [as a certain punctuation of his words], and without feeling: "No había más que inteligencia y ortografía" (I, 492). [There was nothing but intelligence and spelling.] Thus, Fermín establishes for Ana that their relationship will be verbally centered, and asserts that he will be the older brother who controls these words. Fermín seems to recognize that what he needs to provide Ana is a convincing narrative that accommodates and celebrates her superiority, but he begins this campaign indirectly. For example, although Fermín suspects that Ana is interested in a man other than her husband, he does not press her for details because he intuits that the best way for him to win her favor is to show himself to be discreet, dispassionate, and not subject to the common defects of humanity (II, 19). Then gradually, Fermín attempts to assert his control over Ana by channeling her desire to prove herself select. He meditates that he must make Ana climb the "hill of penance" without her noting the incline, and that to do this, he must deceive her into thinking she walks a straight path, until she has entered completely into his dominion, at which point he will take her directly up the steep slope (II, 20). This, then, is one of his plans of attack, but in order to lead her along any path at all, he must come up with a narrative for her to follow, and this is what he endeavors to do.

When he goes to her house to talk to her after she disappoints him by attending *Don Juan Tenorio* on All Saints' Day, Fermín makes further progress in his pursuit of Ana. As they converse, Fermín reveals himself as master of precisely the discourses to which Ana is receptive, and again he gains an advantage over Álvaro. Fermín decides to act with diplomacy, approaching Ana cautiously, but imagining his ultimate goal as ascension. After manipulating Ana by playing the martyr and gaining her sympathy (II, 63), Fermín admonishes her for attending the theater on All Saints' Day. When at first Ana reacts with incomprehension, Fermín returns to his idea of making her climb, determined to use her desire for exaltation for his own purposes: "Pensó, recordando la alegoría de la cuesta: 'No quiere tanta pendiente, hagámosla parecida a lo llano'" (II, 63). [He thought, remembering the allegory of the hill: "If she doesn't want such a steep incline, we shall make it seem flat."] Fermín explains to Ana that although in seeing the play she did nothing wrong, her actions have given fuel to his enemies. Again this application of the plot of *Don Juan* is effective with Ana, who suddenly remembers that Fermín is "un hombre, un hombre hermoso, fuerte; que tenía fama entre ciertas gentes mal pensadas, de enamorado y atrevido" (II, 66). [a man, a handsome, strong man; who was famous according to certain small-minded people for being amorous and forward.] She listens receptively as he next proposes that they sometimes meet outside of church. Just before taking leave of her that evening, Fermín suggests that they hold these meetings at doña Petronila's (II, 78). As Fermín explains, the purpose of these additional meetings is to allow them the freedom to praise Ana. The confessional is the appropriate place to treat sins, but not for extensive conversation: "En la iglesia hay algo que impone reserva, que impide analizar muchos puntos muy interesantes; siempre tenemos prisa" (II, 66). [When in church there is something that makes one hesitate, that prevents one from analyzing many interesting issues. We are always in a hurry.] In addition, Fermín refers to the works of the Arcipreste de Hita and Tirso de Molina, which he assumes Ana has read ("Usted que ha leído" [You who have read]), as testimony to the fact that the confessional only reveals the sinful side of women (II, 66–67). Fermín further encourages her, saying that they need to give attention to Ana's good aspects: "Usted necesita no sólo que la censuren, que la corrijan, sino que la animen también, elogiando sincera y noblemente la mucha parte buena que hay en ciertas ideas y en los actos que usted cree completamente malos" (II, 67). [You need not only to be censured and corrected, but also to be encouraged by someone who would praise sincerely and honorably all that is good in certain ideas and actions that you think are completely wrong.]

Ana then speaks effusively, rewarding Fermín's verbal tactics with words and more words. He receives her declarations happily. Fermín's pleasure at Ana's exclamations relates to his confidence that his own creative imagination has elicited her response, and he listens with delight: "La locuacidad de Ana le sabía a gloria, las palabras expansivas . . . iban cayendo en el ánimo del Magistral como un riego de agua perfumada; la sequedad desaparecía, la tirantez se convertía en muelle flojedad. '¡Habla, habla así!,' se decía el clérigo, 'bendita sea tu boca!'" (II, 68). [Ana's talkativeness was heavenly for Fermín. Her expansive words . . . rained onto the Magistral's soul like a sprinkling of perfumed water. Dryness disappeared, tension became luxurious relaxation. "Speak! Yes, speak to me like that!," the priest said to himself, "Blessed be your mouth!"] Thus, he welcomes her exposition of her ideas, but he does not listen to her or acknowledge her independence of thought, preferring only to revel in the effect of her words on him, knowing that he has inspired her. The final stage of this conversation in the garden of Ana's home is the confession Ana makes to Fermín about the intensity of her reaction to *Don Juan Tenorio,* and his assessment of that reaction. Ana explains that she identifies with doña Inés, and that the play brought her close to God. Fermín attempts to calm her, believing that it is necessary to resist and prevent such dangerous attacks of sentimentality (II, 70).

Fermín then tries to channel Ana's feelings. He recognizes that she might continue to be visited by such attacks of emotion, but warns her that if her virtue is strong and she renounces her identification with sacrilegious stories, she will weather the trauma. Again, Fermín thinks about the fact that he is forcing her to climb a steep incline (II, 71). At this point, we see that the two "hermanos del alma" (soul siblings) are struggling over which narrative to impose on Ana's life. Fermín urges Ana to forget Zorrilla and to become a "beata" [(female) religious fanatic] who observes her religion faithfully and regularly. Clearly, he desires to control and subjugate her as a typical religious devotee, and to fulfill with this new life story Ana's requirement for a narrative equivalent in power to *Don Juan Tenorio.* Fermín explains that if Ana actively participates in church occupations, activities that may at first seem prosaic will become poetic. She will not need the poetry of Zorrilla because she will use her powerful imagination to represent "las escenas de pura poesía del Nacimiento de Jesús" (II, 76). [the scenes of pure poetry from the Birth of Jesus.] In attempting to control her manner of worship, Fermín also proposes that as a model for her life, Ana should adopt Santa Teresa, a writer whose texts provide both religious commitment and romantic sentimentality. After prescribing these narratives for Ana to live by, Fermín recommends that she listen to his sermons, thus claiming responsibility for their shared discourse. Furthermore, he requests that in addition to the works of Santa Teresa she read the lives of other women saints, while still enjoying herself with the harmless entertainments of her social life (II, 76–77). In this way, Fermín brackets her apparently independent choices about her social life with the readings he chooses, and Ana rewards his ingenuity by focusing exclusively on him. However fleeting her attention, for this moment he is her only thought: "Ana salió tras él, ensimismada, sin acordarse de que había en el mundo maridos, ni días, ni noches, ni horas, ni sitios inconvenientes para hablar a solas con un hombre joven, guapo, robusto, aunque sea clérigo" (II, 78). [Deep in contemplation, Ana went out after him, without a thought for her husband, or for the fact that there were days or nights, or times and places in which it was not advisable to speak alone with a young, strong, attractive man—even if he was a priest.]

As time passes, however, Fermín becomes impatient when Ana resists meeting him at doña Petronila's. He notes that his "hija de confesión" [daughter in confession] is not "climbing the hill," and that she persists in her "peligrosos anhelos panteísticos" [dangerous pantheistic desires] (II, 93). She remains attached to the romantic, secular fantasies (her own creations) he has tried futilely to refocus into the religious models of lives of saints (his texts; even though he did not write them, he "reads" them for her and onto her). The recommended readings bore her. Hoping to eventually regain his losses, Fermín tries to appease her with a more romantic presentation of religious activity, in a sort of compromise: "Este sistema de la cuerda floja retrasaba el triunfo, pero le permitía a él presentarse a los ojos de Ana más simpático, hablando el lenguaje de aquella vaguedad romántica que ella creía religiosidad sincera, y no pasaba de ser una idolatría disimulada, según don Fermín" (II, 94). [This system of giving her a lot of slack was delaying his victory, but it permitted him to present himself to Ana as pleasant and sympathetic, speaking the language of that romantic vagueness that she believed was sincere religious expression, and was really nothing more than disguised idolatry, according to don Fermín.] Again, as much as Fermín would like to dismiss as idolatry the discourses that attract Ana, his insecurity in the face of these powerful narratives speaks for itself. When Ana eventually defies him—from the cathedral tower he sees her casting away one of the books he has given her—Fermín confronts Ana and convinces her to meet with him at doña Petronila's, where she promises to do as he wishes. She asks only that he imagine a text for her ("no quiero la virtud si no es pura poesía" [I do not want virtue if it is not pure poetry]), and tells him she longs for his guidance: "quiero que usted me guíe" (II, 107–8). [I want you to guide me] In this way, she lets him know what she is looking for from him, and she tries to convince herself that he has satisfied her request.

As she slowly recovers from a nervous ailment, Ana finally turns to the *Vida* of Santa Teresa, which Fermín had earlier recommended to her. Although at first she cannot concentrate on this text, she eventually reads it, and it speaks to her. She confirms for Fermín that she has decided to follow the model he has proposed for her by writing a letter in imitation of Santa Teresa, and he is thrilled to receive it. In this note, Ana describes Fermín as her brother and only equal in a world of inferiors. She celebrates her relationship with Fermín, commenting that Santa Teresa suffered much longer before she found a confessor worthy of her, and that she (Ana) has been much luckier, because she has received "the protection of God" sooner (II, 194). While Fermín feels genuine happiness after reading the letter, glorying in a passion he sees no need to name (II, 196–97), he next reveals his need to assert his control over Ana by imposing sexuality onto their previously textual relationship. Now outside, Fermín picks a rosebud and feels an intense desire to bite it, to "gozar con el gusto, de escudriñar misterios naturales debajo de aquellas capas de raso" (II, 198). [to enjoy with true pleasure, to investigate the mysteries of nature beneath those layers of satin.] After allowing the bud's petals to fall away as he returns to Vetusta, Fermín puts the heart of the rosebud into his mouth and chews it with "apetito extraño, con una voluptuosidad refinada de que él no se daba cuenta" (II, 198). [a strange appetite, with a refined voluptuousness that he himself did not realize.]

Having dominated the rosebud as pure sensuality, Fermín continues to revel in his authority and to conflate the sexual and the textual. Fermín attends the meeting of a girls' catechism class, and happy to be surrounded by these adoring adolescents, he remembers the rosebud he recently "subdued": "Mirando estos capullos de mujer, don Fermín recordaba el botón de rosa que acababa de mascar, del que un fragmento arrugado se le asomaba a los labios todavía" (II, 201). [Gazing at these budding women, don Fermín remembered the rosebud he had just chewed, a wrinkled fragment of which still hung on his lips.] But these "roses" are different, because rather than biting them, he has injected his words into them. Among these buds that belong to him ("aquellas rosas que eran suyas" [those roses that were his]), one fifteen-year-old stands out, delivering a diatribe against materialism, understanding only part of what she is saying, but speaking with exactly the right tones of pride and intolerance.[10] In contrast to Ana, this girl could never present a challenge to Fermín. Because she cannot make wholly her own the discourse she utilizes, he will always control her: "Era la obediencia ciega de la mujer" (II, 202). [This was woman's blind obedience.] Fermín meditates on his domination of her soul: "El Magistral, con la boca abierta, sin sonreír ya, con las agujas de las pupilas erizadas, devoraba a miradas aquella arrogante amazona de la religión, que labraba con arte la naturaleza, por fuera, y él por dentro, por el alma" (II, 202–3). [The Magistral, with his mouth open, no longer smiling, and with pupils like stiff needles, devoured with his gaze that proud Amazon of the Church, whose exterior was fashioned artfully by nature, and whose soul he himself was building.] He thinks about his ability to decide her destiny—that her "dazzling fanaticism" (fanatismo deslumbrador) was his own work, but that although she was the pearl of his museum of female fanatics, he was not finished forming her yet (II, 203). One day she will emerge from his workshop, but she will never leave Fermín's dominion (II, 203). This obedient girl both flatters Fermín's vanity and intensifies his desire to subjugate Ana in the same way.

Next, Fermín resolves to be as mystical as Ana needs him to be.[11] He remembers his younger days, when he had intended to author his own novels, "una *Sibila* verdaderamente cristiana, y una *Fabiola* moderna" (II, 205). [a genuinely Christian *Sibyl,* and a modern *Fabiola.*][12] At the time that he gave up the idea of writing novels, Fermín believed that novels were better lived than read (II, 205), and this is what he intends to do with Ana. Having confirmed his desire to be an author of lived fictions, Fermín rushes to Ana's house. There Ana tells him again how grateful she is to him, and how she reproaches herself because rather than thinking of God, she thinks of the man He "chose to save her." Fermín is choked with emotion when he hears her say this, realizing that Ana now speaks exactly as he has made her speak in the novels he composed for himself as he fell asleep (II, 206). In thinking this, Fermín reassures himself that he is in control—that despite her verbal excesses, Ana is following a script that he has authored in his fantasies.

A new stage comes when Fermín asserts further control by insisting that Ana perform good works, and that she be religiously active in a conventional (anti-intellectual, nontextual) way. Obligingly, she throws herself into the religious community, and allows her relationship with Fermín to attain a new level of familiarity, although she ultimately expects him to "tell her a story." Their confidences take a physical turn, as when Ana brushes Fermín's mouth and eyes with a rose, but Ana requests, even as she makes this sensual gesture, that he repay it with words, admonishing him: "¡Usted nunca me habla de sí mismo!" (II, 224). [You never tell me about yourself!] When Ana turns to the Magistral for stimulation—she wishes to read him as a book—Fermín imposes the text by which he wishes the two of them to live. Fermín again takes up the story of his persecution by enemies, with particular passion: "Él, elocuente, con imaginación viva, fuerte y hábil, improvisó de palabra una de aquellas novelas que hubiera escrito a no robarle el tiempo ocupaciones más serias" (II, 225). [With a lively, strong, and able imagination, he improvised eloquently one of those novels that he would have written if more serious obligations had not occupied his time.] He suggests that they imagine his story as a sort of confession that he will give to her. Of course, his novel presents him in a favorable light, and her rapt attention consolidates his status as both author and hero. Here, Fermín returns to his narrative strategy of characterizing himself as humble only to better assert his authority. This is the same ploy he used to recover Ana after her "transgression" at *Don Juan Tenorio:* "La confesión del Magistral se pareció a la de muchos autores que en vez de contar sus pecados aprovechan la ocasión de pintarse a sí mismos como héroes, echando al mundo la culpa de sus males, y quedándose con faltas leves, por confesar algo" (II, 225). [The Magistral's confession was like that of many authors, who instead of recounting their sins, take the opportunity to portray themselves as heroes, blaming the rest of the world for their problems, and accepting responsibility only for minor faults, so that they have something to confess.] Thus, Fermín glorifies himself as author, and allows Ana a role in a narrative of shared superiority over their ostensibly inferior Vetustan surroundings. Fermín succeeds in convincing Ana that he is "un alma grande" [a great soul] who has trans-formed the "ambición noble, *elevada*" [noble, *elevated* ambition] of his youth into a desire to save souls such as hers (II, 225, italics in original). Flattered, she then dedicates herself to the protection of this other superior soul in the face of Vetustan mediocrity. In this way, she acknowledges the power of Fermín's story, even allowing it to overshadow the narrative she has authored about her heroic struggle against the temptations presented by Álvaro: "¿Qué cosa mejor que aquella pasión ideal . . . para combatir la tentación cada vez más temible del recuerdo de Mesía?" (II, 226). [What better thing than that ideal passion to fight the increasingly fearful tempta-tion of the memory of Mesía?]

This idyllic state does not last, though, and when the Vetustans who have gone away for the summer return, Fermín loses some of his prestige and his control over Ana. He is particularly disturbed when he intuits that Ana is thinking of Álvaro during Midnight Mass, and he expresses his dis-pleasure to her. When Ana goes to the cathedral the next day, she and Fermín arrange, via an exchange of looks, a meeting at doña Petronila's. Here Ana finds the authoritative Fermín she hopes to use as protection from Álvaro. Ana is about to urge Petronila to stay—there is no need for the mistress of the house to leave her guest alone with Fermín—when Fermín orders her to allow Petronila to leave. He makes this request "con un tono imperioso que a la Regenta siempre le sonaba bien" (II, 288). [with an imperative tone that always pleased the Regenta.] She expects this sort of command from Fermín, which indicates that she accepts him continuing in the role of author: "Eso quería ella, que el Magistral mandase, dispusiera de ella y de sus actos" (II, 288). [That was what she wanted—for the Magistral to tell her what to do, controlling her and her actions.] De Pas confesses to Ana that he has overheard one of Álvaro's companions refer to him (Fermín) as Mesía's rival. His agitation inspires in Ana a further commitment to follow him in his martyrdom, and she confirms his success in creating a "story" for the two of them. She tells Fermín: "¡Ya sé para qué nací yo! Para esto . . . Para estar a los pies del mártir que matan a calum-nias" (II, 290). [Now I know what I was born for! For this . . . to be at the feet of the martyr they slay with false accusations.] Ana remains commit-ted to the fiction of her self-sacrifice for Vetusta's martyr.

Nevertheless, Fermín then loses control by disgusting Ana when he acknowledges that he loves her after she faints in Álvaro's arms at the

Casino ball. Ana eventually gives Fermín another chance after her disillusionment with the fictions of domestic paradise, returning to the Magistral's martyr narration and participating as (his) penitent in the Semana Santa procession. Ultimately, though, Fermín cannot reassert his influence over Ana. She feels humiliated by the parade, and blames the man she believes cast her in her humble role. When she recovers from the trauma during her stay at El Vivero, Fermín visits, but is unable to reestablish himself as author of the narratives she reads. As Fermín leaves El Vivero, soaked to the skin because of his escapade to "save" Ana from the thunderstorm and Álvaro's advances, Pepe the caretaker unwittingly mocks Fermín's missed textual connection with Ana when he tells him: "Anden, anden, ángeles de Dios, que la mojadura puede llegar a los huesos y darles un romantismo" (II, 416). [Go on, go on, angels of God, because the soaking can get into your bones and give you a romantism.] With his deformation of the word "reumatismo" (rheumatism) in a way that suggests "romanticismo" (romanticism), and his address of the two men as "ángeles de Dios" (angels of God), Pepe ridicules Fermín. The Magistral is once again the powerless, inveterate reader of romanticism, humiliated by Trifón Cármenes's verses. Unable to channel his anxieties and insecurities about his readings into the achievement of definitive authorial status, Fermín loses control over Ana and over narratives in general. His visions for Ana's religious life cannot compete with the adventures Álvaro inspires her to compose. Moreover, when Fermín tries at the end of the novel to urge Víctor Quintanar to seek Calderonian revenge for Ana's adultery, he cannot convince him to turn back even to the readings that used to be his favorites. For these reasons, Fermín's pursuit of authorship is ultimately a failure.

ANA

Now, I would like to retell *La Regenta* as the story of Ana as author, revisiting the instances in which the two men appear to dominate her with their stories. I will repeat brief references to the novel's plot, because I hope to demonstrate the validity of rereading these events as Ana's authorial triumphs. Although she ultimately gives in to Álvaro, as an author Ana is consistently superior to the two men who attempt to control her and make her reader of the narratives they compose. Ana displays her greater talent from the earliest chapters of the novel, in which she progresses to the actual composition of poetry in the midst of her conflicts with romanticism, whereas Fermín merely dreams about writing a novel. As an adult, from the time of her first confession with Fermín, she frames the two men—tempter and protector—with her own narrative constructions.

Ana's poetic constructions are based on texts she has read previously, and in that sense she is not an entirely "original" author. But even the most basic consideration of intertextuality and tradition helps us to realize that there are no "pure" texts "untainted" by earlier writings. In any case, whether Ana copies other texts or not, she does not ultimately defer to texts offered by either Álvaro or Fermín. The ideas Fermín communicates to her simply fertilize her imagination.

After her first confession with Fermín, Ana takes a walk, and recalls her conversation with Fermín in a return to nature reminiscent of her preparation as a young girl for the composition of verses for the Virgin Mary. Reclaiming her poetic self, Ana focuses on Fermín's analogy of her unrefined faith as a gold nugget in a river, an image described earlier as articulated fortuitously by Fermín. Whereas the Magistral does happen upon a felicitous comparison, it is Ana who evidences the more liberated poetic spirit. With Fermín's seed (or nugget), Ana creates from this image a story for the two of them: "Ella se había visto con su traje de baño, sin mangas, braceando en el río, a la sombra de avellanos y nogales, y en la orilla estaba el Magistral con su roquete blanquísimo, de rodillas, pidiéndole, con las manos juntas, que no arrojase la pepita de oro" (I, 342). [She had seen herself in her bathing suit with no sleeves, swimming in the river in the shadow of hazel and walnut trees, and on the banks was the Magistral, on his knees and wearing his dazzling white rochet, begging her with hands clasped not to discard the gold nugget.] In this way, Fermín contributes the barest minimum—a tiny nugget, to be exact—to Ana's creative process.

Still, Fermín does perform an important function during this first confession. He allows Ana to recover the poetry she thought was forbidden, justifying this return to idealistic reading by arguing for her special qualities. Ana remembers excitedly that Fermín has celebrated her "special temperament," has given her permission to read books forbidden to weaker spirits, and has promised her access to all sorts of "spectacles" when she attains the ultimate spiritual elevation (I, 345). Ana's reaction to this new vision of herself as superior and able to reincorporate her poetic imagination energizes her. Here again, Fermín's words conform to imagery significant to Ana—her ideas of rising, climbing, and superiority. The problem for Fermín is that this exaltation threatens his authority over her. We see that Ana is already recovering her identity as an author when she characterizes what Fermín offers her as "religión verdadera," and associates it with climbing the mountains where she earlier wrote poetry: "la religión verdadera se parecía en definitiva a sus ensueños de adolescente, a sus visiones del monte de Loreto" (I, 345–46). ["true religion was very similar to the dreams of her adolescence, to her visions of the mountain of Loreto"]

Even though Fermín to some extent defends Ana's poetic sensibilities, he also challenges her independence. As I will now explain, Fermín forces Ana first into a defensive mode, then into a defiant stance which ultimately leads to her (textual) victory over him, and her establishment as primary internal author. Perhaps anticipating the threat of her intelligence, Fermín presents himself as professorial interpreter of texts, and urges Ana into the status of subordinate reader by acknowledging her as cultured, but then reading the classics for her. An example would be the passage cited above, when Fermín reminds Ana of her own previous reading of St. Augustine's *Confessions* only to tell her what she should learn from the text (I, 345). Fermín also insists on his authority over Ana when he suggests that he will be her companion in the exalted realm, referring to himself as her older brother of the soul (I, 343). Thus, in this context, we see that Fermín's references to Ana's prior readings are always couched in a paternalistic, controlling frame. Once we recognize the mechanisms Fermín uses to manipulate Ana, we may also realize that Ana resists this treatment. Ana does not allow herself to be eclipsed by Fermín's apparent magnanimity. She seems convinced of her own exalted status, and of Fermín's, but her conception of Fermín has a self-interested quality, and she is eager to be the hero herself of their shared discourse of superiority. First she speaks of Fermín ("¡Vetusta, Vetusta encerraba aquel tesoro! ¿Cómo no sería Obispo el Magistral?" [Vetusta, Vetusta housed that treasure! Why was the Magistral not a bishop?]), but then quickly switches the focus to herself: "¡Quién sabe! ¿Por qué era ella, aunque digna de otro mundo, nada más que una señora ex-regenta de Vetusta?" (I, 347). [Who knows? Why was she, worthy of another place, nothing more than a former judge's wife in Vetusta?] (At the time of the primary action of the novel, Víctor has retired from his position as judge. Although a new (married) "Regente" has replaced him, Ana is still commonly referred to as "La Regenta.") Like the story of the gold nugget, here Ana also quickly passes from a Fermín-centered "story" to one that she herself protagonizes, in a gesture that bodes ill for Fermín's prospects for restraining her fancy.

In addition, Ana has already begun to entertain doubts about Fermín's manipulation of the exclusive narrative of the two "hermanos del alma," [soul siblings] as seen in the description of birds and animals she encounters on this walk. Although she remembers Fermín's words, she also notices life around her, and her interpretation of nature reveals the progress of her analysis of the interview with Fermín. To understand what she feels, we may compare her reaction to Álvaro before she notices the animals, to her vision of Mesía after she takes this walk. As she sets out, she sees Álvaro on the marqueses' balcony, but Mesía is unable to disturb her concentration on the topics she has just discussed with Fermín (I, 335). Bolstered by Fermín's words, Ana looks at Álvaro indifferently, thinking of him as a puppy who does not bite (I, 335). Prior to her walk in the meadow, then, Álvaro is for Ana a little yapping dog, unable to threaten her. As she walks, Ana contemplates small birds touching a watery surface and quickly taking flight again, and remains confident in her newly discovered freedom to imitate the unrestricted movement of the wagtail ("nevatilla"), because of what Fermín promises her ("algo nuevo, algo digno de ser amado" [something new, something worthy of being loved]) (I, 341). With the bird inspiring rather than unsettling her, Ana allows herself a return to idealism. The reader, however, recognizes her words as an imitation of Fermín ("algo nuevo, algo selecto"). Next, as she remembers Fermín's offer to be her "hermano mayor del alma," ("older brother of the soul") she is interrupted by a sparrow: "Un gorrión con un grano de trigo en el pico, se puso enfrente de Ana y se atrevió a mirarla con insolencia" (I, 344). [A sparrow with a grain of wheat in its beak faced Ana and dared to look at her with insolence.] Even though the swallow with the grain of wheat is a degraded version of Fermín's vision of Ana treasuring the gold nugget of her faith, she still maintains her composure in the face of this potential challenge to her idealism by associating the bird with don Cayetano, the confessor she no longer requires: "La dama se acordó del Arcipreste que tenía el don de parecerse a los pájaros" (I, 344). [The lady was reminded of the Arcipreste, who had the tendency to look like different sorts of birds.] But finally, she is most disturbed by a chorus of frogs and the insolent stare of a toad.[13] She imagines that the toad is mocking her: "Se le figuró que aquel sapo había estado oyéndola pensar y se burlaba de sus ilusiones" (I, 347). [It seemed to her that that toad had been listening to her thoughts and was now making fun of her dreams.] Ana valiantly protects her poetic fancies until the appearance of this toad. Whereas the "puppy," the wagtail, and the sparrow are unable to rattle her, the toad interrupts her religious fantasies, which are based on Fermín's words.

With cumulative effect, all of these animals remind Ana of writing poetry on the mountaintop of Loreto when she was a girl. At this early stage, her poetic fancies were interrupted by a dark bird, which frightened her as it brushed by her face. I suggest here that we read this bird as representing Ana's fear of the uncontrolled sublimity of poetic creation, and as an inherent part of the act of textual composition. Now that Ana is grown, the animals she sees after her confession with Fermín recall this first winged intruder, as well as the challenges of being an author. The Vetustan fauna—particularly the toad—indicate that her romantic, religious illusions are degraded, but only because she is allowing Fermín too much control. Although she believes the animals mock her, they seem also to be her allies, sending her the message that she should recover authorial agency, however frightening the prospect. To do so, she must return to the poetry of Loreto and not be subservient to Fermín's discourse. Not yet comprehending the animals' warning, Ana proves that she is in danger of losing control of her personal narrative when she again meets Álvaro. She reacts to him quite differently than before her walk. Her weakness is made clear by the description of her contact with Mesía: "¿No se abrían nuevos horizontes a su alma? ¿No iba a vivir para algo en adelante? ¡Oh! ¡quién le hubiera puesto al señor Magistral allí! Su mano tropezó con la de un hombre. Sintió un calor dulce y un contacto pegajoso. No era el Magistral. Era don Álvaro" (I, 358). [Weren't new horizons opening for her soul? From now on wasn't she going to have a reason to live? Oh! Who had put the Magistral there in her path! Her hand met with another, which belonged to a man. She felt a sweet warmth and an insistent contact. It was not the Magistral. It was don Álvaro.] Rather than rely on her own strength and creativity, then, she wishes for Fermín to save her, and renounces responsibility for her actions just as she is in danger of forsaking the pursuit of authorship.

While she and Álvaro walk together, engaging in superficial conversation, Ana occupies her understimulated brain by returning to the idea of virtue she explored in her meditations on her confession. She now adds a new element, inspired by the animal's warnings and by Fermín's heavy-handed guidance (in reality, competing authorship). When Ana entertains the possibility that she has imagined the wordless communication that has passed between her and Álvaro, she recognizes that her temptations are her only pleasure (I, 363). She remembers all that Fermín has said to her about virtue (he has promised it will come naturally to her), but she realizes that without the fight against erotic temptation, virtue lacks the poetry she craves: "Sí, era fácil [la virtud], bien lo sabía ella, pero si le quitaban la tentación no tendría mérito, sería prosa pura, una cosa vetustense, lo que ella más aborrecía" (I, 364). [Yes, virtue was easy, she knew that all right, but if her temptations were taken from her, her virtue would be worthless: it would be pure prose—a Vetustan thing, and thus what she most hated.] After intuiting Fermín's manipulation of her during the confession, sensing the animals' reminders of her bonds with nature and her poetic background, and finally rediscovering Álvaro as a blank slate on which her imagination might project poetry at will, Ana emerges from her position of weakness with new resolve. She realizes that it is this discourse of her temptation by Álvaro that she must turn to if she wishes to reassert herself as author in the face of Fermín's attempts to control her, and we soon see that she does so. The story of Álvaro as ideal lover is romantic and quixotic to the core, but it is of Ana's own making, and confirms her authorial selfhood in defiance of Fermín's paternalism. At the same time, Ana also cultivates a competing narrative costarring Fermín, and soon recruits Vetustan society as audience for her drama. Ana first stages this contest between Álvaro and Fermín at a gathering hosted by the marqueses de

Vegallana. She begins by constructing Álvaro, making him into a monument of physical charms. Ana observes Álvaro, focusing solely on his appearance, and ignoring his words:

> Reía con franca jovialidad, abriendo bastante la boca y enseñando una dentadura perfecta . . . don Álvaro tenía que inclinarse para que su aliento, al hablar, rozase blandamente la cabeza graciosa y pequeña de la dama. Parecía una sombra protectora, un abrigo, un apoyo; se estaba bien junto a aquel hombre como una fortaleza . . . don Álvaro al moverse con alguna viveza, dejaba al aire un perfume que Ana la primera vez que lo sintió reputó delicioso, después temible . . . A veces la mano del interlocutor se apoyaba sobre el antepecho de la ventana; Ana veía, sin poder remediarlo, unos dedos largos, finos, de cutis blanco, venas azules y uñas pulidas ovaladas y bien cortadas. Y si bajaba los ojos más, para que el otro no creyese que le contemplaba las manos, veía el pantalón que caía en graciosa curva sobre un pie estrecho, largo, calzado con esmero ultra-vetustense. (I, 489)

> [He laughed with frank cheerfulness, with his mouth open, displaying his perfect teeth. Don Álvaro had to lean down so that his breath, as he spoke, brushed softly over the lady's lovely, small head. He seemed like a protective shadow, a shelter, a support. It was nice to be next to that man who was like a fortress. When he moved quickly, don Álvaro left a perfume in the air. The first time that Ana noticed this, she thought it delicious, but later it frightened her. Sometimes her interlocutor rested his hand on the windowsill, and Ana saw, without being able to help herself, long, delicate fingers, with white skin, blue veins, and well-manicured nails. And if she lowered her eyes more, so that the man would not think she was staring at his hands, she saw his pants, which fell in a pleasant curve over his long, narrow foot in the carefully chosen shoe that spoke to a taste far beyond what was typical in Vetusta.]

Thus, she creates the physical Álvaro piece by piece, on the model of a Golden Age sonne—for example, Góngora's "Mientras por competir con tu cabello," with its enumeration of "cabello, cuello, labio y frente" (hair, neck, lip and forehead). While Ana sublimates overt sexual desire, even her poetic image of Álvaro as protector associates him with the solid physical structure of a fort.

Then turning to Fermín, the other character in the drama Ana is writing, she remembers a letter she has just sent him, thinking of it as a tie that binds the two of them together: "La carta era inocente, podía leerla el mundo entero; sin embargo, era una carta de que podía hablar a un hombre, que no era su marido, y que este hombre tenía acaso guardada cerca de su cuerpo y en la que pensaba tal vez" (I, 491). [The letter was innocent—the whole world could read it. And yet, it was a letter written for a man who was not her husband, and that man might be carrying it close to his body, perhaps thinking of it as well.] Ana marvels at her own ingenuity, as she writes one story for Álvaro and another for Fermín. At the same time, the male leads in her play have only enough ingenuity to dream up an unproductive physical contest (rescuing Obdulia from the swing), as even Fermín is distracted from the verbal battle of wills. Thus, early in the novel Ana is dominant over both men in this competition for creativity and authorship.

Furthermore, in the episodes of *La Regenta* that relate to the Vetustan representation of *Don Juan Tenorio,* Ana is the only author, controlling first Álvaro and then Fermín. At the theater, she creates her own reading of the play, imagining herself living the emotions she sees in Zorrilla's work:

> ¡Ay! Sí, el amor era aquello, un filtro, una atmósfera de fuego, una locura mística; huir de él era imposible; imposible gozar mayor ventura que saborearle con todos sus venenos. Ana se comparaba con la hija del Comendador; el caserón de los Ozores era su convento, su marido la regla estrecha de hastío y frialdad en que ya había profesado ocho años hacía . . . y Don Juan . . . ¡Don Juan aquel Mesía que también se filtraba por las paredes, aparecía por milagro y llenaba el aire con su presencia! (II, 48).

> [Oh! Yes, that was what love was. A potion, a fiery atmosphere, an ecstasy of mysticism—fleeing from it was impossible. It was impossible to enjoy a better fate than to savor love and all its poisons. Ana compared herself to the Commander's daughter—the Ozores mansion was her convent, her husband the narrow religious rule of boredom and coldness she had professed eight years ago. And Don Juan . . . Don Juan was that Mesía who also penetrated walls, appeared miraculously and filled the air with his presence.]

In this way, Ana borrows the play to imagine her relationship with Álvaro. When Álvaro comes to talk with her she imposes this discourse on him: "Dejó caer sobre la prosaica imaginación del petimetre el chorro abundante de poesía que había bebido en el poema gallardo, fresco, exuberante de hermosura y color del maestro Zorrilla" (II, 49). [She let fall over the dandy's prosaic imagination the abundant stream of poetry that she had drunk from the lovely, fresh poem, exuberant in the beauty and color of the master Zorrilla.] Ana imagines that Álvaro accompanies her on this poetic flight of fancy, when in fact her lover resists such a reading (II, 49). Despite his strong negative reaction to her enthusiasm, which I suggest relates to his terror of being as romantic as Ana, Álvaro senses that he should copy literary characters, "hacerse el sentimental disimulado, como los hay en las comedias y en las novelas de Feuillet" (II, 49). [to try to play the discreet sentimentalist like the ones in Feuillet's plays and novels.] He is powerless to resist her "staging" of their relationship, and allows Ana to dictate the (literary) terms of their interaction at the play. Álvaro contemplates the situation, musing "¡Pero la buena señora se había *sublimizado* tanto! y como él, por no perderla de vista, y por agradarla, se había hecho el romántico también, el *espiritual,* el *místico* . . . ¿quién iba a decirle: 'bájese usted, amiga mía, que todo esto es volar por los *espacios imaginarios'?*" (II, 50–51, italics in original). [But the good woman had *gone so sublime!* Accordingly, not wanting to lose sight of her and in order to please her, he had also played the romantic, the *spiritual one,* the *mystic.* Who could possibly say to her, "Come down, my friend, because all of this is just flight through *imaginary realms?*"] Thus, Álvaro makes no attempt to compete with Ana as author, and entirely subordinates his initiative to her construction of their relationship.

The next day, Ana performs an analogous maneuver with Fermín. Like the gold nugget of the first confession, Fermín again plants a seed of fiction, but Ana quickly dominates the new narrative. Fermín explains that he would like Ana to confess in the afternoon rather than the morning, because this would give less cause for gossip to his "enemies": "El Magistral sonrió como un mártir entre llamas . . . le entraron [a Ana] vehementes deseos de defenderle contra todos" (II, 63). [The Magistral smiled like a martyr among the flames. Ana was possessed by an overwhelming desire to defend him from everyone.] To her new vision of herself as solitary defender of Vetusta's martyr, Ana now borrows elements from *Don Juan* to add complexity and interest to her construction of her relationship with Fermín, who she remembers is a man whose enemies consider "amorous and forward" (II, 66). What we read earlier as Fermín playing the role of martyr can also be seen as Ana configuring Fermín as Don Juan, after she imposed the same persona on Álvaro the night before. Let us also look back to Fermín's attempt to secure for himself the professorial role by alluding to Ana's prior readings ("Usted que ha leído," cited above). In the paragraph following Fermín's allusions, Ana does not in fact recall the texts of the Arcipreste de Hita, Tirso de Molina, "y otros muchos" [and many others] (II, 67), nor does she remember the role of personal defender and protector of his ego that Fermín might have prescribed for her, but instead creates an entirely new, "exotic" adventure of feminist emancipation, situated in the New World: "Ya no pensaba en las torpes calumnias de los enemigos del Magistral; ya no se acordaba de que aquél era hombre, y se hubiera sentado sin miedo, sobre sus rodillas, como había oído decir que hacen las señoras con los caballeros en los tranvías de Nueva York" (II, 66–67). [Ana no longer thought about the clumsy accusations of the Magistral's enemies—she no longer remembered that this person was a man, and she would have sat without fear across his knees, as she had heard that ladies do with gentlemen in the trolley cars of New York.] Up to this point Ana has subtly defied Fermín's attempts to control her creativity without drawing his attention to her rebellion. Now she begins to analyze the previous evening's play, and in referring to her attraction to romanticism, she frightens Fermín with her extravagance. Ana insists that her life with Víctor is cold and prosaic, and that the feelings she experienced at the play cannot be sinful, although they sound exaggerated: "Hasta es ridículo, suena a romanticismo necio, vulgar, ya lo sé . . . pero no es eso, no es eso!" (II, 71). [It's even ridiculous—it sounds like idiotic, vulgar romanticism—but it's not, it's not!] Fermín then urges Ana to forget Zorrilla and to become a "beata" who observes her religion faithfully and regularly. Although Ana laughs with tears in her eyes and seems to respond to this new suggestion, the bell of the cathedral tower chimes three times "como un aviso" [like a warning] (II, 73). Again the number three figures as related to the struggle for authorship, realism, and resistance. Whereas *Gerona*'s three authors vie with each other for control of the novel, and still-romantic Manuel Alcázar defies three times Roberto Hasting's attempts to write his life, here the three chimes of the cathedral represent the tenacious authorial will Ana hides behind her tears.

In anticipation of her achievement of further independence, Ana dominates Fermín so that he is forced even to adopt a discourse that frightens him—romanticism. He imitates her language, coloring with sensuality the church he would like her to visit: "A la iglesia, hija mía, a la iglesia; no a rezar; a estarse allí, a soñar allí, a pensar allí oyendo la música de órgano y de nuestra excelente capilla, oliendo el incienso del altar mayor, sintiendo el calor de los cirios, viendo cuanto allí brilla y se mueve, contemplando las altas bóvedas, los pilares esbeltos, las pinturas suaves y misteriosamente poéticas de los cristales de colores" (II, 94). [To church, my daughter, to church, but not to pray—to be there, to dream there, to think there while hearing the music of the organ and of our excellent chapel, smelling the incense of the main altar, feeling the warmth of the candles, seeing all that glitters and moves there, contemplating the high arches, the slim pillars, the sweet, mysteriously poetic paintings of the stained glass windows.] As did Álvaro in describing Zorrilla's play, Fermín takes up romantic discourse for the sole purpose of accommodating Ana: "Poca gracia le hacía a don Fermín esta retórica a lo Chateaubriand; siempre había creído que recomendar la religión por su hermosura exterior era ofender la santidad del dogma, pero sabía hacer de tripas corazón y amoldarse a las circunstancias" (II, 95). [Fermín didn't like this Chateaubriand-style rhetoric very much. He had always believed that recommending religion because of its exterior beauty was to compromise the holiness of religious dogma, but he knew how to adapt to the necessities of his surroundings.] Clearly, both men continue to be less comfortable with their romantic heritage than is Ana, so that their borrowings of this discourse constitute their deferring to Ana's greater force of (romantic) will.

Even though Fermín submits to her leadership in the structuring of their narrative, Ana continues to resist him, arriving eventually at the point of open rebellion. She tosses aside the *Life* of Santa Juana Francisca that Fermín has given her (II, 102), and when he confronts her, she alludes to his inaction: in a statement we read earlier as Ana's gentle reminder to Fermín to provide her with an inspiring text, we can also imagine her request as a reprimand, calling attention to his consistent disappointment of her expectations ("Quiero que usted me guíe" [I want you to guide me], cited above). As she has from the beginning, Ana wants only a "seed" from Fermín, and then she plans to take over. However, all that Fermín can provide is the worn-out story of lukewarm faith, and after making half-hearted attempts to follow his lead, Ana falls ill. During this illness, she remembers excursions when she has imposed on Víctor and Álvaro her reading of the *Quijote* as pastoral, and this memory of herself as author anticipates her next endeavors. She takes up the *Vida* of Santa Teresa that Fermín has recommended, but successfully reads the text only after dreaming of a hell associated with Fermín, which she describes directly to him in these terms: "Mi cuerpo estrujado padecía tormentos que no se pueden describir; y a mí además, por la carne aterida y erizada me pasaban llagas asquerosas unos fantasmas que eran diablos vestidos por irrisión, de clérigos, con casullas y capas pluviales" (II, 193–94). [My compressed, exhausted body suffered indescribable torments. Also, demon spirits ridiculing priests by dressing in their copes and chasubles passed through horrid sores on my frozen, cracked skin.] The frightening specters function as do the birds and animals of earlier experiences—reminders that she will be miserable if she allows Fermín to extinguish her creativity. Spurred on by these omens, she begins to read Santa Teresa independently.[14]

The *Vida* inspires Ana to pursue more aggressively her dream of being an author, and she writes Fermín a letter in imitation of Santa Teresa. After taking Ana's composition to a private spot outside, in ecstasy Fermín reads out loud: "Se le ocurrió mezclar a la cháchara insustancial y armoniosa de los pájaros que saltaban de rama en rama sobre su cabeza, su voz más dulce y melódica, recitando aquellas palabras de espiritual hermosura que la Regenta le había escrito" (II, 193). [It had occurred to him to recite aloud the words of spiritual beauty the Regenta had written him, so that his sweet, melodic voice would mix with the vapid, harmonious chattering of the birds that hopped from branch to branch above his head.] Whereas Fermín chooses to ignore the birds' chirping, again these animals accompany Ana in her creative writing, announcing her persistence as poet. Accordingly, Fermín soon discovers that Ana has acquired a new authorial independence from him, thanks to her solitary reading of Santa Teresa. Initially unsuspecting, Fermín reads as Ana recommends texts to imitate and acknowledges Fermín as the original discoverer of such narratives. Gradually, however, it becomes evident that she is constructing herself as superior even to him. Ana writes—and Fermín reads—"Seguiremos, además de esos monjes alemanes o suecos de que usted me habló, a la misma Teresa de Jesús que, como usted sabe, con buenas palabras y creo yo que hasta bromas alegres que tenía, con purísima intención, con un clérigo amigo suyo, consiguió apartarle del pecado" (II, 195). [In addition to those German or Swedish monks you mentioned to me, we will follow Teresa of Jesus who, as you know, with correct words, and I think even with good-natured jokes of purest purpose, was able to stop a priest who was a friend of hers from sinning.] After employing a phrase similar to the one Fermín used with her in their conversation in the garden of Ana's house, when he acknowledged her as a reader and then made reference to a text (II, 66, cited earlier), Ana recounts the story of Santa Teresa's salvation of her confessor from the temptation of profane love. Although she reverses the roles of these characters ("Aquí el débil no es el confesor, sino la penitente" [Here the weak one is the penitent, not the confessor]) (II, 195), Ana's detailed summary of Santa Teresa's heroism with the debilitated confessor strikes at Fermín's position of authority over her: even if Ana's confessor is reputedly strong, she has taken up the role of Santa Teresa, who dominated her confessor with her virtue. Ana is now the lead interpreter who refers to a text Fermín should remember, just as he spoke to her at her first confession, when proposing they meet to discuss her good qualities. In this case, though, Ana's words appear in writing, as her condescension toward Fermín takes the more permanent form of written text, rather than the spoken discourse he used with her.[15] Again, as author, Ana subjugates, and Fermín is left to read the story she composes for him.

In her exaltation, Ana characterizes Fermín as her brother rather than her father, establishing a relationship more of equals than of paternal authority figure and daughter, even if she does attribute the original idea for the new brotherly model to Fermín. Ana believes that she has been luckier than Santa Teresa, because she has not had to wait as long for support "por mano de quien quisiera llamar mi padre y prefiere que no le llame sino hermano mío; sí hermano mío, hermano muy querido, me complazco en llamárselo" (II, 194). [from the hand of one I would like to call my father, but who prefers that I call him merely my brother. Yes, my brother, my very dear brother—I enjoy calling him that.] After reading Ana's crafty redefinition of their relationship—he cannot criticize her boldness if he has authorized such a stance himself—Fermín notes a passage in which Ana vows to convert Víctor, now deftly shifting herself into the role of spiritual advisor rather than penitent. Fermín sits down and reads silently, perhaps subdued by Ana's replacement of him in this role. He feels threatened by Santa Teresa ("algunos celos tenía de Santa Teresa, de la que veía enamorada a su amiga" [he was somewhat jealous of Santa Teresa, seeing that his friend (Ana) was in love with her]) (II, 196), and the text suggests that this envy originates from his realization of Ana's claims to higher status. She presents herself as having authority over Víctor and, more important, being the author of the texts the Magistral is reading and living. Fermín's apprehensions are confirmed when he visits Ana and recognizes the alteration of the power relations between himself and Ana. When Ana speaks of Santa Teresa, "con entusiasmo de idólatra" [with the enthusiasm of an idolater], Fermín only partially approves of this zeal: "El Magistral aprobaba su admiración, pero con menos calor que empleaba al hablar de ellos, de su amistad" (II, 207). [The Magistral spoke warmly of her admiration (of Santa Teresa), but with less passion than he used when speaking of the two of them and of their friendship.] Also, the narrator repeats: "Don Fermín tenía celos de la Santa de Ávila" (II, 207). [Don Fermín was jealous of the saint from Ávila.] In these passages, then, Fermín struggles with his happiness that Ana directs her effusiveness toward him, and his competing desire to exert control over his penitent "hermana menor del alma" [younger sister of the soul]. Fermín and Ana have built together a relationship based on the processing of texts, but they now compete for the ultimate rights of authorship of their shared narrative. Fermín's position is precarious. He is responsible for Ana's initial contact with Santa Teresa, but in her desire to imitate Teresa, Ana is becoming the very (author) figure who threatens to usurp Fermín's hegemony.

Indeed, he has cause for fear, as Ana's authorial independence increases. When Álvaro leaves for the summer, the emotion Ana has contained within her issues forth in the form of the following fiction: that Álvaro stumbles away from her, not disoriented as he is in reality by anger and resentment of her, but "ciego de amor y pena" (II, 218). [blind with love and sorrow.] She then fights the temptation to assuage Álvaro's alleged heartsickness by turning her eyes to heaven and kissing the cross her confessor has given her. She exclaims, "Jesús, Jesús, tú no puedes tener un rival. Sería infame, sería asqueroso . . . Y recordó la ira de Jesús cuando se aparecía a Teresa que le olvidaba" (II, 219). [Jesus, Jesus, you cannot have a rival. It would be evil, it would be foul . . . and she remembered Jesus's anger when he appeared to Teresa, who had forgotten him.] Thus, in her creative adaptation of Santa Teresa's *Life,* Ana authors this subplot starring herself and Álvaro, with Fermín utterly eclipsed by Ana's directly address-ing Christ, without the aid of her usual mediator. Despite Fermín's in-dulgence of her need for textual stimulation, Ana's preference for the fictionalization of Álvaro continues. As at the performance of *Don Juan Tenorio,* when she transformed Álvaro into a medieval adventurer, Ana reconfigures Mesía when she observes him at Midnight Mass. She studies him, as Álvaro is briefly illuminated by the acolytes' candles, and his drunken half-consciousness appears to her as religious devotion. Again, Ana's fantastic vision of Álvaro accords him added power, and makes of him much more than he really is: "Se le antojó vestido de rojo, con un traje muy ajustado y muy airoso. No sabía si era aquello un traje de Mefistófeles de ópera o el de cazador elegante, pero estaba el enemigo muy hermoso, muy hermoso" (II, 280–81). [She imagined him dressed in red, with a tight-fitting, very elegant suit. She didn't know if this was the suit of a Mephistopheles from the opera or that of an elegant hunter, but her enemy was very beautiful, very beautiful.] When Fermín complains indirectly of this enthusiasm, and takes the bold step of alluding to himself as Mesía's rival, Ana insists on following her own idealistic narrative in opposition to Fermín's crude formulation. Although in calling himself rival to Mesía Fermín claims pedestrian status, his agitation inspires in Ana the vision of him as glorious martyr. Ignoring the pettiness of Fermín's conception of their relationship, Ana refuses to give up her poetry and exclaims—as cited above—that she now knows that she was born to live at the feet of the martyr others crucify with calumny (II, 290).

Nevertheless, Ana quickly loses interest in this particular narrative, and distracts herself with the ball at the Casino. Ana begins the contest with Álvaro, fictionalizing him before he can offer her a text of his own: "Se le figuraban ya todos los caballeros que andaban por allí, don Víctor inclusive, criados vestidos de etiqueta; todos eran camareros, el único señor Mesía" (II, 305). [She imagined that all the gentlemen there, even don Víctor, were dressed-up servants—all were waiters, and the only master was Mesía.] As we have seen, it is at this point, however, that Álvaro begins to gain some advantage with Ana, because he finally acts as an author himself, speaking directly to her of love. At the same time, as we have just noted, Ana writes the romance of Álvaro as Don Juan, specifically characterizing him in this manner at the Casino ball. In this way, Ana remains in control of Álvaro, and continues her manipulation of Fermín. After she faints in Álvaro's arms, Fermín confronts Ana, but she deftly distracts him with a different story, winning him over with the pitiful narrative of her life without a mother (II, 318). However, Fermín then responds to Ana's self-romanticization in a way that is unfortunate for his self-interest. He is unable to mask his personal agenda with any sort of idealistic story and merely succeeds in shocking Ana by revealing that he loves her (II, 321). The only narrative he offers is the story of a priest in love with his penitent, but Ana sees no poetry in this (II, 321–22). She shudders as Fermín's indirect declaration marks an abrupt shift in her conception of their relationship from ideal to material, represented by her feeling that she has touched a cold, slimy body.[16] With this statement, Ana indicates that she is uncomfortable with Fermín's imposing a story of carnality onto her idealized defense of him as martyr. The indistinct, repugnant creature is like that of the other animals and apparitions of the text: reminders to Ana that she must fight rival authors who impose unwanted texts on her.

In defiance, Ana next tries to live a domestic idyll, which she finds unfulfilling. She then attempts to return to Fermín's domain of religion, envisioning herself taking up the role of the Virgin Mary in the Easter Procession, but this act of penance ultimately humiliates her (II, 367–68). She feels that she is crazy, and is ashamed of her literary leanings, saying to herself: "¡Ella era una loca que había caído en una especie de prostitución singular! . . . Allí iba la tonta, la literata, Jorge Sandío, la mística, la fatua, la loca, la loca sin vergüenza" (II, 366). [She was a crazy woman who had fallen into a strange sort of prostitution! There went the fool, the scandalous literary woman, George Sand, the mystic, the conceited one, the crazy woman, the shameless, crazy woman.] Clearly, Ana's shame—which issues forth as a rejection of her romantic self—has to do with her realization that she has submitted to Fermín's control: she is not in fact the author of the story she desperately wished to create and protagonize. For this reason, her romanticism is now an embarrassment. Suddenly afraid of her idealism, Ana cedes some control to Álvaro, so that she may resist religious romanticism with the narrative she has authored for herself and Álvaro. Mesía reinforces Ana's rejection of Fermín after the Easter procession, telling her (as mentioned above) that mysticism was nervous exaltation, and that Fermín was never really a mystic (II, 420). Ana accepts his logic, and applies it obediently to the creation of new stories: "La pasión . . . le sugería sofisma tras sofisma para encontrar repugnante, odiosa, criminal la conducta del Provisor, y noble y caballeresca la de Mesía" (II, 421). [Passion suggested to her one sophism after another, to ensure that she would find Fermín's behavior repugnant, odious, and criminal, and Mesía's noble and gallant.] At the same time, she begins to author stories of another type, as evidenced by her diary, included as part of the novel. For the first time, we read directly long passages that Ana has written. Inspired by her doctor, Benítez, Ana writes odes to her good health. This focus on her body, however, reminds her of erotic discourse, and eventually she returns to her romance with Álvaro.

The ongoing seduction is finally resolved by Ana herself, when she is agitated by two "texts"—the story of the Bacchantes from her readings, and an engraving on the cover of the *Ilustración* called "La última flor" (The Last Flower), which portrays a woman of about her age, clutching desperately at a flower (II, 439). The novel has presented Álvaro as Bacchus, at the conspiratorial dinner at the Casino (II, 173), but although this imagery would have him as authority over the women who worship him (Ana and the other "bacantes"), again we note that it is Ana who has imagined for herself the narrative and subordinate role, so that in this instance, the devotee outshines and controls the master. With Ana prepared by these two unsettling "texts" she waits only for Álvaro to take the initiative, although in effect, because she has encountered the narratives that will guide her (self)seduction, she remains the true author of her affair with Álvaro.

Even after her "fall," and although Álvaro eventually deserts her, Ana continues as supreme author. This is evident if we contrast the other characters' actions with Ana's. Álvaro is unable to control the web he creates with Petra, Víctor, and Ana. Fermín attempts to orchestrate Víctor's return to his Calderonian models of vengeance when Ana's adultery is discovered, but he fails as well. When the characters do enact a degraded version of Fermín's plan, Álvaro ultimately kills Víctor in a duel he never wanted to fight. If we glance again at these examples, they can be seen as proof that Ana is the only competent author of the novel. To begin with, she has conceived of the climactic duel scene at a very early stage in the novel. When she stays home from the theater pitying herself—the same night Álvaro is intimidated by his vision of her as El Cid—Ana fantasizes about Álvaro killing her husband and stealing her away (I, 371). (As mentioned earlier, in her fantasy Ana is married to the *indiano* don Frutos, not Víctor Quintanar, but nevertheless the novel's climax is foreshadowed.) The duel is originally Ana's idea, and she is also the textual authority who gives Víctor his final model for imitation. When faced with his wife's adultery, Víctor chooses the resignation recommended by Kempis's *Imitation of Christ* instead of the violent solutions he has absorbed from Calderón, and which Fermín recommends. Ana, of course, is the vehicle for his access to Kempis; she prescribed this reading when she was encroaching on Fermín's role as spiritual advisor. Finally, Ana's—or as she envisions herself, Mary Magdalene's—coup de grâce is her coopting of the martyr discourse in the final scene of the novel. When Fermín rejects her attempts to confess with him, she falls senseless, and is further degraded by the effeminate acolyte Celedonio's kiss, which leaves her feeling that she has unwillingly kissed the slimy belly of a toad. Ana is now the most "persecuted" creature in Vetusta, because she has outdone Fermín in this final contest. At the end she has the last word: she definitively protagonizes the martyrdom Fermín has earlier monopolized, and stages her personal drama for an unlimited audience—beyond the inhabitants of Vetusta, for all of Clarín's readers pity her.

Staying far from the train tracks on which Anna Karenina brings about her own end, and Emma Bovary's poison, the imaginative romantic Ana de Ozores lives on as an unlimited feminine authorial impulse. Even while degrading and confirming her as a martyr, Celedonio (the deliverer of the toad belly kiss) also reminds us of the other animals and birds that have recalled Ana's poetic drive. Returning to Galdós's review of Alas's novel, I would now like to suggest that Galdós, in order to reduce Ana's agency and power, configures the narrative as the plight of a weak woman torn between two seducers. Rather than describing her as a strong author, this influential reader—a novelist himself—dismisses Ana because she might compete with him. If such a reading were not imposed on her, Ana would threaten not only her male adversaries within the novel, but also the external authors who encounter her. When we read *La Regenta,* Ana's persistence continues to challenge us, in the same way that it unsettled her creator, Clarín, and her interpreter, Galdós.[17]

Conclusion: Realism as Reconciliation, or, Recovering Cervantes

WE HAVE SEEN THAT THE FIRST SERIES OF *EPISODIOS NACIONALES, LA lucha por la vida,* and *La Regenta,* all of which may be called realist novels, attempt to come to terms with romanticism, idealism, and quixotism. We have considered the stories of Gabriel Araceli, Manuel Alcázar, and Ana de Ozores as acknowledging the continuing pull of a romantic or poetic vision, even if such a worldview is in contradiction to realism. We have also delved into a concern with the unruly reader, and have discovered beneath this superficial preoccupation the author-character's (and, I would suggest, the external author's) doubts about him or herself, driven by the unsatisfactory resolution of the contest between realism and romanticism.

Perhaps the most important conclusion to be drawn from this analysis of the *Episodios, La Regenta,* and *La lucha por la vida* is that there is always a loss associated with the reactive renunciation of idealism. Realist authors were certainly aware of the limitations of their narrative style. The elimination of romanticism protects the realist character (and author) from charges of effeminacy, immorality, and foreignness, but at the same time prevents such a character from deriving any of quixotism's possible benefits. For example, these novels raise the question of whether antipragmatic idealism is necessary for the patriotic defense of the nation and for social change. The texts we have examined also ask whether the tenacious individualism linked to romanticism and quixotism is a required component of creative life and of authorship. Thus, we are ultimately left wondering how to handle quixotism if it is undesirably irrational, yet also inherently joined to the concept of heroic patriotism and to the authorial project itself.

In our study of the realist novel's author-protagonists, we looked at *La Regenta*'s Ana de Ozores last. Ana's authorial endeavors are crucial if we wish to draw any conclusions about realism and romanticism in these texts. To begin with, Ana is a strong author. Even in her misery, she persists, when the male protagonists of *La Regenta* are silenced. Moreover, she outdoes these male competitors and would-be seducers at every stage of the novel. At the same time, Ana creates romantic rather than realist texts. This presence of romanticism in Ana's discourse leads us to ask whether her strength as an author might result from the fact that she directly engages romantic narrative instead of resorting to a resistant and defensive realism. In effect, the texts Ana de Ozores produces are more "honest" in their inclusion of both realism and romanticism than are some of the tortured, ineffective discourses of her male counterparts. Ana remains the dominant author in *La Regenta* even in, and precisely because of, her suffering. She ends as a martyred romantic, with an inextinguishable female self.

Still, despite her success as an author, Ana is obviously unhappy at the end of *La Regenta*. She is not socially integrated like the author-protagonists of Galdós and Baroja, Gabriel Araceli and Manuel Alcázar. I would like to suggest that this irony represents the dilemma faced by the external authors of these novels: the author-character who most bravely engages romanticism is the most powerful of the three, yet she is a threat to social stability. In fact, rather than embodying the heroic quixotism of Galdós's Santiago Fernández, Ana de Ozores could even be called unpatriotic, since her adulterous relationship with Álvaro Mesía causes a crisis that unsettles the town of Vetusta. Furthermore, Ana not only undermines her immediate community. She and the dissipation she represents constitute a threat to the entire Spanish nation.[1]

We also note that of the three internal authors, the most persistent author-protagonist is female, with a femininity closely associated with vestigial romanticism. Actually, though, all of the novels examined here exhibit a preoccupation with the feminine that is particularly obvious at the end of each series (or single novel in the case of *La Regenta*). Gabriel humbles himself and allows Inés and Amaranta to "author" his life. Manuel Alcázar extinguishes his romanticism and his ego, while his wife, Salvadora, dominates him, remaining the stronger partner in the marriage. Salvadora also appears as a final Christ figure, intercedes as savior for the dying Juan, and reminds us of Juan's feminine nature. Although Gabriel and Manuel marry seamstresses—apparently humble women who are ostensibly mere technicians of fashion—these "uncultured" ladies end up dominating the author-characters who are the protagonists of the novels.[2] It is ironic that Gabriel and Manuel, the narrators who ultimately achieve the most social success, are nevertheless emasculated and eclipsed by women or femininized men like Juan. In contrast to Gabriel and Manuel, Ana de Ozores remains a strong author-figure—the inexhaustible female authorial ego. Ana persists in her creative, martyrial misery, because she comes closest to accepting the romantic heritage that finally defeats the male author-characters, and plagues the male external authors.

At this point, we must recall that the author-character, or internal author, is of course distinct from the external, historical author. Even so, I believe that we can read as subtext encoded within the novels an extratextual drama featuring the external authors. Realizing that strength in authorship relates to incorporation of romanticism and possibly femininity, the external authors face certain challenges. They would like to be strong, and to ally themselves with the strain of quixotic romanticism seen as patriotic, but they do not want to risk being linked to effeminacy or irrational ideations. Also, they must come to terms with the other facet of quixotism, authorial selfishness—we must remember that the selfish author, as exemplified by Nomdedéu, but also by Gabriel, Manuel, and Ana, is often characterized as particularly *un*patriotic. In other words, we see the preoccupation with egoism of the external authors as reflected in the internal authors' conflicts. Drawing on the lessons of the novels, we notice that for Galdós, Baroja, and Clarín, to be an author is to be "selfish"—to defiantly draw attention to oneself as a creative individual. This egoistic drive is problematic when one is called to be patriotically self-effacing (in the case of Gabriel), a disciplined and humble worker (Manuel), or a conventional married woman (Ana de Ozores). In all cases, these author-characters need to sacrifice authorial self-promotion and ally themselves with selflessness if they wish to contribute to the good of the nation and society. Now, by doing this, the internal authors would escape negative associations with romanticism, selfishness, and femininity. Embracing one aspect of quixotism (patriotic action), they would eschew another (self-glorification). However, they would also no longer be authors. Also, this solution begs the following question: in the sense that it is heroic, is the pursuit of self-sacrificing patriotism not merely another expression of the cult of the quixotic self—the glorious romantic hero? For these reasons, the recommendation made by the novels is not simple.

Still, I believe we have enough information to guess at the external authors' view of these issues. The warning implicit in all of these texts is that if the author (external or internal) takes up realism as a shield from romanticism, rather than confronting idealism as an integral part of realism, that writing subject will find such romantic narrative an unwanted traveling companion on his side of the shield. The task of our realist authors, then, is to work through ever-present romanticism, in order to incorporate the strengths of patriotic and authorial quixotism without abandoning the realism the external authors see as the better discursive option. Thus, rather than a romanticism relegated to a feminine realm, the authors of these novels reclaim romanticism within a frame that showcases their authorial selves, while protecting them from charges of effeminacy and lack of patriotism.

To accomplish this, the external authors perform a simple maneuver. Instead of producing extravagant narratives based on the model offered by the character Don Quijote, the realist authors identify with Cervantes, the unquestioned master of the romantic-realist hybrid. In other words, the external authors come to terms with romanticism by absorbing it into their realist texts, and protecting themselves by controlling the integrated discourse. Just as Cervantes preserves the novels of chivalry even as he engages in their parody, Galdós, Clarín, and Baroja recapture romanticism and tame it, still deriving the benefit of romanticism's seductive discourses, but also figuring as authorities able to contain such volatile fantasies within the "healthier" narratives of realism. In imitating Cervantes, the realist authors of the late nineteenth and early twentieth centuries borrow their protagonists in all their complexity, giving us both idealistic and realistic Quijote characters based on the Don Quijotes at the beginning and the end of Cervantes's novel. Also like Cervantes, these realist authors condescend to their novels' characters—the descendents of Don Quijote—treating them like case studies in their diagnoses of contemporary Spanish pathologies. This superior attitude protects the external authors from possible accusations that they revel in idealism, even though such romantic discourse forms the skeleton of their novels. Galdós, Baroja, and Clarín thus appropriate idealism by enclosing it within a realistic narrative, and promote themselves as enjoying control of the synthesis of romanticism and realism, in the same way that Cervantes incorporates the chivalric novel in order to create his parody.

Returning to Galdós's essay "Observaciones sobre la novela contemporánea en España" (1870), and to José España Lledó's call for a contemporary Cervantes, we realize that the external authors Galdós, Baroja, and Clarín figure as the new leaders who would end Spain's "idealismo desaforado" (excessive, unbridled idealism) by merging the excitement of idealism with Cervantine realism. In offering their integrated prose as healthier than extravagant romanticism, the realist authors reveal their desire to be considered patriotic, manifested in their imitation of Cervantes's cleansing of the chivalric excesses of his nation. With this gesture, Galdós, Baroja, and Clarín recover the quixotism of patriotism, while shielding themselves from associations with irrationality, because as authors they remain safely at one remove from becoming quixotic characters. Because these realist authors take Cervantes as a model, they can write romanticism and draw on its power within their realist narratives without identifying with female romantics. Cervantes, their male mentor, protects them from charges of effeminacy. In this way, they capture the strength of the Ana de Ozores who outdoes her male counterparts by recuperating romanticism instead of writing reactive realism, and at the same time, they identify with a male precursor, rather than with Ana's powerful yet threatening feminine spirit. The male external authors who recover Cervantes hope to go beyond Ana de Ozores, replacing her social maladjustment with a constructive, even patriotic literary project that will heal their illogical nation. Thus, by calling on Cervantes as precursor, the external authors of the realist novel process romanticism so that they are seen as masculine heroes rather than effeminate romantics. In adopting the identity of the male external author who created the dual discourse of romantic realism, Galdós, Baroja, and Clarín synthesize and subdue the quixotism of both heroic authorship and self-sacrificing patriotism, while claiming that their masculinity is unassailable.

Notes

INTRODUCTION

The second epigraph to this chapter is quoted in Geoffrey Wall's *Flaubert: A Life*, p. 239. Wall observed that Flaubert contradicted himself. At times he claimed that the character of Madame Bovary represented his own subjectivity, whereas on other occasions Flaubert described the story as pure invention. If a male author like Flaubert identified in any way with a female protagonist of romantic tendencies, it makes sense that he would have felt conflicted about such a parallel.

1. My use of the term "realistic" rather than "realist" allows me to generalize about these three authors' novels without implying that they all belong to what is considered the realist generation, or that their different versions of realism are in any way "pure" or uniform. In the rest of the text I simplify the term as "realism" or "realist," and ask the reader to keep these qualifications in mind. Baroja especially is not usually considered a "realist"—he is often characterized as an "impressionist" (Earle, "Baroja y su ética de la imposibilidad," 66; González López, "*Camino de perfección,*" 451), who used elements of reality to create texts significantly different from those of Galdós's and Clarín's generation. It is precisely because of this disparity that I find it stimulating to trace similar patterns in the interaction of realism and romanticism across generational lines.

2. See Wellek, "Romanticism in Literature," 195–96; Abrams, *Glossary of Literary Terms,* 5th ed., 152; Kaufmann, Prologue to *I and Thou,* by Martin Buber, 47.

3. Hemmings, *Age of Realism,* 36.

4. Close, *Romantic Approach to* Don Quixote, 1.

5. Because their opponents tend to conflate and interchange the terms romanticism, idealism, and quixotism, I use these words somewhat indiscriminately, thus conveying the viewpoint of poetic extravagance's enemies.

6. Núñez Ruiz, *La mentalidad positiva* 12, 96–109. All translations are my own.

7. Davis, "Spanish Debate," 1653. The Ateneo (Atheneum) is a club that was founded in 1829 to encourage the intellectual development of Spain.

8. Bretz, *Voices, Silences and Echoes,* 41, 81. Here we might conceive of the later nineteenth-century Spain's interest in Krausism as part of idealism's heritage. For a thorough discussion of this intellectual movement, which could also be termed philosophical, ethical, and even religious, see López Morillas, *El Krausismo español.*

226

9. Gullón, "Parodias del sentir," 181.

10. Lucas, *Decline and Fall,* 14.

11. Hartman, "Heroics of Realism," 34. According to Hartman, "modern realistic fiction . . . has kept its attachments to romance and myth. to characters that bear a 'daimon' which cannot be morally or psychologically reduced" (33). I pursue this vestige of romanticism in the realist "hero" who is also an internal author.

12. Despite my criteria for selection, my choice of novels and authors remains arbitrary. One could analyze many novels using the method I practice, with equally interesting results. Rather than an exhaustive study of the legacy of romanticism in realist-based novels of Spain, I hope to offer a limited number of readings of a phenomenon common to many novels of the age.

13. This campaign for selfhood is itself a romantic project, particularly as it implies a struggle or contest. John Koethe described this dynamic: "The central impulse of romanticism is, I take it, the affirmation of subjectivity. While this affirmation may, in concrete instances, be embodied in or disguised by a championing of individualism, the presentation of the heroic, the picturesque, or the languorous, or the celebration of nature, the underlying movement of romanticism is a contestatory one, in which subjective consciousness seeks to ward off the annihilating effect of its objective setting." ("The Romance of Realism," 725–26). According to F. W. J. Hemmings, "Romanticism is nothing if not self-expression" ("Realism in the Age of Romanticism," 66).

14. For more on this topic, see John Reed's "Inherited Characteristics."

15. Ramos-Gascón, "La literatura española," 87.

16. Close, *Romantic Approach to* Don Quixote, 50.

17. I use the masculine pronoun for the sake of simplicity, and also because I eventually argue that the author-character parallels the external (male) author of the realist novel. Nevertheless, this discussion of the internal author applies also to female Quijotes, such as *La Regenta*'s Ana de Ozores.

18. According to the German philosopher Wilhelm Dilthey (1833–1911), literature was a central formative influence for nineteenth-century thought, and the novel prepared for the convergence of biography and historiography that took place during the nineteenth century (Gilman, *Galdós and the European Novel,* 11). Also, Galdós's generation of writers produced works of fiction unlike the great novels of the past, in that the Spanish realist novel merged national and personal biography, as well as public and private spheres (22).

19. Emilio Alarcós Llorach has discussed the chronology of *La lucha por la vida* in detail, and concluded that the trilogy spans the years 1888–1902 (*Anatomía,* 42–50). E. Inman Fox situated the action in 1885–1902 (*Ideología,* 193).

20. The Restoration mentioned here is that of the Bourbon monarchy which returned to power in Spain in the last days of 1874, after losing the throne in 1868. The Restoration years—"los tiempos bobos"—were marked by a stability that masked political corruption, and a loss of faith in the political system (see Cabrera, *Revolución liberal,* quotation on p. 85). The phrase is difficult to translate. The "Foolish Age," or the "Stupid Age," is perhaps the best option.

21. This impulse to fictionalize the nation in certain ways can also be seen as the heritage of romanticism and idealism, particularly of the "Schlegelian Romantic historicism" studied by Derek Flitter (*Romantic Theory and Criticism,* 150).

22. Tsuchiya, *Images of the Sign,* 108.

23. Diane Urey has related Galdós's warning in the Third Series of *Episodios nacionales* to Nietzsche's cautions about "monumental history" ("Monuments to Syllables," 109). Nietzsche's 1874 attack on scientific history called for literature to question the past. In *The Use and Abuse of History,* Nietzsche explained that the student of history must be strong

enough to "break up the past," and to make it useful for living by interrogating it at "the bar of judgment" and ultimately condemning it (20–21). Nietzsche preserves his optimistic faith in the young. He believes in the youth who inspired his critique of modern historical education and his demand that all people learn to use history in the service of life (65). Praising art, Nietzsche suggested an outlet for the historical impulse, and anticipated the fictional representation of national history which we see in the Spanish novels of the late nineteenth and early twentieth centuries. In these novels, in which author figures analyze themselves, using historical fiction as national interrogation serves well, given that the personal and the national are intimately related.

24. Gilman, *Galdós and the European Novel,* 57–59.

25. Fox, *Ideología,* 180–81. Jorge Rodríguez Padrón paints a similar picture in "Divagaciones en torno a un centenario" (see particularly pp. 15–16). The comparison of Baroja's treatment of history with that of Galdós has been a contested issue. Pedro Laín Entralgo's *La Generación del Noventa y Ocho* emphasized differences in the narration of history found in the writings of Galdós and the Generation of 98. For Laín Entralgo, Galdós represents traditional history whereas the younger writers, particularly Baroja and Valle-Inclán, write intrahistorically, taking a fragment from the past and portraying it novelistically, "from within" (166–67). Carlos Longhurst has disagreed, explaining that Laín's insistence on differentiating Baroja's novelizing of history from Galdós's by identifying Baroja with Unamuno's *intrahistoria* led the critic astray. For Longhurst, Laín's implication is that Galdós dehumanized history, which he found to be an incorrect assumption (*Las Novelas históricas de Pío Baroja,* 255). According to Juan Ignacio Ferreras, rather than possessing a historical criterion different from that of Galdós, Baroja lacks such a criterion altogether ("Tensión y negación," 298).

26. The work of Gabriela Pozzi is relevant here; all three of these novelists wrote at the end of the nineteenth century or the beginning of the twentieth. Pozzi found that as the nineteenth century progressed, more was required of the implied reader: "Si al principio del siglo XIX, el lector implícito es una figura pasiva, según avanza el tiempo, se va haciendo paulatinamente más activo y complejo; la actualización del texto requiere cada vez mayor participación del lector" (*La Novela del XIX,* 142). [If at the beginning of the nineteenth century the implied reader is a passive figure, as time passes, that reader slowly becomes more active and more complex. The actualization of the text requires an ever greater participation by the reader.]

27. Godzich and Spadaccini, "Literature in Nineteenth-Century Spain," 29–31. For histories of the *novela por entregas,* see Botrel, "La novela por entregas"; Ferreras, *Novela;* and Romero Tobar, *La novela popular.* Martí-López's *Borrowed Words* is particularly helpful for this history, for the clarification of terms related to the popular novel, and for the definition of the *folletín.* (See note 46).

28. On this point, Germán Gullón remarked on Baroja's continuation of Galdós's awareness of the construction of the authorial subject within the text, and explained that Galdós (and by extension, Baroja) successfully transmits the essence of modern man, trapped between the tendency to believe in the ideal and the reality of everyday events ["la esencia del hombre moderno, atrapado entre la tendencia a creer en lo ideal y la realidad del suceder cotidiano"] (*Novela del XIX,* 47).

29. Fox, "Unamuno, Ganivet," 56.

30. Barzun, "Romantic Historiography," 318. Again, Derek Flitter's *Spanish Romantic Literary Theory and Criticism* is relevant here.

31. Bann, *Romanticism and the Rise of History,* 5, 21.

32. Ibid., 5, 44.

33. Many of my quotes exemplifying the fear of the novel's possible unhealthy influence on readers come from texts produced prior to the novels of the authors I study here—

particularly Baroja. As might be expected, the preoccupation with unruly "readers" (people) as a collectivity is less noticeable in Baroja than in Galdós, and even Clarín, although there is clearly a concern with potential inappropriateness of readings evident in all the novels I examine.

34. Fernández, *Apology to Apostrophe*, 42.

35. Goldman, "Sociology of the Novel," 181; Jagoe, "Disinheriting the Feminine," 229; Sieburth, *Literature, Mass Culture, Uneven Modernity*, 5.

36. "Tanto la prensa periódica como la popularización de la novela fueron posibles gracias al desarrollo de la educación y la enseñanza popular" (Zavala, Romero Tobar, and Benítez, "La realidad del folletín," 381). [The periodical press as well as the popularization of the novel were possible thanks to the development of the education of the general population.]

37. See Zavala, *Ideología y política*, 232–35, 254–69, 274–78, 284–91, 308–17. Quotation is from p. 266.

38. Ibid., 266.

39. Jagoe, "Disinheriting the Feminine," 227.

40. Martí-López, *Borrowed Words*, 34.

41. José España Lledó, qtd. in Zavala, *Ideología y política*, 316.

42. Sieburth, *Literature, Mass Culture, Uneven Modernity*, 6.

43. José España Lledó, qtd. in Zavala, *Ideología y política*, 317.

44. Ibid., 318. For an extensive study of the topic of Cervantes in Galdós's work, see Benítez, *Cervantes en Galdós*.

45. Jagoe, "Disinheriting the Feminine," 228.

46. With women writers rejected because of their idealism, "we can trace the emergence of a new discursive tactic linking the novel's inferior literary value with feminization, as male writers began to equate what they saw as the need to improve the aesthetic standards of novels with increased textual virility" (Jagoe, "Disinheriting the Feminine," 230). Furthermore, with reference to one of these supposedly inferior literary forms, Martí-López explains, in "Historiografía literaria y folletín," 116, "el folletín carece propiamente de autor" [strictly speaking, the *folletín* lacks an author]. For this reason, realist authors striving for strong authorial presence as defenders of national culture would wish to avoid association with this "authorless" genre. To clarify, "folletín" refers to either the novel fragment inserted in a newspaper, or a specific section of newspapers or magazines dedicated to critical and cultural essays (Andreu, *Galdós y la literatura popular*, 34–35). The word came to be associated primarily with serialized novels, and the *folletín* gained fame as a mouthpiece for campaigns for social justice, "no solo por razones políticas y económicas, sino por razones humanas" (Zavala, Romero Tobar, and Benítez, "La realidad del folletín," 381, 384). [not only for political and economic but also for human reasons.] The *novela por entregas* was thematically and stylistically similar, but was published independently (385). See also Note 27.

47. "Lo que esta primera novela realista propone es la emancipación del hombre; ataca la injusticia social directamente, los privilegios, el sistema de explotación del hombre por el hombre" (Zavala, Romero Tobar, and Benítez, "La realidad del folletín," 382). [What this first realist novel proposes is the emancipation of man; it directly attacks social injustice, privilege, the system of man's exploitation of man.]

48. Sieburth, *Literature, Mass Culture, Uneven Modernity*, 33, italics in original.

49. According to Carlos Moreno Hernández, in "Realismo y romanticismo," Pedro Alarcón is the author who best represents the heritage of romanticism as revealed in realism. At the same time, I believe that the three realist authors I study here also preserve romanticism's rich heritage. For additional work on realist authors' ties to romanticism, see Valis, "Romanticism, Realism, and the Presence of the Word" and "Pardo Bazán's *El cisne*

de Vilamorta and the Romantic Reader"; as well as Ciplijauskaité, "El romanticismo como hipotexto en el realismo."

50. Sainz de Robles, Introduction to *Obras Completas,* by Benito Pérez Galdós, 147; Montesinos, *Galdós,* 85; Bonet, Introduction to *Ensayos de crítica literaria* (see esp. 28–29); Fuentes, "El realismo integral," 54; Ríos-Font, *The Canon and the Archive,* 116.

51. Elizabeth Sánchez, "Beyond the Realist Paradigm," 102; Valis, *Decadent Vision in Leopoldo Alas,* 104–5; Kronik, "La modernidad de Leopoldo Alas," 126; Larsen, *"La Regenta* and the *Symposium,"* 176; Davis, "Critical Reception of Naturalism," 104; Gullón, "'Clarín,' Novelista moderno"; Sobejano, *"La Regenta:* De su final," 70.

52. García Morales, *Literatura y pensamiento hispánico,* 19; Hindson, "Clarín como intertexto de *La Regenta,"* 472; Ife, "Idealism in Clarín's *La Regenta,"* 294.

53. Mandrell, "Popularity of *Don Juan Tenorio,"* 38; Rogers, *"Donjuanismo* and Death in Clarín," 337–38; Roberto Sánchez, "Clarín y el romanticismo teatral," 216.

54. Ouimette, "Liberalism of Baroja," 22.

55. Regalado García, "Verdugos y ejecutados," 26. Juana de José Prades examines romantic connotations in Baroja, and cites E. Allison Peers as also having noted Baroja's ties to romanticism ("Un héroe romántico de Baroja," 552).

56. Franz, "Baroja, Machado, and the French Symbolist Connection"; González López, *Arte narrativo de Baroja,* 159.

57. Martínez Lainez, "Sentimiento político de Baroja," 194; González Mas, "Baroja y la novela de folletín," 167; Fox, *Ideología,* 196; Blanco Aguinaga, *Juventud,* 252; Fernández García, "Lo grotesco en Baroja," 1742.

58. Carlos Blanco Aguinaga, for example, finds "extraordinary objective realism" in *La lucha por la vida* ("Realismo y deformación," 308).

59. Fox, *Ideología,* 193.

60. See Rutherford, "On Translating *La Regenta,"* 55–57, for a discussion of the pitfalls of translating the name "La Regenta" into English. There is no exact equivalent.

Chapter 1. Setting the Stage

1. For seminal work on *La corte de Carlos IV* as Gabriel's semiotic apprenticeship, see Tsuchiya, *Images of the Sign.* Also convinced of the novel's importance, Germán Gullón refers to *La corte de Carlos IV* as "el grado cero del narrador realista" (*Novela del XIX,* 34). [degree zero for the realist narrator.]

2. For a thorough discussion of the relationship of the maritime adventure to the process of writing, see Diane Urey, "La historia y la lengua." For a summary of *Trafalgar's* commonalities with the picaresque novel, see Urey, "Galdós' Creation," 631.

3. References to the Galdós novels will be given in parentheses in the text.

4. As Urey explains, the rejuvenation of Alonso and Marcial recalls that of the "narrador 'resucitado'" (resuscitated narrator) of the first chapter ("La historia y la lengua," 1528).

5. Later in the series, in the novel *Cádiz,* Gabriel will again return to his birthplace, and will accordingly "start over" in his assessment of himself as author.

6. In *Gerona,* Gabriel uses this same technique to contain the narration of Andrés Marijuán.

7. Later, in an attempt to inflate his own literary authority, Gabriel criticizes Moratín, but at this early stage Moratín's portrayal is positive by default, representing all that is rejected by the benighted Pepa.

8. On Galdós's portrayal of Comella, see Cabañas, "Comella visto por Galdós". On the general topic of works of Spanish literature in Galdós, see Benítez, *Literatura española.*

9. Clearly, Galdós also hints here at autobiography, suggesting the connection between internal and external authors that I explore here.

10. For the topic of Moratín in the work of Galdós, see Cabañas, "Moratín en la obra de Galdós."

11. We can imagine an interesting parallel in Galdós, debating with himself over the responsibility of the author to please, in that at the time he wrote the First Series of *Episodios,* he was starting his own writing career.

12. Godoy was awarded this title after the Treaty of Basel (1795) (Tomlinson, *Twilight of Enlightenment,* 93).

13. It is interesting to observe the various ways in which the *Episodios* express a desire to control Moratín for posterity. As mentioned, the lighting of the theater replicates the action of *El sí de las niñas,* so that the novel absorbs the play. In addition, Gabriel plays a role in the reception of Moratín's work when he begs the author's pardon: "¡Sombra de Moratín! ¡Perdón mil veces!" (285). [Ghost of Moratín! A thousand pardons!] Whereas Gabriel pleads for Moratín's forgiveness, the *Episodios* nevertheless include a critique of the earlier writer's classic Enlightenment drama. In this way, through his surrogates Gabriel and Godoy, Galdós processes for his readers the cultural icon Moratín.

14. The marqués is Amaranta's uncle, and he is as untruthful as José María de Malespina of *Trafalgar,* but in a different way, in that the marqués does not alter historical fact, but merely claims to be an actor in all important events (303).

15. By "specularity" I refer to the mirroring of one character by another.

16. For further work on Galdós's use of pictorial art, see Hazel Gold's discussion of the *novelas contemporáneas* (*The Reframing of Realism,* 123–47).

17. Although in the play Othello is incorrect in his assumption of his wife's guilt, Isidoro discovers on stage the proof that Lesbia has betrayed him with Mañara.

18. When he conceives of the notion that the countess Amaranta might love him and provide him access to power, Gabriel imagines himself in control of the country, remedying the ills he sees around him. Briefly, he believes himself destined to be "generalísimo de los ejércitos de mar y tierra, gran almirante, ministro y quién sabe si rey de algún reinito chico" (308). [supreme commander of troops on land and sea, great admiral, minister, and who knows if maybe even king of some small kingdom.] If his dreams of reform remind us of don Quijote, his ultimate goal recalls Sancho Panza's desire for an island.

19. This disavowal comes, of course, only after he has used all the arts of deception that he has learned from Amaranta herself to manipulate his erstwhile "protectress." See Tsuchiya, *Images of the Sign,* 106–28, for a complete discussion of Gabriel's semiotic apprenticeship with Amaranta, and the implications of this literary training for the development of his consciousness and skills as a narrator. Also, for the topic of Gabriel and Amaranta, see Urey, "Engendering Style" and "Woman as Language."

20. Godoy's undecided nature in Galdós's novel establishes intriguing parallels with the historical Manuel Godoy. Many wondered how Godoy arrived at his position of immense responsibility and power at such a young age and without formal education. Nevertheless, the lack of personal distinction may have been what drew the Spanish rulers to him, because Godoy's insignificance provided the monarchs with a bland surrogate through whom they could rule—a "new man" Carlos and María Luisa could manufacture, "moulding him to their liking" (Lynch, *Bourbon Spain,* 382, 386). In fact, even when he wrote his autobiography, Godoy left his life open to speculation by avoiding disclosures about his personal life (Hilt, *Troubled Trinity,* 4), and we can see this decision as his encouragement of the fictionalization to which he was subjected by the public. Thus, *La corte de Carlos IV's* production of the different stories of Godoy links him as character to the historical figure whose legacy is doubt and rumor.

21. This resistance to the temptations of fantasy anticipates the actions of Manuel

Alcázar (*La lucha por la vida*) in his first campaigns against quixotic readings of reality, and recalls as a contrast the failure of the narrator of Galdós's *La novela en el tranvía* to reject poetic melodrama.

22. Here, Gabriel's comments about the printing press anticipate the contrast between quixotic idealism and the materiality of the press we will see played out in the experiences of Manuel Alcázar in *La lucha por la vida*.

23. Lady Holland, qtd. in Lynch, *Bourbon Spain*, 385.

24. The Spanish rulers authorized Godoy to concede favors and decide destinies in an arbitrary use of power that "filled his lobby with *pretendientes* (petitioners or suitors) and gave him a shifting *clientela*" (Lynch, *Bourbon Spain*, 385).

25. With people now taking to the streets, *El 19 de marzo y el 2 de mayo* frequently portrays them as lacking individual behavioral controls—as the typical "psychological crowd" described by Gustave Le Bon. Prior to the composition of the *Episodios*, in *La Fontana de Oro* (1870), Galdós had already expressed many of the ideas that Le Bon would publish later, demonstrating that mass psychology was "in the air in Europe by the end of the nineteenth century," and that Le Bon's treatment of the crowd was a synthesis of accepted ideas (Zlotchew, "Galdós and Mass Psychology," 5). Thus, it is not surprising that we find Le Bon–like portrayals of crowds in the *Episodios* as well.

26. Godoy protected the periodical press and established *Amigos del País* societies, and claimed with some justification that his country had become the "refuge of the lights that were elsewhere feared" (Herr, *Revolution in Spain,* 359). Godoy also acted as patron and protector of the Royal Academy of Fine Arts and the Pestalozzi Institute, founded in Madrid by a royal order of 1805, and based on the Swiss pedagogue Heinrich Pestalozzi's theories of primary education (Tomlinson, *Twilight of Enlightenment,* 110–11).

27. Especially in view of Galdós's concern for the public's reading habits and reception of various literary forms, as evidenced by the "Observaciones" essay of 1870, we might read the *Episodios'* implicit criticism of the brutal treatment of Godoy as Galdós's personal attack on the uncritical reception of culture and national history. The anxiety that prompted Galdós's largely successful attempts to marginalize certain literary genres and styles shows through even in this passage of the *Episodios*. For provocative discussions of these marginalizing gestures in Galdós's "Observaciones," see Jagoe, "Disinheriting the Feminine," and Santana, "The Conflict of Narratives."

CHAPTER 2. THE NATION FIGHTS BACK

1. Gabriel was treated by an "albéitar," which can also be translated as "quack," but the fact that the word can be rendered as "veterinarian" suggests the blurring of the line between human and animal—a common practice in the *Episodios*. Significantly, animalization here affects Gabriel himself, and reminds the reader that Gabriel, still in the early stages of establishing his identity and critical sensibilities, is barely human.

2. Santorcaz is actually Inés's father. Because he is a commoner Amaranta's family did not accept him as a potential husband for her, and he turned to radical politics and moral dissipation in France. Andrés is the young man who will narrate the *episodio Gerona*.

3. Brace, *Making of the Modern World,* 444. At the time the battle of Austerlitz took place, occurring soon after the French-Spanish loss at Trafalgar, Spain was obligated by an alliance to participate in French military entanglements (Carr, *Spain,* 81).

4. Diane Urey has noted the similarity of Gabriel's memoirs and Santorcaz's tales, and the parallel narrative projects and goals of the two "authors." Urey observed that Santorcaz's visions "are essentially the same as Gabriel's memories of his own youthful exploits, the central focus of the Series"; and that Santorcaz "eagerly recounts his experiences in

Napoleon's army, wanting his audience to visualize them, just as Gabriel does when he writes his life" ("Resurrection," 209).

5. In Roque's imagining of the contents of the paper before reading it, this passage also anticipates *La Regenta,* when Ana de Ozores mentally creates Santa Teresa before reading the saint's work.

6. I will eventually argue that the author-character's presentation of himself as Cervantes rather than don Quijote mirrors the agenda of the external authors of all the novels I study here.

7. Brian Dendle has noted perceptively that the book scrutiny of *Napoleón en Chamartín* occurs in chapters 6 and 7 of the novel, and the equivalent exercise appears in Cervantes's novel in chapter 6 (*Galdós,* 53). I use Charles Jarvis's translation of Cervantes's chapter title.

8. Gabriel says directly: "Yo le contesté que lo de mi ciencia latina era una equivocación, y que el licenciado Lobo me daba aquella fama usurpándola a otro" (578). [I answered him that this business of my Latin learning was a mistake, and that the Bachelor Lobo gave me the credit deserved by another person.]

9. In this *episodio,* the terms "poetry" and "prose" represent the idealist-romanticist and the realist mentalities, just as they do in *La Regenta.* Here, I respect the terminology of *Zaragoza,* but I call the reader's attention to the equivalence of these terms to those I have been using all along, romanticism and realism.

10. Agustín later replicates Gabriel's association of Mariquilla with the Virgen del Pilar when he explains that his family worships the saint by dedicating candles to the image of her that they have at home: "Yo la miro, y para mis adentros, le digo: '¡Señora, que esta ofrenda de velas sirva también para recordaros que no puedo dejar de amar a la Candiola!'" (686). [I look at her, and inside myself say to her: "My lady, let this offering of candles serve also to remind you that I cannot stop loving Candiola's daughter."]

11. For the topic of the various saints of Zaragoza, see Collins, "Sainthood for a City?"

12. Dendle has studied *Zaragoza*'s treatment of women in his *Galdós,* 58.

13. Here, Gabriel focuses on the constancy and persistence of these three females associated with quixotism. As I argue in the Conclusion, the external authors seem to be particularly concerned with the staying power of romantic, creative women. I believe this fixation derives from the external authors' sense that such women authors are their competitors.

14. Rojas, *La Celestina,* 232–36.

15. *La Regenta* also presents the epic as featuring a romantic mentality opposed to realism.

16. Again, I call attention to the association of the epic with romance.

17. Diane Urey draws on the ideas of Derrida (*Dissemination*) to explain "Gabriel Araceli's apology for altering Marijuán's style," which she sees as exemplifying what Derrida "has shown to be primary functions of the preface or prologue: a desire to control how the book is read, a narcissistic absorption of the body of the text into the prologue, much like the absorption of the son into the father" ("Nested Intertexts," 183). This, then, would be another model for seeing Gabriel's gesture as an appropriation of Andrés's embedded text.

CHAPTER 3. WAR FOR INDEPENDENCE

1. Gabriel's rebirth coincides with the founding of the modern Spanish nation in the Cádiz of 1810—the inauguration of the Regency government, the meeting of the Cortes, and the proclamation of the Constitution.

2. Here, Gabriel gives a specific example of birth, filiation, and youth as related to the newspapers when he tells the story of *El Concisín* and *El Conciso:* "Sacaron un diminuto papel, húmedo aún, como recién salido de la prensa, el cual era una especie de suplemento, hijuela y lugarteniente de *El Conciso* grande, y en su lenguaje figuraba un niño que venía a contarle a su papá lo que ocurría por las Cortes" (902). [They got out a slight paper, still wet, as if hot off the press. It was a sort of supplement, daughter and lieutenant of the big *Conciso,* and in its language there was revealed a child who was going to tell his father what was happening in Congress.]

3. In the first *episodio,* well before the events of the War for Independence, Gabriel personally experiences the idea of *la patria.* Nevertheless, he also assesses English national pride, concluding that the English also had their "patria querida" (dear homeland) to defend (227). Later, as he watches Spaniards and Englishmen fraternize, Gabriel sees terror and hope in all faces, and recognizes the feeling of humanity and charity as a motivation shared by all (232).

4. The persistence of don Pedro as part of Spain's unwelcome cultural heritage recalls Diana Pamp de Avalle-Arce's argument about the literary archetypes of Don Juan and Juan Ruiz in the work of Galdós. She sees these two characters as "the dark side, the self-destructive side of the national character. . . . This resurgence of personalities of antique stamp from the unquiet grave of the Middle Ages and even the Romantic era, is, for Galdós, like ghosts walking, inappropriate and unwanted, impeding the march of progress. If Don Juan is, as he says, immortal, then Spain dies a suicide" (Literary Archetypes in Galdós," 39).

5. As confirmation of the linking of the bombastic hero to Spain's political situation, Diane Urey explicitly associates don Pedro with the new government that marked the birth of modern Spain, explaining that "the quixotic absolutist Don Pedro de Congosto . . . becomes a literal synthesis of the theatricalized and burlesque aspects of the Cortes" ("Duelling Discourses," 575).

6. The older version of Gabriel would be a literate Quijote—still a Quijote in spite of himself, as I suggest throughout this text.

7. The context for this list is the following: "¿Se ha ajustado ya vuestra cuenta (Has your count been adjusted), ¡oh Empecinado!, Porlier, Durán, Amor, Mir, Francisquete, Merino, Tabuenca, Chaleco, Chambergo, Longa, Palarea, Lacy, Rovira, Albuin, Claros, Saornil, Sánchez, Villacampa, Cuevillas, Arostegui, Manso, el Fraile, el Abuelo?

"No sé si he nombrado a todos los poqueños grandes hombres que entonces nos salvaron y que, en su breve paso por la Historia, dejaron la semilla de [I don't know if I have named all the small, great men who saved us then and who, in their short appearance in History, left the seed of] los Misas, Trapense, Bessières, el Pastor, Merino, Ladrón, quienes a su vez criaron a sus pechos [who in their turn nursed at their breasts] a los Rochapea, Cabrera, Gómez, Gorostidi, Echevarría, Eraso, Villarreal, padres de los Cucala, Ollo, Santés, Radica, Valdespina, Samaniego, Tristany, varones coetñeos que también engendraron su pequeña prole para el futuro" (976). [contemporary men who also engendered their small offspring for the future.]

8. Because Miss Fly and Gabriel have traveled to Salamanca together, the English officers are initially suspicious of his close relationship with her.

9. His begging for death also recalls the quixotic *guerrilleros.*

10. The characters Molichard and Tourlourou, upon suspecting that Gabriel was a spy, entrusted him to Jean-Jean, who promised to see that justice would be done. It was at this point that Gabriel seduced Jean-Jean with promises of money and the story of his nobility and his tragic love affair.

11. Juan de Dios also parallels Gabriel earlier in the novel, when he suddenly reappears as a penitent friar, tortured by visions of Inés and his frustrated love for her. The return of

Juan de Dios as alter ego for Gabriel suggests a lack of progress in Gabriel's development, in that this pairing was a feature of the first half of the series.

CHAPTER 4. ESCAPE FROM ROMANTICISM

1. Gabriel often appears as a "typical" hero—making significant contributions to the war effort, winning his lady's love, righting wrongs in general—Manuel is more of a turn-of-the-century or even decadent hero—inactive, interiorized, and disappointed with the world. For this topic, see de la Fuente, "Patología," particularly 87–89; and "Mundo fenoménico."

2. Manuel remembers that in the small town where he has been living with relatives, the school teacher compared his academic abilities to those of his brother Juan: "aseguraba que Juan llegaría a ser algo: a Manuel le consideraba como holgazán aventurero y vaga-bundo que no podía acabar bien" (265). [he assured everyone that Juan would end up being something: he considered Manuel a lazy, vagabond adventurer who couldn't help but turn out badly.] References to the three novels are given in parentheses in the text.

3. "La patrona solía llamarle el paje don Rompe Galas, recordando un tipo desastrado de un sainete que doña Casiana vio, según decía, representar en sus verdes años" (269). [The landlady often called him the Page don Rompe Galas, recalling a scruffy character from a play doña Casiana had seen, as she used to say, in her younger days.]

4. The baroness and her daughter, Kate, two more of the boarders, later play an important role in Manuel's life. Kate eventually marries Roberto.

5. Antonio Risco describes the parallelism between Manuel's identification with Roberto and the narrator's rejection of idealist rhetoric, in the following way: "Así, la literatura picaresca se afirma como *antiliteratura* a la vez que el pícaro se confiesa cínica-mente un antihéroe" (268, italics in original). [In that way, picaresque literature identifies itself as antiliterature at the same time that the *pícaro* cynically confesses to being an antihero.]

6. Emilio Alarcós Llorach has noted that don Alonso attracts Manuel because of the older man's idealistic tendencies (*Anatomía*, 33).

7. I read this description of Balzac's novels as Baroja's commentary on his own text, among others. Many novels of the period mix realism with romanticism.

8. Stephanie Sieburth classifies works by these two authors as *folletines* of seduction. Her helpful discussion of these texts and related novels is found in *Reading* La Regenta, 11–12.

9. Custodio and his wife charge Manuel with escorting Justa to and from her friend's wedding. While at the celebration, she meets el Carnicerín, and then refuses to return home when Manuel insists. Humiliated by her rejection and ashamed of his emotions, Manuel deserts her. We learn in *Mala hierba* that el Carnicerín ultimately deceives Justa, infects her with a venereal disease, and then leaves her. Her dishonor leads to her parents' break with her, and her turn to a life of prostitution.

10. Here, the parallel with Gabriel Araceli should be evident. Both work at a printing press as they attempt to negotiate their escape from romanticism. The association with the press reminds the two young men that they are mere tools in the literacy industry, and their resulting insecurities are a feature of their contradictory programs to both rely on and gain independence from their more cultured "benefactors."

11. When he arrives at Manuel's home in Madrid, Juan supplies the story of his life in Barcelona and Paris, where he lived after leaving the seminary and before coming to Madrid (531–33).

12. About his reaction to the scandal, Juan explains: "Desde que me enteré de estas cosas, no sé lo que me pasó; al principio sentí asombro; luego, una gran indignación contra toda esa tropa de curas viciosos que desacreditan su ministerio. Luego leí libros, y pensé y sufrí mucho, y desde entonces ya no creo" (512). [Ever since I found out about these things, I'm not sure what has happened to me. At first I felt surprised, and then I felt a great indignation toward that whole army of corrupt priests who discredit their ministry. Then I read books—I thought and suffered greatly, and lost my faith.]

13. The two artists might be the French Aristide Maillol and the Belgian George Minne, who produced revolutionary (postimpressionist) works of sculpture around 1900 (Janson, *History of Art,* 659–60).

14. This negative reaction is significant because when Manuel discusses with Perico Rebolledo his relationship with Salvadora, he contextualizes his insecurity about whether he and Salvadora love each other by saying that at least with Justa, he knew she loved him (523).

15. Domingo Pérez Minik, in "Al cruzar el siglo xx," believes that here, Caruty voices the opinion of Baroja himself: "Cuando Pío Baroja nos grita en *La lucha por la vida* 'Viva la anarquía. Viva la literatura,' nos está afirmando su muy seguro criterio del valor que le da a las palabras, que sólo son eficientes si no las convertimos jamás en acción" (59). [When Pío Baroja cries out to us in *La lucha por la vida,* "Viva la anarquía. Viva la literatura," he is affirming to us his confident judgment about the value of words, that they are only useful if we do not ever put them into action.]

Chapter 5. *La Regenta*

1. References to *La Regenta* are given in parentheses in the text. See Aranguren, "De *La Regenta* a Ana Ozores," 199–205, in which this critic speaks of "el debatirse entre el que ella cree amor espiritual de don Fermín y el que imagina amor verdadero aunque prohibido, de Álvaro" [(her) interior struggle between accepting Fermín's love, which she believes is spiritual, and accepting Álvaro's, which she imagines to be sincere, although forbidden].

2. I agree with Stephanie Sieburth, that Fermín and Álvaro are " 'diabolical' readers, who use books of any kind as tools to manipulate others" (*Reading* La Regenta, 92). The two men do succeed in artfully managing other characters, but they also display at times a distinct lack of control of their own readings, when these texts come back to haunt them.

3. For more on this topic, see Robert Archer, "*La Regenta* and the Problematics of Reading."

4. These are Ana's thoughts, as articulated by the narrator, who uses the indirect free style to communicate characters' interiority. See Rutherford, "On Translating *La Regenta.*"

5. The passage related to Víctor is the following: "En general don Víctor envidiaba a todo el que dejaba ver la contera de una espada debajo de una capa de grana, aunque fuese en las tablas y sólo de noche. Conoció que Anita contemplaba con gusto los ademanes y la figura de don Juan" (II, 44). [In general Don Víctor envied anyone who revealed the tip of a sword protruding from under his red cape, even if it was on the stage and only at night. He recognized that Anita contemplated with pleasure the gestures and appearance of Don Juan.]

6. See Roberto Sánchez, "Clarín y el romanticismo teatral," 227–28, on Clarín's affection for Zorrilla's play.

7. *La Regenta* features many examples of sublimated homoeroticism, as same-sex pairs are formed—or repressed homosexual desires are expressed—by Víctor and Frígilis, Víctor and Álvaro, the Marqués and Álvaro, Álvaro and Paco, Álvaro and Ronzal, Ana and Obdulia, Ana and Visitación, Paula and Teresa, and Álvaro and Fermín. For a thorough

treatment of the topic of homosexuality in *La Regenta,* see Cristina Mathews, "Making the Nuclear Family." Mathews argues convincingly that Alas characterizes homoerotic bonds as threatening to the nuclear family he wished to champion.

8. "Ana se encontró sentada entre la Marquesa y don Álvaro. Enfrente don Víctor, un poco alegre, fingía enamorar a Visitación y recitaba versos de sus poetas adorados" (II, 306). [Ana found herself sitting between the marquesa and don Álvaro. Opposite her, don Víctor, who was a bit tipsy, was pretending to woo Visitación by reciting verses from his beloved poets.]

9. On the topic of the *folletín*'s triumph over classical literature at the end of *La Regenta,* see Rivkin; and Sieburth, "*La Regenta* as Quixotic Novel."

10. "La rubia hermosa, con brazos de escultura griega, no entendía cabalmente lo que iba diciendo, pero adivinaba el sentido de su arenga, y le daba el tono de intolerancia y de soberbia que le convenía" (II, 202). [The beautiful blond, with arms like a Greek statue, did not really understand what she was saying, but she guessed the meaning of her harangue, and she gave it the necessary note of haughty intolerance.]

11. "Afortunadamente él tenía arte para todo: sabría ser místico, hasta donde hiciera falta" (II, 204). [Fortunately, he had all sorts of skills. He knew how to be a mystic, and would play one no matter what.]

12. See Gonzalo Sobejano's edition of *La Regenta* (II, 205) for a discussion of these novels, by Disraeli and Wiseman, respectively.

13. For a thorough discussion of the significance of the toad in *La Regenta,* see Sieburth, "Kiss and Tell."

14. Noël Valis has noted that Ana's vision of Hell (which we have seen as related to Fermín) comes directly from Santa Teresa's autobiography ("Hysteria," 336). This link between Ana and the saint's writing allows us to read Santa Teresa as another being, like the birds and animals throughout the text, who reminds Ana that she is in danger of losing her claims to authorship.

15. Here, rather than making an outmoded theoretical argument about the written text's primacy over spoken discourse, I simply mean that Ana has recorded her words on paper, and Fermín has not.

16. Gonzalo Sobejano astutely observes the anticipation, by this sentence, of the final words of the novel (*La Regenta,* II, 322).

17. Although she studies Ana as reader instead of author, Catherine Jaffe's characterization of Clarín's reaction to Ana is relevant here. She finds that "Alas's portrayal of Ana as a reader and his representation of gendered reading practices in *La Regenta* reveal profound ambivalence toward reading practices culturally gendered as feminine and an uneasy awareness of their relation to the creative process" (20). I suggest that Clarín's channeling this ambivalence into a portrayal of Ana as author is a logical counterpoint to his configuration of her as a reader.

CONCLUSION

1. Again, see Mathews "Making the Nuclear Family" for the topic of Ana as defying the nuclear family and Spanish society.

2. Of course, Inés is actually of noble birth, but her employment as a seamstress together with her lack of formal education mark her as untutored.

Works Cited

Abrams, M. H. *A Glossary of Literary Terms.* 5th ed. New York: Holt, Rinehart and Winston, 1988.

Alarcós Llorach, E. *Anatomía de* La lucha por la vida. Madrid: Castalia, 1982.

Alas, Leopoldo ("Clarín"). *La Regenta.* Ed. Gonzalo Sobejano. 2 vols. Madrid: Castalia, 1987. [1884–1885]

Andreu, Alicia. *Galdós y la literatura popular.* Madrid: Sociedad General Española de Librería, 1982.

Aranguren, José Luis L. "De *La Regenta* a Ana Ozores." *Estudios Literarios.* Madrid: Gredos, 1976, 177–211.

Archer, Robert. "*La Regenta* and the Problematics of Reading." *Modern Language Review* 87.2 (April 1992): 352–57.

Bann, Stephen. *Romanticism and the Rise of History.* New York: Twayne, 1995.

Baroja, Pío. *Obras completas.* Vol. 1. Madrid: Biblioteca Nueva, 1946. [1904–5]

Barzun, Jacques. "Romantic Historiography as a Political Force in France." *Journal of the History of Ideas* 2 (1941): 318–29.

Benítez, Rubén. *Cervantes en Galdós.* Murcia: Universidad de Murcia, 1990.

———. *La literatura española en las obras de Galdós.* Murcia: Universidad de Murcia, 1992.

Blanco Aguinaga, Carlos. *Juventud del 98.* Barcelona: Edición Crítica, 1978.

———. "Realismo y deformación escéptica: La lucha por la vida según don Pío Baroja." *Pío Baroja.* Ed. Javier Martínez Palacio. Madrid: Taurus, 1979, 307–53.

Bobes Naves, María del Carmen. "Técnicas narrativas en *La Regenta:* Efectos especulares." In Laurenti and Williamsen, 319–29.

Bonet, Laureano. Introduction. *Ensayos de crítica literaria.* By Benito Pérez Galdós. Barcelona: Península, 1972, 7–112.

Botrel, Jean-François. "La novela por entregas: unidad de creación y de consumo." *Creación y público en la literatura española.* Ed. Jean-François Botrel and S. Salaün. Madrid: Castalia, 1974, 111–55.

Brace, Richard M. *The Making of the Modern World: From the Renaissance to the Present.* New York: Rinehart, 1955.

Bretz, Mary Lee. *Voices, Silences and Echoes: A Theory of the Essay and the Critical Reception of Naturalism in Spain.* London: Tamesis, 1992.

Brownlow, Jeanne P., and John W. Kronik, eds. *Intertextual Pursuits: Literary Mediations in Modern Spanish Narrative.* Lewisburg, Pa.: Bucknell University Press, 1998.

Bush, Peter. "*Montes de Oca:* Galdós' Critique of 1898 *quijotismo.*" *BHS* 61.4 (October 1984): 472–82.

Cabañas, Pablo. "Comella visto por Galdós." *Revista de Literatura* 29 (1969): 91–99.

———. "Moratín en la obra de Galdós." *Actas del Segundo Congreso Internacional de Hispanistas.* Ed. Jaime Sánchez Romeralo and Norbert Poulussen. Nimega, Holanda: Instituto Español de la Universidad de Nimega, 1967, 217–26.

Cabrera, Hilda. *Revolución liberal y restauración borbónica.* Madrid: Altalena, 1978.

Carr, Raymond. *Spain: 1808–1975.* Oxford: Clarendon, 1982.

Cervantes, Miguel de. *Don Quixote.* Trans. Charles Jarvis. New York: Oxford UP, 1992.

Ciplijauskaité, Biruté. "El romanticismo como hipotexto en el realismo." In Lissorgues, 90–97.

Clarín. *See* Leopoldo Alas.

Clarín y La Regenta en su tiempo. Actas del Simposio Internacional, Nov. 26–30, 1984. Oviedo: University of Oviedo, Caja de Ahorros de Asturias, 1987.

Close, Anthony. *The Romantic Approach to Don Quixote.* Cambridge: Cambridge University Press, 1977.

Collins, Marsha S. "Sainthood for a City? Hagiography and Galdós's *Zaragoza.*" *Anales galdosianos* 29–30 (1994–1995): 87–99.

Correa, Gustavo. "Galdós y el platonismo." *Anales galdosianos* 7 (1972): 3–17.

Cueto Alas, Juan. "The Critical Reception of Naturalism in Spain before *La cuestión palpitante.*" *Hispanic Review* 22.2 (1954): 97–108.

———, ed. *Hitos y mitos de La Regenta.* Oviedo: Caja de Ahorros de Asturias, 1987.

Davis, Gifford. "The Spanish Debate over Idealism and Realism before the Impact of Zola's Naturalism." *PMLA* 84 (1969): 1649–56.

Dendle, Brian. *Galdós: The Early Historical Novels.* Columbia: University of Missouri Press, 1986.

Earle, Peter G. "Baroja y su ética de la imposibilidad." *Cuadernos Hispanoamericanos* (July–Sept. 1972): 66–76.

Embeita, María. "*La lucha par la vida.*" *La picaresca. Orígenes, textos y estructuras. Actas del I Congreso Internacianal sobre la picaresca organizado par el Patronato "Arcipreste de Hita."* Ed. Manuel Criado de Val. Madrid: Fundación Universitaria Española, 1979, 877–92.

Fernández, James D. *Apology to Apostrophe.* Durham: Duke University Press, 1992.

Fernández García, María Nieves. "Lo grotesco en Baroja." *Actas del X Congreso de la Asociación Internacional de Hispanistas.* Vol. 2. Barcelona: University of Barcelona, 1989, 1741–49.

Ferreras, Juan Ignacio. *La novela por entregas: 1840–1900.* Madrid: Taurus, 1972.

———. "Tensión y negación en la obra novelesca de Baroja." *Cuadernos Hispanoamericanos* 265–267 (July–Sept. 1972): 293–301.

Flitter, Derek. *Spanish Romantic Literary Theory and Criticism.* New York: Cambridge University Press, 1992.

Fox, E. Inman. *Ideología y política en las letras de fin de siglo (1898)*. Madrid: Espasa Calpe, 1988.

————. "Unamuno, Ganivet y la identidad nacional." *Negotiating Past and Present: Studies in Spanish Literature for Javier Herrero*. Ed. David Gies. Charlottesville, NC: Rockwood Press, 1997, 54–75.

Franz, Thomas R. "Baroja, Machado, and the French Symbolist Connection." *Hispanic Journal* 10.2 (Spring 1989): 49–62.

de la Fuente Ballesteros, Ricardo. "Mundo fenoménico/mundo nouménico: una clave finisecular (Unamuno/Ganivet/Baroja)." *La independencia de las últimas colonias españolas y su impacto nacional e internacional*. Ottawa: Dovehouse Editions, 1999, 245–60.

————. "Patología y regeneración: en torno al héroe ganivetiano." *Siglo diecinueve* 4 (1998): 75–91.

Fuentes, Víctor. "El realismo integral de *La Regenta* y *Fortunata y Jacinta*." *Hispanic Review* 57.1 (Winter 1989): 43–56.

García Morales, Alfonso. *Literatura y pensamiento hispánico de fin de siglo: Clarín y Rodó*. Seville: Secretariado de Publicaciones of the University of Seville, 1992.

Gilman, Stephen. *Galdós and the Art of the European Novel*. Princeton: Princeton University Press, 1981.

Godzich, Wlad, and Nicholas Spadaccini. "Introduction: The Course of Literature in Nineteenth-Century Spain." *The Crisis of Institutionalized Literature in Spain*. Ed. Wlad Godzich and Nicholas Spadaccini. Minneapolis: The Prisma Institute, 1988, 9–34.

Gold, Hazel. "De paso por el museo: sociedad y conocimiento en *La Regenta* de Clarín." *Actas del X Congreso de la Asociación Internacional de Hispanistas*. Barcelona, Aug. 21–26, 1989. 2 (1992): 1285–93.

————. *The Reframing of Realism: Galdós and the Discourses of the Nineteenth-Century Spanish Novel*. Durham, N.C.: Duke University Press, 1993.

————. "Show and Tell: From Museum to Novel in Clarín's *La Regenta*." *España Contemporánea* 3.1 (Spring 1992): 47–70.

Goldman, Peter B. "Toward a Sociology of the Modern Spanish Novel: The Early Years." Part 1, *MLN* 89.2 (1974): 173–90. Part 2, *MLN* 90.2 (1975): 183–211.

González López, Emilio. *El arte narrativo de Pío Baroja*. New York: Las Americas, 1971.

————. "*Camino de perfección* y el arte narrativo español contemporáneo." *Cuadernos Hispanoamericanos* 265–67 (July–Sept. 1972): 445–62.

González Mas, Ezequiel. "Pío Baroja y la novela de folletín." *Pío Baroja*. Ed. Javier Martínez Palacio. Madrid: Taurus, 1979, 165–75.

Gullón, Germán. " 'Clarín,' Novelista moderno: focalización y narración en *La Regenta*." In Cueto Alas, 50–53.

————. *La novela del XIX: Estudio sobre su evolución formal*. Amsterdam: Rodopi, 1990.

————. "Parodias del sentir: la pervivencia de lo romántico en la novela realista (Clarín y Galdós)." *Siglo diecinueve* 4 (1998): 179–88.

Hartman, Geoffrey H. "The Heroics of Realism." *The Yale Review* 43.1 (1963): 26–35.

Hemmings, F. W. J. "Realism in the Age of Romanticism." *The Age of Realism*. Ed. F. W. J. Hemmings. Harmondsworth: Penguin, 1974, 36–68.

Herr, Richard. *The Eighteenth Century Revolution in Spain*. Princeton: Princeton University Press, 1958.

Hilt, Douglas. *The Troubled Trinity: Godoy and the Spanish Monarchs.* Tuscaloosa: University of Alabama Press, 1987.

Hindson, Jean. "La crítica novelística de Clarín como intertexto de *La Regenta:* un diálogo entre el espíritu y la materia." *Romance Languages Annual* 1 (1989): 468–73.

Ife, Barry W. "Idealism and Materialism in Clarín's *La Regenta:* Two Comparative Studies." *Revue de Littérature Comparée* 44.3 (July–Sept. 1970): 273–95.

Jackson, Robert. " 'Cervantismo' in the Creative Process of Clarín's *La Regenta.*" *MLN* 84 (1969): 208–27.

Jaffe, Catherine. "In Her Father's Library: Women's Reading in *La Regenta.*" *Revista de Estudios Hispánicos* 39.1 (January 2005): 3–25.

Jagoe, Catherine. "Disinheriting the Feminine: Galdós and the Rise of the Realist Novel in Spain." *Revista de Estudios Hispánicos* 27 (1993): 225–48.

James, Henry. Preface to *The American. The Art of Criticism: Henry James on the Theory and the Practice of Fiction.* Ed. William Veeder and Susan M. Griffin. Chicago: University of Chicago Press, 1986, 271–85.

Janson, H. W. *History of Art.* 3rd ed. New York: Henry N. Abrams, 1986.

Kaufmann, Walter. Prologue to *I and Thou.* By Martin Buber. Trans. Walter Kaufmann. New York: Charles Scribner's Sons, 1970, 9–48.

Koethe, John. "The Romance of Realism." *New Literary History* 28.4 (1997): 723–37.

Kronik, John W. "El beso del sapo: configuraciones grotescas en *La Regenta.*" In *Clarín y La Regenta en su tiempo,* 517–24.

———. "La modernidad de Leopoldo Alas." *Papeles de Son Armadans* (May 1966): 121–34.

———. "La retórica del realismo: Galdós y Clarín." In Lissorgues, 47–57.

Laín Entralgo, Pedro. *La Generación del Noventa y Ocho.* Madrid: Espasa-Calpe, 1979. [1947]

Larsen, Kevin. "Another Guest at Dinner: *La Regenta* and the *Symposium.*" *Revista Hispánica Moderna* 45.2 (December 1992): 169–80.

Laurenti, Joseph L., and Vern G. Williamsen, eds. *Varia Hispánica. Homenaje a Alberto Porqueras Mayo.* Kassel: Edition Reichenberger, 1989.

Le Bon, Gustave. *The Crowd.* New York: Viking Press, 1960. [1895]

Letemendía, Emily. "Galdós and Bécquer." *Romance Notes* 21 (1980): 178–83.

Lissorgues, Yvan, ed. *Realismo y naturalismo en España en la segunda mitad del siglo XIX.* Barcelona: Anthropos, 1988.

Longhurst, Carlos. *Las novelas históricas de Pío Baroja.* Madrid: Guadarrama, 1974.

López Morillas, Juan. *El krausismo español: perfil de una aventura intelectual.* México: Fondo de Cultura Económica, 1956.

Lucas, F. L. *The Decline and Fall of the Romantic Ideal.* New York: Macmillan, 1937.

Lynch, John. *Bourbon Spain.* Oxford: Basil Blackwell, 1989.

Mandrell, James. "Nostalgia and the Popularity of *Don Juan Tenorio:* Reading Zorrilla Through Clarín." *Hispanic Review* 59.1 (Winter 1991): 37–55.

Martí-López, Elisa. *Borrowed Words: Translation, Imitation, and the Making of the Nineteenth-Century Novel in Spain.* Lewisburg, Pa.: Bucknell University Press, 2002.

———. "Historiografía literaria y folletín: notas para un debate crítico sobre el siglo XIX español." *Siglo diecinueve* 4 (1998): 109–30.

Martínez Lainez, Fernando. "El sentimiento político de Pío Baroja." *Revista de Occidente* 21 (1968): 185–203.

Mathews, Cristina. "Making the Nuclear Family: Kinship, Homosexuality, and *La Regenta.*" *Revista de Estudios Hispánicos* 37.1 (January 2003): 75–102.

Montero-Paulson, Daria J. "Nombres, símbolos, personajes y textos literarios: una evocación del romanticismo en la obra de Benito Pérez Galdós." *Siglo diecinueve* 4 (1998): 169–78.

Montesinos, José F. *Galdós.* Vol. 1. Madrid: Castalia, 1968.

Moreno Hernández, Carlos. "Realismo y romanticismo: el caso de Alarcón." *Siglo diecinueve* 4 (1998): 149–67.

Nietzsche, Friedrich. *The Use and Abuse of History.* Trans. Adrian Collins. New York: Macmillan, 1957.

Núñez Ruiz, Diego. *La mentalidad positiva en España: desarrollo y crisis.* Madrid: Tucar, 1975.

Oliver, Walter. "Galdós' *La novela en el tranvía:* Fantasy and the Art of Realistic Narration." *MLN* 88 (1973): 249–63.

Ordóñez, Elizabeth J. "Revising Realism: Pardo Bazán's *Memorias de un solterón* in Light of Galdós' *Tristana* and John Stuart Mill." *In the Feminine Mode: Essays on Hispanic Women Writers.* Ed. Noël Valis and Carol Maier. Lewisburg, Pa.: Bucknell University Press, 1990, 146–63.

Ouimette, Victor. "The Liberalism of Baroja and the Second Republic." *Hispania* 60 (1977): 21–34.

Pamp de Avalle-Arce, Diana. "Literary Archetypes in Galdós: Don Juan Tenorio and Juan Ruiz." *Selected Proceedings: 32nd Mountain Interstate Foreign Language Conference.* Ed. Gregorio C. Martin. Winston-Salem, N.C.: Wake Forest University, 1984. 33–40.

Pattison, Walter T. *Benito Pérez Galdós.* Boston: Twayne, G. K. Hall, 1975.

Pérez Galdós, Benito. *Obras completas.* Vol. 1. Madrid: Aguilar, 1951.

———. "Observaciones sobre la novela contemporánea en España." In Zavala, 317–31.

Pérez Minik, Domingo. "Al cruzar el siglo XX. Pío Baroja en el panorama de la novela europea." *Cuadernos hispanoamericanos* 265–67 (1972): 55–65.

Pozzi, Gabriela. *Discurso y lector en la novela del XIX (1834–1876).* Amsterdam: Rodopi, 1990.

Prades, Juana de José. "Un héroe romántico de Baroja." *Estudios de literatura española de los siglos XIX y XX: Homenaje a Juan María Díez Taboada.* Ed. José Carlos de Torres Martínez and Cecilia García Antón. Madrid: Consejo Superior de Investigaciones Científicas, 1998, 551–57.

Ramos-Gascón, Antonio. "La literatura española como invención historiográfica: el caso del 98." *Eutopías. Teorías/Historia/Discurso* 3.1 (Winter–Spring 1987): 79–101.

Reed, John A. "Inherited Characteristics: Romantic to Victorian Will." *Studies in Romanticism* 17.3 (Summer 1978): 335–66.

Regalado García, Antonio. "Verdugos y ejecutados en las novelas de Pío Baroja." *Papeles de Son Armadans* 41 (1966): 9–29.

Ríos-Font, Wadda C. *The Canon and the Archive: Configuring Literature in Modern Spain.* Lewisburg, Pa.: Bucknell University Press, 2004.

Rivkin, Laura. "Melodramatic Plotting in Clarín's *La Regenta.*" *Romance Quarterly* 33 (1986): 191–200.

Rodríguez Padrón, Jorge. "Divagaciones en torno a un centenario." *Cuadernos Hispano-americanos* 265–67 (July–Sept. 1972): 11–25

Rogers, Douglass. "Don Juan, *Donjuanismo,* and Death in Clarín." *Symposium* 30 (1976): 325–42.

Rojas, Fernando de. *La Celestina (Tragicomedia de Calisto y Melibea).* Madrid: Alianza, 1986. [1499]

Romero Tobar, Leonardo. *La novela popular española del siglo XIX.* Madrid: Fundación Juan March, 1976.

Rutherford, John. "On Translating *La Regenta.*" In Valis, *"Malevolent Insemination,"* 47–66.

Sainz de Robles, Federico Carlos. Introduction. *Obras completas.* By Benito Pérez Galdós. Vol 1. Madrid: Aguilar, 1941, 9–173.

Sánchez, Elizabeth D. "Beyond the Realist Paradigm: Subversive Strategems in *La Regenta* and *Madame Bovary.*" In Valis, *"Malevolent Insemination,"* 101–16.

———. "From World to Word: Realism and Reflexivity in *Don Quijote* and *La Regenta.*" *Hispanic Review* 55 (1987): 27–39.

Sánchez, Roberto. "Clarín y el romanticismo teatral: examen de una afición." *Hispanic Review* 31.3 (1963): 216–28.

Santana, Mario. "The Conflict of Narratives in Pérez Galdós' *Doña Perfecta.*" *MLN* 113.2 (1998): 283–304.

Sieburth, Stephanie. *Inventing High and Low: Literature, Mass Culture, and Uneven Modernity in Spain.* Durham, N.C.: Duke University Press, 1994.

———. "Kiss and Tell: The Toad in *La Regenta.*" In Valis, *"Malevolent Insemination,"* 87–100.

———. *Reading* La Regenta*: Duplicitous Discourse and the Entropy of Structure.* Amsterdam: John Benjamins, 1990.

———. "*La Regenta* as Quixotic Novel: Imitation and Intertextuality." *Romance Quarterly* 35.3 (1988): 319–29.

Sobejano, Gonzalo. "*La Regenta:* de su final a su finalidad." *Homenaje al Profesor Antonio Vilanova.* Ed. Adolfo Sotelo Vázquez and Maria Cristina Carbonell. Vol. 2. Barcelona Departamento de Filología Española, Universidad de Barcelona: 1989, 699–724.

———, ed. *La Regenta.* By Leopoldo Alas ("Clarín"). 2 vols. Madrid: Castalia, 1987.

Tomlinson. Janis A. *Goya in the Twilight of Enlightenment.* New Haven: Yale University Press, 1992.

Tsuchiya, Akiko. *Images of the Sign: Semiotic Consciousness in the Novels of Benito Pérez Galdós.* Columbia: University of Missouri Press, 1990.

Urey, Diane. "Desire and Death in *El 19 de marzo y el 2 de mayo.*" *Anales galdosianos* 27–28 (1992–1993): 157–75.

———. "Duelling Discourses in Galdós's *Episodios Nacionales: Cádiz.*" *Romance Languages Annual* 2 (1990): 575–81.

———. "Engendering Style in the First Series of Galdos's *Episodios nacionales.*" *Revista de Estudios Hispánicos* 22.2 (1988): 25–43.

———. "From Monuments to Syllables: The Journey to Knowledge in *Zumalacárregui.*" *Anales galdosianos* 21 (1986): 107–14.

———. "Galdós' Creation of a New Reader for Spain Through the First Series of *Episodios Nacionales.*" *Romance Languages Annual* 1 (1989): 631–38.

———. "La historia y la lengua en la primera serie de los *Episodios Nacionales* de Galdós." *Actas del X Congreso de la Asociación Internacional de Hispanistas.* Vol. 2. Aug. 21–26, 1989, University of Barcelona, 1525–33.

———. "Mythological Resonances in Galdós's Early *Episodios nacionales*." *Hispania* 81.4 (December 1998): 842–52.

———. "Nested Intertexts in Galdós's *Gerona*." In Brownlow and Kronik, 179–200.

———. "Resurrection and Reinscription in *Bailén*." *A Sesquicentennial Tribute to Galdós, 1843–1993*. Ed. Linda M. Willem. Newark, N. J.: Juan de la Cuesta, 1993, 204–21.

———. "Woman as Language in the First Series of Galdós's *Episodios nacionales*." In Brownlow and Kronik, 137–60.

Valis, Noël. *The Decadent Vision in Leopoldo Alas: A Study of* La Regenta *and* Su único hijo. Baton Rouge: Louisiana State University Press, 1981.

———. "Hysteria and Historical Context in *La Regenta*." *Revista Hispánica Moderna* 53 (2000): 325–351.

———. "Pardo Bazán's *El cisne de Vilamorta* and the Romantic Reader." *MLN* 101.2 (March 1986): 298–324.

———. "Romanticism, Realism, and the Presence of the Word." *Media, Consciousness, and Culture: Explorations of Walter Ong's Thought*. Ed. Bruce E. Gronbeck, et. al. Newbury Park, Calif.: Sage Publications, 1991, 90–102.

———, ed. *"Malevolent Insemination" and Other Essays on Clarín*. Ann Arbor: Michigan Romance Studies, 1990.

Wall, Geoffrey. *Flaubert: A Life*. New York: Farrar, Straus and Giroux, 2001.

Wellek, René. "Romanticism in Literature." *Dictionary of the History of Ideas*. Ed. Philip P. Wiener. Vol. 4. New York: Scribner, 1973–1974, 187–98.

Zavala, Iris M. *Ideología y política en la novela española del siglo XIX*. Salamanca: Anaya, 1971.

Zavala, Iris M., Leonardo Romero Tobar, and Rubén Benítez. "La realidad del folletín." *Romanticismo y realismo*. Vol. 5 of *Historia y crítica de la literatura española*. Ed. Iris M. Zavala. Barcelona: Crítica, 1982, 380–91.

Zlotchew, Clark M. "Galdós and Mass Psychology." *Anales galdosianos* 12 (1977): 5–19.

Index